Dream Trippers

Dream Trippers

Global Daoism and the Predicament
of Modern Spirituality

DAVID A. PALMER
AND ELIJAH SIEGLER

The University of Chicago Press
Chicago and London

The University of Chicago Press, Chicago 60637
The University of Chicago Press, Ltd., London
© 2017 by The University of Chicago
Published 2017
Printed in the United States of America

26 25 24 23 22 21 20 19 18 17   1 2 3 4 5

ISBN-13: 978-0-226-48176-0 (cloth)
ISBN-13: 978-0-226-48484-6 (paper)
ISBN-13: 978-0-226-48498-3 (e-book)
DOI: 10.7208/chicago/9780226484983.001.0001

Library of Congress Cataloging-in-Publication Data

Names: Palmer, David A., 1969– author. | Siegler, Elijah, author.
Title: Dream trippers : global Daoism and the predicament of modern spirituality /
    David A. Palmer and Elijah Siegler.
Description: Chicago ; London : The University of Chicago Press, 2017. |
    Includes bibliographical references and index.
Identifiers: LCCN 2017016255 | ISBN 9780226481760 (cloth : alk. paper) |
    ISBN 9780226484846 (pbk. : alk. paper) | ISBN 9780226484983 (e-book)
Subjects: LCSH: Taoism. | Globalization—Religious aspects—Taoism. |
    Spirituality—Taoism. | Pilgrims and pilgrimages—China—Hua Mountain
    (Shaanxi Sheng). | Taoists—United States. | Taoists—China. | Taoism—United States.
Classification: LCC BL1923 .P35 2017 | DDC 299.5/14—dc23
LC record available at https://lccn.loc.gov/2017016255

Contents

Illustrations follow page 24.

Acknowledgments

We began the research for this project in and around Qingcheng Mountain in Sichuan Province in the summer of 2004, and in the intervening twelve years, we have accumulated a mountain of thanks owed.

We offer our sincere gratitude to our home institutions over the past twelve years for giving us time and funding—for Elijah, the Department of Religious Studies at the College of Charleston, and for David, the Department of Sociology of the London School of Economics, the École Française d'Extrême-Orient, and the University of Hong Kong (Department of Sociology and Hong Kong Institute for the Humanities and Social Sciences). We thank our department heads, Lee Irwin and Zeff Bjerken (College of Charleston), Nikolas Rose (LSE), and Karen Laidler and Lui Tai-lok (HKU), and institute directors Franciscus Verellen (EFEO) and Angela K. C. Leung (HKIHSS), as well as John Burns, dean of social sciences at HKU, for their support and encouragement. The HKIHSS provided a generous publication subsidy for the production of this volume. Much of David's writing for this book took place while he was on a Taiwan National Science Foundation fellowship at the Department of Chinese of Yuan Ze University in the summer of 2013, and on a fellowship at the Asia Research Institute of the National University of Singapore in the summer of 2014. We are grateful to Chong Yun-ying and Prasenjit Duara for hosting him and providing excellent conditions for his writing work. As well, the College of Charleston and the University of Hong Kong supported our visits to each other—Elijah spoke at the University of Hong Kong in 2010, and David at the College of Charleston in 2013.

We offer our thanks to our students who have read and commented on various drafts over the years. Students in David's graduate seminar in the fall of 2015—Cheung Wai Leung, Liu Qing, Liu Zhao, Peng Qiaoyang, Temily Tianmay Jaya Gopan, and Fabian Winiger—read through the entire draft and offered especially detailed comments and suggestions. David's research assistants Martin Tse Man Him and Deng Xili provided precious help in the transcription and editorial process.

Over the years, we tested out our ideas at venues and conferences around the world. We are grateful to David Mark Shields, Steve Humphries-Brooks, Chen Jinguo, Lu Yunfeng, Peter van der Veer, Gordon Matthews, and Benjamin Penny for invitations to give presentations at Bucknell University in Pennsylvania, Hamilton College in New York, the China Academy of Social Sciences, Peking University, the Max Planck Institute for the Study of Religious and Ethnic Diversity (Göttingen, Germany), the Hong Kong Anthropological Society, and the Australian National University; and to Wilt Idema, Glenn Shive, Vincent Goossaert, K. E. Kuah-Pearce, Livia Kohn, Liang Yongjia, Knut Aukland, Michael Stausberg, Franciscus Verellen, and Gai Jianmin for inviting us to present drafts at international conferences on Asian studies (ICAS, Shanghai, 2005), modern Daoism (Harvard, 2006), Chinese religious life (EFEO and CUHK, 2006), Quanzhen Daoism (UC Berkeley, 2007), Asian heritages at the crossroads (HKU, 2007), Daoist studies (Hong Kong Institute of Education, 2007, and Loyola Marymount University, 2010), religion and ethnicity in China (National University of Singapore, 2011), religion and tourism in Asia (Frankfurt, 2014), Daoist lives (EFEO and EPHE, Aussois, 2015), and the thirtieth anniversary of the Institute of Daoist and Religious Studies of Sichuan University (Qingchenshan, 2015).

Portions of this book have previously been published in Nova Religio, Ethnos, and Cahiers d'Extrême-Asie, and in volumes published by the University of California Press, the Institute of East Asian Studies at UC Berkeley, and Berghahn Books;[1] we thank the editors and publishers for their permission to reproduce sections of these works here.

We also thank Priya Nelson and Dylan Montanari at the University of Chicago Press for their patience and enthusiasm, and the three anonymous reviewers for their careful critical reading.

We have been friends and collaborators since we were both high school students in 1984, and creating this book together seemed a natural extension of this collaboration (see the appendix for more details). Together, we presented our research in progress at the conferences of the American Anthropological Association in New Orleans in 2010 and the American Academy of Religion in Baltimore in 2013 (in a panel organized by David Mozina and Elena Valussi). We wrote and discussed together in a rooftop garden in Hong Kong, several restaurants in Chengdu and Charleston, a scruffy hotel courtyard in Beijing, and a leafy backyard in Toronto. All this took time away from our families, and to them we owe more than thanks—we owe everything.

Finally, this book would not have been possible without the willing participation of its subjects. Many thanks to all those participants of the China Dream Trips, to Daoist monks, to Mantak Chia, Livia Kohn, and Mark Johnson, to Masters Hu, Hao, Hei, and Pu.

Most of all, we thank our three main protagonists—Chen Yuming, Louis Komjathy, and Michael Winn. We thank them not only for their patience and candor while sitting for hours upon hours of repeated interviews—and for allowing us to participate in their retreats, classes, and lectures—but for their overall support of and enthusiasm toward our project. This support and enthusiasm manifested itself uniquely in their detailed comments after reading a full manuscript of *Dream Trippers*; we have incorporated many of their insightful responses into the final text. Of course, any errors that remain are fully our responsibility.

Thus, we dedicate *Dream Trippers* to our friends Chen Yuming, Louis, and Michael. We hope we have told your stories and expressed your opinions faithfully, even if you may not fully endorse our conclusions.

DP and ES
Toronto, Canada
July 2016

The Subject

When the Daoist monks at the Jade Spring Monastery at the foot of Mount Hua conduct the ritual to the Dipper on the day of Gengshen, the temple, closed to tourists for the evening, is deserted save for the monks gathered for the recitations in the main shrine devoted to Chen Tuan, a patron saint of inner alchemy. But, on May 30, 2006, a different scene presented itself. On either side of Chen Tuan's statue, eight Daoist monks in their dark blue robes and black caps solemnly chanted the *Scripture of the Northern Dipper*, following the dreamy cadence of knocks on a hollow wooden fish, reverently holding tablets with both hands, bowing, kneeling, and standing, their backs to the temple's central court. Darkness had fallen and the light in the shrine only faintly illuminated parts of the court, into which meandered wafts of incense smoke that hesitated between motion and stillness. Around the heavy round incense burner in the middle of the courtyard, scarcely visible bodies turned in the shadows, some in unison, stretching and contracting, and others in spontaneous motion. Still others sat in quiet meditation on steps and ledges, a few in the lotus position, some with their knees to their chests, dispersed at various spots in the small temple enclosure. A young couple held each other in embrace, their minds mingling like clouds of vapor, in the obscure stillness punctuated by the monks' grave chanting and hollow knocking.

They came from the Americas and Europe, thirty of them, doing *qigong*, tai chi, inner alchemical meditation, yoga, or just sitting there. There was a martial arts teacher from Mexico, a Sufi seeker from Seattle, a *fengshui* consultant from Toronto, a shaman from Colorado, a therapist from Turkey, a few enthusiastic youths, others rather jaded, a banker, a brain scientist, several retirees, and a French vineyard owner. They were travelers on the "China

Dream Trip," a tour of Daoist sacred sites organized by Healing Tao USA, one of America's main providers of courses and workshops on Daoist practices of meditation, healing, and the body.

At the inner altar, the Daoist monks chanted, stood in a single line and bowed, facing South; in the outer courtyard, the Dream Trippers exercised and meditated in all directions, many of them facing North: two groups, their backs to each other, in their own worlds, doing their own rituals. But both groups felt each other's presence and each other's pursuit of Dao, and consciously contributed to the shared atmosphere. After the ritual ended, the monks distributed the fruit offerings—watermelon and bananas—to the foreign group members. Few words were exchanged that night, but a sense of peaceful communion was felt by all.

The Dream Trippers had arrived by tour bus after a two-hour drive from Xi'an, across the dusty yellow plains of central Shaanxi, coming within sight of a chain of mountains to the South thrusting upward out of the earth, a forbidding wall separating North and South China. The crown of these summits is mount Hua, its towering cliffs propping up, like a stem, a ring of peaks shooting out of a central bulb, akin to the petals of a flower, thus the Chinese name Huashan or "Flower Mountain."

The "China Dream Trips" are organized once every two years. At Huashan, the participants spend a week climbing the mountain, meditating in secluded caves, and learning Daoist practices from monks and the hermit tending the caves. On the 2004 trip, they then set off by bus for Louguantai, some 500 miles to the west—a place the group leader, Michael Winn, lauds for its "intensely spiritual vibration," where, 2,500 years ago, the sage Laozi is reputed to have transmitted the *Daodejing*, the *Book of the Way and Its Virtue*, and disappeared into the Kunlun Mountains.

As soon as the Dream Trippers arrived at the Louguantai guesthouse, filling the hotel with English chatter, an American couple who had already spent a night there closed the door of their room, packed their bags, checked out of the hotel, and hurried off. They, too, were on a spiritual journey to Daoist sacred sites in China—but emphatically did not want to be associated with Winn's "Dream Trip." Louis Komjathy (b. 1971) had recently received his doctorate in religious studies; his dissertation on the early history of the Complete Perfection (Quanzhen) order of Daoism would soon be published as a 550-page tome,[1] and he would become an important contributor to academic teaching and discussion on the comparative study of contemplative traditions. His companion, Kathryn "Kate" Townsend (b. 1962), a longtime Daoist and Chinese medical practitioner, had a private practice in Chinese medicine. Tired of the superficiality and commercialism of the dominant American Daoist scene, they had come to China to attend a major conference on Daoist Studies and to go on a pilgrimage to important Daoist sacred sites. They were in China in search of the authentic expressions of China's ancient spiritual tradition—and not to meet a group of American "spiritual tourists."

On hearing our account of the monks of Huashan, Komjathy and Townsend set off to the Jade Spring Monastery. When they arrived, they sat down for tea with the vice-abbot, Master Chen Yuming (b. 1969), who had seen the Dream Trippers off only two days earlier. Komjathy stressed to Chen that he did *not* have the same approach as Healing Tao USA. The young scholar-practitioner complained to the young monk about the absence of true Daoism in the West—and that the Dream Trips were the perfect example of everything that was wrong with "so-called American Daoism." Komjathy told Chen that, instead, he hoped to deepen his own Daoist self-cultivation and determine if he had an authentic connection to Daoism. They also discussed the issue of lineage and ordination as requirements for Daoist identity and affiliation, and Komjathy asked how to establish and develop "authentic Daoism" in the United States, especially one rooted in lineage and tradition.

"I pretended that I didn't understand," Chen told us[2] a few months later, reluctant to agree to Komjathy's proposition. "I don't think we should pay too much attention to these outward forms of Daoism. He is right to want to bring the container over, but one must not be too rigid: the purpose of the container is only to carry the water inside. On the other hand, Michael Winn wants to take the water, without a container to hold it. As a result, he can't hold the water."[3]

This book is about the transnational circulation of the "water" of Daoism, as it spreads outside and beyond, but also flows back toward, its traditional institutional "container." It is about the people in China and America who "cultivate" themselves with this "water," and about their encounters, interpenetrations, and appropriations. In the words of Winn, responding to our project, this book is "catching it in midair. You're saying, 'Hey, there's an appropriation going on. Let's record it while the actual act of appropriation is happening, and the counter reappropriation.'"[4] And the book is a reflection on the anxieties that are produced by these encounters, flows, and appropriations—what we call the "predicament" of a modern, global spirituality that both rejects and feeds on its connection with local traditions, their sacred places, their traditional masters, and their broken institutional containers—raising vexing questions about authenticity and authority. How do transnational circulations transform the meaning of spiritual practice, authenticity, and authority for a globalizing, indigenous tradition such as Daoism—both at an individual and collective level?

✳

This book is a study of the encounter of two groups of Daoist practitioners, coming from vastly different cultural and religious backgrounds, at a common sacred site. Both the Chinese monks and the Dream Trippers share the experience of practices of Daoist body cultivation and meditation, but live worlds apart in terms of the social trajectories and environmental contexts of their "Daoist" experience. Both groups cross paths on Huashan, physically and figuratively, in monasteries, in caves, and on mountain trails, at different points of their trajectories in life and in their paths of spiritual cultivation. On Huashan they pass through spots that are meaningful or "powerful" on their "spiritual path"; their "way"; their "Dao."

For the Chinese monks of the monastic order of Complete Perfection, Huashan is steeped in sacred history as: one of the Five Imperial Sacred Peaks (*wuyue*) of China, a major Daoist Grotto Heaven (*dongtian*), an important site in the historical genealogy of the Daoist esoteric tradition of inner alchemy, and a way station in the past and present practice of "cloud wanderings" (*yunyou*) of Daoist monks in their travels from one monastery to another throughout China. For Master Chen, Huashan is the spiritual home of his own master, the place where he came of age as a Daoist and encountered the Immortals of past ages—but which, he feels, has become an oppressive place, where bureaucracy, politics, and backbiting have destroyed the spiritual atmosphere.

For the international spiritual travelers, Huashan is a stop on the itinerary of China Dream Trips, group tours organized by the flame-haired American Michael Winn (b. 1951), former war correspondent in Africa, kundalini yoga instructor, and, since the early 1980s, a student and close associate of Mantak Chia, a Thai Chinese who is one of the best-known teachers of Daoist body cultivation practices in the West. Winn's organization, Healing Tao USA, is one of the leading American providers of training programs in the traditions of gentle breath, body, and mind exercises commonly known as *qigong* (pronounced "tchee-gong"). The Dream Trip itineraries combine sightseeing, shopping, and *qigong* practice and meditation at major Daoist temples and mountains. The international participants, for the most part, have little knowledge of or interest in the geographic, historical, and religious significance of these sites: for them, the mountains are spaces for generating embodied experiences through *qigong* practice, and for connecting with the powerful energetic imprint left by past generations of anonymous Daoist hermits and cultivators.

For the scholar-practitioner Komjathy, on the other hand, Huashan is an important Daoist sacred site and a pivotal way station on his personal initiatory journey. It is one of the key links in his Daoist lineage and transmission, the precious and precarious connection between an authentic Chinese tradition and his own project of establishing a "tradition-based" Daoist practice and institution in faraway America.

These encounters between Chinese monks and primarily Western spiritual seekers and scholar-practitioners are moments in the "return globalization"[5] of Daoism, when practitioners of an Americanized Daoist practice meet with indigenous exponents of the tradition. China's indigenous religion has, during the twentieth century, spread to North America and Europe, breaking out of its Chinese cultural matrix and finding a home in the world of alternative spiritualities, natural health practices, and academic scholarship. This book is a study of a moment in the globalization of Daoism: the moment when, having spread overseas through the emigration of Chinese masters, an Americanized Daoism is now making its way back to China, bringing the process full circle. This is the moment when Daoism becomes truly "global"—after its outward dissemination and acculturation in various countries, a new stage begins—a maturing Westernized Daoism returns to China, not only to connect with its roots, but also to bring something back to its ancestral soil, which, after decades of revolutions and reforms, has also undergone deep changes.[6] The encounters characteristic of this "moment" have been occurring with increasing frequency in the past few years, with the arrival in China, for short or long stays, of Westerners committed to varying degrees to the study, practice, and promotion of Daoism. Among these, it is "Daoist *qigong*" tours that have the greatest visibility and impact: international groups of ten to forty people, primarily but not exclusively Westerners, organized by associations and enterprises active in the small but growing "Daoist" niche in the market for oriental spiritual practices and experiences. Such visits began in the early 2000s, are increasing in frequency, and are now offered by most American Daoist organizations.[7]

The encounters that produce such transnational spaces are multiplying through the circulation of practitioners, monks, scholars, and visitors between locations in China and overseas. This multiplication of encounters has become increasingly evident since we began researching this book in 2004. Each of these links occurs in discrete times and places, connecting different networks of Daoists in China and abroad. No two are the same, and the encounters we describe here should not be seen as representative of all. But it is the increased frequency of all these encounters—the multiplication of these localized spaces of transnational Daoist discourse and practice—which, ultimately, creates the broader contours of global Daoism.

How do these encounters change the protagonists? What happens when "Western Daoists" come back to the "roots" of Daoism in China, and meet with "real" Chinese Daoists? Does the encounter change them? Does it change the Chinese Daoists? What do these encounters tell us about the search for spirituality in the condition of late modernity? Through these encounters, it is the spiritual and religious histories of China and the West that intersect, collide, and interpenetrate—revealing the paradoxes and dilemmas of the search for spiritual authenticity in a globalized world. If Chinese and American Daoists are practicing the same or similar techniques derived from the same tradition, are they doing the same thing? Are they on the same path? Are they leading to the same Way? These are some of the questions we explore in this book.

Forming Spiritual Subjects:
Toward an Anthropology of Spirituality

Our Daoists are engaged in what, in the modern context, is often called a "spiritual practice" or "spirituality." Like countless others, in myriads of contexts and traditions, they are constituting themselves as *spiritual subjects*—as conscious and reflexive agents in realms perceived as transcending the world of immediate materiality and visibility.[8] This is a study of how people are constituted as spiritual subjects through their practices, their experiences, their travels and trajectories, their encounters, their conversations, and their participation in social groups, networks, and institutions. These are processes in which a specific type of subject is "constructed" or "cultivated"—a subject who is engaged in processes of ontological transformation, discovering or attaining his essence as being more than mortal flesh, and living in, interacting with, and aligning himself to a meaningful cosmos that extends deeper or beyond the immediate materiality of the world as it appears to the senses.

Contemporary popular parlance in the West tends to define spirituality in opposition to religion, seeing "spirituality" as rooted in inner, subjective experience while "religion" is considered to be based on external institutions, ritual, and dogma. But this discourse forgets that the term and concept of *spirituality* emerged within the highly institutionalized and religious context of medieval Catholicism;[9] and that disciplines of spiritual subject formation, as we define spirituality, exist in a variety of cultural and religious contexts—the institutions of Daoist monasticism in China being one of them. Through the encounters we describe in this book, different approaches to Daoist spirituality confront and question each other, while linking each other into a global network through which influences flow in both directions.

In this study, we hope to contribute to an anthropological approach to spiritual subject formation. Some questions that might be asked in a comparative anthropology of spirituality would be: what are the forms of knowledge, practice, and social relations through which people constitute themselves as spiritual subjects? And how do spiritual subjects transform knowledge, practice, and social relations? What kinds of subjectivities are generated by different regimens of spiritual subject formation? These regimens constitute what Adam Chau has called the "personal-cultivational modality" of doing religion: "This modality presupposes a long-term interest in cultivating and transforming oneself . . . the goals of this transformation and cultivation are different in each religious tradition: to become an immortal in Daoism, to be reincarnated into a better life or to achieve Nirvana in Buddhism, and to become a man of virtue or to be closer to sagehood in Confucianism. But the shared element is the concern with one's own ontological status and destiny, something akin to a Foucauldian 'care of the self.' In other words, the practices in this modality provide 'technologies of the self.' "[10]

"Technologies of the self" were theorized by Michel Foucault as "those intentional and voluntary actions by which men not only set themselves rules of conduct, but also seek to transform themselves, to change themselves in their singular being, and to make their life into an oeuvre that carries certain aesthetic values and meets certain stylistic criteria."[11] As "spiritual technologies," the practices we are interested in here aim to go beyond the outward, aesthetic or stylistic cultivation of one's life: they seek to effect an ontological transformation of the self of the practitioner. As argued by Komjathy, they are "techniques of transformation" that "aim to facilitate and initiate a shift in ontological condition from habituated being to realized being"[12]—from the self constituted by the unreflexive habits of daily life, to a self that strives to become conscious of, to experience, or to encounter a spiritual, sacred or ultimate reality.

Komjathy, in his study of the early Complete Perfection tradition, enumerates the following typology of religious training regimens: "(1) Ethical; (2) Purificatory; (3) Meditative; (4) Ascetic; (5) Dietetic and Hygienic; (6) Slumberic (sleep/dream); (7) Alchemical; (8) Respiratory; (9) Gymnastic (broadly understood); and (10) Ritualistic."[13] All of these can be found in the Daoist tradition, which uses a range of terms to discuss forms of practice: *fa* 法 ("method"), *gong* 功 ("exercise"), *lian* 煉/錬 ("refine"), *shu* 術 ("technique"), *xing* 行 ("practice"), and *xiu* 修 ("cultivate").[14] These technologies constitute regimens for the "cultivation of the self," which Foucault defined as "an attitude, a mode of behavior; it became instilled in ways of living; it evolved into procedures, practices, and formulas that people reflected on, developed, perfected, and taught. It thus came to constitute a social practice, giving rise to relationships between individuals, to exchanges and communications, and at times even to institutions. And it gave rise, finally, to a certain mode of knowledge and to the elaboration of a science."[15] Self-cultivation regimens set individuals on paths of ontological transformation but, no matter how intimate and personal such paths may be experienced and construed, and no matter how transcendent their goals of personal or social liberation, they are socially constructed, elaborated, and enacted. They emanate from and give rise to traditions, lineages, institutions, and organized systems of knowledge. These traditions, practices, and systems of knowledge lead people to "embody a coherent set of dispositions" in which the self is oriented in the world in terms of its positioning in relation to a nonhuman, divine or spiritual other, constituting what the anthropologist Thomas Csordas has called the "sacred self."[16]

The Daoist techniques of inner alchemy, of meditation, and of *qigong* that are practiced and/or discussed by the Dream Trippers and Chinese monks are typically referred to in the English language academic literature as practices of "self-cultivation." But what is the "self" being cultivated? Does the term presuppose the self as a bounded ontological entity—as assumed by much of the Greek and Western intellectual tradition and popular culture—and the object of the Orientalist spiritual search? As expressed by Thomas Merton, the famous Catholic mystic and popularizer of Asian spiritualities: "For me to be a saint means to be myself. Therefore the problem of sanctity and salvation is in fact the problem of finding out who I am and of discovering my true self."[17] On the other hand, the techniques are called "cultivation and refinement" (*xiulian*) in Chinese Daoist terminology, describing a process of transformation, in which the first character *xiu* has connotations of gradually bringing into order and alignment, while the second character evokes the cooking and transmutation of mineral elements in the alchemical furnace. The Chinese term does not evoke the "self" as the beginning, end, or ultimate purpose of the practice. If we include these techniques under the rubrics of "self-cultivation," the "care of the self" or "technologies of the self," it can only be if we see the self as a *process*, rather than as an entity or goal. Building on the work of Maurice Merleau-Ponty, Thomas Csordas, and Tim Ingold, we thus understand the self being cultivated to be an embodied process of orientation in the world.[18] This orientation involves the perception of embodied states, of the environment, and of social interactions and forces—all of which contribute to the formation of the self.

Generally speaking, American spiritual seekers can be said to begin their quest and practice within a framework of "ontological individualism," in which spirituality consists in discovering, nurturing, and expressing one's own "deep

self"; Daoist cultivation, on the other hand, is based on a process of "cosmological attunement" in which spirituality consists in the harmonization of the dynamic structure and forces of the body/mind with the corresponding dynamic
structure and forces of society and of the cosmos. To what extent, if at all, do the
Dream Trippers shift, in their self-cultivation, from ontological individualism
to cosmological attunement? To what extent can these approaches be detached
from their cultural matrix and embodied by people with little or no relevant
cultural knowledge or experience? What happens when these two approaches
to spiritual subject formation confront each other, or become imbricated with
each other? What are the implications of this interpenetration?

As people constitute themselves as spiritual subjects, advancing in the trajectories of their lives, they position and orient themselves in relation to the
forces they encounter. While the discourses and practices of many religious
traditions, and certainly the Daoist tradition, specifically address the bodily,
environmental, cosmic, and spiritual forces in relation to which we position
ourselves, less explicit, but always present as well, is the alignment of the practitioner with or against different social and cultural forces, and her interaction with those forces. These forces also contribute to constituting spiritual
subjectivity; consciously or not, the practitioner also contributes to reproduc-
ing or transforming those social and cultural forces. Daoist practices, in their
introduction to the West, do not come into a vacuum: they enter the highly
contested field of Western cultures of the body, health, and spirituality; within
this field, they become positioned in affinity with other sets of discourses and
practices, and against still others.

Indeed, in the West, Daoism is often explicitly defined by its practitioners
and advocates in opposition to the dominant church-style Christian religion
that is derided as oppressive, dogmatic, ritualistic, patriarchal, and with an
unhealthy relationship to the body, nature, and sex. More implicitly, Daoism
is positioned in contrast to secular Cartesian or "mechanistic" worldviews
that posit a dualistic division between mind and body, and between humans
and nature. Daoist ideas and practices are, instead, aligned with "holistic" approaches to health, healing, and spirituality, whether they originate in Western esoteric tradition, Oriental religions and philosophies, or Native American shamanism; practitioners often circulate between yoga, tai chi, shamanic
peyote cults, angel channeling, and Tibetan Buddhism. In this field, Daoist
self-cultivation practices seem to be the quintessential form of modern Western spirituality: a path grounded in the inner exploration of the individual
body and its energies, in which the stress is on subjective experience rather
than moral precepts (it even provides for the enhancement of sexual life!),
which can be practiced alone by the individual, without a community. It can

2500 years ago

be done through the practice of rationalized sets of techniques, rather than faith in religious dogma. Ritual or organization is unnecessary. Its key text, the *Daodejing*, is associated with a feminine, holistic, and ecological consciousness, as well as the undermining of traditional authority. Could any form of practice be more attuned to the spiritual sensibilities of a hyperindividualistic, postmodern West?

And yet, these practices emerged in China over 2,500 years ago, and have evolved in a religious field structured by the dynamic tensions between the imperial center and local societies, between the canonical traditions of Confucianism, Buddhism, and Daoism, and between communal ritual traditions and salvationist movements.[19] Through its interactions with the elements of this field, the Daoist tradition has accumulated a vast repository of forms of knowledge, practice, and social relations aiming to form spiritual subjects.

But these forms are deeply embedded within broader cultural and social practices, institutions, and contexts. What types of spiritual subjects are constituted by Daoist practices in different cultural contexts? What are the consequences of the migration of spiritual practices from one cultural context to another? Do practitioners from different cultural backgrounds become similar spiritual subjects? What happens when they meet? The forms now spreading in the West were developed and refined in China through centuries of interaction with an authoritarian, patriarchal culture that, to say the least, has little in common with the individualistic culture of the baby boomers who have welcomed them onto the American soil. The techniques, and the context of practice, have undoubtedly been changed through their introduction to Western societies— just as they had already been transformed in China itself in modern times, through over a century of reforms and modernizations. And, like any living tradition, they have constantly been reinvented and reinterpreted from the earliest days. Elements of Daoist culture have been selectively adopted and adapted into a new social and cultural context, producing something new.

Individual experiences and pathways can never be fully dissociated from collective trajectories, that is to say, from social and cultural history. The American spiritual travelers and Daoist monks whom we met are each on their own journey, but each one is also the carrier of, and is carrying forward, a long collective trajectory, a history which is embodied in their orientation toward techniques, experiences, interpretations, and life narratives. Through this encounter between Chinese and Western Daoists, then, we perceive— embodied in the interactions between discrete individuals—the encounter between two histories of the care of the self, two histories of spirituality, histories that intersect through the transmission of Daoist spiritual technologies. However, the direction of each collective trajectory is curved by the weight of historical memory and of contemporary sociocultural dynamics in China and America. Are the trajectories converging or diverging?

Spiritual Circulations

In this book, we consider the genealogies of the trajectories that have intersected at this encounter, as ongoing strands of the "interactional history"[20] or "circulatory history" of cultural, religious, and spiritual flows between Asia and the West.[21] The intersection of these trajectories produces the emergence of what we call "global Daoism." The globalization of religion is not a new process: over a thousand years ago, the Silk Road trade routes were pathways for the spread and transformation of Buddhism; five hundred years ago, the transatlantic trade route disseminated and changed African religions and Christianity, to name only two examples. But Daoism is relatively new to this process; only in the past few decades has it taken root outside the traditional sphere of influence of Chinese civilization in East Asia. Most significant is that this process is occurring at a time when the global circulation and interpenetration of religious cultures has reached an unprecedented scale and intensity.

At a time when colonial expansion facilitated the circulation of texts and practices of the different religious traditions of the world, the modern field of "spirituality" opened a space for people to make connections between the practices and ideas of different traditions, enabling a universalism that "bridges various discursive traditions around the globe."[22] Modern concepts of spirituality have appeared in tandem with secularism, offering a space for free and rational individuals to explore spiritual reality outside the authority and boundaries of the church. In parallel with the disenchantment of the traditional world in the West, other paths of "reenchantment" appeared. Magnetism, Mesmerism, Spiritualism, and Theosophy all proposed purportedly "scientific" methods for communicating with occult forces, the souls of the dead, angels, and God, all in secular contexts outside the confines of orthodox religious institutions, and often linking, integrating, and reinterpreting the teachings and practices of Asian religious traditions. The technologies of modern spirituality typically aim to train practitioners to open channels to reenchant their lives, while maintaining the autonomy, self-control, and reflexivity of what the philosopher Charles Taylor has called the "buffered self"[23]—the disenchanted, self-contained, and autonomous self of the modern secular world. Indeed, secularity also generates a desire for reenchantment within the limits of individual autonomy, which can be accessed through modern reformulations of spiritual technologies such as Daoist practices of the body. "Modern spirituality" thus situates itself in an uneasy and ambiguous location in between the two poles of enchantment and disenchantment—between a completely disenchanted, buffered, self-contained self at one extreme, and a completely enchanted, porous self lacking individual agency at the other.

The export of Daoist practices can only occur through a process of radical decontextualization. Csordas has suggested that two aspects of religion can "travel well" cross-culturally: "portable practices" and "transposable messages."[24] Portable practices can be learned easily, require relatively little esoteric knowledge or paraphernalia (although their esoteric "secrets" are one of their selling points), are not held as proprietary or necessarily linked to a specific cultural context, and can be performed without commitment to an elaborate institutional apparatus. Csordas identifies yoga as an "archetypal instance" of portable practice; similarly, the Chinese mind-body techniques of meditation, *qigong*, martial arts, *taiji quan* (tai chi), and so on are also quite portable when separated from their original social contexts. Michael Winn himself used the same terms when he told us,

> One thing I figured out is that while I was working in the third world as a journalist and photographer, I needed a portable health system. That's originally why I got into the yoga. . . . The Daoist practices were the most portable of all. You can do them standing, anywhere. Yoga you have to have a place for sitting. Qigong you can stand and no one even knows you're doing it; you can be doing it internally. It's perfect for me.[25]

Although the techniques do have elaborate esoteric meanings and cosmologies, one only needs one's own body, grown in any culture, to try the techniques out; and the degree to which one learns about and adheres to their underlying cosmologies and esoteric teachings is entirely a matter of personal choice. As for "transposable messages," Csordas refers to "religious tenets, premises, or promises [that] can find footing across diverse linguistic and cultural settings"; at the same time, these messages are "susceptible to being transformed or reordered without being denatured." Daoist notions of the ineffable Dao, of spontaneity and naturalness, of harmony and relaxation, of an embodied spirituality and of experienced *qi*, are examples of "transposable messages" which can find new homes and transformed meanings in the context of the Western counterculture, holistic spirituality, and alternative therapies.

The anthropologist Tulasi Srinivas, in her study of the highly globalized Sai Baba movement, analyzed four stages in the process of transnational cultural mobility: (1) Disembedding, in which specific practices or concepts are extracted from their originating cultural matrix; (2) Codification and universalization, in which the often unspoken, inexplicit, and unsystematized notions, practices, and modes of transmission are codified and packaged into explicit statements, discourses, procedures, and staged levels of practice that can be easily transferred and made meaningful in any context; (3) Latching and matching, in which the transferred forms "are given latching mecha-nisms that enable them to match up with the interpretive maps of meaning within other cultures"; and (4) Contextualization and reembedding, in which the exported form is incorporated and embedded within the broader ecology of meanings and practices of the host culture.[26]

All of these stages can be identified in our account of the transnational diffusion of Daoism; and we pay special attention to the "latching and match-ing" and "reembedding" processes by which Daoist techniques and ideas are "latched and matched" onto American ideas and notions of selfhood, spiri-tuality, and the body, and embedded into a milieu of alternative healing and spiritual networks that create a new context and meaning for Daoism. We also look at the reverse process of the return to the originating culture, in which self-identified American Daoist practitioners "latch and match" back onto elements of the sacred geography, lineages, and contemporary social practices of Daoism in China.

The most truly "portable" practices and "transposable" messages have been disseminated by universal religions which emphasize a split between the tran-scendental and the mundane.[27] Thus, it has been possible for a core of teach-ings of Buddhism, Christianity, and Islam to become packages of portable prac-tices and transposable messages, able to fully take root in any cultural context, and to retain their religious identity throughout a long process of localization and indigenous acculturation. Daoism, however, presents a different scenario. The tension between the transcendent and the mundane is far less radical in Daoism than in those world religions; the search for transcendence in Dao-ism has always been deeply embedded in the immanent body, in local so-ciety, history, and memory. Unlike the paradigmatic, foundational moments of the lives of the Buddha, Jesus or Muhammad, there is no point of rupture when "Daoism" as a universal religion broke out of the cultural matrix of its emergence; it is impossible to draw clear lines between Daoist religion, the rit-ual structures of local Chinese community life, and the general patterns and worldviews of Chinese culture. The complex ritual systems that historically—more than meditation and body cultivation techniques—have directly struc-tured the lives of Chinese people through communal festivals, funerals, and exorcistic rites cannot be understood or practiced outside the context of local social structures and deity cults. These are not easily portable or transposable. It would thus be legitimate to argue that exporting Daoist body technologies involves such an extreme level of disembedding and decontextualization that what is exported is either not Daoism at all, or a Daoism deeply mutilated and reduced. Is it still Daoism, or does it become something completely different? The transnational encounters we study here further complicate the issue, producing not only confrontations between different discourses of spiritual authority and authenticity but also fields of common experience and understanding. At stake is the meaning of Daoist identity and authenticity. Is this all a superficial sham, or does it, as Winn claims, open up the possibility of freeing Daoism from the fetters of centuries of historical and cultural baggage, allowing it to release its full potential?

The Emergence of a Global Daoist Field

In order to situate this process within the dynamic context of sociocultural change, we make critical use of the concept of a "religious field." For the sociologist Pierre Bourdieu, a religious field comes into being when a class of specialists appears that attempts to centralize, systematize, and control a body of knowledge, simultaneously disqualifying the nonspecialists or laypeople and creating a field of power between those who hold religious authority and those who do not. When political or ecclesiastical elites elevate one religious system over another, the displaced beliefs and practices associated with the vulgarity of the common people become stigmatized as "magic," "sorcery," and "superstition,"[28] or perhaps, in contemporary America, as "new age mumbo jumbo." Here, we take the concept of the religious field further by considering how those marginalized beliefs and practices form into an alternative tradition that occupies a specific location in the religious field, defines itself in tension with the dominant religious institutions, and attempts to elaborate its own norms of authenticity and authority.

Daoism fits into such a dynamic in both China and America—albeit in different ways, which explain the structural differences between "Chinese" and "American" Daoism: Chinese Daoism having evolved over 2,000 years in tension with the centralized imperial state and its Confucian ideology in the Chinese religious field; and, on spreading to the West, being recontextualized into the tensions of an American religious field in which esoteric, "alternative," and "holistic," spiritualities have evolved in tension with the dominant Christian church as well as with the disenchantment of the dominant secular institutions.

Spirituality is thus not a purely individual pursuit, but involves the construction, orientation, and embodiment of the self as a spiritual subject within a specific religious field. The encounters we describe in this book thus represent an encounter and mutual interferences between the Chinese and American religious fields, each of which has its own historical trajectory and internal dynamics. What begins to arise from these encounters is a global Daoist field in which an array of Western and Chinese actors, some of whom are the main protagonists of our account, engage in a contest to define and appropriate the meaning of authentic and authoritative Daoism.

By "global Daoism" we thus do not mean simply the spread of Daoism to different parts of the globe,[29] nor even, as described above, the return to China of forms of Daoism that have been indigenized overseas, bringing the process full circle. Our study shows how Chinese and Western, practitioner and academic, constructions of Daoism have elaborated their own multiple discourses on Dao—and in the encounters we describe here, these discourses become conscious of each other, respond to and influence each other. "Global Daoism" thus appears when a transnational field of Daoist practice, discourse, and authority claims opens up.

In the case of the encounters we study here, the Dream Trippers and the Huashan monks both claim the "Daoist" label, and they recognize each other's claim, notwithstanding the vast gulf that often separates their understanding of Daoism. And it is on the basis of this mutual recognition that they engage with each other, forming a new network that is based on its common "Daoist" identity. These encounters generate contested discourses on authenticity among participants, in which they seek authenticity, make claims of authenticity, and sometimes challenge the authenticity of the others.

Indeed, the protagonists of our story are acutely sensitive to the perception that an "American" Daoism could only be a form of superficial "New Age" spirituality, and go to great lengths to distinguish themselves from such an association—notably by stressing their connection to an authentic transmission of Daoism from China. With the opening of a global Daoist field through the encounters we relate here, such claims are contested by Daoists in China; at the same time, Chinese claims to authenticity can also be contested by Americans.

Komjathy, in the website of his Center for Daoist Studies, defines two categories of "American Daoism," essentially the authentic form that is directly affiliated to Chinese tradition, and with which he identifies himself; and the "fabricated" form of "Popular Western Taoism" (PWT), in which he places Healing Tao USA and the Dream Trippers:

> On the most basic level, "American Daoism" (a.k.a. "American Taoism") refers to anything identified as "Daoism" in America. In a more technical sense, it refers to two distinct dimensions of contemporary American society: (1) Adherents and communities associated with the Chinese Daoist religious tradition; and (2) Individuals who embrace a popular construction of "Daoism" rooted in colonialist, missionary, and Orientalist legacies. Only the former is Daoism per se.[30]

For Komjathy, modern Daoism in the West can be described as a spectrum of "tradition/transmission—innovation/adaptation—appropriation/fabrication."[31] Locating himself on the "tradition/transmission" end of the spectrum, he suggests that most groups that claim the Daoist label in America can squarely be placed at the "appropriation/fabrication" end:

> At the farthest reaches of popular Western appropriations and exploitations of Daoism are adherents who are best understood as members of a new religious movement (NRM), or, following their own self-representations, an ancient but new and perennially relevant form of "spirituality." That NRM may be labeled "Popular Western Taoism" (PWT), with "Taoism" pronounced with a hard "t" sound. In the case of the United States, PWT adherents and groups are the most publicly visible self-identified "Daoists." They are most likely to construct Daoism as "ancient philosophy" and (trans-religious) "spirituality," wherein the Dao (Tao) is identified as an abstract first principle or "energy field," and wherein Dao-ists just "go with the flow" (read: follow their own desires and egoistic motivations). Such accounts of "Daoism" are characterized by ahistorical, acultural and anti-religious views. Here the *Daode jing* (Tao-te-ching) is read, most often in inaccurate popular translations (e.g., by Ursula LeGuin, Stephen Mitchell), as the "Daoist Bible," as source of "universal wisdom," and as a guidebook for alternative spirituality. When people read such "translations," they are not reading a Daoist scripture (sacred text written in classical Chinese), but rather a contemporary American cultural production.[32]

Michael Winn admits the existence of such "New Age" American Daoists, but sees himself, and many of the Dream Trippers, as having attained a different plane of cultivation. He places American practitioners and Dream Trippers in between two poles: at one end is the New Age Daoists who rely on "instant Tao pop culture" to "expand their subjective identity to fill the cultural-religious void within their alienated, disenchanted world. Their identity is seeking a community and cultural ground and may be viewed as ultimately frail." At the other end are those who "appropriate a deep level EXPERIENCE of Daoist cosmology that is part of the appropriation of authentic inner alchemy practice. This requires months or years of training and a whole-body/mind experience of transformation into a higher cosmological level of causality than is offered by even a 'reenchanted' subjective self."[33] "They turn the cosmos into the solid ground of their identity.... The surrounding field of Western culture is a secondary aspect of their identity, not primary. Culture is just a part of the human playing field, but they do not measure their material and social success in it as the primary measure of identity." Some Dream Trippers, says Winn, could be situated in between those two poles—they experience Daoist cosmology, "But unless they have the discipline to practice it regularly and ultimately combine it with other internal meditation methods of neidan [inner alchemy], they may find their identity floating in between ontological individualism and cosmological attunement."[34]

The anxieties generated by the coexistence of "tradition-based" Daoism and "fabrications," of grounded practice and "Pop Tao," are precisely symptoms of the "predicament of modern spirituality." What we call the "predicament" refers to a condition in which, having rejected the authority structures of traditional religion, modern spiritual seekers exercise individual agency and choice in constructing their own spiritual path and identity, and are no longer forced to follow any religious authority. But this freedom is exercised at a time of unprecedented uncertainty, in which all of the structures that had previously grounded the self—whether tradition, community, religion, or ideology—are disintegrating. Free and atomized individuals are thus, paradoxically, thirsty for a stable ground of authenticity and authority. The ease with which one can experience, package, and consume "spiritual wisdom" generates anxieties about the authenticity of spiritual practices, and struggles over determining who has the authority to define authenticity in the religious field and on what criteria.

In the discussions and debates that we relate in this book, we find our protagonists evoking and contrasting several norms of authenticity and sources of authority. We list them in table 1. As we show, Chinese and American practitioners variously evoke one or several of these sources of authenticity or authority to defend their own claims and to dispute or doubt the claims of other actors. It is through these contested claims that the global "Daoist field" comes into being.

At one level, this book adds to a growing academic literature on how alternative religions, new spiritual practices, and appropriations of Asian traditions in the West merely reinforce the global neoliberal order they propose to transcend.[35] Our conclusions, however, both go further and are more qualified than this literature. Academics find it all too easy to offer devastating critiques of spiritual entrepreneurs. On the other hand, they often give a free pass to more tradition-based forms of religiosity. The appropriative agenda of the "plastic medicine men" and "white shamans" who hawk their wares on tour is contrasted with the authentic work of the Native American healers who live full-time on the reservation.[36] Or the consumerist discourse of the Western "mindfulness meditation" movement is shown lacking compared to the original intent of Theravada Buddhist *vipassana* texts and teachers. In this book, on the contrary, we examine a more "authentic" Daoism as practiced in China in the Quanzhen monastic order and find that it also suffers from a deep crisis of authenticity and authority. Finally, with our chapter on

TABLE 1

Source of Authenticity	Associated Source of Authority
Subjective experience. The authentic Dao is to be found within oneself, and can only be verified through one's own experience.	*The self.* Each individual is the sole authority to judge and to express his own Dao.
Visible embodiment. A cultivator's authenticity can be perceived through the way he embodies and manifests Dao, through the virtuosity of his body, his healing powers, his virtuous conduct, and/or his wisdom.	While such visible expressions can potentially be perceived by anyone, it is *the community of advanced practitioners* who have the discernment to appreciate, to judge, and to argue about the degree to which such embodied powers represent a person's authentic accomplishment of Dao.
Fidelity to tradition. A cultivator's authenticity is based on the degree to which she conforms to and masters the knowledge, disciplines, and practices of the Daoist tradition in a comprehensive manner.	The *senior members of the community* of practitioners who are committed to upholding a specific tradition.
Technical knowledge. A cultivator's authenticity is based on his mastery of practice and discourse on sophisticated Daoist cultivation techniques.	*Technically accomplished practitioners* who are capable of assessing and comparing techniques, their effects, and others' ability to practice them.
Scripture. The authentic Dao is contained and expressed in Daoist scriptures. Authentic practice requires the regular reading and study of scripture.	*Knowledgeable practitioners* who are able to guide students in the understanding of scripture.
Lineage transmission. Formal initiation, through the appropriate rites and ceremonies, of a lineage identity, name, knowledge, and position within a genealogy of masters and disciples, is a requirement for the authentic transmission of Dao.	*Holders of the lineage transmission* who, according to the rules of the lineage, have the authority to initiate disciples and to formally transmit the lineage identity.
National essence. Daoism is central to the essence of Chinese civilization; only a Chinese person can have an authentic understanding of Dao.	In a broad sense, only *Chinese people* can assess the authenticity of one's Daoist claims; more specifically, *the Chinese state*, as the embodiment of the Chinese nation, claims to possess such authority.
Transmission among the people. Owing to millennia of political interference and instrumentalization of Daoism, authentic Daoism is not to be found in state-defined orthodox institutions but is to be found hidden among the common people.	The *local masters* and transmitters of obscure and forgotten traditions.
Location in Daoist sacred mountains. The authentic Daoists are the hermits who have withdrawn from this world and attained the Dao in the mountains.	*Daoist hermits* who have no attachments to this world and are in communication with Dao.
Encounters with Daoist immortals. Daoist immortals will descend and confer powers and techniques to those who have attained an authentic level of attainment in cultivation.	*Daoist immortals.*
Empirical knowledge. Claims to Daoist authenticity can be verified by assessing their conformity to validated historical, textual, or ethnographic knowledge.	*Scholars with academic credentials* and who are recognized by their peers with expertise on Daoism have the authority to assess such claims.

scholar-practitioners, we take a self-reflexive look at the academic critique of New Age spiritual entrepreneurs. All three of these constructions of authenticity in a globalizing Daoism are implicated in the predicament of modern spirituality. In this book, we do not presume to take sides, to locate the "authentic" Daoism in these encounters; it is the *search for, experience of, construction of,* and *contestation of* authenticity that we try to convey.

An Ethnography of Transnational Encounters

This is a comparative anthropological study of the practice, experience, and social embedding of spirituality among American and Chinese monastic Daoist practitioners, as their similarities, differences, and mutual influences are laid bare through the crossing of their trajectories. These trajectories concern the "care of the self" as it has constituted itself through discourse and practice—in China, through the technologies of the body that are at the foundation of Daoist ascetic regimens, and in the West, through the practice of searching for, knowing, and expressing the "self" as an ontological reality. Our goal here is not to present a systematic comparative history—a far too ambitious undertaking—but to identify some of the attitudes, dispositions, and tensions which remain embedded within and continue to orient the contemporary cultures of self-cultivation with which our Daoists are engaging, be they in China or America, and that inflect the encounters between them.

What we aim for here is not a broad survey of the globalization of Daoism but rather a focused ethnographic study of one chain of encounters in the process. Rather than typical representatives of static ethnographic "tribes" of monks, spiritual travelers, and scholars, our protagonists, though unique in their views, their orientations, their experiences, and their perceptions, embody historical currents in the spiritual and religious evolution of post-Mao China and post-boomer North America. The result is necessarily limited and we cannot yet firmly assert that the conclusions reached here can be generalized: we have focused on only one of several American organizations operating Daoist tours in China. The case of the Dream Trippers should definitely not be generalized to all Western groups; European organizations, specially French and German, also organize Daoist tours to China, but often have a very different approach, with a stronger focus on history and culture, and/or on rigorous training. Our study also focuses on only one Daoist site in China. Altogether, according to the monks at Huashan, the total number of Western Daoist groups they had hosted (excluding groups which did not arrange to interact with the local Daoists) was not higher than a few dozen: the type of encounter studied here is far from a mass phenomenon, although it is increasing in number and impact. However, the Healing Tao network is one of the most well-rooted, active, and influential within popular Western Daoist circles; and Huashan, thanks to the works of Hedda Morrison and Deng Ming-Dao,[37] occupies an important place in Western Daoist lore and is therefore an indispensable stop on any Daoist tour to China.

Based on ethnographic research at multiple sites and interviews conducted in China and the United States, as well as one trip to Tao Garden resort in Thailand, this book unpacks these encounters between 2004 and 2016, using the narrative of their individual interactions, trajectories, and intersecting paths to identify and analyze the broader cultural and historical processes which come into contact and tension through the encounters. In following these moments of contact and tension, we follow Anna Tsing's metaphor of *friction*:

> [A] study of global interconnections shows the grip of encounter: friction. A wheel turns because of its encounter with the surface of the road; spinning in the air it goes nowhere. Rubbing two sticks together produces heat and light; one stick alone is just a stick. As a metaphorical image, friction reminds us that heterogeneous and unequal encounters can lead to new arrangements of culture and power.[38]

These frictions play themselves out through the embodied experience and appropriation of sacred places, the practice of pilgrimage and spiritual tourism, the production of religious knowledge and authenticity, and the aspirations of a modern spirituality in a context of globalization. To see the encounters in terms of friction, however, does not imply that they must be sites of conflict, of contest and resistance; they may well be points of collaboration between "heterogeneous and unequal" actors with different purposes and understandings—but they are generative of new and unexpected outcomes and trajectories, "new arrangements of culture and power."

Srinivas has identified three theoretical strands in the academic literature on cultural globalization.[39] The first is concerned with the commensurability, or not, of different cultural systems, and the implications of their interactions in a globalizing era;[40] the second has focused on cultural flows and the resulting combinations described as "hybridity," "mélange" or "creolization,"[41] and the third has considered how the weakening of bounded and inherited identities reinforces the modern construction of self and identity as a reflexive project.[42]

This book combines all three of these strands of analysis. In relation to the first strand, we sketch the historical evolution of ontologically incommensurable approaches to spirituality. We show how Daoism in America has been appropriated within a tradition of ontological individualism that has a

fundamentally different approach to spiritual subject formation than t
mological attunement that the Daoist tradition has aimed for in the C
cultural context. In relation to the second strand, we explore the "h
ity" of these two approaches to spirituality in a globalizing Daoism. We trace
how they are expressed and combined through the intersecting trajectories,
experiences, and encounters of practitioners. We point to the emergence of
a global Daoist field within which practitioners circulate and are connected,
and within which claims of authenticity and authority are communicated,
contested, and negotiated. And in relation to the third strand, we explore
how practitioners attempt to overcome the "predicament" of modern spirituality by connecting to the Chinese source of Daoism, or by reaching out to
Westerners—as they try to navigate between the fragility of the autonomous
self that is the subject of modern paths of individualistic spirituality, and the
dissolution of the norms of authenticity and authority that could, in other
times, provide a stable framework for constructing and transcending the self.

Outline of the Book

There are many bifurcations and junctions on the paths to the summit of
Huashan, and when you reach the top, there are several peaks and multiple
points of view. Similarly, in our story, Huashan is a node which connects not
only the trajectories of our protagonists, but several strands of discourse and
analysis, ranging from the history of Daoism and the hermeneutics of authenticity, to the anthropology of spiritual tourism and the sociology of modern subjectivity. Our narrative of Huashan leads us into the world of globalizing Daoism and, from there, draws us into a meditation on the predicament
of modern spirituality.

In this introductory chapter, we have set the ethnographic stage of our
account, presented the main protagonists, and introduced the key conceptual
issues of our study. In chapter 2, "The Mountain," we ascend the valleys and
peaks of Huashan, describing how the mountain is a source of enchanting
experiences for both Dream Trippers and the Daoist monks of the order of
Complete Perfection. While many Dream Trippers perceive these experiences
within the framework of ontological individualism, others use Primordial *Qigong* practice to connect and attune to the energies of the mountain within
the framework of a Daoist cosmology that is independent of history and culture. For monks, however, an important dimension of cosmological attunement occurs through connections with the Immortals of Daoist history and
lineage. With chapter 3, "The Trippers," we join the international circuit of

Daoist energy tourism, connecting retreats such as Tao Garden in Chiang Mai (Thailand), Tao Mountain in North Carolina, and the lives of the founding figures of Healing Tao, Mantak Chia and Michael Winn. We situate the emergence of American Daoism in the twentieth century and its connections with spiritual orientalism, Chinese immigration, and the counterculture and spiritual quests of the baby boomer generation; and offer a sociological analysis of the location of Daoism in the American religious field. We show how the American appropriation of Daoism has turned it into a paradigmatic expression of American spiritual individualism, in which the self is the ultimate spiritual authority. In chapter 4, "The Cloud Wanderers," we enter the Daoist monastic community at Huashan, presenting its daily routines and factional dynamics, and its historical and contemporary positioning in relation to other Daoist traditions. We discuss the current situation of religious life at Huashan under China's socialist regime, and introduce the spiritual biographies of Master Chen and two other monks—Master Hu and Master Hao—who play key roles in the encounters with the Western Dream Trippers and scholar-practitioners. We show how traditional Quanzhen authority and transmission have for centuries been deeply connected with the authority of the Chinese state. Under the current configuration, Daoist cultivation at Huashan is encapsulated within the structures of modern state and economic development; "cosmological attunement" can be pursued only within a restricted and frayed residual space. In chapter 5, "The Encounters," we follow the conversations between the Chinese monk-hermits and the Dream Trippers, as they meet and interact at the temples and caves of Huashan and other Daoist sites. Recounting their dialogues, we uncover their misunderstandings, humorous quid pro quos, and moments of "transnational communitas," as they approach each other with an ambiguous mix of expectation and condescension, search for a common language to talk about the experience and requirements of Daoist cultivation, and confide to us about each other. We show how they manage to break through barriers of culture and social positioning to experience a shared sense of seeking after Dao—but that they remain worlds apart in their understandings of self, practice, virtue, lineage, tradition, and authenticity. Chapter 6, "The Scholar-Practitioners," traces the influence of Western scholarship on popular American Daoism, and evokes the trajectories of ethnographers who became initiated into Daoist lineages as a way to deepen their research. Others have combined a personal spiritual practice with academic investigation, and some have begun to play an active role in the growth of Daoism in the West, not as an academic field but as a community of practitioners. The chapter focuses on the case of Louis

Komjathy, who is highly critical of both the commercialism of the energy entrepreneurs and the detached textualism of most academic studies of Daoism. We follow Komjathy in his struggles with both the "New Age" and academic worlds of Daoism, his quest for an authentic Daoism in China, and his apprenticeship with Master Chen at Huashan—who was also the first host of the Dream Trippers. Komjathy's story highlights the struggle over defining Daoist authenticity and authority in the West. Finally, in chapter 7, "The Predicament," we discuss the dilemmas facing Daoism as it is reconstructed as a modern, globalized spiritual path. American Daoism, with its emphasis on the body, subjective experience, and self-fulfillment, is a recent expression, and perhaps the fullest consummation, of a long history of spiritual individualism in the West, tending toward the complete disembedding of religious practice from place, tradition, and collective identity. Daoist self-cultivation may appear to be the ideal Oriental counterpart to this Western spiritual individualism—but, in China, it has historically tended to express a tendency *toward*, and not away from, embedding in locality, tradition, and Chinese national identity. The encounters at Huashan reveal the impasse which threatens both trajectories today, in a condition of high modernity: the fragility of a fully autonomous spiritual self on the one hand, and the crumbling away of the traditional authority of Chinese Daoism on the other. For both, there is a temptation to find another source of authenticity by crossing over to the other side. Either way, the protagonists face an impossible choice: taking refuge in a broken lineage and tradition, or a flight into pure subjectivity? In the concluding pages, we consider how our main protagonists see the solution to the predicament of modern spirituality. Winn and Komjathy each propose a "Third Culture" that would, in different ways, overcome the structural tensions between Daoism and modernity, and between the Chinese and American source and receiving cultures. But we question whether these solutions might simply reproduce the ontological and sociopolitical conditions that they hope to transcend. In the epilogue, "The Cosmic Orgasms," we narrate Winn's evolving views on the relationship between Daoist cultivation, sexuality, and marital monogamy, and end with an ethnographic description of what may be the climax of all the Dream Trips—two invented "Daoist wedding ceremonies" that were conducted on the summit of Huashan in June 2012, including that of Michael Winn himself. For this epilogue, we have refrained from engaging in theoretical analysis, giving the last word (or the last "healing sound") to the Dream Trippers, and we give you, the reader, the freedom to interpret the scene. Finally, in the appendix, we discuss how the research and writing for this book was conducted, our relationships with the object of the study and with our interlocutors, and how we influenced the unfolding of the story that we narrate. Reflecting on our experience, we question the insider/outsider distinction in the study of religion. Finally, we discuss how our three main interlocutors, Winn, Chen, and Komjathy, responded to the draft of this book after we had shared it with them, and we reflect on the personal and disciplinary contexts for the biases that they pointed out.

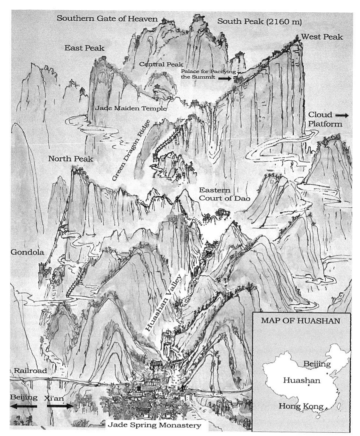

Map of Huashan (Courtesy of Vincent Chau)

Master Chen Yuming speaking to the Dream Trippers at the Jade Spring Monastery, beside a portrait of Wang Changyue, founder of the Dragon Gate lineage of the Daoist order of Complete Perfection

Daoist monk at Cloud Platform

Two Huashan monks

Xue Tailai, Chen Yuming's master (Courtesy of B. Porter)

Michael Winn meditating at Huashan (Courtesy of M. Winn)

Dream Trippers practicing Primordial *Qigong* at the Jade Spring Monastery

Travelers ascending the Green Dragon Ridge, from the North Peak up toward the Gate of the Golden Lock

Two Dream Trippers at a cave at the Cloud Platform where they spent the night

Louis Komjathy teaching at the Green Cove Daoist Association, Olympia, Washington, 2007 (Courtesy of Kate Townsend, Daoist Foundation)

The Mountain

The Dream Trippers whooshed up the eastern flank of Huashan in a gondola lift. This is the opposite side of the mountain from the traditional path taken by Daoists and pilgrims over the centuries, and still by thousands of tourists every day—a route which starts by gently meandering along a creek up the Huashan valley, but then abuts a sheer cliff, towering over 7,000 feet—the brave travelers ascend it, climbing through crevices in the cliff, up the almost vertical steps carved in the massive limestone. The gondola, on the other side, glides over a newer path up Huashan, opened up in 1949 by a Red Army detachment to capture the mountain from some of the last holdouts of Chiang Kai-shek's forces in northwest China.

Tourists spill out of the cable car at the North Peak, but here they still need to hike for a few hours, up the "stem" of the mountain, on a narrow stone flight of stairs atop a sharp ridge, until they reach the other four peaks of the "flower" of Huashan. The Dream Trippers settled for three days at a temple nestled in a depression near the Western Peak. This temple, the Zhenyuegong or "Palace for Pacifying the Summit," is a dilapidated wooden and concrete building turned into a tourist guesthouse. At our first visit to the mountain in 2004, blaring hip-hop music—provided by the managers of this guesthouse—dispelled any sense of silence and solitude. Ten years later, the passenger terminal to a new gondola lift leading directly to the Western Peak was blasted into the rock at this location, and now continually disgorges hundreds of tourists onto the temple grounds. The temple/guesthouse houses a shrine to the Lord of the Western Sacred Peak, and, in the cliff, a cave shrine dedicated to the King of Medicine. For the whole first day, the Dream Trippers dispersed along the forest paths connecting the peaks. Some sat in meditation on the windy

summit of the Western Peak, while a few adventurous souls tried the peril-
ous wooden platform overhanging the steepest drops at the Southern Gate
of Heaven. One Dream Tripper, writing after his return to the United States,
described his experience of practicing *wujigong* ("Primordial Chi Gung")—
the *qigong* method that Winn had taught to the participants—on a deserted
promontory:

> I spent three days at the group's "secret spot" atop Mt. Hua. During Primordial
> Chi Gung I saw the clouds mystically rise like angels and dragons and dag-
> gers. I could sense the clouds as the dragon's breath. I stripped naked once,
> and laid down on the rocks, my spine aligned with the spine of the gran-
> ite mountain. Now that I am home, I am feeling my spine aligning with the
> mountains. I rode a cloud dragon up a spiral toward heaven, taming my wild
> mind as the wind washed through me, playful & euphoric. I thought: THE IM-
> MORTALS ARE THE MOUNTAINS. I saw them through the eyes of the dragon, a
> bat, and a butterfly. I feel altered forever. I still ride the dragon now that I am
> home.

At each of the vistas of Huashan, the Dream Trippers peered down the
spectacular cliffs and across toward the other mounts and crags, feeling the
yang energy surging up from the entrails of the earth, their gaze following
the bulges, the folds, and the sheer vertical smoothness of the white rock faces
which shoot upward from distant gullies below and poke at the firmament
above. Sitting on ledges, some of them in the lotus position, over the abys-
sal drop of 7,000 feet, the Dream Trippers watched the sunset on the western horizon as it splashed its orange, red, and dark violet rays over the moun-
tainsides. And they took turns taking digital snapshots of each other beside
the glowing solar disk. Back at the temple, as they reviewed their pictures,
one young American in his early twenties spotted a bright white winged
creature, that looked strangely like an angel, in the foreground of one of
his photos. And in another shot, a translucent white globe, also in the foreground. Shocked and amazed, he excitedly showed the picture to his fellow
travelers, causing quite a stir. "Now I really believe this stuff," he exclaimed,
and vowed to fully soak in the rest of the trip, which, he admitted, he had
not fully enjoyed until then. For him, the Dream Trip was now becoming
an enchanting experience. For one of the travelers, what the photos had cap-
tured were simply flies or specks of dust that happened to have flown in front
of the camera flash. But for Master Hu, the Daoist monk who was accompanying the group, "Those are the Immortals of Huashan. I see them all the
time."

Enchantment as Subjective Experience or
Cosmological Attunement

Huashan is one of a string of "energetic hot spots" on the itinerary of the Dream Trips, a venue with spectacular scenery, welcoming monks, and reliable access to caves for meditation. The passage of growing numbers of foreign practitioners through these sites, and their experience of the mountains, contributes to inscribing the sacred topography of Chinese Daoism into the personal and collective memory and spiritual landscapes of popular American Daoism. Meanwhile, for the thousands of chattering tourists crawling up and down Huashan's ridges, steps, ledges, and observation terraces every day, Huashan is a gondola ride followed by a challenging climb and rewarded by scenic photo opportunities at the top; they are oblivious to the small handful of those, Chinese or foreign, for whom Huashan has deep spiritual and personal significance.

In this chapter, we show how the experience of Huashan is an enchanting one for both the Dream Trippers and the Daoist monks who live on the mountain. But we argue that there are different types of enchantment, based on the "integrative schema" through which enchanting experiences are structured and interpreted. In the previous chapter we contrasted the integrative schema of ontological individualism and cosmological attunement. In the former, subjective experience is crucial to the enchantment of the individual self; while in the latter, enchanting experiences confirm the correspondences between the cosmological structures of body, place, and history. Are the Dream Trippers experiencing Huashan as ontological individualists, or do they tend to cosmological attunement? To what extent do they complete this ontological shift, or combine the two integrative schema? We also consider how these integrative schema structure the practice and experience of pilgrimage and spiritual tourism, and the construction of Huashan as a sacred mountain.

Secularization has been described by Max Weber and others as a process of "disenchantment," as society evolves into the "iron cage" of rationality.[1] The philosopher Charles Taylor, in his monumental *A Secular Age*, analyzed the specific type of self and subjectivity that arises in a secular world, one that he calls the "buffered self." According to Taylor, in a disenchanted world, all meaning is "in our own mind." We give meanings to things; there is no meaning intrinsic to anything in the world. It's all "in our heads"—"the only locus of thoughts, feelings, spiritual élan is what we call minds; the only minds in the cosmos are those of humans (grosso modo, with apologies to possible Martians or extra-terrestrials); and minds are bounded, so that these

thoughts, feelings, etc. are situated 'within' them."[2] Thoughts and meanings
occur only in human minds, which are inward spaces. But in an enchanted
world, not only is there meaning intrinsic to the world, to the cosmos, to
objects or to invisible agents such as gods or spirits—but these agents can
communicate meaning to us, even meanings and ideas that we would not
expect. In other words, in an enchanted world, *we are in communication with
the visible and invisible world around us*, while in a disenchanted world, we
can only communicate with other humans.[3] But this communication is not
between firmly bounded entities: the enchanted self is porous, there is not
always a clear line between personal agency, the influence of other beings and
powers, and impersonal forces. In the buffered self of the disenchanted world,
on the other hand, the self becomes a bounded entity that has its own, unique
private inner space over which it can aim to be the sole master.[4]

In a secular context, experiences and processes of "reenchantment" are
important aspects of the formation of spiritual subjects. Techniques of spiritual cultivation can produce and reinforce embodied and perceptual dispositions that enhance the probability of such experiences occurring. As we show
in this book, the experiences generated through practices of *qigong* and Daoist inner alchemy, as well as experiences at sacred sites such as Huashan, are
the source of many enchanting experiences for both the Chinese monks and
the Dream Trippers, in which immaterial entities, forces, and coincidences
make unexpected irruptions into their bodies, their consciousness or their
lives. These enchanting experiences interpellate them as spiritual subjects, inflect on their self-orientation, and become part of their individual narratives
of transformation.

Enchanting experiences are culturally shaped, interpreted, and acted on.
The flow of perception is structured and mediated by what the anthropologist Philippe Descola calls "integrative schemas." These schemas selectively
give salience and significance to certain perceptions rather than others, organize thoughts, feelings, and actions according to standardized scenarios,
and provide a common language and interpretive framework for members of
a community.[5] Integrative schemas consist of cosmologies or ontologies that
identify, classify, and interrelate the basic components of the world.[6] This is
not the place for an extensive discussion or evaluation of Descola's method;
for the purpose of our study, we simply retain the contrast between what he calls
the "naturalist" and "analogical" ontologies. In the naturalist ontology—as
opposed to animist ontologies which posit that all beings have interiority—
humans and nonhumans share a material exteriority that follows the same
laws and principles of physics, chemistry, and biology, but only humans
have interiority. However, the interiority of each individual, or the collective

interiority of each cultural group, is absolutely unique. Subjectivity and communication are only possible between humans, who are thus radically different from other beings. This corresponds to the disenchanted, "buffered self" of Charles Taylor. The naturalist ontology, which first appeared in Europe in the sixteenth and seventeenth centuries, now structures discourse, social relations, and individual subjectivities in modern cultures around the world, including, to a great degree, contemporary China. When, in this book, we speak of "ontological individualism," we refer to an integrative schema of the self that is rooted in the naturalist ontology.

In an "analogical" ontology, on the other hand, there is no strong distinction between exteriority and interiority. All beings are made of infinitely changing combinations of heterogeneous elements, forces, and energies in circulation, which are differentiated from each other only by degree. Different orders of reality all have analogical structures—that is to say, they are considered to be structurally similar, by analogy to a basic ontological or cosmological pattern. Descola classifies the cosmologies of several ethnic groups into the "analogical" category, but he uses Chinese thought as his paradigmatic case, quoting the famous sinologist Marcel Granet who wrote that, in Ancient China, "Society, humanity and the world are the object of an all-encompassing knowledge that is constructed through the sole means of analogy."[7] Indeed, scholars of Chinese religion have typically described Chinese cosmology as the "cosmology of systematic correspondences," or as a "correlative cosmology," which expresses much the same meaning. The cosmos is made up of the interactions between the forces of yin and yang and of the five phases. These forces are conceived of as analogical to the movements of the cardinal points, the seasons, the times of day, the copulation of male and female, etc. They operate and resonate with each other at all levels, from the whole universe to the individual body. The body is a microcosm of the entire cosmos. When, in this book, we speak of "cosmological attunement," we refer to this integrative schema.[8]

In ontological individualism, spirituality consists in penetrating deeper into one's own, unique interiority, knowing and expressing "the true me." In cosmological attunement, on the other hand, the cultivation of a spiritual subject consists in aligning the relationships between the substances, energies, and forces of the mind/body with the relationships of the corresponding components of the cosmos, attaining the underlying unity that transcends the division between interiority and exteriority, and between all the diverse elements and forces of the body and the cosmos. Daoist self-cultivation practices aim to transform the body so that it is attuned with, and fully embodies, the cosmology.

The Dream Trippers embody the cosmological practices of *wujigong*, but within a subjectivity and in a culture that are conditioned and structured by the ontological individualism that underpins self-knowledge and social relations in America. This has far-reaching implications because, as we show, cosmological attunement is not a simple theory, belief system, or subjective experience: it is a process of aligning and structuring the relationships between humans and nonhumans, as well as social and political relations. Do American Daoists assimilate the symbols and experiences of Daoist cosmology into the integrative schema of ontological individualism? Or, on the other hand, do their Daoist practices and their Dream Trip experiences draw them out of the individualist framework, leading them to seek cosmological attunement in their positioning in relation to other humans and to other beings and forces in the cosmos? Or both?

By setting up an analytical contrast between ontological individualism and cosmological attunement, we hope to avoid going down the route of evaluating to what extent Daoism is being "Westernized" or "Americanized," or making our own judgments about what type of Daoism is "authentic" or "traditional." One might imagine different spiritualities, individualist and cosmological, claiming the label of Daoist. One might imagine Chinese ontological individualists, and Westerners seeking a path of cosmological attunement. One might also ask if the two integrative schema are incommensurable, or if they can be combined.

Consuming Huashan as Modern Spiritual Tourists

The Dream Trippers come to China as a package tour, appealing to a niche market of spiritual seekers and energy practitioners. The format of these tours—in which the ascent of Daoist mountains and meditation sessions are sandwiched between sightseeing visits to the Great Wall and the Terracotta Warriors—may strike some as jarring, juxtaposing, in successive days, the search for sacred, mystical experiences in lonely caves, and then joining the crowds of jostling tour groups taking snapshots and buying souvenirs in the tired locales of China travel guidebooks. Online promotion of the Dream Trips included one participant's testimony about experiences of sensuous dancing at a bistro in Dali, hinting that the nature of the trips is far from being exclusively transcendental. Are the Dream Trippers pilgrims on a sacred journey, or tourists on a superficial whirlwind?

"In the Western discursive universe, which is heavily imbued by Christian patterns that are still casting long shadows over scholarly discussions, pilgrimage and tourism occupy two diametrically opposite semantic poles," states the scholar of tourism and religion Michael Stausberg. Thus, "pilgrimage is positively valued—travel as a spiritual, transformative ritual; tourism is travel as materialist holiday, [and] serves as a distraction."[9]

Theorists such as the historian of religions Mircea Eliade or the anthropologist Victor Turner have defined pilgrimage as a journey to the sacred symbolic center of one's religious world.[10] The conventions of tourism, on the other hand, "tend to domesticate these novel places by commodifying the experiences that visitors have of them."[11] These definitions of tourism and pilgrimage may imply a dualistic understanding of the place as *other*, separate from the visitor, so that it can only be either approached with awe, through pilgrimage, or profaned, through tourism. Either way, they can be associated with ontological individualism, in that they posit a clear boundary between self and other, and emphasize the quality, in terms of depth or superficiality, of the subjective, inner experience of the self.

A more nuanced view sees tourism not as opposed to pilgrimage but as a modern or secular form of pilgrimage. Tourists aim to have authentic experiences at the sacred or, at least, legendary sites of the modern world—the Mona Lisa, the leaning tower of Pisa, the Grand Canyon. For the anthropologist Nelson Graburn, tourism is "supposed to renew us for the workaday world"; he contrasts the "sacred/nonordinary/touristic and the profane/workaday/stay-at-home."[12] Dean MacCannell calls the tourist's "to do" list—a collection of places, structures, and objects—"sight sacralization."[13] Unlike traditional pilgrimage, however, the tourist's search is oriented away from one's own religious center. Tourism, as a product of modernity, finds authenticity in the cultural other (the mystic East, the exotic, the primitive, the ancient, etc.). But, because the authentic is always being staged and re-created, at a remove from the traveler, tourism is often experienced as ultimately unsatisfactory. This unsatisfactoriness may be one reason for tourism's self-disavowal, what MacCannell calls the "touristic critique of tourism." In other words, travelers never want to be called tourists, and disdain places that are too "touristy." As Michael Winn said at a banquet at Huashan: "We came here not as tourists but as cultivators."

In our interviews with Dream Trippers while on the trip and via e-mail afterward, we asked respondents their favorite and least favorite parts of the trips. The Daoist mountains (Qingchengshan, Huashan, and Weibaoshan in Yunnan Province) were a clear favorite. The least favorite place was Beijing, which was seen to be crowded and "touristy." Several respondents also mentioned that the temples, whether in the city or the mountains, also seemed "too touristy."

In the West, tourists aim for an authentic travel experience, while criticizing "bad" tourists as crass and shallow. At Huashan, as at so many "scenic spots" in China, tourist infrastructure cannot hope to keep up with the rapid growth of domestic tourism in China. Indeed, Huashan's North Peak, where one of the cable cars and both footpaths up the summit end, is so packed with people it can resemble Times Square more than a Daoist hideaway. Other than in slogans and regulations on "civilized traveling," China does not (yet?) share this normative discourse on touristic behavior. "China's lack of the distinctly modern, romantic, exploratory, and self-bettering discourses of tourism that emerged in the West after the Enlightenment" manifests itself today in the way that famed tourist destinations in China (and, as visa restrictions are eased, increasingly Southeast Asia, Europe, and America) are filled with Chinese tourists who unselfconsciously buy, smoke, spit, snack, shout, and snap photos.[14] As Pal Nyiri puts it, "the good tourist" in China is not "one who recognizes the authentic and approaches it in an authentic way (as in the Western discourse) but one who learns the canonical representation of the sites he is planning to visit"; this value is still practiced in modern times and Nyiri quotes a pocket tourism encyclopedia from 1988 in support of this: "Each famous mountain and great river has its specifics. Mount Tai is heroic; Huashan is dangerous."[15]

For Chinese tourists and the officials charged with developing the travel industry, Huashan represents a "scenic spot"—in Chinese, *jingdian* or *mingshengqu*. These terms have been used to mean beautiful scenery since the Qing dynasty (1644–1912). The canonization of "scenic spots" has been shown by scholars to be a project of state power involved in maintaining the empire and its boundaries. The Ming dynasty (1368–1644) saw the publication of catalogs with illustrations of specific views of "scenic spots" as tourism became a culturally approved activity for the literati. These catalogs were reproduced in various official gazetteers.[16] With the rise of modern tourism in the late twentieth-century People's Republic of China (PRC), this "canon" of "scenic spots" remained important, and indeed was expanded to include communist sites, but access became more controlled by the state with the addition of ticket gates and fences.[17]

In such ritualized, "canonical" tourism, the purpose is not authentic subjective experience but the alignment of travelers' bodies and perceptions with collective memory, evoked through the ubiquitous calligraphied verses of famous poets, generals, sages, saints, and emperors engraved onto stones, temples, and monumental gates at "famous scenic spots." As we elaborate further below in the case of Huashan, this is often an imperial collective memory constructed through the inscription of the site into a broader cosmology. The alignment of bodies, localities, polity, and cosmology is part of the historical process of cosmological attunement in China.

In contrast to canonical tourists who participate in the performance and construction of collective memory and consciousness, authenticity-seeking tourists wonder if the stories they are told are true, distrust their guides, suspect friendly locals, ironize about staged performances, and fear being cheated by their servants.[18] One common way to avoid misgivings about the authenticity of the tourist experience is to seek powerful bodily sensations. "Because of their overwhelming and undeniable felt physical reality, such sensations are experienced as existing beyond the corrosion of commercialism."[19] Such authenticating physical experiences include extreme indulgence in food and drink, adventure tourism in jungles and mountains, high-risk sports such as white-water rafting and kayaking, skydiving, surfing, hang gliding, and bungee jumping, and even sex tourism.

Spiritual tourism also aims to create authentic experiences; in the "energy tourism" of the Dream Trippers and trips to other "energy hot spots," these experiences involve not only connections with sacred places rich in history, culture, and meanings, but also sensations of powerful flows of energy linked to those places—while avoiding the dangers of some of the high-risk activities mentioned above. Although its more distant origins are in Romanticism, when British poets visited the English Lake District and the Swiss Alps, Western spiritual tourism has its proximate origins in the counterculture of the 1960s, with the rise of backpacking as a means of travel and as a statement against group tours, cruise ships, and other "establishment" forms of travel. Hippies traveled to India, Nepal, and beyond: destinations that were exotic, inexpensive, and offered easy to come by drugs and spiritual enlightenment. Guru-centered spiritual tourism to India stretches back into the nineteenth century when Madame Blavatsky and her Theosophical Society decamped for Adyar, India. With the rise of the New Age movement in the 1970s, a new set of "power places" or "power spots" emerged, which are associated with "ley lines," energy vortexes, etc.[20] Already famous tourist spots, such as Stonehenge in England, the Egyptian pyramids, and Machu Picchu in Peru, are given an additional level of "spiritual" meaning. Other destinations become well known solely because of their spiritual quality, most notably Sedona, Arizona. Nazca in Peru and Glastonbury in the UK are two locations where tourists go to experience the "earth energy."[21] "Shaman tourism" takes seekers to meet indigenous healers in Peru and Siberia.

Like much of the counterculture, by the 1980s spiritual tourism had gone upscale and corporate. "New Age" tours became a new subset of spiritual tourism, with its own organizations. In 2007 the *New York Times* reported that "New Age-style sacred travel, or metaphysical touring, is a growing branch of tourism." The report put the beginnings of this iteration of spiritual tourism in 1987, with the harmonic convergence, a culminating event in the New Age movement when "many in the metaphysical community traveled to sacred sites around the world for prayer, meditation and ceremonies."[22]

The growth of "energy tourism" solves MacCannell's touristic conundrum. For the Dream Trippers, an authentic experience is possible, because for them authenticity is based primarily on the experience of *qi*, located in the deeply personal reality of embodiment and subjectivity—unlike, as we show, in Complete Perfection Daoism in which lineage, ritual, and virtue are more important indicators of authenticity. The Dream Trippers can thus be compared to the New Age tourists studied in other destinations: they are "deep tourists" who "do not simply go to see a place, lay out on the beach or take pictures—they participate in and become part of the destination through meditation, prayer, and other rituals."[23]

The idiom of "energy" or *qi* (pronounced "tchee") also provides a language for enchanting travel experiences, such as: "I felt a strong energetic connection with the mountain." Or, one of the Dream Trippers stated that the "energetically most powerful experiences" she had had were "the food, the meals, the conversations, the friendship." Or others said, "The group is very good, there are very good energies, nobody is complaining, there are excellent vibes."[24] This idiom could also be used for negatively evaluating touristic experiences according to "energetic" norms: instead of saying that a place was too crowded, or that one was tired, participants in one tour to Daoist sites in China said, "There was bad energy at the top. It was better down below"; or, about a hotel with surly staff or problems with the room: "This hotel has bad *qi*." Or, speaking of a masseuse who, like most in China, was a twenty-year-old peasant girl with minimal training who lived like an indentured servant in the massage parlor: "This one just has techniques, no energy."[25]

Huashan is added to spiritual tours because it meets a certain number of standard criteria for "energy power spots," which would include places sufficiently off the beaten track but within convenient access to comfortable accommodation and transportation, places and activities producing distinct energy experiences, extraordinary scenery, and a special atmosphere of religious authenticity—the presence of "real" monks, for instance, who are genuine Daoist cultivators and able to impart teachings to group members. For each of these criteria, the uniqueness of the locality is highlighted, but within a standardized, ahistorical framework of expectations that allows Huashan to be placed in a sequence of other sacred energy sites in the itineraries of global spiritual tourists. Group members are consumers, whose relationships may not last beyond the three-week trips to China. The Western Daoist organizations and networks within which many of them circulate in America and other countries are mostly commercial operations selling retreats, courses, books, and, increasingly, tours to China.

Chinese mountains outside of Tibet remain largely unknown in these global circuits of energy spots, but Michael Winn and others, through their Daoist trips to China, are helping to put Huashan and other Daoist mountains "on the map." In between his biannual Dream Trips, Winn regularly travels alone to China as an energy prospector, a "connoisseur" who samples the *qi* from different mountains. He describes Huashan as especially powerful: "Just knock-your-socks-off. . . . That's the power mountain in China. All that yang earth energy, the granite, the fire. The *fengshui* with the five petals . . . it's just the consummate Daoist mountain."[26]

Doomed to Disenchantment? Western Tropes of Huashan

Dream Trippers, who started visiting Huashan in 2000, tread the footsteps of a small number of Western writers, who, since the 1930s, have inscribed Huashan in the Western imagination of Daoism. When China's Five Sacred Peaks (*wuyue*) are mentioned in English-language literature, Huashan is singled out for special praise. Brock Silvers, an American businessman who, while working in China for many years, developed a deep interest in Daoism and published a guide to the religion, recommends, for Huashan, spending "four to five days to explore this gem of a mountain."[27] Meanwhile, a coffee table book that surveys sacred mountains around the world states that "of the five sacred mountains [of China], the loveliest is Hua Shan," and describes how "for centuries Chinese poets and painters have evoked in unnerving detail the dizzy hollow-stomach sensations inspired by its fathomless views. The landscape of the sacred mountain easily matches the wildest fantasies of the kind of airy place where sages commune with the stars in heaven."[28]

In 1935, the British spiritual seeker and adventurer John Blofeld (1913–1987), whose books were among the first to bring Chinese Buddhism and Daoism to a mainstream Western audience, was riding the train from Xi'an to Beijing when, as he wrote in his memoirs, "about two or three hours along the way I suddenly saw a sight of such magnificence that it tumbled my soul. It was a high and mighty mountain that soared like a tower straight up to the sky."[29] It was Huashan. Blofeld felt compelled to get off the train, found a local willing to carry his bags up the mountain, and started up. They climbed in falling snow, and stayed at a small monastery halfway up the mountain, unable to make it to the summit. Blofeld described the hospitality of the Daoists and their homespun wisdom.[30]

Another early Western visitor to Huashan was Hedda Morrison (1908–1991), a German photographer who, like Blofeld, hiked on Huashan in 1935. A book of her striking black and white photographs of the mountain was published in 1974, with an introduction by the sinologist Wolfram Eberhard.[31] Morrison thus described the Jade Spring Temple: "The place was charming and the monks courteous and friendly. I felt welcome and, in their enlightened company, all the troubles of the outer world seemed to vanish."[32]

The next major English language account of Huashan is *Chronicles of Tao: The Secret Life of a Taoist Master*, first published in 1983 by the Californian Chinese artist and author Deng Ming-Dao.[33] Damned by scholars and practitioners as a "forgery," it is the purported biography of Deng's Daoist master, Kwan Saihung. According to the *Chronicles*, Kwan was born in 1920 to a wealthy family in Shaanxi Province. At sixteen he met "the grand master of Huashan," and was accepted as a disciple. The three volumes contain various episodes of Kwan receiving advanced Daoist training at Huashan, leaving the mountain, and then returning, in between tales of him commanding a brigade in the anti-Japanese war, and becoming an opera star, a bodyguard in the Shanghai underworld, a solo bicycle traveler in Europe, a student at Yenching University, an aide to Chinese premier Zhou Enlai, a deputy in the Peoples' Congress, and finally an American immigrant in 1951 (all this before he turned 32). In 1954, he was summoned back to Huashan by his master. He found few Daoists left, and most temples ruined. Toward the end of the book, he is conned out of his life savings. Despondent, he plans to meditate himself into the next world. Then he meets a young man in the park who wants to learn from him. "Taoists traditionally met students by chance," the *Chronicles* tell us;[34] and we realize that the whole narrative serves as an advertisement for the "real" Kwan's martial arts seminars.[35]

After living in Taiwan for many years, first in a Buddhist monastery and then at a hermitage, the writer Bill Porter traveled to China in the spring of 1989 in search of hermits in the Zhongnan Mountains. The book he produced—*Road to Heaven: Encounters with Chinese Hermits*—combined travelogue and popular history. He climbed Huashan and met Master Xue Tailai, seventy years old at the time, who had been living at the mountain's summit for forty-five years. Xue was Master Chen's master; his story is related in chapter 4 of this volume. Porter wrote: "Huashan had a special power to attract veneration. Its form was unique among mountains. And to climb it required great courage and great desire, desire not of the flesh but of the spirit. For Huashan was one of China's earliest spiritual centers, a place where shamans came to seek visions."[36]

These Western accounts of Huashan focus on the mountain as the site of a mysterious and mystical tradition, where a spiritual authenticity could once be found that has disappeared in the modern world. But this spiritual quality of Huashan is portrayed as rapidly receding into the past, and, in the *Chronicles of Tao*, as a commodity that can now only be approached through the consumption of commercial seminars in San Francisco. The Western trope of Huashan mirrors the process of disenchantment, in which the last, aging Oriental monks are caught on camera or in text: as the living spirit of the mountain disappears, its last traces are recorded in books to be consumed or lessons to be purchased.

The Dream Trippers Reenchant Huashan

Given this lore on Huashan in Western writings, we initially thought that Huashan had become an obligatory stop for the Dream Trips because Michael Winn had read about the mountain in Blofeld or Morrison or Porter, or perhaps in the quasi-fictional peregrinations of Kwan Saihung. But, in fact, what attracted Winn to Huashan was none of these literary antecedents. It was the accounts of an old friend, and a series of coincidences. Juan Li (b. 1946), an American-educated Cuban of Chinese descent, was, like Winn, an early student of Mantak Chia, as well as the illustrator of Chia's book covers and posters. According to Winn, Li

> went on a pilgrimage around China, didn't speak any Chinese, didn't have a guidebook, he got a list of sacred mountains and he went there, he just bumbled his way around China, and spent some months going around and taking pictures. And I saw his pictures of Huashan and, of course, I immediately fell in love with it, like, "I've got to go there." [. . .] He would climb the mountain, it was like a pilgrimage, where each step you would be initiated into the mountain. And you were getting the *qi* of the mountain into you by climbing it. And by the time you actually climbed it, you had it inside you. So that's the way he approached it. That was a lovely teaching and an inspiration to me.[37]

The Dream Trippers' narratives of Huashan thus never evoke past Western accounts of the mountain, nor do they mention previous Chinese visitors. The Huashan they describe is entirely one of embodied experience. They talk of connecting to the energies of past cultivators in the sacred mountain, who remain unnamed—it is only their energies which are felt. In contrast to the

earlier Western accounts, theirs is not a narrative of disenchantment. Michael Winn himself described powerful, enchanting experiences in one of the
Huashan caves:

> After I finished saying all my thanks, an extraordinary thing occurred. My
> mouth was suddenly filled with a ball of pulsating energy, which slowly moved
> down my throat and esophagus into my stomach. Remarkably, this chi ball
> stayed in my gut during my time in the cave, and I am certain accounted for
> the fact that I never once felt even slightly hungry for the entire five-day cave
> fast! Since this occurred immediately after my meditation thanking the cave,
> it felt like a clear communication from the mountain. [. . .] Some invisible
> presence within Huashan mountain seemed to be actively pushing me deeper
> into Daoist practice at every moment.[38]

Such descriptions, and the testimony of tour participants, are highlighted
in tour promotional materials, attracting other practitioners to experience the
mountain's powers as well:

> The Qi (chi) I experienced in China was simply mind blowing. I got a trans-
> mission from being in those mountains that has totally opened up new levels
> of my inner vision.
>   But then some crazy stirrings happened in the lower tan tian. Rumbling,
> earthquake . . . explosion in my head. Feeling pressure . . . mouth open wide,
> eyes shut tight, indescribable feelings in whole body . . . then boom!! It ex-
> pressed through me as great laughter, I laughed like never before, my whole
> body was shaking in laughter, my lungs gasping for breath, my eyes tearing
> like crazy from laughter. . . . Then crying . . . like never before crying and cry-
> ing. . . . Then dancing and spinning like never before.[39]

These testimonies of powerful experiences, published on the Healing Tao
website, provided narratives to which future participants could aspire to connect to. And Dream Trippers whom we interviewed on Huashan had similar
experiences to tell:

> This trip again gave me the incredible opportunity to connect with the land and
> people in places of the world where there has been an ancient and continuous
> presence of powerful meditation practitioners. The result of this has been that I
> have developed a deeper connection with my inner self through the inner self of
> many other people (as well as the earth self) as a collective experience.
>   A very soft energy, welcoming, spiraling, as if someone was sending me
> energy.

One young American spent a week in the caves of Huashan, then sent a poetic e-mail to the group:

Inside the domed womb of a small cave, lost in the depths of internal thun-
der . . . for three days, slowly being inducted into the collective self of Huashan;
the immortals, the deep earth energy and the primordial self, pulled into the
dark womb of the mysterious female. My deep collective inner self slowly
filled with the shimmering sound of crystal light.[40]

The narratives of Huashan by the Dream Trippers clearly involved describing and experiencing the mountain as a site laden with powerful energies that open their "inner vision," connecting them to their "inner self."
These experiences break through the "buffered self" of a disenchanted world:
the Dream Trippers find themselves in communication with an "invisible
presence," "the inner self of many people," a "welcoming energy," "the collective self of Huashan," which is derived from "an ancient and continuous
presence of powerful meditation practitioners."

While Winn admits that some Dream Trippers are "spiritual tourists" who
"will go home feeling some satisfaction at adding a new layer of exotic memory to their hypersubjective Western bubble-self," others, however, will "be
converted to become pilgrims" as they sense a connection to the Daoist cosmology; for some of them, their lives are transformed, they return to China
on successive Dream Trips or even move to China,[41] or see their Dream Trip
as a key stage in their spiritual path.

They are NOT "consumerist" experiences of Qi, eaten one day and forgotten the
next. They are LIFE CHANGING for them, i.e. permanent. They open up a new
bedrock in their spiritual identity that stays with them. Many Dream Trippers have told me that "I've been digesting the China trip for YEARS." When
you consume a meal, or a movie, or a book, or even a lover for a one-night
stand of sex, its enjoyment is more temporal and superficial, and soon forgotten. Consumerism SPENDS YOUR QI. Deep Daoist self-cultivation BUILDS QI in
one's core identity.[42]

These comments raise a question that we return to throughout this book: Do
the Dream Trippers' experiences merely reinforce ontological individualism,
an enchantment that provides a deeper and more "authentic" subjective experience than ordinary tourism, or do they experience a shift into processes
and practices of cosmological attunement?

The living Daoists of today are only secondary to what the groups are
seeking, namely, the energies opened up by the cultivators of past eras: "That's
why we come to China," said Winn. "The Daoists have been in communication with these nonhuman energies for thousands of years. The channel of
communication has been opened by them. These energies exist elsewhere
too, but in those places they have not been communicated with. Here, the

energies are used to being communicated with over such a long time. We tread along a path that has already been treaded."

> The vibration of the ancients is there in the earth, in the mountains, and when you go there you feel it. Even if there were no Daoists living there, you would go there, you feel it. It's been immortalized. It is the energy of the Dao Immortals. They've merged with that aspect of nature, so the vibration is there. It's very different than going to mountains in other countries that haven't been worked, haven't been meditated with alchemically, and the consciousness in the mountain is not the same, it hasn't awoken, so these Daoist mountains really do have a different consciousness, and people who are sensitive enough will experience it. Not everyone will experience it or [is] conscious of it, but I feel they are still impacted by it very powerfully.[43]

In other words, contact with living Daoists is less important than "feeling" the vibrations of dead (or immortal) Daoists. This confirms Stausberg's observation that "it is not always the current religious situation at the destination which is of primary interest to the tourist; in many cases contemporary religion is of little or no interest, or even perceived as a disturbance."[44] Who those past Daoist cultivators were—their names, their lives, their lineages—is of little interest to most Dream Trippers. What matters is that they have opened energy channels which can now be directly accessed—but only after the Dream Trippers "reopen" the channel, which had closed up through long years of neglect, by "taming" the energies. Said Winn:

> At first, a few years ago, the energies were no longer used to being communicated with [owing to so few Chinese cultivators in recent times and to the unprecedented arrival of foreigners], so the experiences were hard to deal with. Now, they are more used to it; there have been more foreign meditators here; the powers have become more manageable. . . . The first trip that came there, it was not so easy. The vibrations in those caves were not used to foreigners. We can call them vibrations—it was really the consciousness that was residing there, the spirits. They were not used to foreigners and the people who spent that first year in those caves had some frightening experiences—dragons showing up, or feeling like astral stuff was attacking them and saying, "What are you doing in my cave?"—it was terrifying. After that they [the cave spirits] said, "Oh well, you guys are OK, you're serious; you're really coming here to meditate." They became supportive and people who came there felt supported.[45]

The powers that the Dream Trippers thus reopen now support them, and allow them to communicate with the collective planetary consciousness. In Winn's words:

Mountains are just natural pyramids; their axis acts as a double vortex between the center of the earth below and the stars above. My experience of Huashan, a giant "earth flower" made of solid granite, is that the mountain is a vast initiation chamber for those who can attune to its inner frequency. When you align your human body axis to [the] axis of the mountain, it becomes a pathway for communicating with all that the "mind of the mountain" is communicating with. Huashan is thus just an individual outlet for the collective planetary consciousness, like any ley line or sacred place. The more a place gets used for spiritual awakening, the more powerful and skillful it becomes at using the natural chi field to communicate with humans. For those following the path of the Tao, this is the major reason to visit China's sacred mountains.[46]

After a trip to Changbaishan (the Eternally White Mountains) in China's far northeast in the summer of 2013, searching for the origins of his own Daoist lineage, Winn wrote ecstatically that he had discovered "China's crown chakra" in an account in which he compares the mountain to his energetic experiences on the Great Pyramid of Egypt, Mauna Kea in Hawaii, and the Greek Island of Santorini,

Changbai is an incredibly powerful portal for transformative Qi. . . . I've never had such easy, deep and powerful kan & li (water & fire) alchemical meditations. Every cell in my body, my deepest jing (bone marrow, sexual essence, and DNA-RNA) felt like it was being vibrated at a super high frequency in a cosmic pressure cooker. . . . In my attunement to Changbai's Present Moment, I felt what a powerful Earth Portal this volcano is, a vast highway into the core of the earth. . . . Every volcano is a portal. But Changbai's unique fire & water energetic balance I found allows for much greater stability in penetrating into the very core of Mother Earth. Attuning to Changbai is like entering deep into Mother Earth's mingmen, our planetary gate of destiny.[47]

Dream Trippers' enchantment narratives can be situated somewhere between the two integrative schema we have discussed earlier. On the one hand, the emphasis on the subjective experience of energies and on the discovery of the inner self can be associated with the framework of ontological individualism. On the other hand, the connections to a "collective planetary consciousness" and to "Mother Earth's *mingmen*"—an acupoint at the lower spine, meaning "gate of destiny" and a key node in the body's energy circulation—seem to display a tendency to cosmological attunement, sometimes in an analogical mode. But these discourses of attunement posit a direct connection between the self and a rather vague collective consciousness or cosmic motherhood, without specified intermediaries. Even the Immortals of the past, whose energies they are attuning with, remain unnamed.

The Monks' Attunement with Huashan

When Master Chen spoke of the mountain to the Dream Trippers, he did not mention experiences of energy or vibrations; he only privately disclosed such experiences to us after several years of conversations. Instead, to the Dream Trippers, he listed the genealogy of great Daoist figures such as the Yellow Emperor, Laozi, Lü Dongbin, Hao Datong, Chen Tuan, Qiu Chuji, and Wang Changyue, among others, who are said to have cultivated on its peaks and in its caves. These figures stand on their own in Daoist history, however, and are not associated exclusively with Huashan or any other Daoist sacred site. At Huashan, the Daoist can connect with the memory of these figures, and through these figures can connect with the broader mythology and cosmology of Daoism.

In the monastic practice of "cloud wandering" (*yunyou*), in which monks travel from one monastery to another across the realm, staying a few months or years in one place before moving onward, they travel through, in their embodied experience, the cosmic geography of the Daoist tradition, connecting their own trajectories with those of past generations of "wanderers."[48] It is in this body of memory—recorded in texts and in the narratives of great Daoists in history—that the Complete Perfection monks dwell. When they move into Huashan, the place they attune to is much more than the physical mountain and its field of forces; it is also a mountain of memories and of associations, a specific location in the Daoist cosmos. The experiences of the body and of sacred places are significant only insofar as they can help to draw the practitioner into that cosmos, and within that cosmos, to further progress toward the ultimate generative Origin. For the monks of the order of Complete Perfection, which sees itself as the most refined and complete expression of the Daoist tradition—and has for several centuries been the most highly institutionalized and elitist form of Daoism in China—the experiences generated by the practice of body techniques, and/or one's presence in a powerful sacred site, can only be seen as *part* of the process of cultivation, which embeds and embodies the person into a far vaster process of cosmological attunement.

When Master Chen told us of his experiences in caves and at Huashan, they always connected with the lineage and history of Huashan and of Daoism in general. In one story, for example, he linked a cave he had discovered to historical records of a Daoist hermit who had declined an invitation to the emperor's court:

Once I was climbing the mountain. It was snowing, and white all over. I was facing north, looking at the mountain northwest, and felt that, there must be a cave there, and if there isn't, if I were to dig a cave I would do so at that spot. In the past, those cultivators who dug caves could certainly not have neglected this spot. So I went to have a look. It was a bit dangerous. As I was crawling over, I almost fell down the cliff. It was snowing heavily, at one point my feet slid into the void. I grabbed the chain, but my body was already hanging out. Then I kept going, holding onto the chain. I went down a few dozen meters, and there was a cave there, a very big one. It was square. It was partly natural and partly man-made. And it was extremely well dissimulated, impossible to see it from outside. But from inside, you could see the entire view of the mountain. It was beautiful. After returning to the monastery, I checked some historical materials, and found that in the Sui and Tang dynasties, there was a Daoist patriarch who stayed there; he was the one who found that cave. According to the story, he enjoyed playing the flute. He carved his flutes, and played them for a while, and then each time he threw his flute down the mountain from the cave. This patriarch lived as a hermit. At the time of Tang Taizong, during the years of Zhenguan, the emperor invited the hermit. He came to this spot, and invited him to the court. But the hermit declined. His style gives me a very deep impression. I like his style, even though I don't know what he cultivated.[49]

Master Chen also spoke of another cave, located in the highest cliff on the West Peak. This cave cannot be seen from outside. According to his master, Xue Tailai, before Liberation, there was a pole platform and ladder leading to it. "Now, seeing with your own eyes, it's impossible to know the way to the cave." There were no steps carved in the cliff leading to it; it was accessed with ladders made of dried poles. But these no longer exist. Chen did not physically visit this cave, but he claims to have been there in a "fantastical" way, and to have met an Immortal there, "appearing in my mind," who was the founder of the "Ancient Huashan lineage" during the Han dynasty (206 BC–AD 220). Although we have verified the existence of this Immortal in Daoist history, Chen stated that his connection to Huashan, and his Huashan lineage, has been largely forgotten; and he requested that we not disclose his name, for fear of it being instrumentalized for the tourist or cultural development of Huashan.

I feel that I have a strong predestined affinity [yuanfen] with [this Patriarch]; that he has close concern for me. For me to learn about him isn't the result of my consciously searching to discover him; it feels like in Christianity or Judaism, the idea of a calling: he attracted me to go, and he gave me a lot. There are many immortals that I worship, unconditionally, but I haven't seen their form. But this immortal and his cave, I have seen them; he has appeared before me. He has given me very much and called on me. His influence on me is extremely great.[50]

This Immortal was, in Chen's account, the Patriarch of the "Ancient" Huashan Lineage, which is distinct from what contemporary academic accounts categorize as the "Old" and "New" Huashan lineages. The latter, "new" one is the Huashan lineage of the Quanzhen sect; it is divided into two branches: the "Southern" branch whose ancestral temple (*zuting*) is the Southern Gate of Heaven temple on the South Peak, and the "Northern" branch, whose ancestral temple is at the Cloud Platform, a cave complex located on a mountain facing Huashan. The Northern branch was founded by Suo Wu Sou, in the Ming dynasty. Chen recounted his "encounter" with this Immortal on a snowy evening atop Huashan, around 2004:

There was a lot of snow, and I was feeling very relaxed, in an excellent mood. I had walked around three kilometers, and then I heard someone calling behind me: "Xuuuu wuuuu! Xuuuu wuuuuu!" and then a sound of "Tuck! Tuck! Tuck!" After a moment, this sound came closer; after turning around a peak, an old man approached, wearing very old clothes and a hat; they looked like the uniform of a monk. He was very tall. His clothes were so old and disheveled, it was hard to tell if he was a Buddhist or Daoist monk. I couldn't tell his age. His hair was peppered in black and white; I couldn't tell what kind of person he was. He kept walking ahead, toward a tree, and then again, he called, "Xuuu wuuu!" It seemed that he was searching for the void [*xuwu* in Chinese]. I joked aloud, "This old man is seeking after the void!" I leaned against the railing and watched for his reaction. Then, it seemed as if the old man became conscious of me, and walked toward me. I don't know why, but suddenly I felt my heart beating faster; at that moment I wanted to bow down to him on the spot. I don't know where that idea came from, but it was an extremely powerful feeling. But I didn't move. I froze, because I saw people walking over and I was afraid they would laugh at me. But I still wanted to bow down to him, so I kept following him. He kept walking and calling, "Xuuuu wuuuuu," in a calm tone. The strange thing was that, although I was quite young at that time and could run quite fast, I couldn't keep up with him. When I had almost reached him and tried to kowtow, he suddenly was far away. I felt embarrassed and he became conscious of it, so he stopped for a moment, then walked again, but after his steps turned behind a mountain, I could see him no more. I felt it was a pity, and couldn't determine what kind of person this was. But it was getting dark and I needed to work the next day, so I went down the mountain. As I climbed down, I turned toward the direction of that old man, and with a reverent heart, I also called, "Xuuuu wuuuu!"

At that time it was around Chinese New Year, on the fourth day of the first lunar month. The strange thing was, exactly a year later, on the fourth day, I met with an old Daoist monk, whose surname was Suo; he has since passed away. As I was chatting with him, I asked if there had been any Daoists in history of the same surname, and he said that at the third generation of the Huashan lineage, there was a patriarch surnamed Suo; he was not clear if he was an immortal or not, but his name was Suo Wu Sou. I asked what "Suo Wu Sou" meant, and he said, it means "the old man who seeks the void." I suddenly remembered that, exactly a year earlier, I had seen him—he was the old man who seeks the void.[51]

Through the narrative of these experiences, Master Chen connected himself to the founders of the spiritual lineages of Huashan, whether the Patriarch of the Ancient Huashan Lineage, or Suo Wu Sou, the founder of the Northern branch of the New Huashan Lineage of the Complete Perfection order. These connections linked him to the origins of the main techniques of Daoist cultivation, in the case of the Immortal of the Ancient Huashan Lineage; or conveyed something of the essence of Daoist teaching, in the case of "the old man who seeks the void," or of the Immortal who threw his flutes down the cliffs and declined the emperor's invitation. While many of these stories have a paranormal dimension that has an enchanting effect, the focus, in the end, is not those unusual experiences in themselves, but the deepening connection to Daoist lineage and tradition.

For Master Chen, our life in this world can be compared to being confined in a small box, in which we can't perceive the complete reality of our existence. Spiritual phenomena are simply the result of coming into contact with reality beyond the confines of that box; it may be frightening at first, but then you realize it is perfectly normal and ordinary. The Huashan that we can see is only one space of the mountain; it also has many other spaces. Because Huashan is such an incredible place, it attracts the attention of many beings, including humans, tourists, animals, and Immortals, as well as ghosts and amazing energies. There are many spaces in this world, and there are many links and passages between these spaces; and there are ways and passages for a person to travel from this space to another space.

The Chinese term for "grotto" or "cavern," *dong*, is similar in sound and meaning to *tong*, meaning "to flow unobstructed, to communicate, to reach"; thus, a "Grotto Heaven," *dongtian*, is also a passageway, a gate, with direct access to a heavenly space. Some spots are special "holes" at which Immortals have left special energies, some of which may be good or harmful; but these energies are like clouds of vapor that may dissipate after a long time.

Master Chen enjoyed climbing into the most remote caves of the mountain, which often required passing dangerous paths and cliffs to reach. At these spots, the sounds of noisy tourists could not be heard, and he listened to what he called the "sounds of the heavenly Dao" while meditating, interacting with chipmunks, and watching the pine trees sway at the cave entrance. He described feeling a sense of true liberty and communion with Heaven and Earth and with specific Immortals. He recounted how once, as he meditated one night in a cave, he felt extraordinarily happy and broke into fits of uncontrollable laughter—and then he saw, in front of him, a small human-looking figure, with long hair, wearing clothes made of tree leaves. A while later, he disappeared. Master Chen considered him to be an Immortal—thus linking his experience to the cultural lore of the Daoist Immortals of Huashan.[52]

In some caves, Immortals left words carved into the rock that sometimes give hints and methods on how to cultivate. For example, Chen described a cave he had discovered in a remote and inaccessible location in which there was a platform for sleeping, and a small altar space. Two stones had been carved, with two lines of characters carved into them, which referred to a Daoist meditation method:[53]

二六時中息氣
一腔子裡存神

Which could be approximately translated as

At every moment, calm your breath
Hold your spirit in the cavity of your body

While the Dream Trippers' narratives of enchanting experiences tended to focus on the embodied experience itself, the monks at Huashan were generally reticent to discuss such experiences. And when they did, the experiences were narrated as forming connections with specific Immortals and lineages in the history of Huashan. Cosmological attunement, for the monks of the order of Complete Perfection, does include a direct experience of the "sounds of the heavenly Dao"—but it also includes attunement to the specific personages, events, and places that constitute Huashan as a sacred mountain, as well as to Daoism as a historical tradition. And as we shall see in the next section, the sacralization of the mountain itself is part of a process of cosmological attunement.

Cosmologizing Huashan

The practice of visiting sacred sites has a long history in China, going back at least to the fourth century BC.[54] Pilgrimage has never been a clearly defined, obligatory requirement of any Chinese religious institution or doctrine; it has evolved in a great variety of forms, but typically involves ascending to the peak of a mountain said to be imbued with the numinous or efficacious (*ling*) power of a deity, burning incense at the temple on the peak, and stopping and worshipping at other *ling* spots along the way. Thus, a traditional Chinese term for pilgrimage, *chaoshan jinxiang*, means "paying respect to a mountain and presenting incense." This expression implies that the mountain, or its deity, is a living, powerful Lord, comparable to a king or emperor that one approaches with reverence and with offerings, with entreaties and supplications, hoping that the Lord will confer blessings and protection unto those who ritually acknowledge its power, but also enhancing it. But it is also a place whose deity and power have been subdued and domesticated by Daoism and/ or Buddhism. In his description of a paradigmatic Daoist mountain, Thomas Hahn writes:

> High under the roof of the entry portal, the "tablet for pacifying the mountain," salutes the pilgrim. It seems to signify the subdued potency of the mountain, giving the pilgrim or other traveller a sense of security: glancing at the tablet, he knows instinctively that the powers of the *kaishan zushi*, the religious patriarch of spiritual acumen who dared to "open" the mountain, continue to ensure the success of the ascent.[55]

In the local lore of Huashan, the mountain's powers, considered the lair of sprites, demons, and ogres, have been domesticated by the sages and Immortals of Daoism as a supralocal religious institution.[56] Even today, monks speak of their fear of demons, ghosts, and strange apparitions at unopened paths and deep valleys unprotected by temples or caves of Immortals. In one story, a Huashan monk had taken a long, unused and overgrown path, and was resting on a stone when suddenly the clear skies were covered by thick fog, and two persons dressed as ancient opera singers appeared behind him and began to follow him. He ran away as fast as possible, until the two opera characters disappeared; he turned around, and saw two intertwined giant cobras. He ran from the path as fast as he could, and never dared to return. In another story, a group of monks took a wrong turn and walked into the deep reaches at the end of Huashan valley, and they entered a cave. One of their party disappeared, and the rest of the party returned to the Jade Spring Monastery. Several days later, the lost monk returned, but he was unaware that several days had passed; he thought it was the same day, and was angry that the party had not waited for him. But he died not long thereafter. Their fears stoked by such tales, monks and locals do not dare to venture to the wild areas, far from the temples and caves opened by Daoist Immortals.

Near the Western Peak of the mountain lies a temple, the Palace for Pacifying the Summit (*Zhenyuegong*), whose name implies the act of possessing and subjugating the mountain, and enshrines the mountain's tutelary god.

The Daoist domestication of the mountain and its god involved cultivators and Immortals taming the god's energies, and giving him a rank and title in the Daoist pantheon—as the Great Lord of the Western Marchmount, *Xiyue dadi*—honoring his powers, but subordinating him to even higher Daoist divinities.

In his study of Tibetan Buddhism in China, Dan Smyer Yü has provided some useful insights to understand the connection between religious practitioners and the power of a landscape. Central to his argument is a distinction between two modalities of sacred place: the first is vertical and transcendental, of which Mircea Eliade's "theophany" that opens the "axis mundi" between heaven and earth is the best known formulation, and which can be applied to some of the most majestic Tibetan sacred mountains such as Mount Kailash. These mountains place humans in awe before an otherworldly, transcendent realm. More common, however, is a horizontal, "intersentient" sacrality in which common people, souls, spirits, and the forms of the land are all animated, in constant interdwelling and reciprocal relations, with worldly concerns at the fore. In this intersentient modality, "mindscape" and "landscape" shape each other and become one. Mountains are the abodes of human souls, "humans ensoul and spiritize the landscapes in which they live." A sacred mountain may be the abode and the materialization of a heroic figure and bring protection to the communities surrounding it—but the human communities must also respect and protect the mountain; failing to do so, it would lose its spiritual potency; the soul it enshrines would also be destroyed. Through ritual acts, human communities engage in reciprocal give-and-take with the powers that surround them, all the parties, human and nonhuman, seeking protection, power, and prosperity. At this level, there is no fixed hierarchy but a constant negotiation between humans, spirits, and animated landscape features. Tibetan landscapes typically embed local, pre-Buddhist spirits which have been converted to Buddhism by great incarnate lamas, domesticating them and turning them into lower-level Buddhist guardian spirits. In their relations with the spiritual forces of the place, then, although local spirits may have more supernatural powers than humans, humans can subdue them through the Buddha Dharma.[57]

A similar logic applies in the domestication of Huashan by Daoist masters and Immortals, in which local spirits are pacified and incorporated into the Daoist pantheon and cosmology. Cosmological attunement is a political process, a negotiation and reciprocal relationship between humans and nonhuman forces and beings, often described in terms of violent battles. Daoist cultivators and Immortals play a pivotal role in this process, as they use the power of their own spiritual alignment to attune humans, spirits, and places with a broader and overarching cosmology—a cosmology that the Chinese imperial state itself sought to attune itself to and to embody.

The Daoist memory of Huashan is thus one of the conquest, domestication, and integration of the mountain's powers into the sacred structure of the imperial Chinese state and into the universal cosmology of the Daoist religion. The sacrality of Huashan is thus constituted in this supralocal cosmological framework, which, today, no longer exists politically, but lives on as a powerful presence in collective memory.

Stories of Huashan as a sacred site go back as far as the fifth century BC.[58] The *Book of Mountains and Seas* (*Shanhaijing*), an early cosmo-geographic text, describes Huashan as a site inhabited by countless fairies and Immortals. The *Book of Documents* (*Shangshu—yugongbian*) describes it as the place where the Yellow Emperor—the mythical ancestor of the Chinese people and noted as the ancestor of the arts of governing both the nation and the body— encountered the concourse of Immortal spirits. Legend has it that near the end of the Zhou dynasty (1046–256 BC), Laozi passed by Huashan on his travels to the Kunlun Mountains of the West, and left behind several stories associated with sites on the mountain such as the "alchemical furnace," the "platform of the reclining ox," and so on. The *Zhuangzi* contains a story about a sage visiting Huashan, where he is mocked by a Daoist hermit. Other texts of the period describe the miraculous feats and powers of Daoists having stayed at Huashan, attesting to the early fame of the mountain as a powerful place for attaining transcendence and immortality.[59] In the beginning of the later Han dynasty, Huashan was one of the most important sites for the worship of the Queen Mother of the West, who is associated with China's earliest known millenarian movement.[60]

During the Han dynasty, Huashan was integrated into the official cult system of the Chinese empire as one of the Five Sacred Peaks or Five Marchmounts (*wuyue*), corresponding to the five cardinal points of the realm: Hengshan (North), Taishan (East), Hengshan (South), Songshan (Center), and Huashan as the Western Marchmount. The emperor, as the Son of Heaven, periodically set forth on tours of the realm, stopping at each of the five Marchmounts to worship and subordinate the local deities, conferring titles on them and patronizing their cults. These acts were part of cosmological attunement as a political process: the mountain god of Huashan was thus integrated into the imperial civilizing cosmology as one of the Lords of the Five Marchmounts, the sacred mountains marking China's five cardinal points, forming the imperial realm into the unified sacred space of "all under Heaven" (*tianxia*) and guarding the frontiers on all sides against barbarian and demonic invasion. The emperor, in his tours of the realm, conducted rites to honor the Great Lord of the mountain at the sprawling Temple of the Western Marchmount (*Xiyuemiao*) built in the plain near the mountain's foot, with a layout similar to that of the Forbidden City in Beijing.

Indeed, as the historian of Chinese religion James Robson put it, in China it is "relatively rare for sacred mountains to be venerated merely for their glorious heights"; rather, these "mountains have generated feelings in China ranging from fear and awe to sublime wonder and religious reverence" based on their symbolic placement in a cosmic structure.[61] The Five Marchmounts actually mirror other quintets in traditional Chinese cosmology, all of which are correlated with the cosmological system of the five elements (*wuxing*) of Wood, Fire, Earth, Metal, and Water.

Within this analogical cosmology, Huashan, as the Western Marchmount, is associated with the element of Metal, which is associated with the West, each Marchmount being associated with one of the five elements and five cardinal points. And Huashan itself, with its own five peaks, replicates the cosmological system, with each peak also associated with one of the five elements and cardinal points; the five peaks also constitute an alchemical body, with each peak corresponding to one of the Five Organs: the North Peak is the kidney, the East Peak is the liver, the South Peak is the Heart, the Central Peak is the spleen, and the West Peak is the lung. The Western Peak of Huashan is thus the western peak of the Western Marchmount, the Metal peak of the Metal mountain. The domestication of the mountain also involved erecting a shrine to the god of fire (*huoshen*) at the Western Peak, since, in the "conquering" cycle of the five elements, Fire conquers Metal; the extreme tendency to *yin* of the double West/Metal can thus be corrected and balanced by worshipping the *yang* spirit of Fire.

In Daoist circles, the Five Peaks were interpreted as the five fingers of the cosmic Laozi, part of a rich and complex sacred geography in which the ascent and penetration of mountains became the physical and symbolic site for the transformation of the body into immortality. By the eighth century, Daoist texts integrated the sacred landscape into a system of ten major and thirty-six minor Grotto Heavens (*dongtian*) and seventy-two Blissful Realms (*fudi*), imagined as a network of caves and mysterious passages connecting each mountain to each other and also to the Immortals' palaces in heaven, which are emanations of pure *qi* while, in the words of Master Chen, the "fairylands on earth" are "made of pure *qi* wrapped in a hard shell of dense matter."[62]

As described by Master Chen, Huashan, as one of the Grotto Heavens, is connected to the Daoist conception of cosmogony:

The great Dao is the origin of all beings. The original expression of Dao is *qi*. There is pure *qi*, and turbid *qi*. The pure ascends, the turbid goes down. So there is a distinction between the pure and the turbid. The pure *qi* is of perfect clarity. The pure *qi* rises up and joins with the Celestial *qi*. In the heavenly realms, there are no stones, everything is made of *qi*.

The great Dao is perfect. Then, matter appeared, all kinds of *qi* appeared and separated from each other, becoming different forms. The pure energies (*qi*) ascended to the heavens, and became the heavenly Immortals. Some essential *qi* became wrapped up in turbidity, and descended to the realm of humans, and became the caves in the famous mountains. They became the immortal realms (*xianjing*) within the famous mountains. Through the caves, then, humans can access the heavenly realm. In the legends of the five dynasties, it is said that some caves have small openings, but if one steps inside, one will find the whole universe inside. That's why they are called grotto heavens, because they are wrapped up "bubbles" of heavenly *qi*.[63]

Daoist texts identify Huashan as one of the Lesser Grotto Heavens. Master Hu thus described the distinction between the "Greater" and "Lesser" Grotto Heavens:

In the Greater Grotto Heavens, there are traces which have been left behind by great Immortals from the distant past, such as the Yellow Emperor, who cultivated here. These are incredibly high-level Immortals, so the realm which they have attained is very high. Their level of realization was innate to them. But in a Lesser Grotto Heaven, there have been patriarchs who have attained a high level through their own cultivation of techniques using their own body.[64]

Sacrality as Experience or Social Construction

In the accounts of both the Dream Trippers and the monks of the Complete Perfection order, the relationship with the sacrality of Huashan differs from conventional Western concepts of the sacred. The "powers" of the mountain are at least partly associated with other humans (the cultivators and Immortals of the past), rather than from a purely transcendental reality; and the cultivation of current practitioners is understood as having an effect on reenergizing "dormant" caves. How can we understand the feedback loops between the physical environment, individual practice and experience, and collective memories and powers?

Parallel to the theories of tourism and pilgrimage discussed above, most theories of the sacred posit a dichotomy between subjects and objects of sacrality—the "sacred" is either something preexisting and distinct from the subject, which erupts into his experience, or is an artifact purely dependent on social constructions. The first type of dichotomist view, exemplified by Mircea Eliade, sees the sacred as essentially Other: "In actual fact, the place is never 'chosen' by man. It is merely discovered by him; in other words, the sacred place in some way or another reveals itself to him." Elsewhere, he states, this "is not a matter of theoretical speculation, but of a primary religious experience that precedes reflection on the world." In a more recent, popular iteration, we can cite Edwin Bernbaum, who notes that "mountains have an extraordinary power to evoke the sacred" and that "people have traditionally revered mountains as places of sacred power and spiritual attainment." Sacred places thus share a mystical unity with the ultimate being or reality; the best approach to them is thus to let them be, and approach them with awe and reverence. Therefore, pilgrimage should be an unmediated experience of the sacred reality, leaving it untouched and pristine. Or, in the words of Belden C. Lane: "Sacred place, we have said, seems to have an unaccountable identity distinct and separate from those who move in and through it."

In radical contrast to this essentialist view of the sacred, a social constructivist perspective would claim that the sacred is first and foremost the product of social and cultural forces. In his definition of religion, Emile Durkheim argues that all cultures classify things and ideas into the two categories of sacred and profane, conceived of as "separate genera, two worlds which have nothing in common." The boundaries between the two worlds are marked in any culture; approaching the sacred always requires special rules and procedures; and entering the sacred world involves a process of metamorphosis or transformation. However, the idea of the sacred does not emerge from the sacred objects themselves; rather, it comes from the experience of the moral force of society which is impressed on individuals through the imposition of norms of conduct and through the "collective effervescence" of periodic rituals. The sacred object is a mental representation of this moral force, which is transferred onto the object; the sacred object is thus perceived as imbued with a divine power that is none other than the power of society. In the Durkheimian analysis, then, the sacred experience is entirely of a social nature, and the choice of sacred things is purely arbitrary—the sacred is the result of social agency. Ritual acts at sacred places are not so much designed to establish and manage contact between humans and an essentially other reality, but to construct or reproduce a certain place or thing as a representation of the social power. And such a construction is thus always an act of a group's appropriation of the place. In the words of Chidester and Linenthal, "Sacred space is inevitably contested space, a site of negotiated contests over legitimated ownership of sacred symbols. . . . Power is asserted and resisted in any production of space, and especially in the production of sacred space. Since no sacred space is merely 'given' in the world, its ownership will always be at stake. In this respect, a sacred space is not merely discovered, or founded, or constructed; it is claimed, owned, and operated by people advancing specific interests."[65]

Our study at Huashan shows the possibilities and limitations of both the essentialist and constructivist perspectives. On the one hand, the place imposes itself even to the untrained observer; the experience of awe, power, and beauty that it impresses on the visitor or pilgrim is hardly arbitrary. On the other hand, the site is heavily overlaid with cultural and historical connotations, and inscribed within several cosmological and political schemas symbolically linking the mountain to the essence of the Chinese empire or nation and its collective power. The Daoist sites and practices on the mountain use a culturally determined framework of techniques, narrative, and lineage to induce practitioners into a heightened sensitivity to the sacred powers of the mountain. As a sacred site, Huashan is associated with dense strands of history, memory, and experiences of power. It is this sacred dimension which attracts monks and spiritual tourists today; which the imperial state tried to harness in past centuries; and which, as we discuss in chapter 4, the Maoist state tried to obliterate a few decades ago.

The Dream Trippers come with their own memories and sets of meanings and are engaged in a process of appropriation, often in tension with the multiple layers of meaning and sacrality attached to the mountain by other religious groups, institutions, and political regimes. Indeed, there is a dialectic between the place as a source of raw, unmediated, powerful experience, and the sociocultural constructions which induce, reproduce, record, interpret, and structure those experiences.

Both the essentialist and social constructivist perspectives thus produce a dichotomy between the perceived environment and human subjectivity and agency. In the former, the sacrality of a place is possible only insofar as it is completely external to and untouched by human agency; in the latter, insofar as the significance given the environment is the product of human agency, the external environment in and of itself is of no significance, it is only the cultural representations and social appropriations of the environment that matter. Both perspectives can be associated with ontological individualism, in which the sacred, whether it is real or a mere social imagination, is entirely outside the self, and then subjectively experienced by it.

Both perspectives reproduce a naturalist ontology that is critiqued by the anthropologist Tim Ingold in *The Perception of the Environment* (2000). Rather than seeing organisms, objects, and the environment as discrete entities acting on each other, Ingold argues that the human being should be seen as "a singular locus of creative growth within a continually unfolding field of relationships," whose characteristics arise "as emergent properties of the fields of relationship set up through their presence and activity within a particular environment."[66] From such a perspective, the question becomes how, by walking, climbing, breathing, stretching, meditating, and engaging in other sequences of embodied activities at different locations on the mountain, a field of relationships comes into being within which a person's growth unfolds. This field puts in relation with each other the vital unfolding of the practitioner, the range of perceptions arising from the plants, trees, stones, temples, statues, cliffs, clouds, and other beings enveloping the practitioner, the other individuals present, their words and actions, and, we argue below, the remembered knowledge, symbols, and narratives evoked by the setting.

At the same time, for Ingold, a place is also an organic process, a locus of relationships and transformations between beings, both animate and inanimate. A mountain such as Huashan, for example, is not merely a mound of static, empty, undifferentiated matter onto which humans affix external cultural concepts and meanings: it is the expression of the interplay of countless cycles and rhythms, ranging from geological movements and chemical transformations spanning hundreds of millions of years—giving the mountain its powerful upward thrust and its clashing sharp ridges and colossal molten curves—to the life cycles of the soils, trees, plants, animals, and insects inhabiting, layering, burrowing, and crisscrossing its surfaces and crevices, to the centuries of human paths being worn down, caves being dug, temples being erected, and the rhythmic flows of monks, pilgrims, and tourists ascending and descending, entering and transforming, meditating, praying, and photographing, over the cycles of day and night, and of summer and winter seasons.

In Chinese cosmology, these fields of relationships between beings that are in perpetual movement, growth, decline, and transformation are expressed through the circulation of *qi*. Michael Winn commented on a draft of the above paragraphs as follows:

> Ingold's [theory] is a very complicated attempt to get to Daoist correlative cosmology but lacks the simplicity and completeness of the latter, which can explain ALL the relationships listed as exchange of Qi.
>
> The meridians in the feet and leg absorb the Qi from the land. Qi holds memory. The more one walks on the land, the more information one absorbs and comes into deeper resonance. Essentially, it is possible to access the Energy Body of a place. . . . I think your text could emphasize that Qi is the medium by which humans can easily cross the boundary between human body and nature's body.[67]

Chinese sacred mountains are, indeed, over the centuries, constantly enriched with human additions, inscriptions, and constructions. As explained
by the historians Susan Naquin and Yü Chün-fang,

> Although pilgrimage in China was traditionally directed toward a temple at
> the top of a mountain, most sites were much more extensive, complicated,
> and multifocal. Mountain often referred to a range of peaks, but even a simple
> summit usually involved many paths of ascent and descent and a variety of
> sights and nodes of interest. The intrinsic numinosity of nature—summits,
> cliffs, vistas, caves, springs, and trees—was the foundation on which much
> could be built, physically and imaginatively. Stupas, tombs, inscriptions, ritual
> arenas, shrines, sculpture, paintings, and pavilions were constructed over a
> wide area; relics and texts were imported and produced; religious specialists
> were drawn to set up residence nearby; records of facts and myths were set
> down and published. Part of the heterogeneity of a site came from the physi-
> cal diversity. Part came from the variety of pilgrims-cum-patrons, past and
> present: Ch'an and ordinary Buddhist monks, professional Daoists, hermits,
> tourists, and lay pilgrims.[68]

Among the heterogeneous crowds of people climbing China's sacred
mountains, there were groups of lay devotees of the main mountain deity, organized by "incense associations" and coming from near and afar: Buddhist
and Daoist monks wandering from monastery to monastery; officials making
a detour on a tour of duty; poets and literati tourists; hermits; and a rowdy
assortment of peddlers, porters, guides, beggars, and brigands. Indeed, by the
seventeenth century, some of the most famous mountains had several thousand daily visitors, and a tourist industry serving them, complete with travel
agencies, package tours, and sprawling inns employing dozens of theatrical
troupes and hundreds of waiters, bellhops, and prostitutes to cater to every
need of the traveler.[69]

To walk on Huashan, then, is to bring the field of relationships of one's
own life-course into the current and historical field of relationships of the
mountain, each inflecting the other. But not all visitors will engage with the
mountain with the same depth and intensity. For many, a visit to Huashan
is little more than passing by, both literally and figuratively, touching only
the surface of the mountain. Others, however—including our monks and
spiritual tourists—engage more fully with the place, seeking and finding deep
significance in spots, experiences, and encounters along the way, and literally
penetrating the depths of the mountain by sojourning in its caves.

The sacrality of a place, then, emerges from the intense interpenetration
of the fields of relationships of human life-courses, collective memories, and
of the place itself. The sacred place becomes a node at which these fields

continue to interact in time and history, leaving an imprint on the place itself, the chains of memory, and the lives of those individuals who orient themselves in relation to the place.

To be attentive to the landscape in such a way, and to enhance one's capacity to enter into relation with the place, one generally needs to undergo a process of attunement, of education in practice and perception.[70] This education undermines the boundaries of the secular "buffered self" and facilitates the occurrence of enchanting experiences. It is through such a process that the Chinese Daoist monks and international Dream Trippers move into the environment of Huashan, and perceive and engage with the mountain in a manner different from most tourists, relating to what they perceive to be the spiritual powers of the mountain. Part of the process involves training in the Daoist disciplines of body, breath, and mind, which sharpen the organism's dispositions and perception of environmental forces and settings.

It is in this light that the Dream Trippers are taught the exercises of *wujigong* (Primordial *Qigong*), and practice them at temples and at "powerful spots." This method, claims Winn,

> bonds the group into a unified or coherent Qi field, and accelerates their ability to penetrate quickly into the sacred landscape. . . . By doing the form collectively in powerful places, the group energetically matures and becomes a phalanx of Qi Cultivators. Their Qi, focused by repeated ritual ceremonies, begins flowing like a powerful river of collective will that makes it easy for even neophyte cultivators in the group to cross the boundary between their mundane, conditioned subjective bubble of a body-mind and the sacred field that has been prepared before them by generations of Daoist cultivators. . . . The ability of wuji gong to tap into larger cosmological cycles beyond their ordinary consciousness is built into the design of the form. The adept never leaves the center of the ritual movement space, as s/he ritually connects to the four cardinal directions, heaven above and earth below, through symbolic gestures and focused intent.[71]

The organism's sensitivity is thus enhanced, and a landscape which, for the untrained observer, is primarily visually perceived and thus differentiated only in terms of color, texture, and perspective, as if it were seen on a flat screen, becomes, for the skilled practitioner, a world of moving forces, energies, and even intentions. These are perceived and experienced by the whole organism, itself a field of circulating energies and interactions, which intentionally interacts with and may even attempt to transform the environmental field of forces. The "sacred" place, then, is one that is differentiated from other places by the high intensity of such perceptions, forces, and interactions. The dichotomy between the essentialist and constructivist views of the sacred is

here overcome by the fact that practitioners *do* experience something powerful beyond themselves and which is associated with a particular spot, but it is
through a social process of human interactions and learning that the organism gains the dispositions which enhance its sense of "attunement" to a spot
and its holistic sensitivity to, and engagement with, the field of forces brought
into consciousness by their moving into that spot.

This process, however, is not limited to the mastery of a regimen of embodied disciplines. The environment in which the organism moves is not
only physical, but symbolic as well; significant places at Huashan are marked
by temples, poems carved in stone, shrines, deity statues, and other features
which trigger responses and associations in the practitioner's memory of previous experiences and knowledge of the symbol systems from which they are
drawn. Enchantment by attunement is also a process of growing into, dwelling in, experiencing, and adding to a collective web of memory, itself generated through the experience of the place. An enchanted place is characterized
by a high density of collective memory; to approach and enter it is to viscerally
experience and interact with these memories, and to recall, enrich, and reinforce them. The field of relations brought into play by pilgrimage and the
encounter with a sacred place thus connects the pilgrim, the place, and the
symbols and memories associated with the place and with past pilgrims.

The Chinese and international practitioners are linked to different pathways of coming and going; they connect to and reenact different collective
memories and narratives of journeys previously made to Huashan. We thus
need to consider where the actors are coming from and where they are going in
their lives, how they pass through the mountain, how they engage with it and
experience it, and how they situate Huashan in broader narratives, memories,
and cosmologies. We find that the movement of the Dream Trippers is one of
cultural, historical, and social disembedding: the journey is one of individuation, of discovering and expanding the self; and the encounter with Huashan
seeks to both break the self out of its "buffered," hypersubjective state, and to
directly experience and activate the mountain's powers, disembedding them
from Chinese history and lineage and creating a direct link to Daoist cosmology
itself. Winn is very explicit about this goal of disembedding:

> Daoist correlative cosmology, while originally expressed in the Chinese lan-
> guage and arising within Chinese culture, is in and by itself a cosmology that
> is completely independent of Chinese culture. The "Qi" does not originate in
> China, it originates in the Source of the cosmos, taiyi [The Supreme Oneness] or
> wu ji [the Primordial Origin] or tao which preexist Chinese culture and cannot
> be named exclusively or definitively by any language (line 1 of the *Daodejing*:
> "The Tao that can be named is not the eternal Tao").

So when any Daoist cultivates their Qi WITHIN THE CONTEXT OF DAOIST
CORRELATIVE COSMOLOGY, they are no longer embedding themselves in the
hypersubjective western culture of individualism. . . . Likewise, a mirror process happens with serious Chinese cultivators—the shift to experiencing the
universal flow of Qi to source removes them from being limited by or embedded primarily in Chinese culture and history and its hypercollectivist culture.[72]

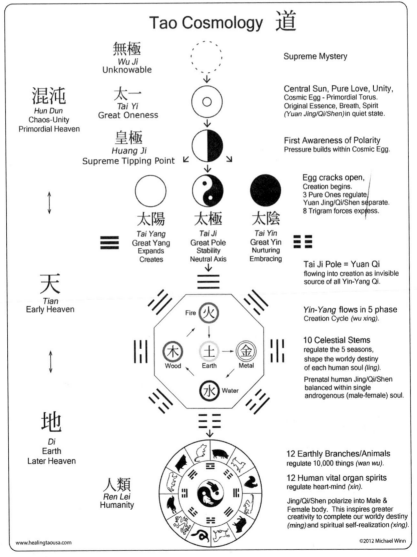

FIGURE 1. Daoist cosmology as rendered by Michael Winn (Courtesy of M. Winn)

In the previous chapter, we referred to Srinivas's phases of "disembedding" and "codification" in the process of constructing "transposable messages" in the globalization of religion. Figure 1 is the "codification" of the Daoist cosmology, a depiction of the cosmos that *wujigong* aims to attune practitioners to. Winn stresses that "none of the elements of this cosmology are dependent on local Chinese individuals or places or lineage—these are cosmic laws underlying all cultures . . . it is irrelevant if you are American or Chinese or German—the Qi field has no nationality."[73]

The Complete Perfection monks, on the other hand, emphasize the deep memory of place and history, and they experience and construct Huashan as a gateway into the world of Daoist lineage. Their movement involves activating memories of specific, named former monks and Immortals who walked on, lived in, and even crafted the mountain in bygone times; the path of cosmological attunement, for them, involves embedding oneself into locality, lineage, and history.

Huashan is an enchanting mountain for Dream Trippers and Chinese monks—but they experience the enchantment differently in their respective paths in life and spirituality. For the "spiritual tourists" among the Dream Trippers, Huashan is a fountain of raw, consumable energy on a path of individuation and self-discovery; for those among the Dream Trippers who are deeply committed to Daoist practices, Huashan is a powerful gateway for attunement to a universal and disembedded Daoist cosmology; for monks on the mountain, Huashan opens communication with the Daoist lineages, personages, and history of the order of Complete Perfection and even earlier traditions; for the emperors of bygone dynasties, Huashan was the Western pillar of a ritual system for attuning the imperial realm into a totalizing cosmology.

3

The Trippers

At the foot of Huashan lies the filthy town of Huayin, a single street of dingy hotels, variety stores, and noodle shops leading to the Jade Spring Monastery. The 2012 Dream Trippers entered the outer court of the monastery, an elegant traditional garden where the wooden pavilions, steles, and stones carrying poetic inscriptions by famous visitors offer pleasant perspectives and photo opportunities. They peeked into the shrines, took their snapshots, and continued into the inner court. That evening there were no Chinese monks or worshippers present, leaving the entire temple courtyard to them. The temple was deserted. All the shrines and offices were closed; and only the occasional monk or layman passed by. Michael Winn stood on the ledge of the main temple, his back to the shrine, and the Dream Trippers took up position in the courtyard, facing him, to begin their collective practice of *wujigong*. All stood in silence. Winn began with an invocation, asking the Dream Trippers to align their intentions.

> To call on, to ask that the great Taiyi [the Supreme Oneness], and all the deities and beings of Huashan, may help us to find what we need in our spiritual destiny at Huashan. Call on the great Taiyi, and all of the Daoist cultivators who have cultivated in this mountain, including Chen Tuan, and the sun radiating light and love, and the moon, and the dipper, and all the beings, to help us on this path.

The group practiced two sets of exercises, each of which lasted around twenty minutes. The second set, conducted in groups of four, turning and changing positions in unison, looked like a slow form of square dancing. Both sets involved the collective recitation of the "six healing sounds," in six musical notes, creating a beautiful, soothing tune, almost like Gregorian chant,

reverberating in the still courtyard. After the practice, all sat in quiet meditation for a few minutes.

The group then stepped out of the monastery, and onto the plaza. In contrast to the stillness inside the monastery courtyard, there was much anima-
tion right outside. In front of the monastery, a large public square is dedicated
to Chen Tuan, known as the patron of Huashan, a famous Daoist hermit who,
in his years at the mountain, is said to have developed several forms of martial
arts, body cultivation, and meditation, including a form of sleeping practice.
An enormous statue of Chen Tuan, lying on his side in sleeping meditation,
dominates the middle of the plaza. Around the statue, however, the crowds
of local people showed no interest in Daoist meditation—whether sleeping,
standing or sitting. The energy filling the square that evening in June 2012 was
not cosmic *qi* but that of hundreds of bodies in motion, mostly portly wives
in their fifties and sixties, dancing to loud, rapid disco beats, all in unison, in
neat rows, in a postmillennial variation on Mao-era mass calisthenics—free
daily exercise for all, keeping the people fit, a common scene in public squares
and spaces in China's cities.[1] Meanwhile, younger couples twisted in freestyle
under Chen Tuan's nose, and mothers chased after their toddlers pedaling
their wagons in zigzags through the rows of dancers. Some of the Dream Trippers joined them. Enjoying the scene, one of them, Peace,[2] a red-haired mystic,
angel-channeling former flower child exclaimed how much she loved China.
"Look at how connected the Chinese people are! Look at them, dancing like
that. They just are connected, you can see it."

For Peace, "grooving" to the beat of pop, was as much an expression of
spiritual connectedness as quiet meditation in a secluded temple. For a former hippie, there is, indeed, a connection between rock 'n' roll and Oriental
meditation—both of which, for the countercultural generation, are ways of
connecting to and expressing your true self. While Peace was moved by the
"dancing mamas," Chinese tourists at Huashan were intrigued by the sight of
her practicing *qigong*:

> It was lovely to have people come around and ask "what are you doing," espe-
> cially when I was alone. Because I went to the mountain alone by myself a lot,
> and just found a place and did my practice. The older people all knew, but the
> young people had no idea. "What is this?" they asked. This is *qigong* [I told
> them]—it came from you! . . . I was floored that they don't know this. . . . I told
> them as best as I could, you know, that this is *qigong*. And with some of the
> people, I would show them, and they would do it with me, which was so nice.
> But I would tell them that this is a practice, a daily practice. It's movement. It
> is energetic. But not having the language, I couldn't tell them a lot. But I could
> show them. I could do this with them—energy balls, *qi* balls—and show

them. They could feel it. Oh, my God, it was just. . . . It was just so incredibly fabulous to have that perspective.[3]

Wherever the Dream Trippers go and practice Daoist cultivation, meditating in caves, doing *qigong* in temples, hugging trees, or even staging wedding ceremonies on mountain peaks, they are the only ones doing these things—Chinese bystanders, when they are not ignoring them, are bemused by what they see; they are sometimes curious, sometimes even excited, but always surprised. Indeed, for many Chinese, be they Daoist or not, it is simply impossible for a foreigner to understand Daoism. As recounted by Winn, "I have been personally confronted by Chinese who told me, to my face, 'You don't understand *qi*. You are not Chinese. You don't know what *qi* is, and never will.' I just couldn't help laughing in his face, you know, like, 'Buddy, I probably know more about *neidan* (Daoist inner alchemy) than you do!' "[4]

And with his knowledge of inner alchemy, Winn knew what to do to communicate with the spirits of Huashan. In fall 2001, on one of his first trips to the mountain, Master Chen had brought Michael Winn to a secret cave. Saying goodbye to Chen, Winn sat in the cave's mouth to meditate. As he later wrote:

> I focused first on my gratitude to the mountain for being such a powerful presence. The massive West Peak of Huashan towered 4,000 feet of sheer wall above my cave. To get to my cave, I first had to climb up a 200-foot cliff with loose rocks, grasping at the roots of bushes, while wearing a backpack filled with camping gear. One misstep, or leaning too far back, and I would've been in a grave instead of my cave. I silently thanked Chen Yuming and other monks who had helped arrange my stay. I thanked the spirits of Taoists past for sculpting this cave space, and asked them to share with me their secrets. Finally I thanked the cave itself, and any rock elementals who cared to listen, for being such a grand cave. After I finished saying all my thanks, an extraordinary thing occurred. My mouth was suddenly filled with a ball of pulsating energy, which slowly moved down my throat and esophagus into my stomach. Remarkably, this chi ball stayed in my gut during my time in the cave, and I am certain accounted for the fact that I never once felt even slightly hungry for the entire five-day cave fast! Since this occurred immediately after my meditation thanking the cave, it felt like a clear communication from the mountain.[5]

After this "clear communication" in which the mountain bestowed its valuable gift on Winn, he settled into a five-day routine of various *qigong* forms and meditations, and, in his own words, "began to merge into the cycle of night and day of cave life." During the pitch-black night he slept in a sleeping bag on a disused stone altar in the middle of the cave and did "Daoist dream practice." He awoke at 4 a.m. to meditate. He wrote: "The boundaries between the two halves of the physical cycle of night and day began to dissolve as I sank deeper into the mind of the mountain itself."

As in any good dramatic narrative, unexpected adversity brought out hidden strengths:

> After two days of not eating or drinking water, I awoke on the second night with a swollen tongue and feeling very overheated. I self-diagnosed myself, and decided it was the lack of water flowing through my kidneys that was causing my heart to overheat. I had brought water, but had decided on arriving in the cave to not drink any, to more quickly test my body response to the deprivations of cave life that might have been experienced by earlier Taoist adepts. I recalled that one of my western friends had a Taoist spiritual guide who taught him how ancient adepts drank their urine and then refined it with internal alchemy. Since this put no new water into my system, and was a well-tested method used by sailors to survive at sea, I began drinking my urine.[6]

Why was Michael Winn meditating in an obscure cave on Huashan? How did the son of an Army surgeon, who grew up on a military base in Texas and later in a comfortable suburb of Sacramento, California, come to ingest an energy ball offered up by the mountain? Why did a middle-class American who had studied Russian literature at Dartmouth College choose to fast for five days and drink his own urine in pursuit of spiritual enlightenment? To answer these questions we need to ask more fundamental ones: How did Winn arrive on this path, why did he see this path as Daoist, and how did this path become a spiritual option available to him and other Westerners like him?

In this chapter, we sketch the historical and social context out of which the Dream Trippers emerged, in what we call "popular American Daoism." We begin with the first appearance of Daoism in the American consciousness, in the late nineteenth and early twentieth centuries, as a timeless wisdom apprehended through the lens of spiritual Orientalism, which continues to inflect contemporary Western Daoist practitioners until today. We then trace the appearance of several Daoist organizations and masters in North America in the 1960s and 1970s. Among these, most relevant to our story were Mantak Chia and his student and associate Michael Winn who, by the beginning of this century, was organizing the China Dream Trips. After sketching their trajectories and presenting how the Dream Trips are organized and experienced by the participants, we propose a sociological analysis of American Daoists and their emergence from the worlds of the American counterculture and alternative spiritualities. We explain how Daoism was appropriated by, and became an exemplary expression of, American spiritual individualism—in which the self is sacralized as the only authority in spiritual matters.

The Orientalist Legacy of the Early American Engagement with Daoism

Daoism, more so than most other Asian religions, was imported to the West as a set of ideas, rather than as practices. America's earliest firsthand accounts of Daoist religious practices came from Christian missionaries who looked on them as satanic and wholly incompatible with the modern, Christian West. In the late nineteenth century the new field of sinology, which developed concurrently with the "science of religion," valued the classical traditions of China, found in ancient texts, while despising its modern, "degraded" manifestations. Twentieth-century scholars, while bringing to light new information on Chinese religions, in particular Daoism, helped to construct a romantic picture of Daoism that might cure the illnesses of the modern West. Popular writers took this idea further, seeing Daoism as a perennial philosophy that could be conserved in the West and restored to its original purity.

In the nineteenth century European thinkers, as a whole, turned away from China and looked to India as the mystical source of Indo-European culture. But the nineteenth century also saw the appearance of professional sinologists, French scholars who translated the Chinese classics, as well as the first sustained English and American interest in China as Protestant missionary societies sent hardy men and women into the field.

Overall though, Daoism was little known. The nineteenth century saw great interest in Hinduism and Theravada Buddhism but, as historian Carl Jackson put it, Daoism "was to remain the least known of the Oriental religions until the twentieth century."[7] In all the many important points of contact between nineteenth-century America and Asian religions—the Transcendentalist appropriation of Vedanta, the Boston Brahmin sympathy for Buddhism, the Theosophical move from Egypt to Asia, and the emergence of Oriental studies as an academic discipline—Daoism was barely noticed. According to Thomas A. Tweed, "Taoism continued to be veiled in a relative obscurity that would be lifted only partially at the end of the nineteenth century."[8] Indeed, the academic study of Daoism is perhaps one hundred years behind the academic study of Buddhism and Hinduism.[9]

At the World's Parliament of Religions held in 1893 in Chicago, Illinois, for the first time, representatives of many religious traditions began to speak on a more or less equal footing with their Anglo-American hosts. Significantly, Daoism was represented not by a living interlocutor but by an anonymous essay which lamented modern-day Daoism as having "deteriorated" and expressed a hope that someone would "restore our religion, save it from errors."[10]

At the Parliament, an audience member named Paul Carus made contact with the interpreter for a visiting Zen abbot, a young Japanese man named D. T. Suzuki, who would later become the great popularizer of Zen. In 1898, the pair produced the first American translation of the *Daodejing*. Carus saw the book as an example of the perennial philosophy, which paralleled Christianity in many ways; for example, Carus compared the word "Tao" with the "Logos" of the Gospel of John.

Carus's work was the first translation of the *Daodejing* published in America but it would not be the last: by 1950, there were ten in print. The most widely read edition of its day was the 1942 "literary" rendition by Boston poet and saloniste Witter Bynner (1881–1961), which was the first of many English renderings of this short text by Americans who knew no Chinese. It was likewise noticeable for containing, in the introduction, the definitive statement of Western dualism about Daoism: "Taoist religion is an abuse of Taoist philosophy," wrote Bynner. The Western public's fascination for the *Daodejing*, as well as its status as the second most translated text in the world (after the Bible), can be attributed to its brevity, its lack of proper names, and especially its multiplicity of possible meanings. These traits continue to make the *Daodejing* central to the contemporary practice of American Daoism.

The language of Daoist cultivation found its way into the popular discourse via scholarly translations, for example, Carl Jung's reading of Richard Wilhelm's German translation of the Chinese inner alchemical text *Secret of the Golden Flower* or Thomas Merton's rendering of the *Zhuangzi*.[11]

Later, popular scholarship argued that China had a "healthier" attitude toward sex while titillating readers with hints of an "exotic" sexuality. An important source for these ideas was Dutch diplomat Robert van Gulik's (1910–1967) *Sexual Life in Ancient China*, written in 1961.[12]

By the early 1960s a basic "Daoist" vocabulary (Tao, *qi*, yin-yang) had found a home in the Human Potential movement, a generic name for a gamut of therapeutic techniques based on self-transformation, and indeed, the growing popularity of the *Daodejing*, the *I Ching* (*Yijing*), and the practice of tai chi can be historically and conceptually linked to the famed California retreat center, Esalen, often seen as the birth of the Human Potential movement, where important popularizers of Daoism such as Gia-fu Feng (1919–1985) and Al Chung-liang Huang (b. 1937) first taught tai chi.[13]

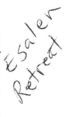

The Birth of Popular Western Daoism

Daoism's globalizing trajectory is conspicuously different from those of Buddhism or Hinduism. Daoism was not first exported from China by immigrant communities, nor by missionaries, but rather as an act of literary imagination. One part of the story of the popular Western appropriation of Daoism has been told quite frequently and quite well. Scholarship has demonstrated how popular conceptions of Daoism owe much to Victorian-era Orientalist prejudice that emphasizes the philosophical origins and "mystic essence of Daoism" in collusion with late-Qing-dynasty literati whom K. Schipper has referred to as "Confucian fundamentalists."[14] Thanks to this research, we know why bookstores throughout the West sell multiple translations of the *Daodejing* while the contours of Daoist practice, both current and historical, are usually ignored, derided, and/or misunderstood.

But there is another story that needs to be told about the westernization of Daoism, a story that ends with the creation of popular Western Daoist groups. The 1970s saw the birth and growth of self-identified Daoist organizations in America, mostly led by Chinese masters with Western followers. This development was due to the 1965 changes in the immigration laws of the United States and Canada, which brought more Chinese to North America. Since the 1960s, the Chinese population of the United States has been doubling every decade and, by 2010, it was well over three million. This growth had several effects on the consumption of Chinese religion in the West. First, with so many Chinese living in North America, Chinese culture—from martial arts to eating with chopsticks—no longer seemed so exotic as it did before the 1970s.

Second, a handful of these immigrants were experienced in various Chinese meditation and body techniques and were eager to teach these skills to willing Americans. At approximately the same time, young North Americans' search for spirituality outside traditional institutions (often called "the new religious consciousness") led them to embrace teachers and practices from Asia. Thus, the situation was ripe for the creation of American Daoist masters and organizations.

What did these immigrants bring with them from China that they used to create American Daoism? They were not Daoists in terms of any formal institutional affiliation. Their most important common characteristic was a background of displacement and a sense of loss. Fenggang Yang thus describes the Chinese immigrant experience:

> In the 1950s to 1970s, many Chinese immigrants were uprooted and rootless people. They were born in the mainland under the rule of Guomindang's Re-

public of China, escaped from wars or fled the Communist mainland, then wandered around in several places—Taiwan, Hong Kong, or Southeast Asia— before coming to the United States. Meanwhile, many also have a strong attachment to their birthplace in Mainland China and hold a vision of a united and strong Chinese nation.[15]

American Daoist teachers, indeed, have been particularly "uprooted and rootless" and have shown "a strong attachment to their birthplace." Their own sense of displacement, of belonging to a nation and a culture that no longer exists as they remember it—not just the physical China but the social, educational, and cultural nexus of the Qing dynasty literati—was an important factor in creating American Daoism. Daoist masters' strong attachment to (and their nostalgic vision of) the China of their memories manifests itself in the utopian and restorationist character of American Daoism that persists to this day.

The first self-identified Daoist organization officially recognized as a tax-exempt religious institution in the United States was the Taoist Sanctuary, founded in North Hollywood, California, in 1970. However, the founder of the Sanctuary was not Chinese—though he often played one on TV (most famously as the Red Chinese agent Wo Fat on *Hawaii Five-o*). Khigh Dhiegh (1910–1991) was of Anglo-Egyptian descent and was born Kenneth Dickerson in New Jersey. Nonetheless, his Sanctuary was the first comprehensive popular Daoist religious organization in North America, teaching tai chi, martial arts, the *Daodejing* and the *I Ching*, and conducting seasonal Daoist rituals (albeit invented by Dhiegh himself). Several notable Chinese immigrants taught at the Sanctuary, including Share K. Lew (b. 1917), who had been trained at a Daoist monastery atop Luofushan in Guangdong, China. After Dhiegh relocated to Tempe, Arizona, the Taoist Sanctuary moved to San Diego, where it is directed by Bill Helm, a former student of Dhiegh's. Carl Totton, another longtime student of Dhiegh's operates the Taoist Institute in North Hollywood.

Mark Johnson was a student of the Taoist Sanctuary who hailed from rural Pennsylvania, and had previously lived in a Hare Krishna ashram in Florida. He had moved to California to be an assistant to Alan Watts, a famous popularizer of Buddhism and Daoism through lectures and books.[16] After Watts' untimely death in 1973, Johnson trained full time at the Sanctuary.

In 1976, Johnson and two other students of the Taoist Sanctuary went to study Chinese medicine in Taiwan. There, they met a Chinese doctor with extensive knowledge of Daoism, whom they invited to the United States. Hua-Ching Ni (birthdate unknown) settled in Malibu, California, opened a shrine called the Eternal Breath of Tao, and began teaching classes privately in a venue he named the College of Tao. Over the years, Ni-sponsored organizations have multiplied. His private acupuncture clinic was known as the Union of Tao and Man. He also founded the Yo San University of Traditional Chinese Medicine in 1989, an accredited degree-granting college. His sons, Maoshing and Daoshing, now head both the clinic and the university while Master Ni lives in semiseclusion.

Mark Johnson was one of Ni's closest disciples and lived with him for several years until 1981 when Ni sent Johnson to New York City in order to establish an East Coast center for Ni's teachings. There, Johnson met another Chinese immigrant teaching Daoist methods that were somewhat comparable to Ni's. This man, younger than Ni, was extremely friendly to Johnson, inviting Johnson to his home for dinner and letting Johnson use the studio he rented in Chinatown for free.

The man was Mantak Chia. Johnson realized Chia wanted him to set up a meeting with Ni, whose Chinese-language books Chia had read, and, accordingly, a meeting was arranged between Ni and Chia. There are different reports of its outcome, including accounts that Ni called Chia a "junior master," that Ni asked Chia to interpret a passage of the *Zhuangzi* to test his philosophical depth, and that Ni demanded that Chia stop teaching. It is impossible to verify the accuracy of these stories.

Ni and Chia had both arrived in America with the express purpose of teaching "esoteric" Daoist practices. Both men have successfully adopted a commercial approach, marketing themselves as "revealing ancient, oral, secret teachings" to the masses. Indeed, Chia proudly claims to reveal Taoism's "secrets" to all by teaching them in public and publishing them in plain, demystified language. "Master Chia sees that the age has come when the public needs and deserves a clear teaching of this healing power, which was shrouded in China by the same secrecy that surrounded medieval alchemy in Europe," wrote Michael Winn.[17] Winn credits this openness to Chia's Euro-American students: "Editorial collaboration by myself and other senior students with Mantak Chia resulted in the conversion of what had been a one-to-one 'ear-whispered' transmission in China into an open and detailed curriculum of progressive courses that Westerners could pay for and take when they were ready."[18]

  pay for play!

Mantak Chia and the Healing Tao

Mantak Chia (b. 1944) is a Thai-born Chinese man who was trained in Hong Kong and has a background in both Oriental and Western medicine as well as in traditional Daoist practices. According to his autobiographical narrative, of his many teachers, his most influential was apparently a Daoist hermit who lived in the hills behind a temple in Kowloon. This teacher, called Yi Eng (in English, "One Cloud"), gave Chia a mandate to use the "Nine Formulas for Immortality" to teach and heal. Yi Eng had trained in a Daoist monastery in the Changbaishan range in Manchuria for thirty years, where a "grandmaster," White Cloud, had taught him the "nine formulae of immortality." After mastering these, Yi Eng was displaced by the Japanese invasion and the civil wars and wound up in Hong Kong, where Mantak Chia was a high school student at the Pui Tseng Chinese-language boarding school. Chia was a fan of martial arts novels, and his senior classmate once invited him to see a master of martial arts, who also had a reputation as a healer, in the mountains north of Kowloon. As recounted by Chia, several friends had decided to see the master together, but, other than the classmate, only Chia showed up at the master's home at the appointed time.

> He put his finger on me, pointing at my dantian, and I felt a lot of *qi*. After that he said, "ok, go home and practice, you feel anything, come and tell me." But that night I could not sleep, so much energy running. Next day I felt the energy moving. I went to see the master in the evening, he said, "oh, you are quick!" He said, "ok, this is the first step you need to do."[19]

According to his account, he learned the Nine Formulas from this master, and also met another master in Hong Kong.

Chia systematized the various teachings he had received, and in 1974 he opened a clinic in Bangkok called the Natural Healing Center, a place where "for a few pennies people sat on a large platform, charged with a negative ion current strong enough to detoxify chronic ailments."[20] In 1978, Chia moved to New York City. He posted advertisements that claimed: "open your microcosmic orbit—money back guarantee!" Leaders of a holistic healing center in Chinatown investigated his claims, and on being convinced of his skills, they offered him free accommodations in the center. "I didn't need to pay rent or find students. They would send patients, I would open their microcosmic orbit, they would heal."[21] Later, he opened his own healing and acupuncture center in Chinatown which he called the "Taoist Esoteric Yoga Center." By 1981, Chia's center, now named the Healing Tao Center, had attracted a coterie of Euro-American students.

The Healing Tao became one of the most widespread institutional forms of popular Western Daoism.[22] Open to all, Healing Tao teaches a popularized system of breathing, visualization, meditation, and postures based on the Daoist practice of Inner Alchemy (*neidan*). The introductory course and the prerequisite for any further study is called "Tao Basics" and consists of simple techniques to visualize the body's "five organs" and meridians. These include Microcosmic Orbit (guiding the body's *qi* flow), Inner Smile (relaxing the organs), and Six Healing Sounds (a specific vocalization directed to each internal organ). Other introductory courses include short form tai chi and "iron shirt" *qigong*. The Healing Tao's intermediate level classes introduce students to the techniques and symbolism of internal alchemy. According to a participant-observer, in the class known as "Fusion," "practitioners proceed from mere channeling of energy into techniques of mixing energies for the purpose of producing superior, pure quality energy."[23] The advanced levels, whose techniques are not revealed to noninitiates, are "the highest stages of Taoist internal alchemy. . . . attained only after many years of living the lower and intermediate practices."[24] In practice, however, an eager student could proceed from Tao Basics up to the advanced Congress of Heaven and Earth over the course of a single summer of workshops, or via audio and videotapes.

Of course!

Chia's first book, published in 1983, was titled *Awaken Healing Energy through the Tao: The Taoist Secret of Circulating Internal Power*. But it was his second book, *Taoist Secrets of Love: Cultivating Male Sexual Energy*, published a year later, which, with its combination of practical advice and titillating expectations, "catapulted him to fame, and sold hundreds of thousands of copies with virtually no advertising."[25] According to historian of American religion J. Gordon Melton, *Taoist Secrets of Love: Cultivating Male Sexual Energy* appeared at approximately the same time as "a variety of new books on various teachings concerning . . . Tantric yoga, sex magick (a la Aleister Crowley), and New Age sexuality. Thus, the sudden popularity of Chia's book may have had little to do with the American appropriation of Taoism, but rather Chia's inadvertently stepping into another popular American subculture."[26] Chia's book, unlike most earlier books that might be considered part of "popular Western Daoism," did not focus on the perennial mysticism of Laozi or the *I Ching*.

Meanwhile Gunther Weil, involved for a long time with the Human Potential movement and transpersonal psychology at the Esalen Institute, wrote the foreword to *Taoist Secrets of Love*. Here, he backs up Chia's claims with examples from physiology and the history of psychology, citing Sigmund Freud's, Carl Jung's, and Wilhelm Reich's attitudes toward sex. Moreover, Weil's foreword adds a dimension to Chia not found in the texts themselves that are completely practical and technical.[27] According to Winn, he, Weil, and a few others became part of Chia's "brain trust," the individuals who taught him how to give American-style seminars and how to dress "like a Master." They also edited, simplified, and standardized his books prior to publication.[28]

classic packaging !!

Beginning in the mid-1980s, Chia's Euro-American students helped him organize national seminar circuits and his Healing Tao grew into one of the largest Western Daoist groups—and a commercially successful international organization—today comprising thousands of certified instructors in many countries. In 1994, Chia moved back to Thailand to establish Tao Garden, an international Healing Tao Center in Chiang Mai, where Europeans and Americans train to be instructors, while he continues to make regular tours of North America and Europe.

Tao Garden is a carefully constructed tropical paradise that is part time-share, part training center, and part international luxury health spa. Chia built it from the ground up and is now beginning to compete in the international luxury health spa market.[29] It markets itself with the slogan "good air, good water, good food, good chi, good heart, good mind." Visitors and students alike can experience Thai or Ayurvedic massage, colon cleansing, acupuncture, and a huge variety of alternative medical diagnostic and therapeutic techniques, as well as hair and beauty services. An Australian travel writer (and holistic health practitioner) described Tao Garden as "eighty acres of organic gardens fragrant with tropical fruit trees, flower canopied cabanas, and gently flowing rivulets."[30]

Tao Garden is located in northern Thailand, outside of Chiang Mai, the heart of the Thai "traditional culture" industry, a region that supports itself based on tourism devoted to traditional Thai dance, art, architecture, cooking, massage, and Buddhist meditation. Its Daoist pedigree is asserted by the names of the buildings, including Eight Immortals Practice Hall and Laozi Meditation Hut (and photos of these and other Daoist worthies are everywhere). A small outdoor shrine, at the center of the resort, honors the Three Purities (*sanqing*), the supreme Daoist divinities.

By the late 1980s, Healing Tao had become a global movement. Chia spends half his time at the Tao Garden and the rest on the road: in the spring of 2008, for example, he taught in Germany, Poland, France, Belgium, Romania, and Russia. Tao Garden has a Thai support staff, but the overall atmosphere is of a retreat for international expatriates. The Instructor Training Workshop that Chia offers each year truly exemplifies globalized Daoism: he teaches Chinese *neidan* techniques to some twenty French, Italians, Germans, and Brazilians in his center in Thailand, managed by Germans, with alternative health services provided by Italians, Swiss, and Thai. English is the lingua franca of all but the mother tongue of none.

The sinologist Douglas Wile sees Mantak Chia as "the product of cross-cultural influences and uses Western scientific theories extensively to support and even to express his own teachings."[31] As an example, Wile mentions Chia's conflation of acupuncture points and the endocrine glandular system. More recently, Chia peppers his lectures with references to research on embryonic stem cells. He sees Healing Tao as activating the regenerative power of embryonic cells housed in lower *dantian*.

Chia's lectures weave in endorsements of fringe science, such as Dr. Masaru Emoto's controversial theory that water can absorb the emotional charge of the people who handle it. Finally, Chia makes liberal use of such buzzwords of alternative health marketing as "nutri-energetics health system" and "emotional stream integration."

As much as the content of his lectures, Chia's biography reveals his eclecticism. Chia's training and outlook are anything but traditionally Daoist. A biographical account mentions his expertise in Thai boxing, Aikido (a Japanese form of hand-to-hand combat), Kundalini yoga, and a martial art known as "Buddhist palm"; interestingly, the biographical note published with his first two books states that "the author Mantak Chia is himself a Christian, but has used the traditional Taoist methods to help thousands of people heal or improve themselves."[32] The disclosure of Chia's Christianity was dropped in subsequent biographical statements.

Although (or perhaps because?) Mantak Chia is an ethnic Chinese, his first forays into China were unsuccessful. In the 1980s, the White Cloud Monastery (Baiyunguan), the main Daoist temple in Beijing, invited him to teach, "but the condition being that I teach for free, fly for free, pay for everything myself," which he refused. He agreed to pay the monastery to find Daoist grandmasters for him to meet, but this did not lead to any meaningful introductions. He went to Louguantai to seek out Ren Farong, the future chairman of the China Daoist Association, but he was disappointed: "We asked about masters in caves, they said they never met them, even if there are some, the government would not allow [us] to go there. So I never met them, don't know where they are." Many years later, he went to Huashan, and met a monk who had a book on inner alchemy:

> It had content on sexual practice, *kan* and *li*, but very poetic, hard to understand. I asked the priest, can you explain to me that you understand this? . . . I said, I can give you a lot of money, if you explain to me what you know in the book. . . . I said I would give him 600 yuan [approx. US$75] for explaining the book, and he said, "ok, later on." But, after delaying, he said, "Nobody wants to talk about this thing." I blew up into the roof. Then he admitted he didn't know it. He just didn't know [the meaning of the book]. I asked him very pinpointed questions, and he could not answer. So I told Juan Li to give him 300 yuan and let him go.

Chia asked another monk at Huashan, who was said to have discovered how Chen Tuan practiced sleeping meditation, to teach him the method; but the monk only proposed a business partnership in which Chia would invest in making Chinese medicines.[33]

It was only by the early twenty-first century that Chia's connections to the Chinese world seemed to increase. He invited a Daoist monk from Chengdu, Li Hechun, to give regular workshops at the Tao Garden resort; his books were translated into Chinese and published in Taiwan; and mainland Chinese began to undergo training and certification at Tao Garden and then offer workshops in China.

Michael Winn

Meanwhile, however, it was Chia's student Michael Winn who had started the practice of organizing regular Dream Trips to China. Winn had adapted the Healing Tao program for North America; Chia's breakthrough book, *Taoist Secrets of Love: Cultivating Male Sexual Energy*, was "written with Michael Winn," who also contributed the introduction. Winn states he wrote the entire manuscript since, as a former professional journalist, he could craft idiomatic and engaging sentences. Describing the success of *Taoist Secrets of Love*, Winn writes, "The book was written in my sophisticated Western literary voice, infused with insights from my years of Tantric practice, posing as Mantak Chia's voice, the Daoist transmitting his oral tradition."[34]

Before meeting Chia, Winn's first exposure to Daoism had been through reading the *Daodejing* while a student at Dartmouth College, but at that time, he had merely considered it to be "pretty poetry," lacking a practical dimension. His spiritual practice started with his own formulation of Transcendental Meditation, seeking release from stress, but this led him to exploring other spiritual practices. He became intensively involved with Kundalini yoga and westernized Tantrism. As a journalist, he worked in Africa as a war correspondent, and also organized some of his first group tours, assisting Israelis to airlift the Falasha Jews out of Ethiopia. And it was there, in March 1981, that he recounts his first encounter with a Daoist Immortal. He had met Mantak Chia a few months earlier, and started practicing his method. One night in the Addis Ababa Hilton, as he was finishing a story on the black Jews and preparing to leave for his next assignment "to spend a night inside the Great Pyramid," he began to feel nauseous with diarrhea, and unable to eat any food for three days.

By the third afternoon I lay on my bed exhausted, but fully awake. My hotel room suddenly began to slowly spin. The furniture and walls began to soften

and flow in a large vortex around me. An ancient looking Chinese man in a
long robe appeared from nowhere, floating above me as if riding on a cloud.
He had a long wispy white beard, and eyes that strangely seemed to be looking
inward at himself. His skin was so wrinkled I remember thinking, this guy
must be 2,000 years old!

Speechless, I watched as a laser beam of a dense white light shot out of
his navel and into mine. The light felt highly charged and totally solid upon
contact. How can light be solid, I wondered? A split second later, my body immediately exploded. Energy shot up my core and out my crown like the mush-
room cloud above an atom bomb.

I felt myself raining back down in tiny droplets that formed themselves
into a body on the bed. The Chinese man disappeared into nowhere. I lay on
the bed, feeling intense bliss, floating in a pool of divine love for hours. All
symptoms of my illness disappeared.[35]

In Chia's method, he found the "nuts and bolts" that had been missing
from the *Daodejing*. Over several years he used the techniques to undo the
damaging effects of Kundalini yoga: "This shift in my practice led to my
writing collaboration with Chia, which over time produced seven books on
qigong and *neigong* ('inner skill'). Chia taught me the techniques he knew,
and I would test them out on myself before writing about them, often under
his name."[36] Winn also sought other teachers and "hunted down every Chinese guy who came through, everybody who was teaching some *qigong*."[37] He
learned techniques from them and incorporated some of them into his own
system.

Winn taught Chia how to give American-style seminars and how to dress
"like a Master." Indeed, Chia's image has changed over time. The author photograph for Chia's first two published books shows Chia wearing thick glasses,
a tie, and a pinstriped suit, smiling (and referred to in the author biography
as a Christian). In more recent pictures, found on Chia's website and publications, he wears a silk jacket and gazes serenely into the camera, conforming to
the stereotypical image of the Oriental monk.[38]

When Chia moved to Thailand, Winn and other Healing Tao senior
instructors formed a trust called the Healing Tao Instructor's Association
(HTIA), which had the license to certify Healing Tao trainers in North America. Michael Winn and his "Healing Tao USA" organization and website were
by far the most active and visible of these instructors, and regularly invited
Chia to give retreats. But in 2014, after Chia failed in an attempt to take control of Healing Tao certifications away from the HTIA, Winn's partnership
with Chia was severely strained. In June 2016, Chia decided to support the
independence of the HTIA.[39]

Winn spends about half of each year in his home of Asheville, North Carolina, the rest of the time giving workshops in Europe and Mexico and leading trips to China. Asheville is home to a bevy of alternative spiritualities and the people who seek them—an East Coast version of Sedona, Arizona, or Boulder, Colorado. Of course, Winn's popular Daoist techniques must compete with techniques derived from Sufi, Native American, Celtic, Buddhist, and a variety of other traditions that are available in any given weekend in Asheville.

Since 1995, Winn has run the Healing Tao University, which for ten years convened each summer in upstate New York and bills itself as the "the largest summer program of Tao Arts & Sciences in the world."[40] (As of 2007, it meets in North Carolina.) Winn sees his mission as "teaching a full spectrum of Daoist Arts and Sciences, with sexual cultivation and alchemy as the core curriculum."

Winn's revised Healing Tao curriculum, which is available on audio and video, is slightly different in form and philosophy from Chia's. In fact, Winn has added several new techniques and claims his emphasis is quite different from Chia's. The main new component is *wujigong* or Primordial *Qigong*, which he learned from a Chinese *qigong* master, Zhu Hui, in 1997. He claims that *wujigong* has been transmitted through a lineage dating eight hundred years back to Zhang Sanfeng, who is also credited with creating the original thirteen-movement *taiji quan* form; and that, after invoking Daoist Immortals before practice, he received guidance on how to improve the method. He writes in his forthcoming book:

> Please allow yourself to imagine (if it serves you) that this school of Wu Ji Gong was begun after Zhang San Feng was visited by an immortal who taught him this form, and that this interdimensional lineage is available to anyone who practices the form with a sincere heart. Just by doing the form you align with this invisible lineage of immortals.[41]

In general, the survival of Chia's Tao Garden and Winn's Healing Tao is based on merchandise sales and attracting new students. The large number of books, booklets, oils and creams, CDs, and DVDs in Mantak Chia's online Universal Tao catalogue demonstrate this clearly.[42] Michael Winn's online presence is, if anything, more explicitly commercialized. Of course, Winn's revised Healing Tao program is also available on audio CD and DVD. Here is how Winn describes them: "Each Qigong video, book, or audio course will assist your authentic Self to fulfill worldly needs and relations; feel the profound sexual pleasure of being a radiant, healthy body; express your unique virtues; complete your soul destiny; realize peace—experience eternal life flowing in this human body. Now 100% RISK-FREE."[43]

Michael Winn's annual summer program also employs highly commercialized language to describe the benefits of cultivation practices. According to the brochure, students will be able to "learn the science of inner sexual alchemy, and self-generate a feeling of 'whole-body bliss,'" "permanently 'breathe' 6 to 10 lbs. of fat away each week with weight-loss chi kung," and "leave feeling younger, healthier, and more enlightened."[44]

Making the "Dream Trip" Come True

From the 1960s to 1980s, American Daoism's connection to China was purely imaginary and entirely mediated by the personal experience of loss and rootlessness of the emigrant masters, as the Daoist heartland in mainland China was largely inaccessible to international visitors. This began to change in the 1990s, as travel to China became easier, and the growth of *qigong* organizations and networks in the mainland and in the West provided a context for increased exchanges—as exemplified by Michael Winn's first trip described above. It was from the early 2000s onward that Daoist "energy tours" became increasingly common and, indeed, have become an increasingly popular "practice" for Western practitioners. The trips themselves are focused on Daoist practices and experience rather than on Chinese culture or landscapes in a general sense, although they are also crafted to appeal to customers who may have little or no prior experience or knowledge of Daoism.

Michael Winn first visited China in 1985, on a tour with a group of Chinese photographers. These included, according to Winn, "Mao Zedong's private photographer, the daughter of the minister of propaganda, and the son of a top architect who was in charge of renovating the White Cloud Monastery." It was through the latter connection that he was introduced to the head abbot of the monastery, the seat of the official China Daoist Association. There, the abbot showed him a text that had been buried during the Cultural Revolution, which contained

an image of the fire and water coupling which is the *Kan* and *Li* image of what we practice in the Healing Tao, and I got this huge transmission—it just came in, BOOM!, right from that text—it's like "OK, we've been waiting to see you—poof!" It started the whole thing cooking in me and I got a really powerful transmission from, you could say, some immortal Daoist.[45]

Winn first led a tour of China in 1998, under the auspices of the US-based National Qigong Association, which was mostly focused on Beijing medical *qigong* hospitals. After the two weeks in Beijing, Winn went alone to Xi'an, where he met some Daoists; one of them took him to Huashan and introduced him to Chen Yuming. Winn and Master Chen became friends. Chen took Winn to the caves of Huashan, and they meditated together—after Chen called his own master, Xue Tailai, for permission. And Chen agreed to clean out the caves for the groups that Winn would bring over, and to teach them some practices. For Winn, this was highly significant:

> You know how the Chinese are, they're secret from mountain to mountain: "Do we want to want to let you into the Huashan tradition? You're from Wudang? You know, hang out for a while, we'll check you out and we'll see how much we teach you." They're very secretive that way. So I felt this was really a big huge shift, like a crack in the wall, the Chinese wall. . . .
>
> And, of course, Chen Yuming himself was quite shocked by the kinds of questions we were asking him about internal alchemy. Like, how do these Westerners already know this? Where are they getting this stuff from? How could they be asking this level of question, which most Chinese can't even ask, because it was kept secret from them as well?
>
> That's really what our credentials were: "This is what we want to know"— "Wow! If you want to know that, then you already know so much to be able to ask for that."[46]

Winn added Huashan to the next *qigong* tour he organized to Beijing; and on his following trip, which took place in October of 2002, he added a supplementary week in the caves, as an add-on experience, for an extra $795. As his newsletter put it:

> The optional week offers an historic first—Taoist cave practice for more advanced meditators in caves at Mt. Huashan used for centuries by Taoist adepts. Once these caves book up, I've reserved more comfortable yet very powerful space in a nearby Taoist monastery (not open to tourists).[47]

A Dream Trip is made up of not only Michael Winn and thirty-five or forty participants, but also an assistant leader who has previously been on the trip and is returning with responsibilities added in exchange for a lower fee. As well, a Chinese guide/translator accompanies the group.

> When you get a whole group doing *qigong* together, concentrating the consciousness, it's just phenomenal. . . . So I get a big thrill from people having powerful life-changing experiences on these trips. That's the main reason I do them. It's not just that it's interesting and colorful and a great trip, but it's an alignment with my spiritual mission: we're using the tools of *qigong* and the Dao to really transform ourselves. Without that, I think I would have lost interest. . . . That's a key piece for me. That's satisfaction. Spiritual transformation made tangible for others.[48]

The Dream Trippers are mostly from the United States but a growing number of Mexicans have joined in the last few years. Any given trip finds an eclectic assortment of participants. In 2004, for example, a Turkish woman educated in Belgium, a Japanese woman who lived in the Netherlands, and a Romanian who had immigrated to Canada joined the trip. In 2012, the group included people from the United States, Canada, Ireland, Holland, Belgium, and Guatemala. The overwhelming majority of Trippers are white, but there is the occasional Asian—a young Chinese woman who had grown up in the United States, a Vietnamese couple based in Geneva—and the rare black person, such as an Ethiopian American, an old friend of Winn's. Groups include many retirees, some even over seventy, as well as some middle-aged couples, and a few younger participants in their late twenties or early thirties.

Religious or spiritual backgrounds are similarly diverse. Some, though by no means all, participants had experience in *qigong* or other "Daoist-inspired" techniques; virtually none practiced more traditional forms of Daoism. Instead, eclecticism was the common thread. A short list of background experiences would include New Age energy healing, yogalates, Sufi dancing, dowsing, and shamanic drumming.

Michael Winn promotes his Dream Trips in the following terms:

> To experience the spiritual essence of China: to meet & study with the most spiritually powerful Taoists, to do chi kung & meditate in its most sacred and beautiful landscapes, to deeply taste China's ancient culture and peoples, and feast on its local cuisines at sumptuous banquets. To share the very best secrets I discovered on seven previous trips to China before it disappears in China's madly modern rush to forget its rich history. In short, The China Dream Trip I would give to myself, if I could only visit China once. . . . The trips are designed to keep the door open between Western and Asian Daoist adepts, and to deepen the ground of our personal practice. Our qigong practice will connect us to the uniquely powerful Qi currents flowing in China's sacred mountains. If your heart feels drawn to China's mystery, I advise you to trust your soul's guidance, and trust the Tao will supply the time and resources to GO.[49]

With these opening lines, sent as an e-mail to his mailing list of thousands, as well as posted on his website, Winn invites you to take part in a secret, soon-to-disappear China.

The Dream Trips, costing approximately US$5,800 per person in 2014, are fast moving and intense. The 2004 cohort, for example, began their two weeks with a couple of days in Beijing then flew to Lhasa for three days, followed by a stay in Chengdu, including two days in a monastery at Qingchengshan. Next, the group flew to Xi'an, then stayed at monasteries or caves at Huashan.

The travel experience is designed to include shopping, sightseeing, and spiritual cultivation by practicing *qigong* in airports, temples, and caves. Participants range from deeply committed practitioners of Daoist inner alchemy and instructors in other, related traditions such as *fengshui*, martial arts or tai chi, to seekers whose first exposure to Daoism is the DVD of Michael Winn's *wujigong* method, included in the tour package and sent to participants a few weeks in advance.

Other American Daoist Trips to China

Michael Winn was not the first to lead such trips to China. Two American Daoist teachers, Harrison Moretz, leader of the Taoist Studies Institute, and Liu Ming (formerly Charles Beyea), leader of Orthodox Daoism in America, both led tours of private students and family on an occasional basis. Both teachers focused their visits on Qingchengshan and neither advertised publicly.

Two other regularly scheduled Western Daoist trips are led by people who took one of Michael Winn's Dream Trips, and have then replicated them with similar itineraries, including Beijing, Huashan, and Qingchengshan. One trip is run by Solala Towler, the editor of *The Empty Vessel*, a magazine of popular American Daoism, published quarterly since 1993. The 2017 iteration of his Empty Vessel Daoist Study Tour is promoted on Towler's website in a tone that seems much less commercial than the Dream Trip's. "All along the way we will 'talk Tao,' eat incredible food, meet qigong masters, artists, musicians, tea masters, and one cave dwelling hermit," Towler writes.[50]

Mark Johnson and Rebecca Kali also were early participants in Winn's Dream Trip and now run their own tours, which are smaller and more frequent, taking ten people twice a year. Like the Dream Trip, Johnson and Kali begin in Beijing, but spend only one day there "because it is so polluted," Johnson told us. Then they go to Chengdu and Qingchengshan, and more recently have added Yunnan Province to their itinerary, including Lijiang, and a Tibetan area the government calls "Shangri-la" to see a new gold-bedecked Buddhist temple, ending with four days in Lhasa. Thus, the tour is not strictly Daoist anymore, only in the pedigree of its two leaders.

There are other variations on Western Daoist trips to China. These include trips conducted specifically to become ordained in a Chinese Daoist lineage (most notably those trips led by Jerry Alan Johnson and Bernard Shannon). There are also trips led by Chinese who have recently come to America and become Daoist teachers there. These trips allow their Western students to stay in their masters' home temples and to meet with their masters' masters. Though these trips are beyond the purview of the present study, they show that virtually all popular American Daoist groups now organize trips to China.

Responses to the Dream Trip

Longtime students of Michael Winn heard about the trip through Winn's e-mail newsletter. (About half of all Dream Trippers read his newsletters, and many of those have been his personal students, Winn told us.) For them, going on the trip was a form of practice, a search for enlightenment.

Other respondents, those not previously acquainted with Winn or his teachings, when asked why they chose to go on this trip, mentioned coincidences—some reported searching the Internet for "Daoist trip China" only a few weeks before departure, finding a link to Winn's Dream Trip and deciding on the spot to sign up. One Canadian civil servant and *fengshui* consultant had not previously heard of Winn or the Healing Tao before picking up *The Empty Vessel* at a bookstore and seeing the advertisement, but was guided by his intuition to register. "Inner guidance told me to come," another participant told us. One fifty-nine-year-old man from Hawaii, who said he was told to attend this trip by a channeled entity from China, told us: "The trip starts before you leave. From when you signed up, things start happening." Another woman said the trip "called to her" and that "there were energy waves coming off this trip."

Winn's deliberate strategy is to stay out of the way of the Dream Trippers—to let participants have their own spiritual experiences, and connect directly to the energies of temples and mountains, and to each other. The way to implement this strategy is to make the groups as large as possible. As Winn said, "What I found with the China Dream Trips is that the larger the group, the easier it is. Because the groups tend to take care of themselves that way. People find their own subgroups. If you [a tour participant] find a little group of people you like and you're happy with, you can handle anything."[51]

Both the 2004 and 2006 groups had tensions. One 2004 participant, a seventy-one-year-old man, wrote the following:

> Based on my understanding of the group's purpose in making the trip, I would say the group was on a spiritual journey, a vision quest. Well, my observations certainly did not support such a description. In several instances I thought individual members of the group displayed an indifference, a disregard for the Chinese culture. Dancing around shaking your rear end with a prayer wheel in your hand while walking out of one of [the] Buddhist's holiest shrines does not seem appropriate in my book [referring to the Jokhang in Tibet]. Shopping was a very high priority and Mr. Winn's scheduling helped to make it so.

He expressed his complaints most forcefully and publicly; but others also had issues. Winn has learned over many years of leading tours to deflect such complaints: "So when a lot of people start complaining, I just put up my shield, 'OK, that's your problem.' You know, that's what the trip is—live with it. Smile. [. . .] I have my travel agent personality, a tour director personality, where you just learn to deflect and move on and get them to focus on what's valuable. 'Yeah, not everything is perfect here in China, it's rough.'"[52]

In 2006, the tension seemed more directed toward other group members (for not knowing *wujigong*, or not performing it in sync with the rest, or for being too picky about hotel towels and other material comforts). But over all, there seems to be a high level of satisfaction with the trip. "I know much more about Daoist monasteries. I have felt the energy there. The honest and open way we were treated by the monks and nuns we met was rewarding," was a typical response we received. In general, the Dream Trippers have a very positive appreciation of the Chinese people, describing them as "contented," "good-natured" or "friendly"; they did not complain about Chinese people or about them spoiling their appreciation of the spiritual energies of the mountain; nor did they complain about the poor condition of accommodations at Huashan. And despite some intergroup tensions, a few Dream Trippers do form bonds—and in at least one case, as we describe in the epilogue, they have fallen in love and gotten married on the summit of Huashan itself. As Winn put it, "Absolutely, it's a community that's formed. It's a bond that goes on, and they stay friends here [in the United States] and it strengthens their path."[53]

More interestingly perhaps, is that the Dream Trip became part of the personal narrative of the Trippers' spiritual quest. It became worked into participants' construction of their identity in relation to Daoism, part of their narrative of spiritual growth. This constructive process is most clearly observable not from the participants' comments during the trip itself, which of course acts as a sacred time and place, a rupture from ordinary routine, but in their reflections from before and after the trip.

The narratives of change after the trip often featured stories of deepening practice and of the difficulties of getting back into regular life. One Dream Tripper e-mailed us: "My most valued experience came on Qingchengshan (Azure Truth Mountain) where I felt a 'nurturing power' that accepted all and promoted what was most natural. Since returning from China, I can often reconnect with that subtle power during meditation or Chi Kung—and it becomes a very tangible dimension in my practice." Another wrote several weeks after the trip, "Everything is quite vivid & still runs thru me day & night."

This deeply experiential aspect of the trips is stressed by Winn in his promotion of the tours: "Why are China Dream Trips so special, and very different from typical tourist trips? We attract a fabulous group of Tao-minded spiritual adventurers. Not mere curiosity seekers or jaded tourists, but fascinating folks who are excited about literally following in the footsteps of Lao tzu and doing powerful qigong ceremonies in China's highest spiritual energy spots."[54]

One could imagine such a tour introducing participants to a great deal of geographic, historic, cultural, and religious features of China. But what Winn stresses in promoting the trip is the idea of China as subjective body-centered space, not as external actuality. As one might expect from a leader of a high-end specialized tour, Michael Winn sent the thirty-seven "China Dream Trippers" (most of whom had never been to Asia) with a series of e-mail recommendations and preparations. All of them concerned the practice of *qigong*. For example, in an e-mail with the subject heading "Health Tips for China Dream Trip," Winn wrote:

> What's the secret to staying healthy in China? Do chi kung [. . .] every day. If you are the really busy type, at least do lots of the first movement, Ocean Breathing, to open your dan tian (belly) power. The chi flows from there into every meridian in your body, and that is your best defense against any sickness. A daily meditation practice also helps to integrate your immune system. . . . Do chi kung at the airport just before getting on the plane. This improves chi circulation and opens your joints, which will get stiff from sitting. I usually do some small movement chi kung on the plane as well.[55]

After he recommends meditation to prevent jetlag, he closes with, "Finally, don't worry too much in advance! Worry weakens your stomach/spleen."

Spiritual Orientalism in American Daoism

It should be clear by now that American Daoism is not based in the lived experience of Chinese immigrants to North America, and has very little connection with their daily rituals and prayers. It has evolved, rather, from textual scholarship and memories of the Chinese literati diaspora. Therefore, American Daoism is notable for its Orientalist character, conforming very closely to literary theorist Edward Said's seminal definition. Said's primary hypothesis was that Orientalism, as a scholarly enterprise, constructs East and West as polar opposites. Orientalists draw an imaginary boundary line, creating an "Other." This structuration can take many forms, but in general, writes Said, "The Oriental is irrational, depraved (fallen), childlike, 'different'; thus the European is rational, virtuous, mature, 'normal.'"[56] American Daoism espouses a similarly bifurcated discourse but the positive and negative values are inverted, in what might be called a romantic strain of Orientalism. Thus the East, as epitomized by a mythic philosophical and alchemical Daoism, is spiritual, mystical, ancient, timeless, intuitive, nonrational, and conceives of humanity and nature as one. The West, as represented by scientific materialism and the monotheistic mainstream, is judgmental, dogmatic, time-bound, and sees humanity in opposition to nature.

In Said's analysis, the Orientalist scholar admits to positive aspects of his object of study, but any such qualities are placed in the ancient past of the constructed East. As Said puts it: "The 'good' Orient was invariably a classical period somewhere in a long-gone India, whereas the 'bad' Orient lingered in present-day Asia."[57] In the final stage of Orientalism, the West has not only found the lost true classical essence of the East, but preserves it. The West dominated the East through "the finality and closure of antiquarian or curatorial knowledge."[58]

What Said called "the now traditional Orientalist ability to reconstruct and reformulate the Orient, given the Orient's inability to do so for itself" is enacted so often in the popular discourse about Asian religions that it seems not worth noticing.[59] Indeed, all of these stages: bifurcating, historicizing, and curatorial, are present in the discourse of Healing Tao and the Dream Trippers.

The discourse of restoration demands that American Daoism ignore the specific ways that Daoism is rooted in Chinese culture and instead emphasize Daoism's universality. (Even as, paradoxically, American Daoist masters use the trappings of Chinese exoticism to present their teachings: Hua-Ching Ni, Solala Towler, Al Huang, Liu Ming, Carl Muller, and others play the bamboo flute, dress in traditional Chinese tunics, or both.) When we asked our survey respondents whether the Chinese origins of Daoism were important, most respondents emphasized the universal origins of Daoism, while only one or two expressed any interest in deepening their knowledge of Chinese language, culture, or history as a way of approaching Daoism. If American Daoists do not value the Chinese qualities of Daoism, it follows that they would not value the Daoist qualities of the Chinese people. One survey response put it this way: "Most Chinese I have met have never heard of Taoism or Lao Tzu." Al Huang echoes this sentiment:

> Undoubtedly, there will be more freeways and polluting chimneys in the East while most great masters of the Orient are emigrating one by one to the mountains and growth-center retreats in the West. I often prepare my friends and students for the shock of discovering the next Chinese they meet may be

well versed in technological jargon but completely ignorant of *t'ai chi* or Tao. The majority of friends of kindred spirit who have shared my studies of the East have been Westerners.[60]

American Daoist masters have been fairly uninterested in teaching Chinese Americans. Maoshing Ni told us that his father, Hua-Ching, never made an effort to establish himself among the Chinese of southern California because the non-Chinese in West Los Angeles were more "spiritually ready."[61] When these Chinese Daoists in America are considered at all, they are usually disparaged. For example, Solala Towler, reporting on his visit to an immigrant Chinese Daoist temple in San Francisco's Chinatown, told us it was mostly concerned with "bake sales" and "funerals." Towler said, perhaps reflecting his disappointment in not being hailed as a spiritual brother, that these Chinese American Daoists are "hard to gain access to if you cannot speak Cantonese, and even then they won't talk to you anyway."[62]

Winn, however, has recently softened his stance, perhaps because of his attendance at numerous academic conferences, where he has been exposed to the scholarly critique of the Orientalism of Western Daoism, as well as to new scholarship on Daoist ritual and monastic institutions:

> I do value those within that tradition who have held that space and guarded the temples, even if they're just sitting there and ringing a gong every day, it's OK, they're still holding a space there. They have held a space for that tradition, I totally respect them, I totally love them for it. It's just we don't have that infrastructure here in America, we don't have temples to guard and we don't have Daoist mountains. We have to create something new.[63]

American Practitioners' Identification with the Dao

While American Daoist masters often use the trappings of Chinese exoticism to present their teachings, they generally ignore the specific ways that Daoism is rooted in Chinese culture and instead emphasize Daoism's universality. This emphasis accounts for the fact that very few American Daoists express interest in deepening their knowledge of Chinese language, culture, or history as a way of approaching Daoism.

The concept of Daoism is fluid enough that anyone can claim it without fear of contradiction, since it signifies a general mystical attitude as opposed to any specific knowledge. People for whom Daoism provides a basic orientation to life but find the word "Daoist" too limiting might use the expression "to follow the Dao."

For example, Americans who are curious enough to buy a book or magazine about Daoism might soon learn the name Solala Towler, who through his *Empty Vessel* magazine and many books has done more to expose North Americans to popular American Daoism than anyone else. Americans who gain this introduction would soon learn that Daoism is nothing if not fluid. For example, in his *Embarking on the Way: A Guide to Western Taoism*, Towler writes:

> [Daoism] works well for highly individuated Westerners and can be approached on any level, from the rank beginner to the evolved aspirant. There is nothing to join, no vows to take, no special naming, clothing style or diet to follow. It is strictly up to the individual to apply whatever aspect of the tradition he or she wishes.[64]

In fact, throughout Chinese history, becoming a Daoist generally meant joining something, taking vows, and taking up a new name, clothing style, and diet. The historical inaccuracy of this passage is less significant than its succinct expression of the basic tenets of American Daoism (which happen to correspond to popular Euro-American spirituality in general): fluidity, universalism, and individualism.

There are anywhere from ten to thirty thousand self-identified American Daoists in the United States and Canada. Typically, they are well educated, middle-class, and white. The majority of them first heard about Daoism in a college or high school class, was lent a book (typically the *Daodejing* or *The Tao of Pooh*) by a friend or family member, or learned about it through tai chi or martial arts.

Our survey of American Daoists revealed that, usually before joining a specific organization, they had been introduced to Daoism through a Daoist-inspired physical or meditation exercise, through Chinese medicine because of an illness, through a Daoist text, or through some combination of the three. A typical example comes from Solala Towler, who today is a prominent and productive member of the American Daoist community. For twelve years he was afflicted with chronic fatigue syndrome, suffering constant pain, unable to travel, and eventually bedridden for six months. Finally, he cured himself of his ailment by taking Chinese herbs and reading the two best-known Daoist classics, the *Daodejing* and the *Zhuangzi*.[65]

Responses to survey questionnaires indicate that the majority of American Daoists first heard about Daoism in a college or high school class or were lent a book by a friend or family member.[66] Another point of entry into assuming a Daoist identity, we have found, is by ex post facto naming of a previously inchoate experience. Daoism can provide a convenient label for nameless physical-spiritual experiences. For example, a forty-year-old acupuncturist, when asked at a retreat about how she first heard about Daoism, writes, "I left the Christian faith as a sixteen year old, had a 'religious' experience a few months later while backpacking and formulated a personal spiritual vision/philosophy. When I went to acupuncture school ten years later, I learned that 'my' philosophy was, in fact, basically Taoism." A twenty-nine-year-old student of Hua-Ching Ni related a similar narrative:

> When I was seventeen years old in high school, I was experimenting a lot with hallucinogenic drugs and with LSD. Before having any serious contact with Taoism, I once had a tremendous experience with a large dose of LSD where I experienced the indescribable primordial origin of life. For over nine years after this experience, I searched the entire spectrum of religious and spiritual texts and traditions looking for the way of knowledge that spoke of what I had experienced directly. I was only further and further confused by the diversity of traditions that I encountered, and as more and more time passed, I began to lose hope of finding this direct, lucid truth. When I finally discovered Master Ni's work, all feeling of promise returned to my life.

Likewise, a thirty-six-year-old wrote, "I found the cosmology of Daoism to be very dynamic and encompassing. It was an easy fit for my experiences." As these answers attest, for some American Daoists, a kind of spontaneous experience generates their Daoist identity, and experience and identity are mutually reinforcing.

American Daoists are aided by a growing library of Daoist scripture translated into English, much of which provides both specific instructions on techniques that are meant to attain a particular religious experience and descriptions of this experience, albeit in metaphoric language.[67] Clearly, religious experiences of such a visual and somatic nature, even if not part of a ritual and liturgical framework, can be powerful builders of a Daoist identity. Thus, some Americans identify themselves as Daoists without any institutional affiliation at all. These include those who, having read the *Daodejing* or such popular interpretations of Daoism as *The Tao of Pooh* (1982) for class or on their own, liked the concepts enough to proclaim themselves, silently or out loud, to be Daoist, yet with no knowledge of Daoist history, practice, or indeed of Daoists.[68]

Those for whom Daoism is one part of an eclectic and individualist religious identity might find a natural home in cyberspace, where eclecticism and individualism flourishes. Many American Daoist sites can be accessed through one of several web rings, among them the "Wandering Taoists," the largest and most active Daoist ring on the Internet, linked by the easily identifiable logo of a Chinese sage, facing up and left, seemingly walking away from the viewer.[69] Most of these sites reject any kind of historic or cultural definition of Daoism in favor of a gospel of contentment and acceptance, with links to other websites about health practices, *fengshui*, the *I Ching*, the *Daodejing*, and quite often *reiki*, the energy-healing technique. The occasional website represents a "virtual Daoist organization" that allows membership and encourages a more active identification as a Daoist, but still in the most individualist terms. Most notable among these is the Reform Taoist Congregation (until 2006 known as Western Reform Taoism), which was founded in 1998 and had 312 online members as of 2009.[70] Its founder states that he has "created a new form of religious Taoism," and his hope "is simply to bring together people who share a spiritual devotion to the Tao. Of course, for the time being, 'together' will mean 'cyberspace,' as facilitated by this website."[71] Most Daoist websites, though, are purely personal. Here is a typical example: "I am a Taoist, and this could be described as a web site about Taoism, but really Taoism isn't about words. Taoism is really about being and doing."[72]

This quality of not belonging to any particular culture or tradition is self-consciously invoked even by those who demonstrate financial and personal commitment to American Daoist masters and their organizations. For example, we surveyed participants in Al Huang's Living Tao Foundation retreats, people who spend thousands of dollars and several weeks out of each year on learning tai chi–inspired dance and free-form calligraphy. One question asked was "Do you consider yourself a Daoist?" That question received twenty valid responses and there were only two clear positives. There were eleven clear negative responses, including those from a man who identified himself as a Buddhist-Episcopalian and a woman who said she was a "nonactive Unitarian." Two more declared that they consider themselves Daoists "only to themselves," one person responded "sort of," and four people thought the term "Daoist" too restrictive. Among the latter group was this typical response from a sixty-two-year-old male: "I don't like the word 'Taoist'—I find it too limiting. I use the expression 'I follow the Tao.' "

Similarly, we asked participants at the Living Tao retreat whether they engage in other non-Daoist religious activities. Most respondents mentioned a variety of "alternative practices" from channeling to yoga, from Tibetan Buddhism to Taize singing. One woman wrote: "Yes, I am very eclectic . . . I use shamanism and pagan practices, mantras from the Hindu and Buddhist tradition, and silent meditation. I also practice latihan from the Subud group out of Indonesia."

For some, American Daoism functions not as an element of the spiritual quest, but as the end to that quest. The American Daoists we interviewed, for the most part, did not arrive at Daoism directly from their Jewish or Christian religious upbringing. For example, we found that Hua-Ching Ni's senior students were involved in a variety of alternative spiritualities before encountering Ni, including Vedanta, *vipassana* meditation, and the Gurdjieff-inspired group Arica. If we take Solala Towler as an example, his religious journey seems very much a spiritual quest. He grew up in a large, working-class Catholic family in New England, and although he never attended college, he received an education by "hanging out" in Harvard Square in the 1960s and by participating in the psychedelic experiments of Harvard professor Richard Alpert (later Ram Dass). He later practiced yoga, joined the Self-Realization Fellowship, and tried zazen but "found it too artificial."[73] Other subjects mention the other practices in which they engaged before "finding Daoism." A partial list reads like an encyclopedia of alternative spirituality in America: Transcendental Meditation, the Gnostic church, Kundalini yoga, macrobiotics, LSD use, the International Society for Krishna Consciousness (also known as ISKCON or Hare Krishna), Healthy, Happy, Holy Organization (also known as 3HO and now sometimes called Sikh Dharma), and American shamanisms.

While this meandering path to Daoism may seem to be an argument in favor of the eclecticism of American Daoist identity, in some ways it demonstrates just the opposite. According to our surveys and interviews, once having found Daoism, some people abandoned other practices. They turned exclusively to Daoism, as they defined it, which provided a link to tradition and authenticity that their previous eclecticism could not. It is possible that a longitudinal study would reveal that many of the subjects would have moved onto other practices in a few years. But this seems unlikely, since many of them have been grounded in Daoism for upward of twenty-five years. For some American Daoists, their practice is no longer part of a spiritual quest, and they no longer consider themselves seekers.

American Daoism promotes self-improvement and physical, mental, and spiritual health by offering a series of modular, voluntary practices, which both produce and are produced by an overall "Daoist" worldview, and provide both immediate benefits (for example, increased physical stamina and emotional well-being) and more long-term rewards (for example, feeling reconnected to nature and to the cosmos). These practices come from China, but the way they are marketed, conceptualized, and inserted into daily life are North American. Indeed, part of the appeal of these Daoist practices is their instrumentality. They can be taught and learned in discrete units, through a combination of weekly classes and yearly, or seasonal, retreats or seminars, and can be performed individually or in groups, when and where needed. This may well be inevitable in the American context.

Although American Daoists engage in numerous practices, the overall variety is limited and consistent. The most commonly mentioned practices are *qigong*, meditation (including guided visualizations), tai chi, and *I Ching* study. The next most common grouping consists of text study, diet change (including fasting), and Chinese medicine (both as patient and healer). Less commonly mentioned practices include invocations, lucid dreaming, *fengshui*, and calligraphy.

Many American Daoists were involved in a variety of other spiritual techniques before settling on Daoism. Thus, another way to describe the journey made by American Daoists is from seeking to finding a practice. That American Daoism embodies a series of practices is not a controversial proposition, since all religions and worldviews are sustained by practices. As sociologist of religion Wade Clark Roof wrote, "Practices, both personal and collective, are embedded in a tradition's history and serve to 'keep alive' that history and are the means by which a person learns, shares, and participates in its symbolic world. In fact a symbolic world 'rests' on a well-defined and embodied set of practices."[74]

What sets American Daoism apart from other traditions is the primacy of practice over history, values, or even community. Self-identified American Daoists define their "Daoism" less as a tradition or even a philosophy, but more as a series of practices. Examples from the survey suggest that most American Daoists do not engage in certain practices because they are Daoists, but rather they are Daoist because they engage in certain practices. In so stating, we do not mean to imply that American Daoists have no interest in Daoist philosophy. As seen earlier, the mystical philosophy of the *Daodejing* was the point of entry into Daoism for many North Americans. But evidence does suggest that they made the leap to identification as Daoists because of taking up a regular practice.

Interviews of Dream Trippers revealed that the participants who were most familiar with Daoist-inspired techniques of energy cultivation, and had their own intensive regime of practice back in North America, were the least interested in Daoist history, rituals or mythology. For the Western Dream Tripper, the subjective experience in one's own body is the only source of authenticity transmitted by the energy signature of previously present (deceased) bodies.

The central place of subjectivity became apparent in our interviews and follow-up e-mails with participants of the workshops at Mantak Chia's Tao Garden resort in Thailand. We were interested in learning about their experiences of Tao Garden as a place—as a luxurious spa, as a center for traditional

Thai culture, or as a home for Daoist deities. Which of these three senses of place appealed most to the students at the teaching training workshop? In talking to us about their experiences at Tao Garden, respondents made absolutely no mention of any of these aspects. The students did not seem to care about the luxuriousness of the surroundings. No effort was made by the staff or students to connect to Thai culture. We never saw anyone enter or hear of anyone mention the Daoist shrine, nor remark on the Daoist images on the walls of many of the buildings.

Instead, students mentioned the effect the Tao Garden had on their body's subjective space. For example, a French woman wrote to us:

> What my vacation brought me: only good, nothing to throw out, every day was one step forward and one more treasure in my energy body. The richest? Always, always condensing energy in my dantian with one goal: the opening of the heart, always more and more . . . which would permit me to become and remain as big as the universe. This retreat reinforced my connection to the universe.[75]

Other participants mentioned their fellow students or the energy of Mantak Chia as the defining experience (a French man: "When Master Chia guided us in meditation, his energy was very present and supported us all"). Others noted how their bodies felt more energized, balanced, or purified. Tradition, scripture, community, or morality was never brought up at all. Subjective experience was the reason for coming to Tao Garden and the criterion for a successful visit there. In chapter 2, we have discussed in detail how, similarly, the Dream Trips to Huashan focused on the subjective experience of the mountain's powers.

The experience of Huashan by the Dream Trippers clearly involved describing and perceiving the mountain as a site laden with powerful energies to be subjectively experienced. Returning to Winn's "secret cave" narrative, we remember that his week there took place about a month after the attacks of September 11, 2001. These events influenced Winn's internal practice:

> The meditations I did on the global situation from my cave on Mt. Huashan were very profound. I linked my own polarized brain hemispheres and deep energy body channels to the powerful granite meridians of Mt. Huashan. These connected me into the core of the planetary brain that links humanity into a single collective mind. [. . .] In this way, the Spring Flower cave on Huashan became in the inner planes a cauldron of hope and renewal for all humanity. Later, after I left Huashan, I could still feel the chi from Huashan's granite still coursing through my deep channels, and the heart of humanity beating more palpably within my own heart.[76]

focus on the subjective experience

In the end, Michael Winn's dream at Huashan is not a dream about Huashan, Daoism or China, but a dream about himself, about the universe, and about the realization that they are one and the same.

Daoism as American Spiritual Individualism

In chapter 1, we referred to Foucault's conceptualization of the "care of the self," itself derived from ancient Greek practices on the "art of existence," and affirmed that Daoist practices of the body can be seen as forming a regimen of such "technologies of the self." The sinological literature on Daoism typically refers to these practices as "self-cultivation" techniques. However, the usage of the word "self" in these formulations masks a fundamental, ontological difference between the Daoist understanding and transformation of the body in the context of a correlative cosmology, and the Western conceptions of the self that are the soil out of which grows American spiritual individualism. The "self" which is the object of "care" and "technologies" in the Greek and Western traditions is an undivided ontological reality. From Greek speculations on "who am I?" to Hamlet's "to be or not to be," to Descartes' "I think, therefore I am," the Western intellectual tradition has repeatedly postulated the existence of a self that is unique, bounded, and identical to itself. In the Christian context, the spiritual subject is formed in its relationship with the supreme Subject, God, who, as the absolute Other, defines both the potentialities and the limitations of individual subjects.[77] With secularization, this becomes the self that asserts its individual conscience, interiority, and subjectivity in the face of an impersonal universe, and in the naturalist ontology analyzed by Descola—the "bounded self" of the disenchanted, secular world discussed by Charles Taylor.[78] Modern American spirituality seeks to reenchant the experience of the world—but within the limits of a bounded self; enchantment occurs by going deeper into oneself, it is to be experienced subjectively, and it finds expression through untrammeled, authentic individuality.

While ontological individualism can be traced back to a long Greek and Christian genealogy, it is in the modern era, beginning with the Renaissance, the Reformation, and the Enlightenment, that the philosophical, economic, legal, political, and cultural implications of an independent, autonomous, and free self have been worked out and enacted in all dimensions of culture and society, producing the distinctive characteristic and foundation of Western modernity based on a disenchanted, naturalistic ontology. Corollary to the notion of the autonomous individual is the problematization of social life, political order, and religion—since society, the state, and religious institutions restrict individual freedom and are thus antithetical to the full and unfettered expression of an authentic self. The grand narrative of Western modernity and progress has always been one of resisting, opposing, and restricting authority, whether traditional, religious or political. Secular authority is the product of the freely negotiated "social contract," or of the "invisible hand of the market" that expresses the aggregated free choices of autonomous individuals. The subversive freethinking of the Enlightenment philosophers led to the proclamation of freedom of individual conscience and religion in the earliest declarations of human rights, and to the entrenching of secularism as an ideology and institutional structure. In this context, the religious field was strictly circumscribed, with strict boundaries between the secular and the religious being the subject of negotiations throughout the modern era.

The Western religious field is structurally defined by the history and legacy of the Roman Catholic project, during the medieval period, of controlling and monopolizing the social and individual connection with the divine. Other doctrines and practices, marginalized and condemned by the church as heretical, formed the loosely associated current of traditions known as "esotericism," which evolved in parallel, and often in conjunction, with the intellectual development of the Renaissance, modern science, and secularism. Growing out of older traditions often condemned as heretical in medieval and Renaissance Europe, this constellation of ideas, movements and practices has always positioned itself against the dominant institutions of the religious field, and often refuses to be categorized as "religion." It included the deism and freemasonry of the Enlightenment, the magnetism of Emmanuel Swedenborg and Mesmer, the mystical romanticism of Goethe and Blake, and the spiritism and occultism of the mid- to late nineteenth century. These movements were followed by the Theosophical society and by the increasing interactions and circulations between this esoteric milieu, Orientalist scholars, and religious masters and movements from Asia. They influenced Freud's conceptions of the "unconscious"[79]—although he would scarcely admit it—and became central to Jung's school of psychoanalysis. In America, this tradition can be traced back at least as far as the Spiritualist movement of the early nineteenth century and to authors such as Emerson, Thoreau, Walt Whitman, and William James—forming the rich culture of what Albanese has called America's "metaphysical religion."[80]

The esoteric milieu evolved into the world of modern spiritualities and religious exoticism, appropriating and absorbing Asian traditions. This world of "alternative" spiritualities defines itself in opposition to the "dogma," the "rituals," and the "institutions" of a church-like "religion"; it thus participates in the secularist rejection of religion. According to Bourdieu, the monopolization of the religious field by clerical institutions—in this case, the church—leads to the dispossession of the laity, who are barred from direct control of access to the divine.[81] The world of alternative spiritualities expresses the laity's desire to reclaim a direct access to spiritual experience, through mastery of spiritual technologies outside the boundaries and control of religious institutions. This milieu also rejects the radical disenchantment of secularity, seeking "alternative" techniques and philosophies that can reenchant the self, the body, and the cosmos in a modern context. In the 1960s and 1970s, with more relaxed immigration policies, the world of esoteric and exotic spiritualities absorbed a large infusion of Hindu, Buddhist, and also Daoist spiritual masters from Asia. At the same time, with the counterculture of the 1960s, this milieu became a key component of a mass cultural turn against both mainstream religion and conventional secular modernization. This "New Age" was antiauthoritarian, individualistic, body-centered, and sexually liberated. Its utopian, communal impulse was gradually absorbed into a growing therapeutic and spiritual marketplace of commercial entrepreneurs and consultants.

This is what Spiegelberg called the "religion of no-religion,"[82] or what Heelas has called the "self-spirituality" of the New Age movement. While extremely diverse in their origins, theologies, and practices, these spiritualities all shared a rejection of the authority, dogmatism, and sectarianism of the church, opening spaces for individuals to freely explore their inner spiritual selves, to cross boundaries between traditions, and to experience mystical experiences and states with "scientific" approaches and rational discourses. They are expressions of what the French sociologist of religion Danièle Hervieu-Léger has called "the religious productions of modernity,"[83] a new approach to religion that has given birth to reform movements and spiritualities in all religious traditions since at least the nineteenth century and even earlier.

These groups are very different in their structure and teachings, but all invariably use a scientific and antiritualistic discourse that shows an unacknowledged debt to ideologies of modernization. The Healing Tao is a perfect example of "modern" spirituality. It proudly claims to reveal Daoism's "secrets" to all by teaching them in public and publishing them in plain, demystified language. "Master Chia sees that the age has come when the public needs and deserves a clear teaching of this healing power, which was shrouded in China by the same secrecy that surrounded medieval alchemy in Europe," writes Michael Winn.[84] Winn credits this openness to Chia's Euro-American students: editorial work by himself and other senior students converted the informal, oral, and sometimes secret transmission of the Asian master into an open, detailed, and progressive curriculum that could be marketed to a Western audience.[85]

[American] Daoism is taking a different form, not necessarily a religious form, than it is taking in China, with temples and uniforms, and the state religion and all that stuff, that's its history. In the West it's taking more of the form of personal belief and identification with the Dao and the structures of the Dao, kind of like getting back to early Daoism, before all that existed in China.[86]

Healing Tao's modernizing tendencies also include a disdain for superstition and ritual. Healing Tao formulates its Daoist identity not as a religion but in counterpoint to religion—which it opposes to esotericism. As Chia puts it:

The Taoists referred to in this essay are the masters of Taoist Esoteric practice, whose traditionally secret methods were studied by Master Mantak Chia. This is not to be confused with the Taoist religion, whose priests combined elements of Buddhism, Esoteric Taoism, and Chinese culture (folk beliefs, confucianism [sic]) in order to maintain a popular base.[87]

The Healing Tao, on the other hand, is more than a case of "modern" Daoism as seen through antitraditionalism. It goes beyond conventional modernity, exemplifying what cultural critics have variously called "late modernity," "postmodernity," "supermodernity," or "ultramodernity." These terms are the subject of different meanings, nuances, and debates in the writings of various scholars, but for our present purpose it is sufficient to consider how they attempt to convey a passage from classical modernity, which defines itself in critical and self-reflective opposition to tradition, to a new phase in which modernity's critical self-reflexivity turns on itself. Thus, while the term *postmodern* has had enormous currency in the past few decades, what we are witnessing is not the end of modernity, or moving beyond it, but an intensification and radicalization of the modern.

While classical modernity was based on the belief in a narrative of ever-increasing progress, rationality, and scientific development, defined against the obscurantism of religion and tradition, Jean-Paul Willaime has argued that ultramodernity desacralizes the belief in progress—secularization, which under classical modernity relativized the authority of traditional religion, now undermines the core beliefs and institutions of secular modernity itself.[88] One of those core beliefs was in the power of objective and universal reason, which is replaced by the primacy of subjectivity.[89] And while classical modernity accorded an encapsulated space for "traditional" institutions such as religion, ultramodernity is characterized by what Peter Beyer has called "the 'subjectivization' of religion, the idea that religiosity is less and less located in authoritative and 'outside' religious institutions and more and more within the 'internal' control and consciousness of individuals."[90] New Age spirituality, in particular, places "emphasis on the individual as locus of religious authority and authenticity."[91]

A spiritual subject who locates authenticity and authority in personal desire, preference, and experience is the same as a consumer. Theorist of postmodernity Zygmunt Bauman sees the rise of "self-improvement movements that train our consumerist potential" to be a hallmark of postmodernity; these movements package and sell "peak experiences," which were "once the privilege of the selected" but now brought "within every individual's reach [. . .] relocated as the product of a life devoted to the art of consumer self-indulgence."[92] Others have commented that, for these postmodern spiritualities, consumerism itself, disguised as "New Age" spirituality, has become "the new esoteric knowledge."[93]

These movements are thus not reactions against modernity, a rear guard action of an enchanted worldview that is rapidly disappearing. In the West, Healing Tao is a fruit of the conjunction of modern spirituality with the counterculture of the 1960s. According to Heelas, indeed, modern spirituality became one of the three main orientations of the counterculture: the first aimed at changing mainstream society, through political activism galvanized by the struggle against the Vietnam War; the second rejected mainstream values and advocated living a hedonistic life, through free sex, drugs, and rock & roll; and the third sought to find ways to nurture the authentic self, through exploring Asian spiritualities and going on journeys to India.[94] All three of these strands were connected and reinforced each other. The Esalen Institute in Big Sur, California, for example, was a focal point for producing the American fusion of experimentation with psychedelic drugs, the development of body-centered psychotherapies, and the recasting of Indian and Daoist practices into the erotic spirituality that Kripal has called "American Tantra."[95] The spiritual strand of the counterculture evolved into what was, by the 1980s, being called the "New Age" movement.

Paul Heelas has described the "lingua franca" of the New Age movement as "self-spirituality," expressed in phrases such as "your lives do not work," "you are gods and goddesses in exile," and "let go" of your artificial self. Other central characteristics include unmediated individualism: "I am my own authority," "follow your own inner voice," and "you are responsible for yourself."[96]

Broadly speaking, the Dream Trippers and most American Daoists can be linked to what the sociologist of religion Wade Clark Roof, in his study of the American "spiritual marketplace," has called the "metaphysical believers and seekers," as opposed to those with religious identities—a group that has much in common with the "secularists," and can be seen as the most thoroughly modern of all groups, or at the avant-garde of modernity.[97] They are the most

detraditionalized, the most fluid or unclear in their ethnic and religious identities, and the most closely aligned with expressive individualism and therapeutic culture. Commercial enterprise and the consumption of commodified
services is the most common form of social relations among this group.[98]

The ethic of "self-spirituality" sacralizes the individualism that is pervasive
in American culture. In their famous study of American culture and values,
Habits of the Heart, Robert Bellah and his associates affirm that the common
moral discourse of America is one of radical individualism, in which, ultimately, while everyone holds values of goodness and tries to live according to
them, the individual is the sole arbiter of what is good for himself and society.[99]
Bellah et al. argue that, in the second half of the twentieth century, individualism, in both its utilitarian and expressive guises, became increasingly pervasive.
This period is characterized by "the nervous search for the true self," for "a socially unsituated self from which all judgments are supposed to flow."[100]

Indeed, in this culture, there is no transcendent source of values beyond
the self. "One's own idiosyncratic preferences are their own justification, because they define the true self."[101] The self and its feelings become the only
moral guide; each individual is free, within his own private space, to follow
and express his inner feelings, his deeper truth. But this freedom generates
its own spiritual anxiety: if my self is my ultimate authority, then what *is* my
authentic self? Self-discovery becomes an imperative: to be a fully realized
American, you need to know who you are, and to show it. And that "who you
are" needs to be something that you have discovered and constructed for yourself. American spirituality thus becomes a process of the "sacralization of the
self," providing systems of knowledge, techniques, and symbols that can be

used by individuals in their process of self-sacralization. But again, the ground
of authenticity in such a process is none other than one's own experience, and
the result will necessarily be different from others: "I am a sect myself," said
Jefferson, while Thomas Paine wrote: "My mind is my church."[102] And Bellah
et al. quote one of their interviewees, Sheila, who defines her own religion as
"Sheilaism."[103]

But, while Western modernity elevates the autonomous self to a position
of ontological primacy, it paradoxically *alienates* the self through a mechanistic, materialistic, and functionally differentiated organization of life. Dualistic modes of thinking and of structuring institutions severely limit the
space for the self, cutting it off from its body, from its environment, and from
much of the time spent living in a compartmentalized, rationalized, functionally differentiated organization of work. The modern self is thus divided,
wounded, and torn in different directions. It is this characteristically *modern*
suffering that gives rise to what Bellah et al. call the "therapeutic culture,"

which includes the spectrum of psychologists, psychotherapists, bodywork therapists, alternative medicines, holistic healers, life coaches, and self-help gurus. This therapeutic culture greatly overlaps with the New Age and "self-spirituality": all offer a cure to the ailment of the alienated modern individual. The cure is to help people to constitute the self in its wholeness and authenticity, so that it can find its own grounding, and from thence to relate successfully to the demands of society and to find satisfaction. Restoring the wholeness of the self, and connecting the self to the body and to its healing, are core concerns of this therapeutic and spiritual culture that is closely associated with expressive individualism. This common therapeutic culture explains why, in spite of the apparent eclecticism of practitioners of alternative healing and spiritualities—who often progress through a string of disparate techniques ranging from reiki to shamanism and tai chi to kabbalah—there is actually a striking uniformity and standardization among the various spiritualities on offer. As argued by Altglas, decontextualized exotic religious resources are formatted into the psychologized therapeutic culture of the Human Potential movement. The journey of self-realization, they propose,

> involves self-examination and control of thoughts and emotions and the building of self-confidence, self-reliance, and adaptive skills. To achieve this goal, religious teachings are presented as effective techniques one can learn and carry over from workshops, seminars, books, and audio and online sources. Thus, exotic religious resources tend to become relatively similar practical tools for personal growth, while in the quest of useful self-help carry-over, their respective religious particularism loses its significance. This homogenization . . . allows individuals to experiment and to combine many of these religious and therapeutic methods without being concerned with contradictions between them.[104]

In the therapeutic culture, religious resources of different origins are typically given a relatively uniform format as simple and accessible self-help methods that replace doctrines, ritual, and scriptural study with access to direct spiritual experience, with a practical orientation and packaged into classes and workshops to cater to different audiences and levels.[105]

The Dream Trips are a perfect example of what the sociologist Véronique Altglas has called "religious exoticism," in which members of the Western middle class decontextualize, construct, and appropriate the religious beliefs and practices of another culture, in line with their own desires and expectations rather than those of the originating culture. "While exoticism dramatizes and fetishizes differences, paradoxically their domestication involves the neutralization of these differences. . . . This process of domestication also generates a process of homogenization of religion: the doctrines, practices, and modes of transmission of Kabbalah, Hinduism, Sufism, Buddhism, and so forth have been significantly shaped by Euroamerican therapy culture."[106] Altglas argues that, while practitioners assert their individual freedom and authority in their self-construction, in fact,

> the self has become the locus of discipline and conformity to collective norms. Realizing the self entails improving oneself; evaluating and controlling one's thoughts, emotions, and behaviors; learning appropriate techniques (yoga, meditation, etc.) to do so; and cultivating moral virtues. In fact, "spirituality," as a quest for self-realization, presents itself as a process through which individuals become the active and autonomous agents of their own regulation. Ultimately, the realization of the self (and what kind of self is desired to be realized) is not "natural" or even unique to each individual's subjectivity; rather, it reflects the political and economic structures of contemporary Euromerican societies.[107]

In such a context, Daoist cultivation appears as a perfect technology for American ontological individualism: rooted in the body, it uses sets of techniques that act as matrices for integrating a wide range of domains into the care of the self. Indeed, the Daoist tradition contains a rich repository of practical methods, all based on a holistic cosmology, which can be practiced by the individual without requiring belief or adhesion to a specific dogma, and without requiring membership in a collective organization. These methods range from practices for health and healing, for building physical strength through martial arts, for enhancing the meaning and pleasure of sex, for observing and reflecting on the ultimate nature of the body, the natural world and the universe, and for progressing toward spiritual transcendence. Taken separately, all of these domains already seem to match areas of strong interest and concern in the American therapeutic and self-spirituality cultures. Even better: over centuries of Daoist history, all of these functions have been increasingly integrated and systematized around a core foundation through a common discipline of the mind, body, and breath, a common cosmology of the body, and a common foundation of nurturing, working with, and transforming *qi*. Seen from this angle, Daoist self-cultivation seems to be the perfect cure for restoring and creating a holistic, authentic American self. Its "fit" with American spiritual individualism seems to be even stronger than other alternative spiritualities: nontantric Buddhism rejects sex and the body; while the tantric traditions of Hinduism and Tibetan Buddhism place too much emphasis on guru devotion, ritual, and cultic organization. As Winn put it,

"It's too much a guru yoga thing, too much worshipping the teacher. I have my authority issues and I didn't really jibe with that. And Daoism is much more independently minded, much more grounded, much more embodied, and much more medically oriented."[108]

These issues have, indeed, been a source of controversy in relation to the Western adoption of other Asian body cultivation and meditation techniques, especially those associated with Hinduism and Tibetan Buddhism.[109] In an interview for the Buddhist journal *Tricycle*, Alan Wallace, an academic professor of Tibetan Buddhism who is also a former Tibetan monk, decried the disembedding of Buddhist teachings when they are packaged into one-off retreats lasting a few days or a week:

> What's missing here in the vast majority of cases is the profound context: the theoretical context, the context of faith, the context of a mature spiritual community. The teachings themselves, though perfectly traditional, are being introduced in a radically non-traditional context. And this, I think, has on numerous occasions led to terrible misunderstandings and a great deal of unnecessary conflict.[110]

According to Wallace, Americans have little interest in the basic Buddhist teachings of ethical discipline, renunciation, and the cultivation of loving-kindness; and only attend retreats given by visiting lamas on advanced meditation initiations. As a result, many Tibetan lamas consider Western practitioners to be "impatient, superficial, and fickle." In this study, we find the same criticisms expressed by Chinese monks, discussed in chapter 5—and in chapter 6, as a counterpoint, we explore the rejection of the Dream Trippers' approach by the scholar-practitioner Louis Komjathy and his attempts to establish a Daoist practice in the United States which is focused, committed, and firmly grounded in lineage, tradition, and rigorous scholarship. As he writes, "Daoist adherence is a religious path, one involving actual commitments and responsibilities."[111]

But, in a rejoinder to Wallace, a disillusioned American ex-Tibetan Buddhist vividly illustrates the difference between the Tibetan Buddhist and Daoist cases. In an online posting, Tara Carreon attacks the conceit and arrogance of Tibetan lamas, who are "comfortable sitting on thrones, eating good food, and having people serve them. And it seems that many Western Tibetan Buddhists are more than willing to intern as domestic servants and handymen."[112] Carreon vehemently rejects the dream of a complete transplantation in the West of Tibetan Buddhism with its feudal social relations and its emphasis on guru devotion and faith-building rituals—a culture which is profoundly antithetical to Western values. Instead, she asserts that Tibetan Buddhism should adopt the "Western Dharma" of equality, fairness, justice, freedom of speech and belief, optimism, creativity, and the scientific method.

In the case of the Dream Trippers and American Daoism in general, the westernization called on by Carreon has perhaps already been fully realized. The Dream Trippers we met do not romanticize China; there is not a trace of "guru devotion" or charismatic relationships between Winn and the Dream Trippers, between Winn and his own teacher Mantak Chia, or between the Dream Trippers and Chinese Daoist monks. Confident individualists, the Dream Trippers treat themselves as equals, cherish their freedom, and have no qualms about picking and choosing the spiritual practices they wish.

In Daoism, you can have ecstatic sex without becoming dependent on a guru! And, as for other New Age and holistic spiritualities, they offer a smorgasbord of ideas and techniques, but none of them offer such an integrated, practical system covering everything from the food you eat to massage and spiritual enlightenment. On top of it all, American proponents claim—in blissful ignorance of history or cultural context—that the true Daoism has no rituals and dogmas: "esoteric Taoism never assumed the cloak of secret rituals and invocation of religious deities that can make tantra seem strange and ill-fitting when transplanted to this culture."[113] The Dao is for everyone, everywhere. "The Tao is not a religion, as it requires no initiations or ceremonies, but is the outcome of all religions, departing from dogma at the point of truth."[114]

The Cloud Wanderers

Master Hu led the 2004 Dream Trippers on the trail up Huashan, behind the Jade Spring Monastery. Most visitors take the cable car from the eastern flank of the mountain, but the Trippers followed the old route, which begins by meandering up a valley alongside a gurgling, stony brook. As they hiked and passed various temples, the gentle slope of the path got more arduous, the stream narrower, and the segments of stairs longer and steeper until, after three hours, at the head of the valley, they reached a flat meadow, Qing-keping. Beyond this point, the ascent to the North Peak is almost vertical, up steep steps often carved into the cliff face.

The group stopped here, and was assigned rooms in a temple, the Eastern Cloister of the Dao (Dongdaoyuan). The Trippers dispersed around the temple, practicing *qigong* on the verandas or in the pavilions, and explored the meadows and woods behind; some would spend the nights in meditation caves located a few hundred meters away. At nightfall, many of the group members congregated around Master Hu, as he told the story of the Mysterious Maiden of the Nine Heavens, the main goddess enshrined in this temple.

Sitting in the darkness of the mountain dusk on the belvedere of the temple, Master Hu told the Dream Trippers about green-haired fairies who fluttered into the caverns and out into heaven. After hours of climbing and talking of caves, cultivation, and the special powers of Huashan, the rumbling noises of civilization having been left in the dusty plains far below, the spirits of all present were as carried upward by the wispy breezes coiling around the pine trees and temple columns, gliding along the cliff walls, pouring into the grottoes, and spreading into the nighttime void. All became as starry-eyed children listening to a bedtime story. The walls of self-defense and doubt had vanished, and the listeners ingested each of Hu's words like a magical elixir pill. Hu himself was carried into the imaginary world, describing the immortal realms in vivid detail as if he were physically there. Indeed, several of those present, feeling flows of *qi* in their groins and backbones as he spoke and chanted in his grave voice, were even as viscerally transported there. It was as if he had never known of any other world. At that moment, the spirits of Master Hu, the Dream Trippers, and the Mysterious Maiden of the Nine Heavens commingled in a single sacred place, moment, and experience. This time, said Master Hu, "The energy field is extremely strong."

The Dream Trippers left with deep memories of this exchange, but, as we found when we visited Hu a few weeks later at the Jade Spring Monastery, it had left a strong impression on him as well. He was now clearly back into this world of dust, far from the realms of the Mysterious Maiden. Even he didn't seem to "believe" in the green-haired fairies as much as that night on the mountain. But he fondly yearned to be carried away by the winds of Huashan again.

The next time the Dream Trippers came, in 2006, he wore his best Daoist robes, immaculately white and pressed. Clearly, he now eagerly anticipated spending time with them. He explained that the "energy field" (*qichang*) had been extremely good in his interactions with the 2004 Dream Trip. He accompanied the group on its ascent to the summit of Huashan. In the shrine to the god of the Western Peak at the Palace for Pacifying the Summit (*Zhenyuegong*), he began to teach the Trippers the meditation method of the Shining Heart. Just as he had finished explaining the preparatory postures, in the middle of the question-and-answer session, Hu's mobile phone rang. He stepped outside, and never came back. After a few hours, the tour guide, from the bottom of Huashan, called Winn: Master Hu was being interrogated by the police. The reasons weren't clear, and nobody came up the mountain to harass the foreign travelers, who continued hiking around the mountaintop and practicing *qi-gong* on stones, in forests, and on viewing platforms, ethereally oblivious to the machinations of the forces of the state down below.

Three days later, as the Dream Trippers had completed their time at Huashan and reached the Jade Spring Monastery at the foot of the mountain, Winn asked us to find Master Hu and invite him to a thank-you banquet for lunch. The purpose of the banquet was also to provide the temple with a donation on behalf of Healing Tao USA—8,000 yuan (around US$1,000)—in exchange for the hospitality and arrangements made. But we found Master Hu nervous and unwilling to talk the way we had during many long hours together when we had visited the temple alone. This time, he led us into the Daoist Association office and told us the story of his police interrogation: seven officers had interrogated him for hours, constantly asking the same questions about what he had been doing with those foreigners. Their story: on the group's entering China, an immigration official had informed the Ministry of State Security, which had assigned a spy to follow the group for the entire trip. Since at all the other sites the group had only gone sightseeing, they had not interfered, but here, since the Trippers had been in contact with the Chinese Daoists, the police intervened. The officers threatened Master Hu and told him to never again interact with foreign groups.

"I will never do this again," said Master Hu, visibly traumatized by the experience. "Up on the mountain, the energy is good. But down here, the *daoqi*—the energy of Dao—is very bad."

Winn's guide was also interrogated, and then he invited the police for a lavish banquet, to establish good rapport with them and prevent any other interference. They told him there was no problem—just to call them before their next visit. But from then on, Master Hu always avoided the Dream Trippers whenever they came to Huashan.

What was the true cause of the police incident? Besides Hu himself, no other Daoist I interviewed, at Huashan or elsewhere, believed the police's story about a spy following Winn's group. Everyone agreed that the incident was related to internal politics at Huashan, in which contact with foreigners was the pretext, Winn's group was the instrument, and Master Hu the unwitting victim.

Some informants speculated that the police incident with Winn's group was motivated by the Public Security Bureau's desire for (or anger at not receiving) a "cut" of Winn's 8,000-yuan donation to the temple. Another explanation given was that another monk had intentionally called the police to embarrass Master Hu, given the poor relations between them—a combination of personality clash and power struggle. These hypotheses are mere speculation and gossip by various Daoist monks, and I have not been able to verify which, if any, is true. But they reveal the lines of division and tension, as well as what monks consider to be the actual (as opposed to prescribed) behavior of their fellows within the monastic community.

In this chapter, we analyze the inner relations, tensions, and dynamics of the monastic community of Quanzhen monks—the "cloud wanderers" at Huashan. After sketching the historical shift in the role of Huashan in the construction of the Chinese nation and state from the end of the Qing dynasty, we present a portrait of monastic life at the contemporary Jade Spring Monastery. We analyze the tensions generated by the interplay between traditional monastic authority and transmission, and the work-unit management structure imposed by the state, as well as the conflicts between the Huashan monks and the Tourism Bureau over the control of Daoist sites on the mountain. We follow the life stories of Master Hu, Master Hao, and Master Chen, as they try to pursue their Daoist cultivation in the midst of this complicated political environment. Finally, we situate our narrative in a broader historical context, showing how the structure of the Quanzhen order has always been a product of negotiations between Daoist communities and the Chinese state. In the contemporary context, Quanzhen monasticism at Huashan represents a petrified tradition, encapsulated within a modern state and economic structure that defines and uses traditional authenticity for its own instrumental goals.

Sacralizing the Chinese Nation at Huashan

In chapter 2, we discussed the process by which the Chinese imperial state had incorporated Huashan into its cosmology. By modern times, with the collapse of the imperial polity and the rise of Chinese nationalism, Huashan acquired deep sacred associations with China as a nation in the modern sense—Hua, meaning "flower" or "flourishing," is one of the names of China—as well as with the mystical history of Daoism, itself the spiritual root of Chinese civilization. Thus, for some, Huashan is the spiritual center of China itself. This dual national and spiritual sacralization of the mountain came to the fore in the first half of the twentieth century, after the collapse of the Qing dynasty, with the emergence of modern nationalism and the construction of a republican state in the midst of civil war and Japanese invasion. A steady stream of warlords and nationalist generals and intellectuals ascended Huashan to pray for China's salvation, leaving calligraphied poems inscribed into the rocks and boulders along the paths.

Many of them visited Li Yujie, a former student activist and Kuomintang government official, who had become a leading disciple of the Heavenly Virtues teaching (*Tiande shengjiao*), a new religious movement which propagated the mass practice of meditation techniques, breathing exercises, and healing by emission of *qi*. Li lived as a hermit on a remote ledge on Huashan for eight years in the 1930s, where he claimed to have received spirit communications from the great Daoist Immortals Lü Dongbin, Chen Tuan, and the Cloud Dragon Sage, as well as with many other "earthly Immortals" (*dixian*) or eremitic cultivators who came to live with them at various times. These revelations formed the basis of a new method of cultivation, the Heavenly Lord teachings (*Tiandijiao*), which would become a new religious movement and one of the main *qigong* schools in Taiwan from the 1980s onward. Many military officials visited Li on Huashan where, according to his followers, he offered them strategic advice on leading the anti-Japanese war and used his connection with the deities to stop the Japanese advance. Huashan was thus experienced and narrated as a physical and spiritual fortress for defending and rescuing the Chinese nation.[1]

In 1949, in the twilight of the Chinese civil war, Huashan acquired new connotations as one of the last strongholds of the defeated Nationalist Kuomintang (KMT) army. Controlling the only path up the mountain and occupying the monasteries on the peaks, the KMT army seemed to be in an impregnable position—until, following a tip from a local inhabitant, the Communist Red Army troops found another path and took control of the mountain. This feat was immortalized in a revolutionary film of the 1950s, *The Conquest of Huashan*, which celebrated the heroic battle of the Peoples' Army in its treacherous ascent of the mountain to flush out the last remnants of the imperialist and capitalist forces.[2]

The imperial project of cosmologizing Huashan, and the nationalist project, exemplified by Li Yujie, of placing Huashan at the spiritual center of the Chinese nation, came to an end with the new socialist regime. From then on, the story of Huashan is one of the tensions and negotiations between modern state building and the sacred places and monastic community of the mountain.

For the next three decades, Huashan, as a symbol of the "feudal" culture of the old society, was ignored, its temples destroyed, and its monks (many of whom were rumored to be former warlords and KMT officials who had sought obscurity by becoming Daoist monks) forced to marry and return to secular life. In the post-Mao era beginning in 1979, religious life at Huashan was belatedly allowed to resume, some of the old monks returned, a new generation entered the monastic order, and the temples were reopened, though some remained in ruins.[3]

Contemporary Monastic Life at Huashan

The Jade Spring Monastery is modest and graceful, more like the small square courtyard of an old gentry home than the sprawling palace of a god.[4] Even standing, the forty Dream Trippers almost filled up the entire inner court. Each building of the quadrangle exemplifies the forces that conjoin in the contemporary social configuration of monastic Daoism in China: on the southern side, the locus of religious worship—the shrine to Chen Tuan, his back to the mountain; on the northern side, the locus of commercial transactions—the entrance hall containing the cluttered souvenir shop, with its dusty glass display cabinets of amulets and Daoist books for sale, opening up to the market town of Huayin below; in between, the two buildings lateral to the central shrine to Chen Tuan are reserved for state-sponsored management. In the spartan administrative office, containing two wooden desks, chairs, and a black plastic telephone, a board shows the work assignments of the monks to the different temples on the mountain. On the wall, a one-meter-long, black-and-white group picture of the members of the China Daoist Association with Li Ruihuan, a senior leader of the Chinese Communist Party, and various certificates, such as the temple's permit as a Designated Place for Religious Activity, and its legal registration documents. Opposite the courtyard, the association's reception room is the place where association leaders formally receive distinguished guests to the temple for a cup of tea.

One morning during our stay at the Jade Spring Monastery in August 2004,[5] we went to Master Chen's personal quarters, an office and bedroom, in the monks' dormitory, located outside the inner quadrangle. On his desk were calligraphy implements and a traditional tea service. Next to the color TV, sitting on the traditional-style, rather gaudy Chinese ornamented wood chairs and sofas, Chen was playing go (*weiqi*) with another Daoist. They were leisurely oblivious to anything else.

After we sat through the *weiqi* game, we had lunch in the office, eating simple dishes carried over from the dining hall: potatoes, cabbage, soup, and tofu. Later, stepping outside, as we walked around the park, some of the Daoists on duty in different shrines were playing the flute; one was playing the *guqin*, a Chinese string instrument. In the yard outside the dormitory for *guadan* monks—traveling monks from other temples who are admitted to stay at the temple for a short duration—some Daoists played a wind instrument that looks like a conch: a *xun*; an older Daoist was teaching a younger one. Others were playing Chinese chess. This is a kind of cultivation, a monk told us, regulating *qi* and emotions through various musical instruments and games. After dinner, we went back to the dorm. The Daoists were eager to watch a historical soap opera on TV—a program that features heroes in flowing robes and long hair tied into a bun, just as they dressed themselves. These heroes were often Daoist magicians and martial arts virtuosos, which many of the monks aspired to become. Indeed, several told us that it was through reading knight-errant novels (notably by Jin Yong, aka Louis Cha) and watching kung fu films as teenagers that they had become motivated to enter the Quanzhen order. Now, at the Jade Spring Monastery, they tried to embody their adolescent fantasies, blurring the distinction between the period costume soap operas they watched and their own lives in the monastery. When asked why they had joined the order, most monks simply said that they had "predestined affinity" (*yuanfen*) to become Daoists.

Life at the Jade Spring Monastery is leisurely, a re-creation of an imperial-era aristocratic, lettered, and effete lifestyle—*taiji quan*, *weiqi*, the zither, poetry, calligraphy, idleness . . . one does not get the impression of strong discipline; rather, one of boys at play. But this is refined play: unlike young men in the outside world, in their public lives these men do not play cards, smoke, drink, see girls, or play football. No, they comb their long hair, read, watch soap operas, play chess, and blow the flute. The monks are quiet and don't talk much. Monastic routine is simple: breakfast at 6:45 a.m., the morning liturgy at 7:30 a.m., lunch at 11:45 a.m., the evening liturgy at 5 p.m., and dinner at 5:45 p.m. Unlike at some other Daoist monasteries,[6] attendance at the liturgy is not compulsory and, besides the four to six officiants who chant the ritual, others rarely attend. Meals consist of rice, steamed buns, and some simple vegetables. Monks line up to fill their bowl, and then may either eat in the refectory or go back to their rooms. Thus, there are hardly any collective activities that all monks are required to attend. They are scattered; there is not a strong community feeling. But neither are they solitary: the sense of human bonds is there, but loose. Many monks are assigned to attend to the altars at the various shrines in and around the monastery: when visitors burn incense and bow, they strike a prayer bowl that sounds like a gong. They also answer questions, and some of them engage in divination or interpretation of fortune-telling *qian* slips—numbered wooden sticks in a cylindrical container that one can shake in front of the deity statue until one of the sticks falls out of the container. A cryptic poem is associated with the number of the stick; the interpretation of the verses provides clues to one's fortune. In their relationships with lay worshippers, the monks primarily offer moral support and guidance. They encourage them to do good deeds, and give them scriptures such as the *Supreme Lord Lao's Treatise on Divine Retribution* (*Taishang Ganying Pian*), as well as other morality books that use stories to teach the law of karma and exhort them not to do evil deeds.

Master Chen's leisurely pursuits were interrupted later that week with arrangements for a public ceremony. Wu, a Chinese *qigong* master now based in the United States, had come to Huashan to erect a stele and offer a memorial service for his master of *taiji quan* and inner alchemy, deceased three years earlier. A native of Wenzhou who had been active in *qigong* and martial arts circles in Xi'an for over a decade, Wu had immigrated to Portland, Oregon, in 2001. Short and stocky, combining American grunginess (long hair in a ponytail, dirty jeans) and the coarseness of a Chinese man of the streets, with the poorly grounded, foggy gaze typical of some intense *qigong* practitioners, he looked very much the errant *jianghu* martial artist "of the marshes and lakes." His master, who lived in Xi'an, had had deep feelings for Huashan, where he came often, taught *taiji quan* to some monks, and wished to take the monastic vows at an old age—a plan that had been thwarted by his family.

About twenty people from the Xi'an martial arts, *qigong*, and *taiji quan* circles came to the ceremony, which began with speeches from the chairman of the Huashan Daoist Association (HDA) and representatives from various martial arts and *taiji quan* committees in Xi'an. Then, as firecrackers were set off, the red cloth covering the stele was pulled down, and the main representatives stood in line before the stele and bowed before it.

For Master Chen, the ceremony had been nothing more than routine work, something he was relieved to get over with. He had no regard for master Wu as a "*qigong*/tai chi master," and said that he heard that a Chinese person with no skills can do two things in America: wash dishes or teach tai chi. Before going to the United States, Wu was not known as an accomplished *qigong* master, and had not shown much interest in Daoism. Only after going to the United States did he suddenly call himself a "Quanzhen Daoist." In spite of his disdain for Wu, Chen had nonetheless made all the necessary arrangements for the stele-erection ceremony, which cemented the symbolic connection (and legitimation) between Huashan, Wu's master, and Wu's own school of *qigong*. For Chen, this was part of the work of propagating Daoism, acknowledging that all paths lead to a common Dao. And even those who are engaged in the most low-level techniques are, in their own way, seekers after the same Great Dao—especially if, as did Wu, they bring a hefty donation to the temple.

Monastic Discipline

The Daoist Association and the temple committee only manage work assignments and material matters; there is virtually no spiritual direction. Within the limits of their work duties, monks are free to live as they wish, and monastic discipline is notoriously lax. While the diet is vegetarian at the Jade Spring Monastery dining hall, monks relish the opportunity to entertain guests with meat and liquor at local restaurants. There are many rumors of monks visiting their wives, mistresses, or prostitutes outside the temple precincts.

Many conversations involve gossiping about members of the Daoist circle and their purported Daoist skills. Once over dinner, for example, there was conversation about a *qigong* master from Chengdu, whom one monk seemed to admire. Two others disparaged him, saying he had no level of cultivation at all. The former defended him, saying the proof of his accomplishment was that he has lived to such an old age (over eighty) despite diabetes—and his chain-smoking. But for the other two, such a defense was based on a mere "*qigong*" understanding of visible technical powers. No true cultivator smokes. True *gongfu* can be seen through the power of someone's speech, its power to convince, the *qi* it carries and the magnetic field it creates. These two monks also demeaned a *fengshui* master from Beijing, "who knows how to use the Luopan (geomancer's compass), but knows nothing of *fengshui*." This type of gossip reveals something of the rivalries between masters—especially in this case, where *gongfu* is such an elusive ability, impossible to verify objectively. Like martial artists, Quanzhen monks compare their skills while gossiping with each other—but unlike martial artists who can objectively demonstrate their *gongfu* by defeating rivals in physical matches, the competition between monks, whose *gongfu* is invisible and spiritual, is played out largely through gossip and backbiting.

Our main informants, some of whom had held important leadership positions in the temple and were among the main beneficiaries of this system, were unanimous in their descriptions of the poor spiritual atmosphere of the Jade Spring Monastery: "Many monks don't wear their Daoist robes," said one, "they are sloppy most of the time, and don't meditate or cultivate. But as soon as disciples or foreign visitors come, they quickly put on their best robes, and sit in the lotus position. They start talking about Daoist teachings and leave the light on till late at night to give the impression of late-night cultivation." "There are so many 'temple rascals' that if you talk about spiritual cultivation they will laugh at you and tell you to be realistic. So I never let people in the monastery know that I cultivate." Another monk said that few monks could be trusted at Huashan—some were followers of *qigong* masters; some were government spies; and some visit prostitutes in town.

All of these complaints reflect a general sense of malaise that is widespread among monastic Quanzhen Daoists in China. Monastic discipline is widely considered to be increasingly lax, with the exception of some nunneries. Monastic celibacy is increasingly questioned in theory and in practice, especially since the rule was borrowed from Buddhism by the Quanzhen order and arguably does not conform to Daoist teachings: the priests of the other main Daoist tradition, the Zhengyi (Orthodox Oneness), which claims a much longer history, are neither celibate nor monastic; nor are they vegetarian; and they can make a good living by providing ritual services. Increasing numbers of Quanzhen monks are tempted by the Zhengyi model. Several monks lamented the current condition of Daoism and expressed their longing for the appearance of a new reformer, a new charismatic figure such as Wang Chongyang, the founder of the Quanzhen order.

For Master Chen—who, in his public appearances with Winn's group in 2004, appeared the incarnation of orthodox monasticism, but was actually already planning to leave the Quanzhen order—the world of Daoist cultivation (*Daojiao xiulian jie*) is quite distinct from that of Daoist religion (*Daojiao*

zongjiao jie), the two of which, together with Daoist academics (*Daojiao xue-shu jie*), form three overlapping but distinct circles. He laughed at the fact that he and his fellows were being sought out by Western groups because they were "Daoist masters" wearing traditional robes at a famous mountain:

Some people feel reassured when they see someone who seems to live a detached life transcending desire, even though they aren't willing to do it themselves. Just knowing that such people exist, wearing special costumes, gives them a sense of comfort and tranquility: so they will even demand that such people go about wearing their costumes. . . . People think true cultivation is in a mountain or a cave. Actually, it is not: it's in the city. The true cultivator is not someone wearing a costume in a sacred spot, but could be someone sitting right next to you in a restaurant, looking like a common person. That's the true meaning of hidden cultivation (*yinxing*). Actually, when people see a Daoist monk practicing *taiji quan* with a layman, most people think the layman is learning from the monk, but it's quite probable that it's the monk who is learning from the layman.[7]

Lineage and Monastic Organization

The Huashan Daoist community consists of celibate monks of the Quanzhen order. Chinese monasticism is called *chujia*, which literally means "to leave the family." The anthropologist Adeline Herrou has noted that the term *chujia* is a homophone of the term used for the marriage of a young woman, which implies leaving one's own original line of descent to join a new one—in this case, the pseudo-kinship structure that governs relations between Quanzhen monks. But, unlike what happens in marriage, there is no exchange or alliance. The monks cut all links with their families without any new ties being formed between the original families and the monastic communities.[8] Becoming a monk, indeed, means joining a new family: the organization of relations between monks is modeled on the family, with the monks even borrowing kinship terms in referring to each other and in identifying relationships between generations and religious traditions. So the monks form a pseudo-kin group. But this is a pseudo-kin group without conjugal relations. As Herrou has noted in her study of a Daoist monastery not far from Huashan, although monasteries may admit both monks and nuns, there is no strict division in gender roles, and the kinship terms used are exclusively masculine and patrilineal: a female fellow-disciple initiated earlier than another would be, for example, called her "elder brother" (*shixiong*), no regard being paid to biological age. The pseudo-family group expunges all differences between the sexes. But at Huashan, monks and nuns are physically

separated: only monks live at the Jade Spring Monastery, while nuns live in a
few smaller temples at other locations on the mountain.

The Jade Spring Monastery and the other temples of Huashan are controlled by a hereditary succession of masters affiliated to the Huashan lineage
of the Quanzhen order, and who may accept newly ordained monks as disciples; at the same time, a large proportion of the residents are "registered
visitors" (*guadan* monks), who entered the order in other hereditary temples
and cannot take disciples at Huashan. In the terminology of Chinese monasticism, Huashan thus combines the hereditary (*zisun*) and public (*conglin*)
forms of Quanzhen temples. But since the 1950s, it has been restructured into
the work-unit (*danwei*) form of Chinese socialist social organization.[9] In the
contemporary *danwei* system, this dual organization is reflected through the
different political rights of the two groups of monks: all monks have voting
rights at the elections to the Huashan Daoist Association but only monks of
the Huashan lineage can be elected.

Those monks who leave lay life to enter the monastic order (*chujia*) at
Huashan follow the Quanzhen initiation procedure. When they first make
the request to enter the order, the majority are encouraged to go home and
give up. "This is different from Buddhism, which encourages people to leave
family life to enter the order. Daoism doesn't encourage people to leave their
families."[10] Applicants are accepted on the basis of their strong faith in Daoism, their level of education, and their good morality. They should be healthy;
"from their eyes, we can see that their minds are not mentally ill." Applicants
also need to produce a police certificate, showing no criminal record, and
letters of recommendation from their neighborhood committee (*jumin weiyuanhui*). The most important is the police certificate. With it, one can be dis-
pensed of producing the other certificates.

The admitted novice is then placed on two years' probation, during which
he cannot formally choose a master. The Daoist Association will evaluate the
novice on the basis of his overall conduct, his adapting to the milieu, and his
overall qualities. Almost all are accepted at this stage, as long as they have
good behavior and get along well with the others.

After the two-year probationary period, the newly accepted monk can
find a master and be given a Daoist name and a position in the genealogy of
his religious lineage. There is no requirement to master specific knowledge
or skills. As one monk said, "It's not like Zhengyi, which places a greater emphasis on ritual and techniques: Zhengyi Daoists *must* recite scripture and
conduct rituals, otherwise there's no reason for their existence. But Quanzhen
is based in monasteries; there are many different things one can do. If one
can't recite scriptures or master ritual, one can do other things." Most monks

have a low level of education (middle or high school) and health problems are common—as noted by Komjathy, these ailments "often led them either to begin Daoist practice or to enter the monastery as a sanatorium."[11]

According to one of the monastery leaders, many monks are actually not really interested in Daoism; they become Daoists for a variety of reasons: they want to avoid family problems, they cannot do a job in society, or they just want to pass their days idly. These monks are called "temple rascals" (miaohunzi). But they are not punished or evicted. They are given tasks that they can do; as long as they do their job, they are accepted. "There are also higher-level temple rascals (gaoji miaohunzi), who are good at guanxi networking and politics, and end up as directors of the Daoist Association."

Most of the thirty or so monks were of a young age, in their twenties and thirties. The leaders of the monastery were in their midthirties, and the handful of senior monks were hardly to be seen. Almost all of the monks had entered the monastic order in the previous decade or two—members of the post-Mao generation and products of reform-era religious institutions. This is a condition that prevails in most religious communities in China, owing to the generation gap caused by the Mao-era restrictions and the Cultural Revolution (1966–1976), when almost all the monks were forced to return to lay life. When religious life was normalized in the early 1980s, most of the Huashan Daoists were old and nearly senile, having entered the order at least forty years earlier. At the same time, a new cohort of young monks entered the monastery, but they were reluctant to become disciples of the senior masters. Besides the large age differential between the two generations, making communication difficult, the younger monks doubted the religious qualifications of their seniors: during the Republican period, Huashan had been located on the front line of both the Sino-Japanese war and the Chinese civil war (the kidnapping of Chiang Kai-shek by Zhang Xueliang in the Xi'an incident of 1936 occurred in a resort a short distance from Huashan), and had been crawling with warlord and KMT army soldiers and officers.[12] Many of these were rumored to have become Daoist monks in the dying days of the KMT regime in an attempt to erase their past and to find religious refuge from the new political order. Since many of the younger monks had refused to take these senior Daoists as their masters, the newly established Huashan Daoist Association had to force them to take masters. Several then chose to become disciples of dead Daoists, holding discipleship (baishi) rites at their graves and thus inscribing themselves into the genealogy of a lineage. In the words of Master Chen, "The transmission of Daoism has been cut. When I became a monk, there were still some old masters that we could learn from. Although they weren't all cultivators, through them we could see them incarnate a certain tradition. Now most of them have passed away. The young Daoists today have no models to follow."[13]

There is thus an almost complete rupture in the transmission of Daoism between the pre-1949 generation of masters and the new, post-Mao generation of monks. Some continue to describe their spiritual trajectories in terms of becoming disciples to initiatory masters (*shifu*), for those of the Huashan lineage, or supplementary masters (*xiansheng*) for the *guadan* monks, as well as seeking other types of masters such as *yinshi* (inducting masters), *enshi* (role-model masters), and *dushi* (accomplished masters)—but how much such a system continues to operate beyond mere formality remains unclear. One monk, having overheard his fellow explaining these categorizations to us, sneered: "So full of bookish knowledge, and they don't know anything about the reality under their noses."

Monks adopt the lineage identity of their first master; after which they are free to become disciples of other masters of other lineages. One is "adopted" into the lineage by receiving a Daoist name conferred by one's master. The first character of a Daoist name is determined by one's position among the generations in the "lineage poem": each disciple of the same generation has the same character in his Daoist name; the alignment of characters according to the order of generations corresponds to a poem said to have been composed by the lineage patriarch. This practice follows the traditional Chinese custom of lineage generational poems in secular families.

Most monks at Huashan are members of one of two lineages: the Longmen (Dragon Gate) lineage, and the Huashan lineage. The Longmen is the dominant lineage in the Quanzhen order across China; as explained further below, under Patriarch Wang Changyue, it played a crucial role in the institutionalization of the Quanzhen order during the Qing dynasty, in the seventeenth century. Wang Changyue consolidated and systematized all the Daoist precepts; and the Longmen lineage was made the official authority in the transmission of precepts in the ordination of Daoist monks. During the Qing, the transmission of precepts took place during a training period of twelve years; currently, the period of transmission is thirty-six days, under the authority of the state-sponsored China Daoist Association. Precept transmission and formal ordinations (*shoujie*) are periodically held at the White Cloud Monastery in Beijing. Few of the monks at Huashan, including Chen, Hu, and Hao, have received this formal ordination and precepts.

While Master Hu and Master Hao are disciples of the Longmen lineage, Master Chen is a disciple of the twenty-fifth generation of the Huashan lineage. The founding patriarch of the Huashan lineage is Hao Datong, who is one of the Seven Perfected Ones (*qizhen*), who were the first disciples of

Wang Chongyang, the founder of the Quanzhen order. There are many branches of the lineage, which has spread to different parts of China. So, in the words of Master Chen, "The name of 'Huashan lineage' has nothing to do with the place anymore, nor does the generation number. Some branches spread very fast, so they have many generations. Mine spread slowly, so it has only twenty-five generations. Zou, the chairman of the Huashan Daoist Association, is of the thirty-third generation. So, even though he is older than me in age, I am eight generations 'older' than him in the lineage genealogy!"

Like surnames in secular society, these lineage identities need not have any specific content in terms of beliefs and practices. Lineage affiliation is primarily a form of social identity, by which monks claim their affiliation to an authentic transmission, and identify each other's relative genealogical positions, like relatives consulting a family tree. This knowledge is used to determine if a person is a true Daoist monk or not. As Master Chen stated, "If somebody comes to a temple and claims that they are a Daoist monk, they have to be able to recite the genealogy of their lineage. You need to be able to say who your master is, who his master was, etc. So it's a symbol of status. . . . These lineage identities are only forms that exist for religious identity in secular society, so that they can tell secular people what their status and position and role is."[14]

The Politics of a Daoist *Danwei*

Overlaid onto the traditional modalities of transmission is the modern, state-sponsored, classroom-based Daoist training system.[15] During the winter months, when most monks posted in the mountain temples descend to the Jade Spring Monastery, training classes in Daoist culture are held for all the monks, at which knowledgeable Daoists, scholars, and officials give academic lectures to the collective body of monks. One of the monastic leaders emphasized to us that he teaches nothing of substance at these lectures and nothing about true cultivation. But these courses are the foundation for a selective training system in which, through applications and recommendations, monks can apply to complete a two-year primary-level training, a two-year advanced course at Xi'an, and finally, after passing an entrance examination, the three-year program of the Daoist Academy in Beijing, which enrolls fifty students nationwide per intake. According to one graduate of this program, who was then residing at Huashan—and who had nothing but scorn for academic scholarship on Daoism, on which much of the Academy's program is based—the entire course of study was a waste of time and bore no relation to Daoist cultivation. The main result of the courses was to train Daoist officials, monks who could occupy administrative positions in Daoist

associations. Indeed, a few of the leading Daoists at Huashan were gradu-
ates of the Beijing Academy. Equipped with such modern-style training, they
could manage temples according to bureaucratic norms and were socialized
into the *danwei* culture of officialdom, which they share with their counterparts in units such as the local government, the Religious Affairs Bureau, and
the tourism administration.

Temple leadership is nominally attributed according to genealogical succession within the Huashan lineage, but in reality according to the methods of the
United Front,[16] in which members of the religious community who are seen as
possessing both religious legitimacy and impeccable political credentials are
co-opted into leadership positions. The monastic community—consisting of
the sixty or so monks residing at the Jade Spring Monastery and the mountain
temples—is administered by the seven-member Huashan Temple Administration Committee, whose membership is identical to the Huashan Daoist Association. These bodies are elected at irregular intervals every four years or
so. When the time comes to hold elections to renew the membership, agents
representing the United Front department and the Religious Affairs Bureau
travel to Huashan to establish an "election work group" (*huanjie gongzuozu*)
made up of Huashan monks whom they trust. Through private discussions
with members of this group, a consensus emerges on the suitable candidates,
who are usually members of the work group, after the government representatives have made their preferences known. This group decides the conditions
that must be fulfilled for a candidate to be elected: for example, high school
education, administrative experience, etc. Conditions are set which only the
preselected candidates can meet. When the time comes for elections, nomina-
tions are opened; if someone is nominated who is not among the preselected
candidates, the chair of the election work group will reject the nomination of
the person on the grounds that he doesn't fit the conditions.

The Religious Affairs Bureau will try to balance the different interests and
factions in its appointment of elected members. One monk considers that
in consequence, "it is never the monks with high accomplishments who are
elected. . . . It is always the lowly, ambitious rascals who get elected. At elections, they never consider the qualities, but only consider personal interest
and factions when voting."

On election day, the election work group nominates a candidate for each
position and asks for those who agree to clap their hands. While the election
of the key members is predetermined, there can be competition for other
posts, giving expression to factional rivalries. According to one monk, originally elections were conducted by the raising of hands. But since the "raising
of hands" does give a number of votes, and since those elected members may

have different numbers of votes, it can be embarrassing if the chairman is not the one with the most votes. Therefore, at one election, when the government's preferred candidate did not get the highest number of votes, a new system was adopted in which the delegates clap instead of raising their hands, making it impossible to determine the number of votes. The election is thus concluded, with the government's candidate being elected.

As mentioned earlier, only Daoists of the local Huashan lineage (as opposed to *guadan* monks) can be elected to the Daoist Association or appointed to administrative positions. However, according to one account, breaking with this tradition, the newly appointed office director, after Master Chen's departure in 2006, was a *guadan* "outsider" of the Longmen lineage, specifically installed by the government to put a check on the "clannish" power of the local monks. A further check to local power is provided by the Daoist Association's general secretary, since 1997 a political appointee assigned to this post jointly by the Religious Affairs Bureau, the Communist Party's United Front department, the Civil Affairs Administration, and the Tourism Bureau. A Party member, the secretary was a young cadre whose room/office looked like any Chinese dormitory room, with a small sofa, a computer, and a hard bed. His job was to "assist" in the management of the temple, to give political direction, and to transmit policies from the government. As described by one monk, "There are many complicated struggles and relationships at Huashan, just like in any work unit. They struggle over titles and personnel matters. But the relationships are so complex that there is a balance, and nobody will seriously try to hurt another."

Tensions over Tourism

Being a state-sponsored official work unit does not guarantee the Huashan Daoist Association's good relations with its other state-controlled counterparts. Relations with the Huashan Tourism Bureau are notoriously bad, as often occurs between religious communities in scenic sites in China and the local tourist authorities, with disputes frequently arising over the allocation of resources and the development of natural and religious sites.

At Huashan, beginning in the 1950s, the entire mountain and its temples had been under the direct management of a "Daoist Service Unit" under the Daoist Association, run by Daoists until the end of the Cultural Revolution. Then, after the economic reforms began in the early 1980s, in the words of one monk, the old monks were "tricked" by the local government into letting the mountain be managed by hired staff on their behalf. This eventually became the Huashan Tourism Bureau, which was given 30 percent of the revenues from ticket sales, with the remaining 70 percent going to the Daoist Association.

After some time, the government inverted the proportions, with only 30 percent going to the Daoists. At that time, the entrance gate for the mountain was at the Jade Spring Monastery. But violent conflicts over ticket sales often erupted between monks and staff of the Tourism Bureau. Eventually, the bureau built a road bypassing the Jade Spring Monastery, and then there were separate gates for charging entrance fees to the park, collected by the Tourism Bureau, and to the temple, collected by the Daoists. Monks then tried to force tourists to go through the monastery. There were fights every few days. But the local police was allied with the Daoists. Some of the monks, who were risking their safety to defend the temple, considered it their right to reward themselves by keeping a portion of the ticket revenue. There was an arrangement with the police—the police would side with the monks at the fights, and they would keep part of the ticket revenue. As described by one monk, "We used to be in collaboration with the police to sell entrance tickets. That was a huge bonanza. There were three shifts, in each shift there were monks and policemen selling tickets, splitting the money between each other. We used to go to brothels, to fight, and to lead a decadent and dissolute life."

Later, while Master Chen was the Office Manager of Huashan, the arrangement changed again: the Tourism Bureau gave an annual subsidy of 1.3 million yuan to the Daoist Association, which was later increased to 3.5 million. Chen considered that this was sufficient for the needs of the Daoists, who stopped charging admission for the Jade Spring Temple. The subsidy was only a small percentage of the mountain revenues, but the corruption around ticket sales, as well as the fighting, ended.[17] At one point, the Tourism Bureau was also taken away from the control of the local municipal government, and placed under the Shaanxi provincial government.

Perhaps as a result of these tensions, in contrast with other famous Daoist sites such as Qingchengshan or Louguantai, in which "Daoist culture" is strongly promoted by the local government and tourist authorities to draw more visitors, and temples are built and restored for purely commercial reasons, the development and promotion of Huashan as a major tourist attraction makes almost no reference to its Daoist heritage. Informants have variously attributed this situation to the conservatism and lack of vision of the Tourism Bureau or to the highly charged political history of Huashan Daoism as having strong links to the KMT prior to Liberation. Whatever the reason, the consequences are evident in the lamentable state of the temples on the Huashan peaks: the Palace of Golden Heaven (*Jintiangong*), the main temple dedicated to the god of Huashan, which commands the entire mountain from a flat

meadow just ahead of the Southern Peak, destroyed in 1967, remains entirely
in ruins, while the Palace for Pacifying the Summit (*Zhenyuegong*), dedicated
to the God of the Western Marchmount and situated below the Western Peak,
has been occupied by a guesthouse, even though the main shrines remain.
A new gondola lift to the Western Peak, built in 2014, now disgorges tourists
directly into the temple courtyard. The pitiful remnants of these two temples
are nonetheless inscribed as National Key Daoist Temples on an official list of
the two dozen most important Daoist monasteries in China.

Huashan monks speak passionately about how the mountain belongs to
Daoism, and has been unjustly taken over by the Tourism Bureau, which
placed toilets in one shrine and a karaoke bar in another, and at one period
required that monks obtain a permit if they wanted to ascend the mountain.
Master Chen recalls an argument he had, as Office Manager of the Huashan
Daoist Association, with a provincial government official who claimed that
Daoism was an obstacle to the development of Huashan, and insisted that
"Huashan does not belong to Daoism, it belongs to the Nation!" Huashan
monks were notorious for triggering violent incidents in the late 1990s, in
which fights and brawls frequently occurred with corporation staff and even
senior government leaders.

In 1999, over thirty Daoist monks went up Huashan to reclaim the Palace for Pacifying the Summit from the Tourism Bureau, which responded by
sending up the police. It was April 24, just a few days before May Day weekend. The monks planned to occupy the temple over the holiday, so that many
tourists, including foreigners, could witness the standoff, forcing the government to give in to their demands. But the government offered the chairman
of the Huashan Daoist Association several positions in the Peoples' Congress,
the Political Consultative Committee, and the like, and he capitulated. According to one informant, when the Daoist monks walked down, they did not
utter a word, and, on returning to the Jade Spring Monastery, when the chairman spoke to them they all turned their heads and refused to look at him.
After that, they signed a petition to have him removed. This monk-official
was already so unpopular that, fearing resistance from the other monks, the
election to renew his term had been postponed for three years. After this
incident, however, the government assigned him to his new political appoint-
ments, he left Huashan, and a new chairman was elected a year later.

It was only in 2012 that new development plans for Huashan were un-
veiled, which highlighted the mountain's Daoist heritage—as exemplified in
a new district of spas, resorts, and luxury villas at the foot of the mountain,
billed as the "Daoist Life Cultivation Zone." But this high-end consumption of "Life Cultivation" was to be built by real estate investors. The living

Daoists on the mountain were not consulted or involved. Master Chen, who visited Huashan in 2015, mentioned a noticeable improvement in the material prosperity of the Daoist temples and community of Huashan, as well as the planned construction of a new building to house the Shaanxi Provincial Daoist Academy.

Huashan has become the scene of uneasy juxtapositions and "micro-struggles over space."[18] While the provincial and tourist authorities have circumvented the religious community on the mountain to privilege purely commercial development, Huashan continues to live as a sacred space for its monks of the Complete Perfection order. There are thus now two distinct worlds on Huashan, the touristic and the religious, both under the control of the state, in uneasy coexistence, ignoring each other most of the time, each claiming the mountain for itself, and yet in contact on a daily basis as tourists tramp through the courtyard of the Jade Spring Monastery at the mountain's entrance, or burn incense at the shrines and temples on the way and at the peaks. For the overwhelming majority of visitors, the mountain is neither a source of powerful *qi*, nor a sacred mountain of Daoist tradition and history. Indeed, most tourists hardly know or care whether Huashan is linked to Daoism or Buddhism.

The tensions, contrasts, and overlaps between the touristic and sacred uses and creations of space make it clear that distinctions between the two remain; as noted by Bremer in his study of contemporary sacred places,

> Neither their religious quality nor their touristic character can make a total claim on these places—they remain both religious and touristic, occupied by both religious adherents and other tourists whose respective experiences of the site are quite different from each other . . . the hybridity of these sites does not allow a seamless blending of the two; careful observations reveal clear distinctions between the places of religion and the places of tourism, despite the very real overlaps that inevitably constitute religious sites of tourism.[19]

Such is the context in which the Dream Trippers ascend Huashan, almost completely oblivious to the agonistic, conflicted relationship between religion, politics, and business on the mountain.

Spiritual Trajectories

It was in this environment that individual Quanzhen monks pursued the trajectories of their lives. There were many possible reasons and motivations for monks to join the monastic order, and many possible goals and strategies for them to pursue once within its ranks. Deep tests and disappointments were in store for those who were driven by a strong sense of attraction to and cultivation of Dao. These are some of the issues and predicaments we discover, as we explore, in the next section, the personal trajectories of our main protagonists, Masters Hu, Hao, and Chen, as their lives unfold and as they encounter the Dream Trippers.

MASTER HU

Master Hu, with his wide face, full beard, thick smell, and ample body, radiates an earthy serenity and a strong will to become a superhuman through Daoist practice; he cultivates the very image of the Daoist sage. The meditative flow of his steps when walking, the reverential sincerity of his kowtows before the gods, and the graceful beauty of his spontaneous *taiji quan* movements make him appear as if made of a different substance, of a fluid of pure mind and movement, exuding reverence and spontaneity. Each of his moves, gestures, steps, words, and breaths is a conscious expression of his cultivation practice.

Born in a peasant family in 1965, Hu claims to have begun meditating in the lotus position when he was six years old, without anyone telling him how. His mother used to tell him stories about the Eight Immortals while he was in her embrace; this left a deep impression on him. This was during the Cultural Revolution, when there was no religion. He studied hard and well, and prepared very hard for the college entrance examination. But he fell ill, so he couldn't pass. After that he became even more ill. So he started to study acupuncture and Chinese medicine.

Once at a temple fair in his home province, he had a vision of the Immortal Lü Dongbin, and so decided to leave his family to enter the monastic order, and became a monk at a local temple controlled by a hereditary lineage of masters. Later, he went to Beijing for advanced study at the Beijing Daoist Academy. There, he had a second vision of Lü Dongbin in the dormitory. He returned to his home temple. His master died, and he became head of the temple. He busied himself with building the temple. "A high master came to take me as a disciple, but I didn't realize it, because I was too busy with the temple building, so I refused. I deeply regret this opportunity, it was a missed chance. After that, I have had many difficulties in life." Before arriving at Huashan in the late 1990s, he had for a time been the chairman of the Daoist Association of his province.

He practices a unique form of shadowboxing which he calls White Monkey Boxing (*Baiyuan tongbeiquan*). "I learned it spontaneously; it was transmitted to me by the White Monkey Immortal (*Baiyuan zhenren*). When I

start, he comes down into me, and I do the forms spontaneously. In the future, perhaps I will arrange it into a method in stages that can be taught to
others. The White Monkey Immortal first transmitted the method to humans
in the spring and autumn period (770–476 BC), but owing to the poor moral
quality of the inheritors of the method, it was lost. Now, it has been transmitted directly to me by the Immortal."

The White Monkey is but one of the many Immortals Master Hu claims to
have encountered. He also told me of a Perfected One he had met in a room
he was staying in at the Palace for Pacifying the Summit. "When I came into
my room, he was here. He came from the Buddha Realm of the West. He was
over ninety years old, and had come to Huashan looking for a cultivator. He
was holding a spade and a pitchfork. I could feel that he had very high powers: I was cold and the room was cold; but as soon as he came in, the room
became hot, and I started to sweat. We meditated together all night, until 5 a.m.;
I didn't tire for a minute."

Master Hu learned many of his practices through popular *qigong* masters.
He associated with followers of Yan Xin, one of the most famous *qigong* masters in the 1980s. He also attended a training given by another famous *qigong*
master, Wang Liping, based in Hainan Island. These activities were frowned
on by other Huashan monks. At one meeting, the chairman of the Huashan
Daoist Association was reported to have angrily noted that some monks were
practicing *qigong* from outside the temple, instead of honoring the ancestral
masters of the lineage. One monk told us, "To have such experiences is common, but it's not appropriate for a member of the monastic Daoist order to
become so engrossed in this." Monks often gossiped about his tales of hearing
masters and Immortals talking to him.

By this monk's account, the backbiting against him only reinforced his
sense of depression and superiority, in which he compensated for his poor
relations with the other monks through his extraordinary relations with the
Immortals—the sneers of his fellows, in fact, only reinforced his tendency to
seek solace in his enchanted worlds.

We can imagine, then, how profound the experience with the Americans
had been for him—while Chinese Daoists only laughed at him and gossiped
behind his back, the foreigners were willing to be led by him, not only up the
physical steps of Huashan, but also deep into his own spiritual worlds.

Thus, when the Dream Trippers came for a second time in 2006, he appeared more carefully preened than the first time, wearing an immaculate
white robe, and full of attentions for the group. But his involvement with the
Americans appears to have been just the pretext his enemies in the Huashan
Daoist Association were looking for to strike him down.

Master Hu was traumatized by the police interrogation, still mentioning it a year later. He vowed never to deal with foreigners again, and, in order to avoid embarrassing him, we did not seek him out since the incident. But through others, we learned that he was still deeply drawn into the petty conflicts at Huashan. As an outsider *guadan* monk, he had little support among the local Huashan Daoists who controlled the monastic community. But, in the view of one of his fellows, he was poor at managing *guanxi* and easily crossed people. "His problem is that he is not good at being an official, but is willing to be one."—why?—"Because he wants to become a Grandmaster. And, in Daoist institutions, that would be impossible without becoming an official." In spite of his marginalization within the Daoist *danwei*, Master Hu chose to further his career in Daoist institutions and, in consequence, had to end his dealings with the foreigners. Ultimately, he succeeded in his role as a Daoist official.

MASTER HAO

The Cloud Platform, a cave complex on a rock face on the opposite side of Huashan valley, commands a stunning view of the entire length and height of Huashan. This is where all pilgrims and cultivators used to come before the trail up Huashan itself was carved in the Yuan dynasty (1271–1368) over seven hundred years ago; now, all that remains are a few vine-covered stone pillars and crumbling archways half-concealed in the thick foliage, a romantic shadow of the spiritual splendors of times past. Officially closed to visitors, the spot is home to a single Daoist hermit, Master Hao, who tends a small vegetable garden and oversees a complex of meditation caves carved into the rock face. As Master Hao led the 2004 Dream Trippers through an overgrown forest path on the way up to his caves at the Cloud Platform, laughing and scampering over old roots and boulders, there were no more visible signs of the present era—was he a contemporary monk or a Han-dynasty wizard (*fangshi*)?—until he entered our contact details in his mobile phone. There is no electricity at his cave complex, and he hops down the mountain and back up again every few days, just to recharge the battery—although we never heard it ring or saw him making a call during the time we spent with him. He often called himself the "wild man of the mountains," and jokingly encouraged the Dream Trippers to study hard and make a great effort to become "authentic wild men." He affectionately called Michael Winn a "sly old fox who has attained the Dao."

We always enjoyed spending time with Master Hao, with his humor, his lack of pretense, his nimbleness in running along the huge slabs of rock on the steep slopes of the mountain, his wispy beard, his enthusiasm, and his craziness. Hao was, when we first met him in 2004, in his early to midforties; previously a farmer in a nearby township, he has been a Daoist monk since the early 1990s. As a young man, he had dreamt of living a simple life in the mountain forests. "That was my motivation. I wasn't really interested in Dao-ism or being a monk. Once when I was visiting Huashan, in one temple, I met a nun from my village, and she encouraged me to become a monk. So I entered the order at the Jade Spring Monastery."—Who was your master?—"I can't speak of anyone worthy of that title."

Around 1997, he was assigned to the Eastern Cloister of the Dao, a tem-ple at the end of Huashan valley and the last stop on the old Huashan route before the climb becomes treacherously steep. Dedicated to the Mysterious Maiden of the Nine Heavens, whose cult is widespread in Taiwan, the temple draws many groups of visitors from the island, and several Taiwanese temples financed the restoration of the temple in 2007. Hao thus found himself play-ing host to many groups from Taiwan, Hong Kong, and overseas. He taught Daoist scriptures to some of them, and built good relations, so that the Tai-wanese paid to have a phone line installed there. It was at that temple that Hao also met Winn, in 1999.

By Hao's account, the Daoists at the Jade Spring Temple got jealous, and they were angry that Winn had mentioned Hao in his "book," without men-tioning the other Huashan Daoists (in fact, Winn had not published a book mentioning Hao). Other monks didn't specifically mention his foreign friends as a cause for conflict, just vaguely explaining, "You know, he's extremely stub-born. He often had arguments with other monks." So they arranged to have him moved away from his temple, and "exiled" him to the Cloud Platform in 2001. Since there is no income stream from donation boxes at the Cloud Plat-form, the Huashan Daoist Association is not interested in the place, which has an unclear status—although Hao could be assigned there by the association, this entailed him losing his membership in the association, and consequently losing his living allowance. "Now I'm half a monk, half not a monk. Because I'm not a member of the Daoist Association, and because, as a mountain-forest Daoist (*shanlin daoshi*), I have a different type of lifestyle from them."

As a result, he no longer identifies strongly with the Quanzhen order, and once said he situated himself somewhere in between the Zhengyi Heavenly Masters and the Quanzhen traditions. "Quanzhen doesn't have its own scrip-tures, and it doesn't teach how to draw talismans. It only exists on the foun-dation of the Heavenly Masters, having been established after the Heavenly Masters had declined."

Now he lives off the donations of a few disciples, including some from Tai-wan and Shenzhen, who pay for his mobile telephone, which has a Shenzhen number as a sort of direct hotline to their master. Very few people go to the cave complex—some foreigners, some from Hong Kong, some Taiwanese, and some Chinese. Each year, he anticipates the visit of one group of Dream Trippers and one group of Taiwanese. Occasionally, he has had visits from television reporters from China or from the UK, and also some people from Spain. He rebuilt the roof of his house, and was planning to rebuild the front wall, build a dining hall below the terrace in front of his house, and add a concrete floor and drain to the main cave of the complex, which is very damp. All of this in order to be able to be a better host to future groups of visitors from abroad or from Hong Kong or Taiwan.

There is hardly anything left of the old Temple of Purple Tenuity at the Cloud Platform, except for a crumbling arched gateway overgrown with vines. Hao tends a small vegetable plot in the temple's foundations, in front of the five or six cave chambers dug into a cliff. He lived in one of the caves, which was around 8 square meters in area, with a wooden bed on each side of the entrance. Against the back wall, in the center of the cave, an altar was carved into the rock in which were placed two paper deity tablets: at the back, a tablet for Chen Tuan, the patron Immortal of Huashan, and in front, a tablet dedicated to the Supreme Sovereign Lord Lao (*Taishang Laojun*), the deified Laozi. In front of him were placed three copies of the *Supreme Lord Lao's Treatise on Divine Retribution* (*Taishang Ganying Pian*), a widely circulated Daoist morality book and scripture which enunciates the heavenly rewards and punishments for one's good and bad deeds. The altar table was also cluttered with various other odds and ends. On the beds lay messed-up quilts and clothes, and some rubbish lay on the ground floor and in the corners. By the door beside one of the beds, on a little wooden table lay a cup containing a toothbrush and a tube of toothpaste. On the ceiling, exquisite designs were carved into the rock, almost in a perfect circle.

On the first and fifteenth day of each lunar month, Master Hao conducts a Morning Ritual (*zaoke*), which lasts around ninety minutes. The ritual begins with recitations at the altar in the main cave; and at one point he and his disciple walk out of the cave, while chanting and chiming a triangle, to the stone arch gateway of the cave complex some thirty steps away, and then back into the cave. At night, they recite the *Scripture of the Northern Dipper* (*Beidoujing*).

When we visited Hao in 2007, he claimed that Master Hu had come up a few weeks earlier to "check things out" and ask him about the amount of money his foreign friends had donated to him. In fact, although members of Winn's groups had stayed at the Cloud Platform, and provided generous donations to the Huashan Daoist Association, they were not aware of the conflict between it and Hao, and so didn't give him any separate donations.

"I told Hu the foreigners are very cheap! They only gave me a few dozen yuan." And, by Hao's account, Hu had told him about the incident with the police the previous year in a tone that seemed to warn him not to host foreign groups, saying that things had changed under President Hu Jintao,[20] and that contacts with foreign groups were to be curtailed. But for Hao, "I will always continue to play host to foreign tours, regardless of what the Daoist Association says. This is the policy of religious freedom and religious 'internationalization' advocated by the State Administration of Religious Affairs. Tell Winn that no matter what they tell him at the Jade Spring Monastery, he and his groups are always welcome here at the Cloud Platform!" Asked if there was any risk that the Huashan Daoist Association will try to take control of the Cloud Platform to control his activities with foreigners, he replied: "They have no power over me!"

When we went to visit him in the summer of 2008, we climbed to the last rest stop at the end of Huashan valley in the early afternoon, and called him on his mobile phone. He happened to be in town to run some errands, and told us to wait for a few minutes, that he would be there very soon and would accompany us to his caves. He finally arrived eight hours later, his long hair tangled into what looked like dreadlocks, tied with a black silk scarf, wearing a long white loose shirt and broad black trousers. He came with a disciple, a young man from Heilongjiang. After sitting for some time, he laughed his long, hearty laugh, and we set off in the dark, at around 10 p.m., for the climb up the narrow mountain forest path to his caves. Around every twenty minutes, we stopped for a long rest. Hao's disciple asked him many questions about trees and plants. Along the way, Master Hao saw a walnut tree, and we stopped to pick all the walnuts on the tree, using flashlights in pitch darkness. Then, at the next rest stop, we stopped to shell the walnuts. We reached his caves three hours later.

Another disciple, a twenty-year-old high school graduate from Chongqing, was at the caves, wearing black pants and a long, flowing white shirt, somewhat similar to Quanzhen robes. Both of Master Hao's disciples claimed to have met Master Hao by chance while traveling, had a sense of predestined affinity (*yuanfen*), and stayed with him as disciples. They did not seem to be very interested in Daoism, and helped out with errands and chores; one of them rather actively, while the other mostly lounged around and occasionally helped out. But when we returned to see Master Hao in 2013, both disciples had left.

Just a few days before we arrived, an old well, said to be 800–1,000 years old, was discovered by workers as they were clearing the soil near the entrance archway of the cave complex. There were many legends about this well, said to contain "water of immortality," needed for alchemical cultivation and for bringing good health and longevity. Some old people knew about it, but nobody knew where it was. Master Hao saw this as a particularly auspicious sign of vitality and prosperity for his cave complex.

Mater Hao has a paranoid view of his "enemies" in the Daoist community. He claims that they once tried to get rid of him by poisoning the water in the well at the cave complex. "I felt a strange illness, and stayed in bed for seven days and seven nights, and ended up going to hospital. The diagnosis was that I had drunk poisoned water from poisonous mushrooms falling in the well, but later I found a dead snake in the well, which had been tampered with, it had not died naturally. I knew they tried to poison me. Even before I died, they spread rumors about me having become an Immortal at the Cloud Platform. But when it turned out I hadn't died, they couldn't take back their story, and my fame spread."

MASTER CHEN

In contrast to Hu's reverence and Hao's enthusiasm, Master Chen can be characterized in terms of his intellectual brilliance.[21] When we first met him in 2004, he appeared as the very embodiment of Quanzhen monastic orthodoxy, both as an official in the Huashan Daoist Association and as an articulate exponent of Daoist teachings who traced his spiritual genealogy to Hao Datong—one of the Seven Perfected Ones, the disciples of Wang Chongyang, the founder of the Quanzhen order. Winn remarked about Chen, "He would never be able to teach the Dao in the West, because he is so much a part of the monastic tradition, and can never get rid of the weight of that tradition."

Little did we know that, within a year, he would definitively leave Huashan and the monastic community to become an urban hermit in Chengdu, Sichuan, a place famous for its leisurely lifestyle, pursuing his spiritual path in a different way, and full of critical insights on the state of contemporary Quanzhen Daoism, as well as on the growing interest in Daoism among Westerners. An avid fan of football matches on TV, he often talked in praise of idleness, with a fondness for the laziness of Chinese people. He was a great admirer of the Tang dynasty, when anyone who could afford it lived a life of genteel idleness, drinking in inns and composing verses, wearing jade pendants and other types of refined ornaments to display one's high state of moral distinction. He was also quite an admirer of America, which he found to be comparable in many ways to Tang dynasty China, notably in its openness to other cultures.

Born in 1969 in Jinan (Shandong Province), Chen was very naughty as a boy; he loved fighting, and climbing on the roofs of houses, and he learned to speak very late, causing much worry to his parents. Only recently did he find out that his primary school building was located in the premises of an old Daoist temple, one of the buildings of which still remained.[22] Chen describes his attraction to Daoism as follows: when he was a boy, he opened a book on ancient thinkers, and saw the word "Daoism" (*daojia*). He fell in love with the two Chinese characters, which left a deep impression on him. But he was not satisfied with the description of Daoist philosophy in the book, which condemned it for being an instrument of the feudal exploiting classes that, nonetheless, contains some good elements of primitive dialectical materialism. China was in the midst of the post-Mao *qigong* and martial arts "fever,"[23] and Chen began practicing as a teenager; he was especially accomplished at Bruce Lee's kicking style, and enjoyed climbing up walls and jumping from one house to another on roofs. According to one of his high school classmates, he had perfect form in physical education, and his teacher gave him special access to a training room.[24] He started reading books on Daoism and, using a manual, started meditating at home. One night, while meditating, he heard a voice telling him: "*Chujia!*"—leave your family to enter the order! He laughed, but couldn't get rid of the voice. He couldn't sleep. The next day, the voice was still telling him to *chujia*! After a week, the voice was tormenting him. At the time, he was studying Chinese medicine in a junior college. For six months, he tried various ways to discipline his mind to get rid of the voice, but no luck. So he gave up. One day, he learned in a magazine that there were Daoist temples and monks at Wudangshan, a mountain famous for its martial arts. He wrote to the chairman of the Wudangshan Daoist Association, telling of his thirst to learn the true teachings of Daoism, and, at the end, asking if they would accept him as a monk. In its reply, the Daoist Association encouraged him in his search for Dao, but, as for joining the monastic order, "it is not important, the key is faith in Daoism." Regardless, Chen decided to set off for Wudangshan.

His parents were teachers; they staunchly opposed his decision. He promised that he would not "leave the family"; he only wanted to "experience" monastic life, and would return a year later. Chen set off with a backpack. He was twenty-two years old.

At Wudangshan, he was surprised that most monks rarely talked about "Dao," but about ghost stories and miraculous events that he was not interested in. Nonetheless, he was deeply moved by the simplicity of many of the elder monks, and by the words in the scriptures he recited every morning. After the year came to an end, he decided to commit his life to Dao, and to become a monk. His brother was the first to accept his choice, but his mother became desperate. But, after some time she felt that he had become less cocky, more "dumb," and more wise, and that he understood more about life and could give advice on how to manage family affairs.

Chen settled at Laoshan, a Daoist monastery on the Shandong coast, where he spent around four years. It was there that he met his master, Xue Tailai. It happened shortly after he had a dream of an old master coming from Huashan, and that he was to become his disciple. Xue was described by Bill Porter in his book *Road to Heaven: Encounters with Chinese Hermits*, based on Porter's travels to meet hermits at the Zhongnanshan range and Huashan in the late 1980s. In Porter's account, Xue was seventy years old, having spent forty-five years as a monk, and now lived in the Jade Cloud Temple on the West Peak of Huashan. Porter described Xue affectionately as a likeable monk, who was "straightforward in a very gentle way."[25] A photograph in the book shows an old monk with deep-set eyes, a large forehead, and a long, wispy beard, wearing a dark robe and cap.

Master Chen described his encounter with Xue as follows:

> When I was looking for a master, I was not interested in finding someone with much knowledge or accomplishment in techniques, for these things I could find by myself. But I wanted someone of high virtue, who could lead me on that path.
>
> When I first saw Xue Tailai, I was at Laoshan, and the moment I saw him coming into the temple, limping, I helped him along and arranged for others to take care of his needs, and I knew that he was exactly the master that I had imagined. I asked him to be my master, but he said that he was useless. I insisted, and he said that I should take the current Chairman of the Laoshan Daoist Association as my master. I insisted, and he said that I should get the permission of the Chairman.
>
> I went to the Chairman and asked him about that old Daoist. He answered right away that one can see at first sight that he is a man of high cultivation. I asked if I could become his disciple, and he said that Xue would surely not take me. I said, "what if he agrees?" He said, "go and see then." So I told him that Master Xue had agreed. The Chairman got angry, saying that "you can't take a master from Huashan; you need to take a master from Laoshan."

Chen then brought Xue Tailai to the chairman, to help make his case. As the chairman continued to refuse, Master Xue said, "I am a useless and ignorant person, and only want to study. At every mountain I go, I become a disciple of a master. Let me be your disciple, and let Chen be your disciple too, as well as mine. Then he can be both of our disciples." The abbot still refused, but Xue kowtowed to him, and told Chen to follow suit, and they kowtowed to him, and it was done. Master Xue gave Chen his Daoist name—Yuming—, but muttered it unclearly, and Chen didn't know exactly what it was. Later, another monk told him.

Chen was delighted and excited that his dream of finding a master had come true. As it was late in the evening, he told Xue, "Master, I will come and see you first thing tomorrow morning!" But the next morning, his master had already left. Chen was deeply disappointed that his master seemed to have already forgotten him.

Once Chen was accused of embezzling some funds, and was mistreated by his fellow monks. Six months later, it was discovered that the bookkeeper had made an error and he was cleared of all suspicion. At that point the monks came to him and apologized. This was his first painful experience of monastic politics. The next day, Chen packed his bags and left on a journey of "cloud wandering." He visited the Golden Platform Temple at Baoji, where the legendary Zhang Sanfeng had entered the Quanzhen order; the Eternal Spring Temple in Hubei; the Hangu Temple in Henan; and the White Cloud Monastery in Beijing. Everywhere he was disappointed by what he perceived as the flagging religious spirit of Daoism, compared to the prosperity of Buddhism. At Yantai he cried at the tomb of one of the Seven Perfected Ones, Ma Danyang, lamenting the decline of Quanzhen Daoism.

Finally, he reached Huashan. He immediately sought out Master Xue, unsure if his master remembered him. He put his bags down outside of Xue's room, and called out, "My master, I have come!"—and he heard his master's reply: "Yuming, you have come!" Chen was deeply moved and excited that Xue had remembered him.

Chen was deeply attached to his master, and shared the following stories about him:

I have many masters, but he is the one who had the deepest impression on me. His level of technical practice was very low, and he was almost illiterate. But he was extremely devout and sincere, and a man of utter purity, simplicity, and humility. Even though he was barely literate, he was an assiduous reader. When he came across a character he couldn't read, he would sit by the path with a dictionary and humbly ask a passerby if he could kindly spare a minute to explain the word to him or help him to look it up in the dictionary. Often, especially when I was in a turbulent state of mind, I would go to him in his room, where he was always either sleeping or reading. He would say, "Chen, you have come! Sit down." And he would continue reading. And my troubles would vanish.

When he was younger, he once decided to retrace the steps of patriarch Qiu Chuji, and went to Panxi stream. But at that spot, the bridge had fallen into ruins, so, like the Patriarch, he decided to help carry people across the river on his back. So he did this for six years. He was reputed among the local people as an extremely good person (though some people also said he was crazy), and on hearing this, the Army gave him an overcoat, and some money. He donated all of the money to rebuild the bridge. Later, he left that spot, and moved to Huashan.

Sometime later, some of the people from Panxi were at Huashan and recognized him, and were surprised to learn that he was a Daoist monk. But he told them that they were mistaken, that he was not that man.

When I asked him, why did you deny it? He said, "I am a cultivator, and I must do good deeds. Could I say otherwise?" He always insisted that he was ignorant and good for nothing.

After 1949, he was for a period an official at Huashan. Then, at the Cultural Revolution, all the monks at Huashan were rounded up, and told they would have to return to married life. They were given three options: (1) to return to their hometowns, (2) to settle in the local town, and the local authorities would find a girl for them to marry, (3) if they insisted on remaining celibate, they would be sentenced to forced labor. Xue Tailai chose to do forced labor. A Daoist nun felt sorry for him and, to spare him that fate, proposed to marry him, but he said he was diseased (implying that he was impotent) as an excuse, and entered forced labor for a decade, where he broke stones on the roadside.

After the Cultural Revolution, he was the first monk to wear his Daoist robes again. Nobody else dared do it, until they finally heard the change in policy, that religious life was now allowed again. Xue Tailai was rehabilitated and compensated for ten years of unpaid wages, which he spent to build a small shelter for people to rest on their ascent of Huashan.[26]

At Huashan, most of the old Daoists were dying off and the new ones had no master, so Xue Tailai agreed to ordain several of them as disciples. But he insisted that he knew nothing, and that he was doing this only to transmit the lineage, which would otherwise be cut off. Master Xue died in 2003. For this deeply respected Daoist monk, there was a huge funeral procession.

At Huashan, Master Chen began by trying to be an upright monk, but after some time he began to live a dissolute life. "After I became a monk, I met many eminent Daoists. But when I saw how they behaved it was a real shock, especially concerning their celibacy. I was deeply disillusioned. At that time I didn't really understand about my own cultivation, and only cared about how to save people. At the same time, I began to live a degenerate life." At first Chen wasn't interested in the fights and the arrangement with police for splitting money, and stayed in his room while he heard fights outside, but later he joined them too, took part in fights, kept money, went out to restaurants for two meals a day, and brought meat into the temple.

He also got caught up in factional politics. During an election for the chairman of the Huashan Daoist Association, he was expected to support a fellow disciple of Xue Tailai, but considered him incompetent. "In fact, I thought there was not a single qualified person at Huashan. No matter what I did, or did not do, others would see me as their enemy. People would come to me and ask, 'Who do you belong to?' and I would get angry at them. 'I only belong to the ancestral patriarch!' "[27]

Chen was already disgusted with his own poor spiritual discipline, and the factional struggle was the last straw that led him to escape from Huashan.

> I was very unhappy. I decided to stop living like that. The only way was for me to go. So I left Huashan, and went to Yunnan for a few months, and reflected, and found that my two major faults were my pride and my lust. And I set out to overcome these weaknesses. I tried everything against the lust, to no avail. I would curse myself, and even hit myself when the desire arose, but to no avail. Then a master in Yunnan taught me a meditation method which was simple and effective. The reason I had not been able to control myself was simply a lack of skill. I needed to improve my *gongfu*. The method was very effective, and within about three months I was able to control my desire. There were a few relapses, but gradually my sexual urges were completely stilled. Daoist monks have a huge responsibility as models of sexual restraint. If common people have dissolute lives, it doesn't matter, but if it's a monk, it has a terrible impact.

On his return to Huashan, he followed discipline more strictly, and his abilities earned him a position of leadership in the monastic community. But factional politics continued. Chen decided to avoid all factional struggles, adopting a "triple no" policy of not participating in organized groups or factions; not commenting on others; and not explaining or justifying himself.[28] Chen was becoming increasingly respected; and he was destined to be promoted to an official post. In order to avoid being called to an official leadership role, he tried acting crazy and unpredictable, such as running around naked in the courtyard—but still he could not avoid being promoted to deputy chairman and general manager.[29]

Master Chen also decided to adopt a low-key approach to cultivation, in which he didn't pretend to have any accomplishment. While deeply committed to his practice, on the outside he wouldn't pretend to be anything, not acting upright and stern, but just acting relaxed and normal. "Otherwise, people will think you are too distant; they will respect your cultivation but they will not do it themselves because they feel it is too different from them." He also never told any of his fellow monks at the monastery about his cultivation, because, "First, they will test you, to try to put you down. And second, once they recognize your ability, they will seek you out, take you as a model, and seek teachings from you, and bother you."

Perhaps because of his own experience of inner struggle, when he spoke about cultivation it wasn't in terms of abstract principles, and virtue was central to his discourse: "Without virtue, techniques are useless, even like nuclear bombs." But at the same time, he was far from being an ascetic puritan; he enjoyed going out to eat meat and drink liquor with visitors at banquets in town, and was very smooth in his socializing with nonmonastics: cultured, adept at conversation and self-deprecating jokes, at ease with social etiquette, he could talk about anything and always had entertaining stories to tell at banquets. In fact, he was the type of person who would be successful in any line of work in China, such as business or government.

With such talent and knowledge, and at such a young age, Chen was the ideal candidate for a political position within Daoist officialdom. And while he seemed to be a smooth operator as Office Director of the Huashan Daoist Association, and his family pushed him in that direction, he insisted,

> I have no interest in becoming a Daoist politician. Others talk of "proclaiming Daoism" and so on. It's hard to resist such suggestions, because of one's sense of duty. But I have seen through them, and I won't fall for it. My dream is to one day retreat into the mountains. Now I still need this collectivity to learn and to support me, but when I will no longer need it I will leave it, to go into the mountains to cut wood. Well, maybe not to cut wood, but to go into the mountains. This collectivity will always continue to go on without me. It doesn't need me, there will always be thousands of Daoist officials. All I want to do is to cultivate better. Laozi had the most influence, yet he did not go out and "found" a religion. The same with Lü Dongbin. The most influential Daoists were never involved in Daoist institutions. There were only a few of them and they lived centuries apart, but their influence by far exceeds that of thousands of abbots and sect founders. Even today, what could you do by founding a sect? You still would have to defer to Lü Dongbin, you couldn't teach anything new—so what would the point be?

At the time, it was hard to judge if he was sincere or if he was only cleverly saying these things to appear humble and conceal a burning ambition for official position—especially when he mentioned that he would accept an appointment only if it was forced on him. But what sounded like mere ruminations became a reality within less than a year, when he left the monastic order to cultivate in solitude. Not in the mountains, though: "Going into mountains is only for the early stages of cultivation. Then the true cultivation can only be in the city. Then, at a very advanced stage, one can return to the mountains."

He chose the metropolis of Chengdu—because, he said, it's one of the twenty-four dioceses of the early Heavenly Masters movement and, as the center of the Sichuan basin, is the "elixir field" (*dantian*) of China, a good place for cultivating. It's also "a very leisurely culture, where people try very hard to play. They're always playing. Nobody here will notice if I'm not doing anything. In my hometown, people would always ask and worry for me, and offer to help me find work." When he decided to leave the monastic order, his mother was delighted at first, but she was then disappointed that he wouldn't return to normal life, and had actually given up his promising career as a Daoist official. "But I never tried to explain or justify myself," he said. At first, every time he went home, his parents would hold a "family meeting" for him. "But later, they saw how I had changed, so they accepted my choice."

His parents are well off, and don't have financial needs; so they support him financially, and purchased a house for him in Dujiangyan, a small city close to Chengdu and near to Qingchengshan. But he lives in Chengdu, where life is cheap, and he also gives occasional zither, painting, and *taiji quan* lessons.

When I saw him in Chengdu in 2005, he had cut the long hair he had grown in his years as a monk; wearing a T-shirt and cheap pants, he looked like a typical Chinese of modest means. In contrast to the times I met him at Huashan, when he displayed some of the worldly jadedness of an official, chatting about international politics and Chinese history as much as about Daoism, his conversation was now very serious and focused on the theme of spiritual cultivation. His goal, he said, was to hurry up in his cultivation, to have the ability in the future to save people. "At this stage I can't go out and save people." Asked how he intended to save people in the future, he didn't answer clearly, but he stressed that it would not be "by going out publicly, by establishing a religion." "Daoism is much weaker and less developed than other religions in China. At first I was concerned about this, but now I understand that that's the strength of Daoism. If you try to reform, to 'proclaim Daoism,' nobody will follow you, because there is no scriptural basis for doing so. Whereas, in Buddhism and Christianity, there is a clear basis in scripture to go about and spread the religion."[30]

Keeping his location and identity secret, he rents a small and simple room in a suburb of the city. In 2009, he told me he was happy to be living a totally relaxed lifestyle, practicing a bit of *taiji quan* every day, living a simple life. He also practiced still meditation, and also occasionally used more complex methods, mostly from the Shangqing and Lingbao traditions.[31]

His spiritual experience also changed—far from the external environment of Huashan that sustained his previous spiritual practice, he now experienced the power of Dao as something completely internal to himself: "When I was at Huashan, I always felt something outside of me, the *daoqi* that was exactly the same as one thousand years ago at the time of the ancestral patriarchs, as if I was living at the same time as them. It was there, outside of me, and going right into me. But now, in meditation, I have had a completely different feeling, as if that thing was right in me, right in my heart, that it was my heart itself."[32]

He decided to keep an extremely low profile: he is willing to give talks and lessons to foreigners who invite him, but will not create an organization. In spite of his fame in the Chinese Daoist circle, he would never go to public events or give public lessons to Chinese audiences—"because too many people would know about it, it becomes a source of trouble. When I do things with foreigners, Chinese people won't know about it." He regretted having once attended a public event to see his zither teacher; he was then introduced to many people, but hated the hobnobbing, and meeting some Daoist monks who enjoyed the social networking. "These people, because they have no other world, they are attracted to that world. If they live in another, spiritual world, they will not be attracted."

Master Chen is selective in accepting disciples, and has only a handful of formal ones, half of whom are men and the other half women. Some are lay Daoists, some are business people; one is a tour guide; there is also one old lady; and there are also a few foreigners, including Komjathy. Most of his disciples are from the days when he was a monk at Huashan. Some of them were referred to by other monks (who strongly urged him to take them), and others asked him directly.

> I don't go out and look for disciples, and I only take disciples who have a strong faith and desire to cultivate. I don't teach to those, like many monks, who are only curious or take Daoism as a hobby. Some of them come to me, because they want to be able to talk about different traditions and techniques, and compare them, and display their knowledge, but I never accept. I never take monks as disciples. They are too much trouble. I have some disciples who are more at the level of faith, and solving problems of daily life, to whom I transmit the forms of Quanzhen Daoism, and two disciples interested in cultivation, to whom I do not transmit a particular form; I do not talk of different sects.[33]

He claimed that he is not afraid of losing his disciples, and won't hesitate to cut off communications with them in order to punish them for wrong attitudes, strong desires or attachments, or not doing the basics. "For example, one of my disciples, a woman, asked to learn cultivation techniques but didn't even bother to burn incense and worship deities. How could she progress?" He prefers to start training in the qualities of the heart and in virtue, rather than with techniques, in order to give his students a strong foundation for future progress. "If you want to learn a moving exercise, I will teach you to bow down; if you want to learn Daoist theory, then recite Daoist scriptures every day."[34] In any case, he felt frustrated that many of his disciples made no progress. "Some people are lazy and they can't get themselves to practice. Others are extremely diligent and can submit themselves to a rigorous meditative discipline. But no matter what, it's the same, they don't progress." And he concluded that what they lacked was the effort to do good deeds.[35]

And he also directed the same criticism at himself: "I used to neglect this aspect. I used to consider that to maintain a good heart was good enough, but that it wasn't important to actually do good deeds. I saw passages in Daoist scriptures about the importance of good deeds, but I didn't really understand. I considered that the most important was hidden virtue (*yinde*), not externally visible acts." According to Master Chen, Patriarch Qiu Chuji had forbidden his disciples from becoming hermits and isolating themselves from society; they should devote themselves to the salvation of all sentient beings. But he realized that he was acting like a hermit himself. "I was closing myself up. Now I realize that progress in cultivation comes from the virtue one has attained. It might, in such a case, be useful to go into retreat for a period, in order to work on oneself, to consolidate an achievement, but to consolidate a virtue already attained. If one has not already attained that virtue, to go into retreat would mean to close oneself from the possibility of progress. Heaven and the myriad beings will respond and lift you up if you do good deeds, but if you don't, why will they come for you?" After coming to this realization, he felt a new life in him; he felt a new energy that led him to act to help others. "Before, it was like being dead. Now I understand the term *walking cadaver* (*xingshi zourou*). That's what people are doing. They get up, they go to bed, they go to sleep, they get up; there is no difference between living and dying. Then they die and they look for another body to continue being dead like this—is there any difference between such life and death? That's the meaning of the cycle of births and deaths" (*lunhui*).[36] So, while Chen's earlier discourse stressed virtue, by 2009 it increasingly stressed doing good deeds—even though, in a Daoist spirit of spontaneity, he did not advocate planned charitable actions or social engagement, or "being attached to specific plans"—simply jumping at opportunities to help people in need, such as a time when he helped pick up for a deaf woman whose shopping bag had burst and her vegetables rolled all over the place. These mundane helping acts acquired a fundamental spiritual significance in Chen's understanding of the process of Daoist cultivation.

This orientation also found expression in his increasing involvement in what could be called exorcistic healing practices, but which, in fact, he defined in terms of good deeds. For instance, one of his disciples had a pain in his upper back, and tried many ways to treat it, but to no avail, and asked Master Chen for help. The image of an animal came to Chen's mind, so he asked him if he had ever harmed or killed an animal. His disciple thought and thought, but could not think of anything. Finally, he remembered that some time ago he had inadvertently disturbed a bird's nest, leading to the death of a chick. "I told him to burn some incense and some paper money for this bird. He did, and his pain went away." In another case, there was a boy who was very ill, and no matter what treatments were used, he did not improve. His parents called on a Buddhist monk, figuring that he was possessed by a demon, and asked Chen to conduct exorcistic rituals. "But I said, there is an animal spirit near your house, and it is injured and is limping. It is suffering. Don't attack it with magic. At the place I designate, burn some incense and paper money, and also offer some painkilling medicine." After this, claimed Chen, the child got better. Thus, Chen saw his practice as the opposite of exorcism: instead of violently attacking demons, in the manner typical of Daoist priests, you need to "do good deeds" by helping those injured and suffering spirits.[37]

Each summer, when we had long chats with Chen in Chengdu restaurants, coffee shops, and teahouses, he appeared more critical of the Quanzhen institution. By 2007, he stated categorically, "I am increasingly becoming uninterested in the Daoist religion; I am only interested in Dao."[38]

Though he now claimed to be indifferent to Daoist institutions, his opinion of the Daoist clergy was far from neutral. Asked what he thought of the commodification of Daoism by the "Daoist hot springs" developer at Louguantai who had hired him to give lectures to his staff:

> So they are using Daoism for their own purposes. But isn't that what Daoist monks do? They put on their Daoist robes to accomplish their own objectives. If they don't want others to do it, they shouldn't do it themselves. One of my disciples recently told me that he had met a Daoist monk, who was the student of such-and-such, at such temple, of such-and-such generation, etc. Who cares about these things? They are but outer garments. We need only look at the heart. Daoist and Buddhist monks are the most despicable of all people. In a war, the worst people are the traitors. In religion, which doesn't have outside enemies, the traitors are the monks themselves, who completely betray the spirit of the religion.[39]

For Chen, the people who worship at temples are motivated by their need for faith, and by their true admiration for great figures like Lü Dongbin and Zhang Sanfeng—it has nothing to do with the Daoist monks and priests in the temple, or the religious organizations, that have no good influence on people. "Daoism and Buddhism now care too little about doing good deeds, they only care about themselves. They only look after their own interests and not those of society, of humanity, and of the myriad beings. They complain that they have no money, that they are too weak, so they can't do anything. These are just excuses. Buddhists are good at making money, but I don't consider this to be a sign of development."[40]

Chen's views seemed to be coming closer to those of Winn's Dream Trippers: only concerned with Dao and the spirituality of the heart, and utterly uninterested in Daoism as a religious organization. Now that he was out of the Quanzhen order, he certainly was free to develop his ties with such like-minded Westerners. Indeed, he continued and increased his interactions with networks of foreign practitioners: he gave talks for Dream Trippers when they visited Mount Qingcheng near Chengdu; he served as a guide for Russian Daoist tour groups, and, around 2010, he began teaching at an annual two-week Daoist retreat in Belgium. He had met the leader of this Daoist center at Huashan when hosting the 2002 Dream Trip. The Belgian was also a student of Mantak Chia, practices *Baguazhang*, and teaches Daoist practices. "He is the foreigner I have met who has the highest level of embodied accomplishment. When he came to Huashan, I noticed how good he was, and asked him if his master was Chinese; and was surprised to learn that he was not." Master Chen felt that he has deep *yuanfen* with him. At that time he invited Master Chen to Belgium to teach, but for several reasons it took several years for this plan to come to fruition.[41] The visits to Belgium started to have an impact on his religious worldview. His experiences in churches and cathedrals changed his views on Christianity, and he changed his formulation of the hierarchy of deities he worships every day. As his top tier, he continues to worship the Three Purities (*sanqing*)—the three supreme deities and hypostases of Dao—and as his second tier, the gods of the stars and of the Dipper, but, on the third tier, he now worships "all deities and spirits" (*yiqie shenming*), instead of his previous formulation of "all deities and Buddhas" (*yiqie shenfo*)—because, "After my mission changed through my trips to Europe, I decided to include all gods [including the Christian god] and not to accord special treatment to Buddhist ones."[42]

Teaching and interacting with foreigners became an increasingly important part of Chen's own cultivation and mission. It broadens his horizons, he explained, and allows him to test the universality of the Daoist teachings, as well as to correct some of his own concepts on Daoism. At the same time, given the inevitable spread of Daoism to different countries, it is important to ensure that a correct understanding of Dao is transmitted; otherwise, once erroneous understandings and practices become solidified as a system overseas, it will become almost impossible to correct.[43]

Reflecting on his spiritual path over the previous decades, Chen recalled that, when he had started his life as a monk at Laoshan, a master had asked him: "Are you truly interested in cultivation, or is it the life of a monk that you are attracted to? Think about it and answer me in a week." Chen reflected, and finally told him that it was the life of a monk that he desired: wearing the Daoist robes, solemnly walking back and forth in the ceremonies. . . . Later, even though he had little experience of Daoist cultivation, on seeing the crisis in the Quanzhen order, he wanted to do great things, to start a new sect. And later, that urge having passed, he entered a phase of enjoying chatting about Dao (*lundao*), knowing much about theory but having little intuitive knowledge. One day in 2000, a master advised him to go into a cave with only one book, and to meditate on it. So he went into one of the caves at the summit of Huashan, taking with him only the *Daodejing* with the *Heshanggong* commentary. He stayed in the cave for two weeks, reading and meditating, until he was called down for a meeting at the Jade Spring Monastery. It was during this time that, for the first time, "my heart/mind descended into my abdomen, and I felt completely grounded, and completely attuned with the world." It was from then on that he lost interest in idle talk on Dao, his focus shifted to cultivating Dao, and then he decided to leave the monastic order.[44]

The Quanzhen Order and the State

In the above biographical sketches, we have seen how Masters Hu, Hao, and Chen have struggled within the religious institution on their path of spiritual cultivation. In the case of Hao and Chen, they ultimately distanced themselves from the Quanzhen monastic order within which they had acquired their religious training, identity, and lineage affiliation. Though their Quanzhen background predisposed the monks to approach the Americans with benevolent condescension, other factors drew them into a more earnest engagement with the Dream Trippers, an attraction which was reinforced by the strong memories of the moments of meaningful communication with them, as we show in chapter 5. This attraction reinforced their marginalization from the monastic community: the ties with Westerners were possibly the cause of a plot against Hu; they became the center of Hao's dreams for the future development of his hermitage; and for Chen they provided a spiritual role independent of the monastic institution. Their comments, and those of other monks, seem to indicate a state of crisis of authority and authenticity in the contemporary Quanzhen institution as the guardian of Daoist orthodoxy. Although most large Daoist temples and monasteries in China today are controlled by monks of the Quanzhen order,[45] Quanzhen is not the only form of institutionalized Daoist religion in China, and it represents only the visible tip of the iceberg of Daoism in China. During the current socialist regime, in which the legal activities, properties, and personnel of the five state-sanctioned religions (Buddhism, Daoism, Protestantism, Catholicism, and Islam) are managed by official state-sponsored associations at the national, provincial, and local levels, monks of the Quanzhen order virtually monopolize the Daoist Associations and control their temples and monasteries.

While Quanzhen generally follows the institutions of celibacy, vegetarianism, and monasticism modeled on Buddhism, the other main Daoist priestly tradition—Zhengyi or Orthodox Oneness—consists of ritual specialists who live among the people and serve the needs of individuals, families, and communities, usually without an affiliation to a temple. Zhengyi priests can marry, hold other jobs, eat meat, and so on. Besides the Zhengyi, dozens of local traditions of Daoist ritual masters, such as the Lüshan, Meishan, and Yuanhuang lineages, flourish in various regions such as Fujian, Taiwan, Hunan, and Guangdong; like the Zhengyi, these are also lineages of priests operating as local ritual service providers. Nonmonastic Daoist priests generally remain unable to legally exercise their profession, although the Zhengyi order has gained some degree of official recognition since the 1990s, and Zhengyi priests have been able to obtain official permits in some provinces. Such types of priests are not visibly identifiable; they operate independently, live among the people, and, instead of giving moral exhortations, they organize rituals and exorcisms for a fee—they blur the boundaries between the secular and the sacred, and have thus tended to be labeled by the secular state as practitioners of illegal "superstitions."

Beyond these professional monks and ritual specialists, Daoist ideas and practices have been widely diffused among a great variety of professions including healers, pharmacists, opera singers, martial artists, diviners, geomancers, and body cultivation masters, as well as among lay religious movements. These different lineages, sects, and practitioners have never been united in a single institution, and while one can be the disciple of a master or the follower of a specific sect, there has never been a concept of "membership" in Daoism as a unified "religion." The disembedding of Chinese body cultivation techniques from specific traditional social contexts—and their reembedding in new settings, organizations, and traditions—is a process that has been going on in China for millennia. As "portable practices," Chinese breathing and stretching techniques, meditation, and visualization methods have circulated between mystics, literati, healers, ritual masters, warriors, religious devotees, and charismatic sectarians. They have been put to different uses, embedded in different types of social networks and organizations, and inscribed into different genealogies.[46] The system of body cultivation and meditation practice known as "inner alchemy" (*neidan*), which both the Dream Trippers and the Complete Perfection Daoist monks claim to inherit, had evolved into a stable form by the Tang dynasty (618–907), before the monastic Complete Perfection order had even been established.[47]

The Quanzhen order, which appeared in the twelfth century, adopted a form of celibate monasticism largely borrowed from Buddhism as the institutional setting for the practice of inner alchemy.[48] It became and remains until today the most influential and prestigious form of institutional Daoism.[49] The Ming and Qing dynasties (1363–1911) saw the appearance of standardized and progressive sets and sequences of body practices, including some well-known martial arts forms (*taiji quan*, *baguazhang*, etc.), as well as some methods of inner alchemy practice. These sets of techniques, disseminated in the form of published manuals, spread rapidly at a time of increasing literacy, urbanization, and commercialization in the Chinese world. They also made it possible for individuals to learn and practice the techniques without being part of formal lineages or institutions, although all of them remained embedded within a common traditional social structure and cosmology. In the first half of the twentieth century, some lay masters, authors, and organizations attempted to modify the traditions in response to the changes and challenges of the onslaught of Western modernity in China. Some tried to simplify the techniques and remove esoteric symbols and concepts, in order to appeal to the new generation of intellectuals with a modern education.[50] Others used scientific terminology to recast inner alchemy as a uniquely Chinese science with nationalist undertones.[51] New religious movements, known among scholars as redemptive societies, integrated them into new combinations of moral discourse, spirit-writing, and millennialism in their quest to revive China's spiritual traditions in the form of a new universalism.[52] In the 1950s, the new communist regime explicitly tried to extract China's body cultivation techniques from their "feudal" and "superstitious" traditional context, to secularize and integrate them into modern health institutions, under the new name of *qigong*. In the 1980s and early 1990s, during the post-Mao "*qigong* fever," *qigong* was officially promoted as a form of health exercise to be practiced by the masses in parks and public spaces; it was also recast as a new scientific revolution which would release the powers of the mind and of *qi* over matter; and it created a space for charismatic masters to create their own, increasingly religious organizations and movements.[53] Several new religious movements have also disseminated these practices in new contexts in Taiwan.[54]

The spread of Daoist body technologies to the West is thus but one of many instances of the recasting of Daoist spiritual cultivation in new social, political, and cultural contexts. Indeed, the Chinese masters who first emigrated to the West and taught them in the contexts of the counterculture, the New Age movement, and alternative health and spiritualities were, to varying degrees, influenced by these changes and reforms of body cultivation in modern China.

Most of these changes and innovations occurred within lay movements outside of the Complete Perfection order, which remained conservative in its monastic organization and rituals and, by the twentieth century, left individual monks free to follow their own "predestined affinity" (*yuanfen*) in their path of meditation and alchemical practice, if at all.[55] However, although Complete Perfection monks have long been a numerically negligible group among the many providers of spiritual and religious services in China, they have enjoyed an immense prestige and legitimacy, which other practitioners and groups, such as martial arts masters, redemptive societies, spirit-writing halls, and lay cultivation groups, have always tried to draw on, while at the same time rejecting Quanzhen clericalism and institutional forms.[56] An ambiguous relationship was maintained between the elite Complete Perfection monks and the dynamic popular practitioners—a pattern which continues today, between monastics and Chinese *qigong* groups, for example, and which, to a great extent, is merely carried over in the relations between the Complete Perfection order and international practitioners such as the Dream Trippers. The encounters and dynamics we describe in this book should not be seen simplistically as instances of "East meets West": it would be more accurate, therefore, to see the encounters as representing two extremes of a continuum between lay practitioners and monastics of the Complete Perfection order, a continuum that has long existed among Chinese Daoists, and along which practitioners have circulated, moving from lay to monastic life and vice versa, questioning and negotiating the ideals of Daoist cultivation.

Different emperors and dynasties in Chinese history have patronized and supported either the Zhengyi or the Quanzhen tradition, contributing to their respective institutionalization and rise and fall over time. The Quanzhen monastic institution itself is a product of the merging of political structures and technologies of religious asceticism. Wang Chongyang (1113–1170), the founder of the Quanzhen movement, did not create a formal organization and had seven disciples, the Seven Perfected Ones, who each went their own way after his death. Celibate monasticism was rare among Daoists. It was one of Wang's disciples, Qiu Chuji (1148–1227), who ensured the institutionalization of the Quanzhen order under the patronage of the Mongol emperor Chinggis Khan, who placed all monasteries of all religions in North China under Qiu's authority. He exempted Quanzhen followers from taxes and corvée labor, leading to a rapid expansion of the order. Later, however, Quanzhen lost the imperial favor during the Ming dynasty, and is not known to have had a strong organization. It was in the early Qing dynasty that the abbot of Beijing's White Cloud Monastery, Wang Changyue (d.1680), established the rules and forms of Quanzhen monasticism, discipline, precepts, and lineage, along lines favored by the imperial Court and imitating many aspects of Chan Buddhist precepts. With official backing, he was able to impose his standardized Quanzhen institutional forms onto most temples in northern China, under the authority of the Longmen (Dragon Gate) lineage. These are the forms that remain the traditional norm of the Quanzhen order until today. Scholars continue to research and to debate the construction of Daoist institutions in the Ming and Qing dynasties.[57]

For Master Chen, the political aspect of Wang Changyue's reconstruction of Quanzhen institutions justifies his critique of Quanzhen institutional forms as inauthentic and as a national humiliation. Fearing that the new Manchu rulers of the dynasty might try to eliminate the long-bearded Daoists or force them to shave the front half of their heads, Wang Changyue sought an audience with the emperor, and explained how Daoism could help the government in pacifying the people. Daoism was thus legalized, but Wang also obtained the imperial authority to unify the dispersed Daoist temples and masters by imposing and standardizing strict precepts and lineages. While these had previously existed, their formal transmission now became more important than the transmission of Daoist techniques.

Much of the reorganization of the lineages had political aspects. . . . The most interesting concerns Daoist vestments. Quanzhen monks must grow long hair. But Wang Changyue invented a type of cap, which he called the *hunyuan jin*. This type of cap is the official cap of the Manchu/Qing officials, called the horse-foot cap. The Manchu are horse riding people. Their hats were shaped like horse hooves. The hat designed by Wang Changyue looks almost the same as the hat of the Manchu officials. When they wore this kind of hat, local officials would not abuse them or chop off their heads. Because their hats symbolized political power. . . . So the hats sent the message that Daoist monks were in relation with officialdom. . . . From then on, Daoist masters were called *Daoye* (Master of Dao), reflecting their official position. Nowadays, Daoist monks often address each other as *ye* (Master); but this is from the Qing dynasty, not from ancient times. This is a way to protect the religion, requiring monks to wear that hat whenever they went out, just like officials were also required to do so. . . . This protected the lives of the Daoists and gave them the space to preserve their culture. But nowadays, Daoist monks don't know the historical reason for their hats, and they wear them as a tradition without realizing that the conditions requiring the use of those hats no longer exist. The Qing dynasty collapsed so long ago, but they are still wearing those hats! But some people in the Daoist circle know that this is actually a symbol of national insult. After I understood this, I stopped wearing the *hunyuanjing* cap. I refuse to wear it. . . . Now that the Qing dynasty no longer exists, we can revert to the true Daoist culture. . . . In my heart, the *hunyuanjing* has no place. . . . And I also think that the *hunyuanjing* looks ugly. It makes you look like a Buddhist monk, not like a Daoist monk.[58]

For Master Chen, the Quanzhen institution adopted too many Buddhist forms, and put an exclusive emphasis on the mind, while disparaging other Daoist practices such as music, external alchemy, martial arts, *taiji quan*, and *bagua* boxing. "As a result, they became closed off and are not good at these things, they forget that you can find Dao in everything. . . . This could only further remove Quanzhen from the true Dao."[59] Similarly, Michael Winn could claim,

> That 1,000-year "stretch" of appropriation across time and culture within China by Quanzhen is not very different than the stretch required by modern Healing Tao USA adepts appropriating One Cloud's formulas across the Pacific Ocean from modern China to modern USA.[60]

The Quanzhen monastic institution has always been an instrument for the formation of both spiritual and political subjects. On the one hand, it was established to provide a space for adepts to devote themselves to practicing the technologies of inner alchemy, allowing them to pursue the practice of cosmological attunement. On the other hand, it was also designed as an instrument to better organize, regulate, and discipline Daoist practitioners within the framework of state management—encapsulating the religious community within clearly defined boundaries, separating it from society while using it as an instrument of governance. During the late imperial period, the rules of pseudo-kinship and lineage that reproduced Confucian norms within the system of Daoist monastic celibacy were eminently compatible with the patrilineal and patriarchal social organization upheld by the state, while providing a distinct space for Daoist spiritual cultivation.

The modern, secular socialist state has also favored the Quanzhen order over the Zhengyi and other Daoist lineages, because it easily fits with a modern conception of "religion" as an activity and institution clearly demarcated from the secular realm: monasticism, celibacy, vegetarianism, and sacred mountains all point to a sacred and ethical vision of religion that is other and outside of the dominant concerns of secular society, while being easily identified and managed. It is precisely because Quanzhen monks wear "special costumes" that evoke a "detached life transcending desire" that most people "aren't willing to follow themselves," to use Chen's sarcastic words, that the state can readily identify, manage, control, and support them in the name of "religious freedom," "protecting cultural heritage," and "developing tourism."

Socialist work-unit management, however, undermined the political foundation of the traditional structure of monastic authority and transmission. The result was a breakdown in spiritual discipline, and a crisis in the monastic institution. Socialist work-unit culture could not be harnessed to the formation of Daoist spiritual subjects; its only articulation with Daoism could be one of managing and exploiting human, cultural, and material resources. Externally, the encapsulation of monastic Daoism as distinct from the secular world was further radicalized, drawing a line between a materially progressing secular world and the "religious" place of worship frozen in the past—whose "otherness" was no longer spiritual but material—as a historical relic, whose value was seen as separate from, secondary to, and often, as in the case of Huashan, contrary to the goals of economic development through tourism.

Internally, the breakdown of discipline and spiritual authority hollowed out the spiritual "otherness" of the monastic community, and drew its members across the sacred-secular boundary and back into the practices of the "world of dust." Under these conditions, many monks themselves questioned the religious legitimacy of the Quanzhen institution.

The encounters we narrate in this book may appear as encounters between a modern spirituality and an institution deeply rooted in tradition and, perhaps, in resistance to modernity. But a pure tradition is impossible—while we have characterized the Dream Trippers as "ultramodern" in their spirituality, the Quanzhen monks could be described as living a tradition that is "encapsulated" within a modern institutional framework. Their religious life is primarily structured around and legitimized by tradition, however much this tradition may have changed over the past tumultuous century. There is little conscious engagement with modernity among Quanzhen Daoists, except that the practice of "leaving the family" to live the life of a monastic or of a hermit effectively entails "dropping out" of the types of social relations and lifestyle patterns of the modern individual. But this is not an "antimodern" stance—the monks don't hesitate to use modern technology and amenities when they can afford them, and the very "freezing" of the Quanzhen order into a rigid, traditional form is itself a product of the Chinese state's modern ideological and institutional practices, encapsulating Daoism as a distinctive belief system and culture within a radically secular political structure.

Ideologically, the category of *religion* has been defined in China as the opposite of secular modernity, as a tradition whose authenticity can only be found in the past, and which, by definition, is detached from worldly affairs.

While, prior to the establishment of socialist rule in 1949, Daoist temples and priests were deeply embedded in local life, with temples often doubling as markets, the new regime restricted Daoist monasteries to purely religious, transcendental pursuits, and banned the Zhengyi priests' practice of Daoist ritual as a trade. Institutionally, the state-sponsored system of managing temples and religious personnel is deliberately rigid and conservative, and not conducive to the emergence of innovations or new movements that could lead to an increase in the role of religion in society. Instead, Daoist monasteries are marketed as tourist attractions, where modern consumers can experience a brief "taste" of premodern tradition. When we define contemporary Quanzhen monasticism as encapsulated, we thus refer to a condition in which the modern state has "petrified" Daoism outside of and alongside modernity for ideological, political, and economic reasons. Within this context, most Quanzhen monks wear their exotic robes and tend to the shrines, while some pursue their Daoist cultivation, following a path which steps out of modernity without actively resisting it: instead, they seek to transcend worldly concerns through cosmological attunement with Dao. But the visible signs of that transcendence, the exotic sacred lifestyle, temples, and mountains, become commodities prized by the very modern and materialist culture that many adepts of Quanzhen Daoist cultivation "leave the family" to get away from.

The Encounters

On its arrival at the Jade Spring Monastery, the 2004 Dream Trip had been greeted by a slim monk in Daoist robes, his long hair in a bun. This was Master Chen, the vice-abbot and Office Director of all the temples at Huashan, in charge of the day-to-day administration of the sixty monks and the dozen temples that dot the mountain. At thirty-four years old, he had the look of a graduate student, but he was deeply revered for his spiritual accomplishments by many Daoists across China. He led the whole group to the temple's meeting room, in a building to the back. All took a seat around the long oval table, a cup of tea for each participant. Chen, standing at the head of the table under a portrait of Wang Changyue—seventeenth-century patriarch of the Dragon Gate Lineage of the order of Complete Perfection—gave a brief lecture on the history of Huashan, listing the names of the famous meditators who have stayed at the mountain, emphasizing the lineage of Huashan masters. He then taught them the Daoist meditation of the Shining Heart:

> After the opening posture, visualize lights at the level of the Shanzhong acupoint, at the center of the chest: first yellow, at the center, then green, at the left, then purple, at the back, then white, at the right, then red, at the front. Let all the lights converge into the center, illuminate the whole body, all the organs, and even into all the bones. Then let a lotus flower appear, with white petals, and a child in the center. Send off the child and flower, and return to the converging lights. Repeat 49 times for one cycle; each cycle can be repeated any odd number of times (1, 3, 5 . . .) during the day.

Several, but not all, of the Dream Trippers entered into meditative posture during the explanation, and followed the instructions. During the question-

and-answer session, a large, middle-aged, blonde American woman had said that she felt like crying, and had heart palpitations. "Very good," responded Master Hu, "the information (*xinxi*) is penetrating your heart."

Later, Master Hu told us his explanation of what had happened:

> This is called "receiving with your body" (*shenshou*). You listen with your body. Even if your thoughts didn't hear, your soul (*ling*) received it. When I was teaching, there was a woman who started crying. Of course, I didn't want her to cry, because as a Chinese person, I didn't want her to lose face. From the perspective of cultivation, we don't care about face. If deep inside, you want to cry, your heart wants to cry, there are things in your heart that can be expelled through crying, through receiving the spiritual *qi* (*shenqi*), the prenatal *qi* (*xiantian qi*), and being purified by it. At that moment, [the concern for keeping] face is put aside. With face, the circulation is blocked.[1]

Hu's words implied that the American woman had opened up to the power of the prenatal, spiritual *qi* being transmitted by him and Master Chen. Michael Winn later wrote in his website about this transmission—and he claimed it was historically unprecedented. But he described it as the outcome of Master Chen opening up to *Winn*—because he, the American, possessed secrets of Daoist alchemy unknown to even most Chinese Daoists:

> Even today, most Chinese students—and Chinese qigong and meditation teachers—do not have access to these inner alchemy methods [the Seven Formulas taught by Mantak Chia]. On a recent trip to Huashan, one of the most sacred Daoist mountains in China, I described some of these alchemical formulas to my good friend the vice abbot Master Chen. We had had many long talks about Daoism on previous visits, but I was always careful to not probe into his personal practice or discuss mine.
>
> But the abbot had finally opened up, and taught a stage of Huashan inner alchemy [the "shining heart" meditation described above] to a group of my Western students—the first time in Huashan's 3000 year written history. So I shared with him my own practice and the structure of the Seven Alchemy Formulas. He gasped in surprise, and was so shocked he could hardly speak. "These are very secret methods," he said. "There are very few Daoists here in China who even know of what you speak."[2]

In the previous chapters, we contrasted the personal and collective trajectories of the Dream Trippers and Cloud Wanderers, and discussed the integrative schema of ontological individualism and cosmological attunement through which many of them respectively perceive and interpret their experiences on the mountain. In this chapter, we closely examine the interactions between the two groups. We consider their attitudes toward each other, their contrasting views on Daoist cultivation, and the economic dimension of their exchanges, showing the extent to which the encounters set the stage for misunderstanding and miscommunication about the pursuit of Dao. And yet, there are moments of "magic" in the encounters, in which the "energy field" between the monks and Trippers is positively charged, generating what we call moments of "transnational communitas." For some of the participants, these are life-changing experiences that give them a sense of unanticipated personal connection to Huashan, its monks, and its sacred history.

The highlights of the Dream Trippers' itineraries are visits to Daoist sacred mountains and interactions with Quanzhen masters who impart teachings to them—a form of pilgrimage, then, in which the travelers connect themselves with the places of origin and the living embodiments of the Daoist tradition.[3] In other parts of the world, spiritual tourism has found itself in tension with local populations. For example, conflicts have arisen between tourists who want to climb the Uluru Rock in Australia and the aboriginal Anangu who find such behavior disrespectful. Having integrated Uluru into their own spiritual cosmology, New Age travelers will perform their own invented rituals and camp overnight over the objections of the Anangu.[4] Similarly, Dream Trippers hold their own *qigong* practice sessions and Daoist wedding ceremonies on Huashan, unconnected to the practices of local Daoists, as we describe in the epilogue to this volume. Indigenous populations such as the Dakota in the United States and Australian aborigines, who face a real risk of cultural extinction in the face of outside pressures, often resist the appropriation of their rituals, cosmologies, and sacred places by spiritual tourists and New Age practitioners. However, Daoist institutions of the Complete Perfection order, and the monks we interviewed, do not feel threatened by such trends, even if they often do disdain the Dream Trippers. For them, they represent foreigners coming to the realization of Daoist cultural superiority— and bringing economic resources to temples and mountains—in a context of China's growing nationalism and influence on the world stage. They are simply yet another wave in the long history of pilgrims and travelers who have flocked to the mountains over the centuries.

On the surface, the Dream Trips are welcomed by the monastic leaders of Huashan, who see them as part of the process of spreading Daoism around the world, something that will occur "without effort," in the words of one, "simply because it will attract people," leading, in the view of another monk, to the "flourishing of Daoism in the whole world in forty to fifty years." Monks who hosted the tours also saw benefits for Daoism in China: "It will stimulate Chinese Daoists to study harder, give them confidence, and awaken them to the value of what they do"; in addition, "it can stimulate the interest of Chinese people who have no interest in Daoism: when they see foreigners doing it, it awakens their own interest."[5]

Indeed, perhaps more incongruous than the sight of Westerners engaging in supposedly Daoist practices is the fact that very few *Chinese* people do such things. It is unusual enough when a group of Westerners crowds into a quiet Chinese temple—how much more so when this same group begins practicing *qigong* in unison, under the puzzled and bewildered eyes of Chinese onlookers! In China, even Daoist monks never practice *qigong* in temple courtyards, let alone in airports. Even less do they hug trees! The unsettling incongruity, then, is that either (1) the Dream Trippers are completely mistaken about Daoism, pursuing nothing but their own imagined version of it; or (2) if what they are doing *is* truly Daoist, then why are most Chinese so ignorant of this tradition, why are monks so few to practice it, why are these "foreigners" more aware, or at least more earnest, in practicing Dao than most Chinese? Is it that (3) this *is* an aspect of Chinese culture, but one which Chinese rightly consider to be a foolish superstition, and have correctly abandoned and suppressed it? Or is it that (4) the Dream Trippers are doing something that is unquestionably Daoist, but in a new and innovative fashion? Depending on their intellectual and cultural biases, readers will find grounds to support any of the four suppositions in this book, and in the encounters we describe in this chapter.

Meeting as Equals?

Quanzhen monks, and educated Chinese in general—most of whom have little specific knowledge of Daoism other than general notions and feelings that they have gained from Chinese literature, philosophy, and poetry—typically consider it impossible for a foreigner to understand anything of Daoism. Master Hao once told the Dream Trippers that Chinese Daoist texts are so rich in meaning that "if you don't know Chinese, it will be hard for you to reach high levels of cultivation, because how can you come to a spiritual realization (*wudao*) of the deeper meanings of the Chinese text?"[6] An intuitive understanding of Daoism comes with being Chinese and knowing the Chinese language, and lacking that condition, it is unimaginable to have any true understanding of the Dao. When Quanzhen monks were impressed with a Westerner's understanding or attitude, they would often link this disposition to past or future lives. Thus, Master Hu told us that our present contact with Dao was the result of our having lived our past lives in the Song or Ming dynasties;[7] a monk in another monastery turned sternly to a Dream Tripper and told her that she would be reborn as Chinese in a next life, so that she could progress in her cultivation.[8]

Chen and Hu were personally fond of American Daoist tour organizers as friends, but they did not have a high view of their level of Daoist cultivation. Speaking of Mark Johnson, Chen said, "I really like him—he is very endearing. But he blindly follows the wrong teachings of his master. He is simply wrong on many counts, and doesn't want to listen. He even gets angry sometimes."[9] Chen was more impressed by Winn's conjugal loyalty, stating that "Winn is innocent like a child. He thinks he's so clever, even though he's not. But I have great respect for him because he was always so loyal to his wife. Even though she couldn't have a child from him, he remained faithful until she died."[10] But another time he said, "He is completely wrong, just flying around all over, even to India, and completely missing the point. That's why I told him that the most important is Daoist thought."[11] And Hu said of Mantak Chia's Seven Formulas of One Cloud, which Winn had described to him: "The method is very complicated, but good. I had a strong feeling when you described Level One, but no feeling when you described the other levels," hinting that Winn had not reached beyond Level One.[12]

Winn, however, does not see it this way. He was proud to be recognized by accomplished Chinese monks as one of the rare persons to know the highest secrets of Daoism:

When [Western practitioners] start asking high-level questions about internal alchemy, about *neidan*, Chinese people would look like, "What? How can these Westerners know these things? And they know these terms, the Chinese terms. How can they ask these questions?" I mean there was a real resistance, a real shock factor. It was like, "Wait a minute—these are our secrets. This is our stuff. How can you know about that?" Even Master Chen said, "Let's meditate together." . . . He called up his master and said, "Can I meditate with this guy? I have known him for seven years now." . . . And his teacher said, "Well, yes, OK. It sounds like he's alright, he is not going to contaminate you too badly." And then when we meditated, Master Chen was blown away. He said, "Wow, this is powerful." And then I started telling him about the formulas I was studying. He goes, you know, "Those are China's highest secrets. Nobody even in China knows this." There is a whole cultural assumption in China that a foreigner could not know these things. . . . The Daoists there said, "How can you guys be . . . Who taught you this? How could you know about all this stuff?" They had to get over that shock thing. And then, of course, after a while, they have been getting to know me—[they say] "This guy brings over people who are studying alchemy." This is like, "that's the reality."[13]

Master Chen, recollecting this incident, confirmed that he had indeed been surprised to discover that foreigners had systematized inner alchemy cultivation, showing that they had some level of knowledge. But "my surprise was partly out of politeness—I would never have said that nobody in China knows!"[14]

For Dream Trip organizers, awakening the Chinese to their own Daoist heritage was not a mere beneficial side effect of the tours, but a conscious objective. The trips also aimed to reactivate and domesticate the energies left behind by previous generations of cultivators and immortals, both within the mountain and among the Chinese people, as we have seen in chapter 2. Tour participants were given the role of "ambassadors of the Tao"; they had little interest in the religious expression of Daoism as it exists in Quanzhen monasticism, and saw themselves as practitioners of a "true" way they consider was lost in Communist China. This is a form of silent missionizing, then, in which the travelers, through their *qi*, inject a lost authenticity into the sites they pass through and, through their public practice of *qigong*, deliberately aim to shock Chinese observers into reconsidering their own spiritual tradition: "When forty foreigners come to cultivate at Qingkeping," said Winn, "more than doubling the population of Huashan valley, it shakes [the Chinese Daoists] and awakens them to the value of what they are doing."[15] At its most extreme, this attitude is expressed in highly Orientalist and chauvinist language: "The Chinese are more lost than Americans," said one group member, while another considered that: "The Daoists [in China] for the most part, except at Huashan, are far, far behind us practitioners in the West and they don't seem to care. . . . The Chinese people do not have any reverence for the sacred sites we visited. We went there and showed them what they could be again."[16] Or, in the words of another, "It's us the Americans that are going to preserve it. . . . We seem to be the historians. . . . Maybe we will ignite something."[17]

The posture of the American groups, then, is not one of mere sightseeing, nor of coming from afar to seek wisdom from true masters. The tours are not about China or about Chinese Daoism, but about connecting with an energy that is ignored by the Chinese and even most Daoists: "That's the whole point: the Dao is universal. The Chinese people walking on these mountains may or may not be connected to it, but that's not my concern," said Winn. What the groups are seeking is not the living Daoists of today, but the energies opened up by the cultivators of past eras: "That's why we come to China. The Daoists have been in communication with these nonhuman energies for thousands of years. The channel of communication has been opened by them. These energies exist elsewhere, but they have not been communicated with. Here, they are used to being communicated with over such a long time. We tread along a path that has already been treaded."

The Americans go to communicate with the mountain's energies, but not to learn from Quanzhen approaches to them. Far from it, they claim to possess the superior approach of Western science. Returning to Winn:

> The reason for the superiority of the West is that science opened up all the secrets and shared information, leading to the progress of science. In China, the culture of secret is what holds them back. Inner Alchemy will flourish and advance in the West because it is not smothered by the weight of history; it has nothing to do with Western culture. So in the West, the secrets will be opened, they will be shared, and they will stimulate the development of Inner Alchemy in China. It is just like the compass, gunpowder, and paper. It was not the Chinese who fully developed their applications, but the West.[18]

Winn is very explicit in stating, as we noticed in our own observations, that "the lack of interest in China's institutional Daoist orthodoxy is being led by serious Dream Trippers who have trained for 5, 10, 15 years in qigong and neidangong—as I have for 35 years."[19] The more they are seriously committed to their practice, the less they are interested in learning from the monks. "I don't want to learn to chant Chinese-language scripture, or play their ritual music, which is the main practice of many of the monks. I'm happy to witness what they do and share it with the Dream Trippers—but I know none of them are interested in learning those practices."[20] Although Louis Komjathy has published detailed studies of the inner alchemical texts of the early Quanzhen period, "I have seen no evidence of them being much known or practiced on Huashan or other mountains where I have interviewed many monks about neidan. And Chen Yuming would be the first to admit that he never received Quanzhen training in the 36 inner alchemical methods of the Gold Barrier and Jade Lock—he mostly cared about his humble teacher's virtue, which was NOT focused on inner alchemical method."[21] On this basis, Winn could claim that, by virtue of his technical mastery of the Seven Formulas of One Cloud, and of his transmission of *wujigong*, that he was more advanced in Daoist cultivation than most of the Quanzhen monks.

Winn approached the mountain as a technical expert on *qigong*, pleased to develop friendship *as an equal* with the Huashan monks. The talks and transmission of meditation techniques by monks at Huashan, which were included in the tour itinerary, were seen by him as more of an "exchange of views" between expert colleagues than as a transmission between master and student, as the monks expected. Speaking of some Daoist monks at another mountain who were impressed with Winn's knowledge of Huashan, he said, "This is part of the global interaction, learning to talk as equals" between Chinese and Western *neidan* practitioners.[22] On another occasion, he engaged in a technical criticism of the Shining Heart meditation taught by the monks, saying that "Westerners are not sufficiently grounded, so they should start with the *dantian*, not with the heart. Adjustments need to be made to fit the West. The Shining Heart method is suitable for people living in the mountains in isolation, where there are few complex methods and life is celibate. In modern, urban society, it is necessary to be better grounded, so that cultivation should begin at the lower *dantian*."

The Quanzhen monks, on the other hand, far from Winn's egalitarianism, stressed the relationship between a master and his disciples as a fundamental aspect of cultivation. This attitude contrasted with those of the Dream Trippers; for example, one of them, an acupuncturist from Asheville, told us, "I can understand that sometimes a master can give you mojo, push you on, but often you figure it out by doing it yourself, feeling the energy flows in the meridians. Becoming sensitive to different energy qualities and learning to work with them. This you can do yourself, without a master."[23]

But for Master Hu, when Dream Trippers mentioned embodied sensations or energy flows when practicing the Shining Heart meditation or listening to his stories, these responses were not only due to the power of the place and of the meditation techniques, but to the emerging relationship of the group to him as a master. "It's not just a question of transmitting techniques: *it is the power of the master that matters*. Without the master's power, without a lineage, all of these techniques are of no use."[24] While he was satisfied with the flows of energy between him and the group in these instances, he was critical of Westerners' general attitudes to cultivation. First was the tendency to question anything the master said: "Chinese disciples normally have deep faith without a trace of suspicion, because they know that no master would transmit a distorted teaching: to do so would be dangerous and lead to the divine punishment of the master. Westerners, on the other hand, ask objective questions, but show more suspicion, which interferes with the power of the information being transmitted." "The main difference between Chinese and American practitioners is that the Chinese don't ask questions, they just do it. But Americans will always ask many questions, they always want to know *why*. Only once they know, will they do it." By asking so many questions, the Trippers were not respecting them as "masters" in the way they expected from students or disciples. They noted this disrespect for hierarchies in other aspects of behavior as well: Master Chen related how, a few years earlier, he had accompanied five American *qigong* masters up Huashan—"reputedly five of the six top masters in the US"—and halfway up, owing to poor health, he had had difficulty climbing. The Americans had offered to conjoin their *qi* to heal him. "Of course, they were well intentioned, and it's a cultural difference, but in China the students of a traditional doctor would never claim that they could treat his master, nor would the students of a *gongfu* master ever propose to teach him a few moves." This Daoist, even though he had never met the American *qigong* masters before, had no formal relationship with them, and was younger than them, considered, by virtue of the fact that he was Chinese and an ordained Quanzhen monk, that he should automatically have been treated with the deference owed a master by his disciples—and that the disciples could not have the power to heal the master.

But this was not merely a question of respecting hierarchies. For Hu, any trace of skepticism has the effect of interfering with the flow of power from the master to the students, thus damaging the "energy field" (*qichang*) created through the encounter. Referring to an instance when a foreign group came with a skeptical interpreter who ruined the atmosphere, the "energy field was bad" and he didn't want to say anything.

An underlying agenda and attitudes set the stage for misunderstandings and tension between the Dream Trippers and their monastic hosts. Such, in any case, was the assumption we held at the beginning of this study. Considering the American pretensions to be preposterous, we assumed that they would be rejected out of hand by the Quanzhen monks, and that any communication between the two groups could be based only on misunderstanding. And the initial encounters confirmed our assumption—while graciously hosting and humoring the Dream Trippers, in their private comments to us, they were highly critical of the Dream Trippers, while maintaining a condescending attitude of tolerance and optimism that, over time, the Westerners would come to a better understanding of true Daoism.

When talking about *qigong* and other lay masters of Daoist techniques, be they Chinese or foreign, the Quanzhen Daoists always began by emphasizing that all ways lead to one, that some of them do have *gongfu* and transmit the true Dao, and that these practices contain "some very elementary elements of Daoism." As one of them said, "There is no pure Daoist entity in this world, separate from all else. *Qigong*, *taiji quan*, even yoga are passageways to Dao. Many people will come closer to Dao through these practices. Even though, once you have come close to Dao, you realize these things are not important." They saw the American Dream Trippers in much the same light as they saw Chinese *qigong* practitioners and the clients of lay spiritual entrepreneurs— with the added sins of being less deferential and mixing too many things together: excessively concerned with technique and not enough with virtue and the true purpose of cultivation; interested in only a small part of Daoism; and generally of a much lower level than themselves as holders of the full Daoist tradition incarnated in the Quanzhen order.

The Monks' Views on Cultivating Dao

The Quanzhen monks do not identify with the Chinese *qigong* movement or with American Daoism. Quanzhen Daoism at Huashan does not attempt to transform itself into a modern spirituality; in the encapsulated space it holds onto within modern political and economic structures, it remains firmly committed to tradition, to an eternal Dao, that can be known and approached only through the traditions, the genealogies, the masters, rituals, and institutions of the past. In the institutions of the Quanzhen order, Chinese *qigong* and commercialized Daoist health practices are not considered to be legitimate, orthodox forms of Daoism—for the same reasons that the monks criticized the motivations and attitudes of the Dream Trippers: they detached Daoist techniques from their grounding in Daoist faith, cosmology, ethics, ritual, and genealogy, instrumentalizing them for worldly goals of health or personal power.

Master Chen considered that the "Daoist" methods of cultivation popular in America are "simple exercises to which some Daoist terminology and mysticism have been added." Chen claimed that they are merely the "minor tricks" (*xiaoshu*) and "deviant ways" (*zuodao*) of the "sects and secret societies" (*huidaomen*), which "fraudulent masters" used to teach in the turbulent years of the early twentieth century, and which now dominate Daoism in Taiwan, having found legitimacy by claiming to be Daoist. "Now these types of teachings have spread to America," said Chen. "I like to discuss and teach to Westerners, in order to help to correct these distorted teachings, to prevent them from monopolizing the field simply because they were the first ones to spread there."[25]

Indeed, in a subtle fashion, in their talks to the Dream Trippers, and more explicitly in private discussions with us, the Quanzhen monks emphasized that Daoist cultivation cannot be reduced to the practice of the inner alchemical and *qi*-circulation techniques that the Westerners were drawn to. In various contexts and conversations, they repeatedly mentioned that "all these techniques are useless" in the absence of Daoist faith and thought, virtue and morality, lineage and master, and the practice of religious rituals. For them, the practice of techniques could only be understood within the context of *xiulian*, a term commonly translated as "cultivation," which includes the notions, in the character *xiu*, of gradual ordering and perfecting, and in the character *lian*, refinement through smelting, as in the transmutation of elements in the alchemical furnace. The body is the main crucible of *xiulian*, aiming for the transmutation of its unrefined substance into an ethereal, immortal body. A high level of cultivation is typically referred to as *gongfu*, in which the term *gong* can perhaps best be translated as virtuosity, combining the notions of both virtue and skill, and is demonstrated through moral selflessness and extraordinary capacities in wisdom, healing, and compassion.

The experiences of the body and of sacred places are significant only insofar as they can help to draw the practitioner into the Daoist cosmology, and within that cosmology, to further progress toward the ultimate generative Origin. But this cosmology is more than an abstract system of symbols that could be learned intellectually; it can only be penetrated through a comprehensive path of cultivation, which begins with faith in the Immortals—a "faith in supernatural beings, which is the root of virtue, since actions in this world are related to a larger world—otherwise, techniques are of little value." For the Quanzhen monks, this path thus entails, in addition to practicing body techniques, an orientation, through what they call "faith" (*xinyang*) or "thought" (*sixiang*), toward the ultimate goal and stages of the path; the practice of ritual; the embodiment of virtue; and connection to a lineage and discipleship to a master.

Through this discourse on cultivation, the Quanzhen Daoists define themselves in opposition to lay masters and practitioners, be they Chinese or foreign, of Daoist *techniques* such as *qigong*, inner alchemy, martial arts, Chinese medicine, or even sexual cultivation. While the Quanzhen monks don't object to these techniques per se, what they object to is the instrumental use of the techniques, in which the techniques themselves are practiced to achieve a specific goal. The very characteristics that enable these techniques to easily lend themselves to modern, even scientific, instrumental rationality, and have thus become so popular in modern culture—both in China and the West—is what the Quanzhen Daoists refuse: true cultivation, for them, springs from inner motivation or spiritual nature; but it can be expressed, trained, and refined through a variety of practices and techniques. "The main issue in Daoist cultivation is *xinxing* (heart-nature), *dao* and *de* (virtue). This is the difference with *qigong*," said Master Chen. No technique can intrinsically lead to or enhance cultivation, and practicing techniques for instrumental goals does not automatically lead to progress in cultivation. This requires refinement of motivation, for which the nurturing of faith, the understanding of Daoist thought, the strengthening of moral virtues, the emulation of a master, and the practice of ritual are essential. The search for rapid results in the practice of *qigong* was also criticized: Master Hao recounted the story of a young *qigong* adept who, in the early 1990s, had resolved to stay in a cave at Huashan for six months, doing *bigu*—a fasting technique in which one completely or partially stops eating, taking nourishment exclusively from *qi*. "I tried to convince him to eat, but he was stubborn. He wanted to achieve in a few months a level that takes a lifetime of cultivation. You think you can become a high-level cultivator just after reading two books? He wanted to go too fast. In the end this boy gave up and started eating."

From this perspective, body and meditation practices are but partial elements of a much broader and deeper process of Daoist cultivation. "Some people will take little parts or techniques and use them for their own profit. But Daoism is a whole, like Chinese medicine: you can't just take the foot or part of the body in isolation. *Qigong* is like Western medicine, it can only improve symptoms temporarily, while it cannot reach the root," said Master Hu. For Master Chen, speaking of peoples' excitement at feeling flows of *qi* during *qigong* practice,

> I am not willing to talk about the experience of *qi*, which is a rather narrow thing; it's like when a new song comes out, your soul is moved by it; it's an emotional response. Many people feel . . . this experience of *qi* is such a great thing. I think, well, you have forgotten the most beautiful thing; this experience of *qi*, it might be like a song that expresses painful things. You are so happy to hold onto the feeling of *qi*, but that just shows that you are not standing from the perspective of a human being, you are not even at the level of a common animal—even plants have feelings. You can only say it's *qi*, that's too basic! We have a saying that goes: "Vitality begins in the intention; and ends in the *qi*" (Zaiyi zehuo, zaiqi zezhi). You need to understand the meaning of intention, and not keep turning around the *qi*.[26]

From this perspective, the most important thing in Daoism, Master Chen claimed, is Daoist thought (*sixiang*); techniques are secondary. The thought should govern the techniques, and not the other way around. Winn, however, disagreed. "Westerners have very structured mindsets, so they need to be presented with a structured system. If you give them 'Dao' and 'nonaction' right away, they won't accept it. But if you give them a technical system, then they might enter it, and then take an interest in Dao."[27] Chen concurred that in China, historically, it has been the same. But "without the focus on Daoist thought, the result is only common people who may be slightly healthier. There is a tendency in both China and the West to focus on the technical aspects of Daoism, ignoring its core of thought: but this is of no use."

At the same time, the monks did emphasize religious practices per se, but extending beyond body and meditation techniques, to acts of worship as well. "Those who consider that rituals have no connection with cultivation are completely wrong," said Master Hu. Using terms that became common in the *qigong* movement in the 1980s and 1990s, he continued, "The rituals are a form of cultivation. During the Dipper ritual, I was adding information (*xinxi*) to give energy (*nengliang*) to your group." Master Chen noted that Daoism had lost much of its spirit in recent centuries, paying too much attention to outer forms: "In early Daoism, the truest Daoism, there was much less emphasis on outer forms. But over the centuries, outer forms have increasingly accumulated. Until the Ming and Qing dynasties, when this led to the decline of Daoism, and Daoism began to look more and more like Buddhism." At the same time, however, he stressed that the outer forms remain essential: "The problem of people trying to take some techniques and ignore the religion is common, also in China. They try to make a division between 'Daoist philosophy' (*daojia*) and 'Daoist religion' (*daojiao*). So people are surprised that I emphasize that outer forms are not important, but at the same time I say that customs such as burning incense, and popular forms of worship, are essential. Even many Daoists say that such things are unimportant. But if that is so, why have they been transmitted down for so many centuries? There must be a deep significance to such acts."

In the same vein, the organic unity of the Daoist tradition must be respected: commenting on one American he knew who was interested in *qigong*, in tai chi, in Taoism, Tibetan Buddhism, Hinduism, and Christianity, Master Chen said:

It's a trend, and inevitable with the increased communications: people pick a little here and there, I like this and I like that. It's all patched together. While it's inevitable nowadays, it can also be dangerous. Although it is true that all religions have the same essence, most people don't have the ability to make a proper judgment. At a very superficial level, such as different martial artists showing their different methods to each other, it's no problem, but if you were actually to mix the methods together, it wouldn't work. Only masters at a very high level can do it, because they are from a higher position, from which they have a broader perspective, and know what is good and what isn't. They know what the highest principle is, so they know what conforms to that principle. But the average person doesn't know what is important to look for, so they can't wisely pick and choose from different traditions. New religions are typically founded by people who have already a high level of accomplishment in the existing tradition, and have already transcended that tradition and are no longer limited by any religions. Such religions are long lasting. But it is certainly not people who dabble in different traditions, much less who sell courses and training programs with various techniques who will create something long lasting![28]

The comments of the Quanzhen monks thus expressed a constant back-and-forth between an emphasis on detachment, on the formless nature of the Dao, the invisible nature of cultivation, and the intrinsic uselessness of outer forms, and, on the other hand, an emphasis on the essential importance of these outer forms as vehicles for the expression of Daoist cultivation.

Similarly, speaking of virtue, Chen elaborated and emphasized the importance of cultivating virtue (*de*) as a precondition of Daoist cultivation: "Without this foundation, the cultivation of techniques is useless." Hu mentioned that many schools of Dao, *qigong*, and martial arts are fake, merely outward forms, since they lack the cultivation of virtue as the foundation.

From the questions asked by the Dream Trippers, and from our interviews with them, we know that virtue is not an explicit preoccupation for them, nor are masters or lineages: their chief interest is experiencing the *qi* of the mountain, and secondly, to learn meditation techniques. In one anecdote related by Master Chen, he had been hired by a Russian Daoist tour group to take them to famous Daoist sites. "They were glad to learn techniques and mantras, but whenever I spoke about virtue and thought, they smirked and frowned. I told them how important it was, that without cultivating the heart (*xinxing*) all the rest was useless, but they continued to frown. Later they came to me to expressly tell me to stop talking about morality! I felt sorry for them."

Winn's group was less blunt, and he stressed that his *wujigong* method does emphasize virtue, such as the virtue of the heart, of the liver, spleen, lung, and kidney. By *virtue* he meant the powers of the five functional systems associated with the five organs in the Chinese cosmological body, and the manipulation of these powers through meditation techniques—but what Master Chen meant in his talk was virtue in the sense of moral behavior: to always be considerate of others, to do meritorious deeds and virtuous acts, and to adhere to moral behavior, justice, loving respect, filial piety, service, giving, and generosity. For them, the practice of *xiulian* involved not only drawing the consciousness of the practitioner into a higher sensitivity of the organism in relation to its physical environment, but also of its behavior in relation to other people during each moment of life. Such comments reflect the mainstream Quanzhen view on the old debate in Daoism concerning the appropriate balance between *xing* (cultivating one's spiritual purity) and *ming* (refining and prolonging the life of the body), in which *xing* is valued over *ming*.

Winn agreed that "without a mission or sense of *de* [virtue], cultivating one's *qi* is ultimately pointless." But he stressed that "the Daoist sense of *de* arises from within, it is not granted by external/social religious authority," and thus he did not consider it appropriate to "impose myself as an outside authority" by telling practitioners about morality.[29]

The centrality of virtue in the discourse of cultivation can be seen in some of the monks' views on Daoist sexual practices. Michael Winn commented that Master Chen, who had left a deep impression on many of the American group members, owed his accomplishment to his residing on the mountain and absorbing its *qi*, and that he would not be able to achieve the same level in a big city. And, from the standpoint of a Westerner with no hang-ups about sex, and whose career as a promoter of Daoism, in contrast to Quanzhen precepts, *began with* teaching sexual cultivation, he commented on the sexual difficulties of celibate monks. Mantak Chia's and Michael Winn's first books placed sexual cultivation at the *beginning* of the stages of practice. They have published popular books on how to master sexual energy and achieve higher levels of orgasm, with alluring titles such as *Taoist Secrets of Love: Cultivating Male Sexual Energy*, *The Multi-Orgasmic Man*, and *The Multi-Orgasmic Woman*.[30] Master Hu, in contrast, stressed that sexual alchemy is only transmitted to a tiny minority of practitioners, and in our society, with its lecherous morals, is transmitted even less. For Chen, "Many people teach sexual practices (*shuangxiu*) as a form of cultivation. Actually, it's just an excuse for nourishing their sexual appetites. Those methods of the arts of the bedchamber are not necessary for young people in their prime; they are only for old people with weakened sexual stamina. For cultivation, *shuangxiu* techniques are taught only at the highest level, to those who have *already mastered* their sexual appetite."

In the invisible realm of Daoist cultivation, both sides might always consider themselves to be right. But if there was one area in which the monks could *prove* their superiority, it was in the martial arts. One evening during the 2012 Dream Trip, in the Emerald Cloud Monastery of the Western Peak, there had been some arm wrestling matches between one of the Americans, a rather stout and well-built young man, and some of the local staff working in the monastery, who were all much smaller than the American. Most of the matches were a draw, but the American beat the Chinese on a few occasions. The long, drawn-out jousts attracted crowds of onlookers among the tourists and staff at the monastery, who started betting on the matches. The Daoist monks peered at the action from their windows. At this point a monk came out, performed a theatrical martial arts display, challenged the American to an arm wrestle, subjugated him within one quick second, performed another kung fu flourish, and disappeared back into his quarters. The point had been made: the monk's superior virtuosity had saved China's honor.

Questions of Money

From their position of superiority and in their capacity as hosts, the monks were willing to receive financial payments from the Dream Trippers—but they had different understandings of the nature of the exchange. Winn operated as a businessman, willing to pay, but also to bargain for a cheaper price. For the monks, the "payment" should take the form of a "donation," should not be the subject of bargaining, and should not be perceived as a money-making opportunity. Chen explained that he told Winn that other temples had heard rumors that Huashan was hosting foreign groups for free; they were concerned that this might be creating expectations among the Dream Trippers for a free service. The other temples considered that Huashan might have the resources to host them for free, but they were poor and would not be able to do so. So Chen told Winn that he would need to make a "donation" (*bushi*) for the Dream Trippers' visit to Huashan. In 2004, the total "donation" amounted to around US$1,600, to cover room and board in the monasteries, as well as for the cost of sending workers to clean the caves and have wooden cots placed in them for the meditators. For a later Dream Trip, however, the Daoists' "understanding" was that Winn would provide a "donation" of 1,000 yuan (around US$150), a much smaller amount, since the caves did not need to be refurbished this time. But Winn only offered some tea to the monk managing the Jade Spring Temple. So, when the Dream Trippers arrived at the monastery where they were to spend the night, the monks there asked for 2,000 yuan. Winn refused to pay, so the monks refused to let him go. Only after this stand-off lasted for some time did he relent, and agree to pay the 2,000 yuan. Chen stated, "If he had given the donation of 1,000 yuan to the Jade Spring Monastery, he wouldn't have needed to pay 2,000 yuan at Qingkeping!"

As a businessman, Winn would not let himself be swindled. On one occasion, he claimed to have been cheated of 5,000 yuan (around US$800) from another monk. He made a formal complaint about the incident to the chairman of the China Daoist Association, which conducted an investigation and exonerated the monk. "All the Daoists closed ranks," said Winn. "Everyone is losing face here. So they had to basically try to cover it up."[31]

After Chen had left Huashan, he charged Winn 1,000 yuan per day for time spent with Dream Trippers. Once, Winn proposed to Chen that they could cooperate by running a venture like the famous Chinese Daoist *qigong* master Wang Liping—perhaps the most famous *qigong* master still active in China after the Falun Gong crackdown—who charges 800 yuan (around US$100) per day per person for weeklong courses, and US$800 per person per day for foreigners. "Winn says that we could make lots of money that way. He is too interested in money. I told him that I can work with him, and continue the way we work now, and I charge 1,000 yuan per day no matter how large your group is. I don't want to operate like Wang Liping. . . . Winn says, 'I am a businessman.' How can someone who claims to be doing Daoist cultivation say something like that?"[32] It was over Winn's approach to money that Chen ultimately decided not to continue his relationship with him; and for the same reason, he ended his collaboration with the Belgian who had been inviting him to give workshops in Europe.

Michael Winn did make arrangements in 2012 to meet with Wang Liping—until Wang signified that he would charge US$1,600 per hour of chatting together. That was the end of Winn's attempts to connect with his entrepreneurial counterparts in China. The Dream Trippers continued to meet with monks of the Quanzhen monastic order, who wear exotic robes and headdresses, who don't charge a fee for becoming "spiritual commodities" in the package tours—but who are sensitive about the "donations" they expect.

Transnational Communitas

Given the Huashan monks' perception of and attitudes toward the American Dream Trippers, we might conclude that they would humor them as fellow wayfarers for a few days, collect their donations, sigh with relief when they left, and go back to their flutes, chess games, and soap operas. Indeed, the *institutional* attitude of Huashan as a Quanzhen monastic community and socialist work-unit could perhaps be thus characterized. But for the *individual* Daoist monks who had close dealings with the Americans, over time a human and spiritual bond did emerge, leading them out of their aloof condescension to attempt to engage with the foreigners on a deeper level. Indeed, some of the Quanzhen monks were coming closer to the Westerners' point of view, while taking a more critical stance toward their own tradition. This growing attraction was partly the result of the natural affection that grows between friends from afar after repeated visits. But it was strongly reinforced by what we might term moments of "communitas," when conversations between both sides not only broke through the barriers of their respective cultures and expectations, but even created an almost hallucinatory sense of breaking out of the limits of the ordinary world and entering a dreamland of true Immortals.

The anthropologist Victor Turner described a social modality that may occur when people are in a liminal state, having temporarily stepped out of the social structure that defines their roles and identities. In this condition, culturally defined distinctions such as status, reputation, class, caste, or sex cease to be operational, and people experience undifferentiated, egalitarian, and direct interactions that he calls "communitas."[33]

When we began this project, with the initial aim of observing and analyzing encounters, we assumed they could only be based on mutual misunderstanding. This was also the attitude of most of the Chinese monks, even as they humored the American visitors by welcoming their tours and offering them simple teachings. And it is the firm conviction of many scholars. But, as the research advanced, we came to question this assumption: we witnessed several moments of this "transnational communitas," which seemed to indicate the possibility of real communication at the level of shared understanding of experience. These enchanting exchanges show that, in spite of vast differences in cultural backgrounds and expectations, when the Dream Trippers and the Quanzhen monks met, there *could be*, at a basic level, a real connection—because Daoist body cultivation produces experiences which, though subjective and unique to each individual, are similar enough that both Western and Chinese Daoists could talk about them and understand what each other was talking about. There is something universal about the human body, about the possibility of generating experience, and about techniques that can generate such experiences, even when they come from very different social and cultural worlds.

More than this, however, is the sense of yearning that emerged among some Chinese monks for further interactions with the Westerners. The Dream Trippers, naïve and ignorant as they may be of the Daoist tradition, meet the monks with an innocence which comes precisely from their lack of Chinese historical, cultural or political baggage—a shared and often painful burden which many Chinese carry with them, Daoist or not, and which causes many of their interactions to be infected with mutual suspicion and contests of "face," as we described in the previous chapter. The freshness, the simplicity, the unscripted, surprising moments of these encounters offered members of both groups new experiences of the transcendent. Traversing boundaries, the anthropologist Thomas Csordas suggests, can be a transcendent experience. Thus, the *transnational* and the *transcendent* are both mutually reinforcing and constitutive.[34] More than instances of the circulation and interaction of Daoist practitioners and techniques, the encounters we describe here are instances of "transnational transcendence"—liminal encounters which, however momentarily, thrust the participants out of their localized pathways and routines, and produced new, unexpected intimations of the transcendence they seek in their spiritual practice.

To understand how these moments of transnational communitas oc-curred, we may reflect on how the conversation between two or more individuals involves the constant generation of a world of consciousness between them. We can consider the metaphor of birds singing, used by Master Chen to describe his communication with fellow monks:

> Once some monks came to debate about scriptures with me. I refused. They asked me why? I said: In a tree, there are many birds, some of which sing beautiful melodies, others that sing plain melodies, but all are free to sing their melodies in that tree. Now if a phoenix were to land on that tree, can one possibly compare the song of that phoenix with those of the smaller birds? Can they possibly sing together? If the phoenix were to begin chanting, all the other birds should quiet down and listen. But the phoenix won't sing, because it has just landed on the tree for a moment, on its way to fly elsewhere.[35]

In this particular instance, the speaker was implying that his level of spiritual accomplishment was so high that, like a phoenix, he would never lower himself to sing with the common birds. We may consider the idea that when there is harmony and compatibility between the different species of birds singing in the tree, the result is a beautiful symphony—but that when there is no such harmony, it is better to keep silent and move on. In the moments of communitas we describe below, the Quanzhen monks—who can be said to have seen themselves as phoenixes—joined the Americans in "singing together" and were unexpectedly carried away by the melodies that resulted.

For Master Hu, the relationship with a master must be one of absolute belief, without a trace of suspicion or doubt. Any trace of skepticism has the effect of interfering with the flow of power from the master to the students, thus damaging the "energy field" (qichang) created through the encounter. In contrast to the Greek and Western tradition of seeking after the truth through doubt and debate, Master Hu's insistence on unquestioning belief aimed not to blindly impose some dogma, but to open the field for the mutual generation of another world, through an untrammeled communication of the imagination, of feelings, and even, through qi sensations, of somatic energies: a total fusion, orchestrated by the master, in which he and his disciples carry themselves away into the worlds they have coelaborated—realms in which the laws and limitations of this world do not apply.

Such worlds cannot be coelaborated without mutual reinforcement between the master and his audience. Responses indicating receptivity—and physical reactions such as tears or sensations of qi—are positively reinforced as markers of progress. Those who have strong reactions are seen as having great potential. For the disciple, the reactions are signs of the master's power; for the master, they are signs of the disciple's receptivity. For both, they are signs of the reality of the alternate world they are drawing themselves into; in fact, they are signs of the relationship's efficacy. When the signs are strong, both may thus nudge each other further, augmenting the reactions and their significance. What these experiences showed Hu was that Americans, too, could be receptive; they could count among the "cocreators" he needed to pursue his journeys in the alternate worlds.

The Goddess of Liberty

A small group of about eight Dream Trippers, among the more intense meditators and adventurous travelers, set out for an optional few days in the Dream Trip itinerary: while the rest of the travelers remained on the Huashan peaks to enjoy the views, this small group would spend the time meditating in caves, in a secluded spot on another mountain directly facing Huashan. They hiked down the Western flank of Huashan, two hours down steps sometimes carved into vertical cliffs, to the head of Huashan valley, and then back up the slope of a neighboring mountain, along a muddy path through woods leading to the cave complex of the Cloud Platform tended by Master Hao.

Hao, with his wispy beard, twinkling eyes, and flowing Daoist robe, darted around the rocks and ledges like a mountain goat. Easily provoked into rolling laughter, he was visibly happy at the arrival of visitors from so far away. He showed the caves to the meditators, who unrolled their sleeping bags in the Cave of Purple Tenuity, the Cave of the Three Origins, and the Cave of the Dipper Mother. Some of them made a vow of silence and fasting for three days of intensive meditation, rarely coming out of their caves, while others were there simply for a new experience. At meal times, Master Hao eagerly distributed stale buns and rice porridge with slices of potato, and asked the participants, with curiosity and humor, about their Sufism, their shamanism, their martial arts, and their sexual liberation, and waxed lyrical about their Statue of Liberty.

In Chinese, the Statue of Liberty is translated as the "Goddess of Liberty" (*ziyou nüshen*). While the term "goddess" is in this case generally understood metaphorically, many Daoist monks seem to consider her to be a living goddess. Master Hu once stated, "Only some people in the West, such as the Goddess of Liberty and Jesus, have reached a high level, they are Immortals. But they have not reached the highest realms of Dao."[36] Master Hao enthusiastically explained that the Goddess of Liberty is a manifestation of the Dipper

Mother (*Doumu*), one of the supreme goddesses of Daoism. "The Dipper Mother has four faces and eight arms, symbolizing the multiplicity of her functions. She can separate herself and multiply herself. Just like, from one peach tree, I can then plant many peach trees. In the same way, the Goddess of Liberty is a manifestation of the Dipper Mother. She is spreading the spirit of liberty around the world. Thanks to her, we are here, people from the United States, China, Canada, Mexico, all talking about Dao together."[37]

The Shaman and the Wooden Fish

One afternoon, Hao was chatting with Larry, a tall, long-haired, dark-skinned man in his forties hailing from Colorado; in his appearance and demeanor a member of the counterculture, an experienced meditator who specialized in Native Shamanism.

Larry had a gift for Hao, a metal bowl with a stick for striking it. "The days spent here have meant a lot to me, I would like to give you this gift," he said.

"Oh, thank you, thank you!" exclaimed Hao, as he struck the bowl and listened to its chimes. "What scriptures do you recite?"

Larry thought a while and replied, "I ask the mountain and it tells me its secrets."

"Oh, very good, very good!" Hao's excitement grew. "There is a country in the northeast, where they practice the religion of shamanism (*Samanjiao*), and don't recite scriptures." (Interestingly, he and Larry hadn't conversed before and he didn't know that Larry was precisely a "shaman.") He started striking the bowl, improvising a rhythm as he went along, appearing to enter a different mental state. He then went into his hut and came back with an old, worn *muyu* or "wooden fish"—a hollow wooden instrument, shaped like a carved fish, that is used to strike a cadence in Buddhist and Daoist temples when monks chant scriptures. He offered the *muyu* to Larry.

"I have used it a lot, it has numinous power" (*ling*).

"I have also used the bowl often in shamanistic rituals. What's this? Why is it called a wooden fish?"

"There was a man cultivating near a river," replied Hao. "In the river there was a fish cultivating, and near him there was a tree cultivating. The fish and the tree were interfering with the man's cultivation. So an Immortal told him to chop down the tree and kill the fish with it. That's what he did, and thus the wooden fish came into being. Now he could cultivate without interference."

At this moment, a huge flying bug, looking like an oversized, four-inch-long bee, buzzed past.

"Do you know what that is?" exclaimed Hao. "It's an ant!"

When we looked puzzled—showing that we hadn't completely entered Hao's world—he looked at us sternly. "You can't understand! It's an ant that has been cultivating for ten years. Ever since it has been here, I have been watching it. [Pointing at Larry] He understands!"

Around the shaman's bowl, the wooden fish, and the giant flying ant, a complicity was established between Hao and Larry, about a world they could understand and communicate about, a secret world that mystifies outsiders.[38]

The Martial Artists

In another exchange, the rapport was created through bodily contact, in demonstrating martial arts moves. This occurred between Hao and Nicolo, a martial arts instructor from Mexico City, a stout, middle-aged man in sunglasses who made no secret of his fascination for Daoist sexual techniques, even taking pleasure in describing his experimentation with them. Nicolo had been practicing martial arts for over twenty years, and is now a martial arts instructor. He has studied many martial arts forms, but now specializes in Wing Chun, transmitted from Hong Kong, which is one of the forms practiced by Bruce Lee. By his account, it was founded by a nun who was one of the only survivors of Shaolin temple after it was overrun by the Manchus. She had devised a soft form of martial arts to resist the oppressor. Her first four generations of disciples were women. The form includes a technique through which, by pressing a finger on an acupoint of the adversary's body, the adversary can be killed. It was a secret technique, which was not to be transmitted to foreigners. Nicolo's teacher's master was reportedly killed by the Triads after he revealed this secret to foreign students.

"Can you demonstrate?" asked Hao, as if to challenge Nicolo.

The Mexican gave a display of his martial arts method, in three different sets. The first set involved only movements of the wrists and hands, the other sets involved more complete movements. After that, he demonstrated some combat moves with his student Isaac, a thirty-two-year-old Mexican Jewish film director who often spoke of his past dreadlocks and rave parties, but now looked very clean-cut and preppy. During the demonstration, Hao also joined in, playfully fighting Nicolo back with light hand strokes.

Hao applauded, saying they weren't bad at all. "You are a good master," he told Nicolo, and, turning to Isaac: "you be a good disciple." In this encounter, the connection was made through the sight and contact of bodies as, for an hour, Hao and the Mexicans joined the same field of *gongfu* practice.[39]

The Elixir of the Western Seas

Another connection was made through discussing a common interest in herbs. Mark, an Asheville resident who went by the name of "Blackfeather," is a stout, slightly chubby, red-haired and bearded man in his late twenties, a student at the Daoist Traditions College of Chinese Medical Arts in Asheville, NC. His parents own a company that imports South American herbal medicines to the United States; since the age of twelve he has been surrounded by herbal culture, attending many herbal conferences and exhibitions since childhood.

"Is there such a thing as Western herbal medicine?" Hao asked him. "Yes," replied Blackfeather, who explained that Western herbs lack the theoretical system of Traditional Chinese Medicine, and that he was trying to integrate Western herbs into it. In Western herbology, he explained, herbs are applied to an essentially biomedical view of the mind and body. But several times, their transmission almost disappeared. First it was the Catholic Church, then biomedicine, which tried to stamp it out, because they wanted control. The "illuminati" have always wanted to stop it, he claimed. But now, said Blackfeather, there is a revival of Western herbs, because now everyone knows that pharmaceutical companies are trying to stop herbs only to make money, for their patents.

"Next time you come, bring me a Western herb!" said Hao.

Blackfeather pulled an herb from his wallet: "Here. This is called Osha. It's good for pimples, skin rash, athletes foot—"

Hao was getting visibly excited. "Next time, come here and we will research together to integrate Chinese and Western herbs!" After more conversation, he asked, "Is there a Western alchemical drug (*danyao*)?"

"Yes, there is," replied Blackfeather. "It has mostly been lost, but still exists among the Indians of South America. How about the Chinese alchemical pill of immortality?"

"It has also been lost. In ancient Daoist texts, there is mention of the elixir pill of the Western Seas (*xiyang danyao*), but nobody knows what it is. . . . There is also mention of the 'Immortal from the Western Seas' (*xiyang xianren*). . . . Next time, come with your herbs and we will research together the Elixir of the Western Seas! I feel that, through you, the Immortal from the Western seas is coming near!" Hao laughed with great excitement.

He went into his cave and brought out a bag of an herbal medicine called "white pine bark" (*songbaipi*), which he offered to Blackfeather. "This is bark from a rare type of white pine. I have collected it myself."

Hao and Blackfeather continued their animated conversation, fellow herbalists "talking shop." Blackfeather was inspired to come the following year with some of his fellow students of herbology. They would talk herbs with Master Hao, help with his gardening, and build him an outhouse. He was also tempted to initiate him to LSD: he had a piece of the drug on him. "He seems to be asking for it, always talking about the Western elixir. . . . The concoction of LSD is a truly alchemical process." For Blackfeather, the Western Elixir spoken of by Master Hao was nothing other than LSD. But he hesitated to give it to him without being able to communicate with him, to guide him on his "trip."

A few days after the Dream Trip ended and most of the participants returned to the United States, Blackfeather, who stayed a week longer in China, returned alone to Master Hao's caves. But this time, Master Hao was not in the usual jovial mood. He seemed sad, for some unclear reason. There was no "communitas" this time, and Blackfeather left Master Hao, wondering. He did not return to Huashan.[40]

The Cave Dream

One Dream Tripper, Caroline, a massage therapist and mother of three sons, saw deep spiritual teachers in the world of nature. As we walked up the mountain path leading to the Cloud Platform, we spotted a lizard basking on a stone. "Look at him meditating! He is teaching us! What a gift!" she exclaimed. Later in the evening, she mentioned that she had seen a cicada, and treated it as a teacher. The rhythm of its song—three short chirps, followed by a long one—was a meditative form.

Caroline stayed with her husband in a cave directly facing Huashan. The first night, she had a powerful dream that led her to discover, the next morning, an old stele lying against the cliff near the cave entrance:

> Our first night in the cave, we had slept on the altar. There were no statues or deities—nobody in the cave. So we had made offerings the night before in our cave. Each of us who was spending the night in the cave, walked in and spoke to the energy or the energies that may have been present in the cave, and made our little ritual. This is what is important to me. [On the altar I put] the picture of [my] three boys. The wheel of the I-Ching, that is important to me—my favorite card picture of the eight immortals. This is me. This is us. Oh, I had found a cicada shell. I put that up there. I found something else too, maybe a pine cone or some needles or something nature gift, some elementals. I put them all on the altar. And then that night, I had a dream with the energy of the cave in it. Inside the cave there was a beautiful deity on the altar. In my dream, I saw somebody who was creating this lineage of what this cave is, who is this cave, and what it represents. I remember feeling the energy of the people who had created that cave, what it meant to them, and how they wanted it to be

honored again, and how they wanted a representation presented, and they
wanted someone to be a temple keeper back at that cave, and to come back
and make offerings in the cave. Oh, my God, it's wonderful! I can't stay and
be a temple keeper, but I hope someone does come to be a temple keeper. It's
kind of the energy I found. And all I could hear was this noise, like a tap on the
rock. I'm like, someone is pounding on the rocks. And the next thing I know I
awoke in my dream to watch a person sitting there in the cave, creating a stele,
pounding on the rock. . . . He was showing me that this cave had been dedicated, and had history and lineage. And I'm like, where is the marker? He told
me that it was right outside the cave. . . . When I woke up that morning, I saw
the stele outside the cave, in two pieces, leaning up against the rock face, just
sitting there, being eroded. What had happened to them? Why weren't they
inside the cave anymore? Why weren't there deities anymore?[41]

In another dream the second night, Caroline saw herself sitting in a courtyard
by the temple, wearing traditional Chinese clothes, having tea with Immortals. And she also saw a shining polar star—the Northern Dipper that is the
most significant constellation in Daoism.

Caroline asked Master Hao about the meaning of these dreams. He told her,

The star you saw was a star of blessing, shining from above. You have a strong
predestined affinity (*yuanfen*) with this place. You are amazing! In Daoism, we
can often see dreams of the future, but these dreams should not be unsealed.
Dreams are signs from the spirits, just as the changes of the weather, but the
common people should not know. . . . With a high level of cultivation, we see
our dreams, and through them, we come to a sudden understanding of the
will of the gods, and we try our best to put it into practice—but without telling
people.[42]

Caroline told me that in her whole life, nobody until now had been able
to understand her dreams. She had never been able to share her dreams with
others and be understood. But, she said, "Master Hao understood," as tears
came to her eyes.[43]

"Mr. Mohammad"

Moments of bonding usually occurred when they were least expected, while,
at other times when both sides consciously attempted to establish a more enduring relationship, they failed. For example, the case of Marvin Rubinstein,
a short, balding Jewish man with glasses, in his early fifties, very earnest in his
appearance and speech, who, in addition to being a *qigong* instructor, ran a
Sufi center in Seattle. He had placed the portrait of his guru on the altar in the
Cave of Purple Tenuity. He told Hao that his students had given him money

to donate to a charitable cause, and that he had decided to donate the funds to the interfaith meditation center Hao had spoken of building at the Cloud Platform, as we discuss further below. "I have been practicing *qigong* for thirty years and teaching it for twenty. I know many *qigong* forms and have inner experience, but what I lack is lineage. One reason I came to Huashan is to find lineage. Can you help me?" "No problem!" replied Hao. "We will have a ritual, and donors like yourself will be invited. All will wear special robes, and after the ritual you will be given a certificate, just like a university diploma." "What are the requirements? How long must one study?" Hao didn't answer the question, stressing that this would be a collective undertaking, that everyone will decide together how to organize it. "All the major investors will be able to take part in the ritual."

Rubinstein then told him about his Sufi practice.

"Just last week I felt that Mohammad would come," exclaimed Hao. "And when I saw you I saw the shadow of Mohammad around you. Isn't that true? Am I not right? You are the successor of Mohammad!"

"Yes and no. I do not transmit the type of Islam practiced by most Muslims."

"You are the only true successor of Mohammad."

"No, there are many others."

"But you are the only true one. May you spread the teaching of Mohammad far and wide! Mr. Mohammad, together we can build this meditation center that will spread religious culture around the world." They then talked more about Sufism, Hao always addressing Rubinstein as "Mr. Mohammad," and then Hao talked more about his plans for building a meditation retreat. Addressing the five or six Dream Trippers who were present, he said: "In this religious retreat, it will not be necessary to become a monk. To be a follower (*xintu*) will be sufficient. Would you like to become followers?" There was a long silence among the foreigners. Marvin hesitated, "Er, maybe. . . ."

Hao, the lone hermit at the Cloud Platform, lived with the fantasy of building an international multireligious meditation retreat, to which believers from all religions around the world could come together, worship, and cultivate. "Not for anybody, but for cultivators." He tried to draw the Dream Trippers into his dream, and was particularly excited when Marvin's philanthropic plans seemed to fit with his own. But in the end, Marvin told us he had decided not to contribute: this type of lineage affiliation wasn't exactly what he had in mind.[44]

Hao claimed to already have friends and supporters in Shenzhen and Taiwan raising funds for his project. It would be a special meditation center, an organization that would bring unity to all the world's religions—because all of the Immortals, including Laozi, Mohammad, Chen Tuan, and the Goddess of Liberty promote the ideal of the "free man." While his plans sound grandiose, when asked about the specifics, he talks about rebuilding the roof of his hut (done), repairing the front wall (maybe next year), building a dining room, and laying a concrete floor and drain in the Cave of Purple Tenuity, which is very damp. Simple improvements, then, so that he could be a better host to his guests from abroad and from Taiwan. All of his plans revolve around the expectation of overseas visitors, including Dream Trippers.

In reality, visitors to the Cloud Platform are few and far between. So when groups of eight or nine members of Winn's groups come up for a few days of cave meditation, it is the most exciting time of the year for Hao. Coming to see us in our cave, he once told us:

> In the past few years, there have been foreign visitors to the Cloud Platform, but very few Chinese. And when the Chinese come, they always come with their business, family, and money problems. They just want to download their problems on others. How can we cultivate under such conditions? The whole point is for us to avoid the problems of the world! Chinese people have very grave limitations in their thinking. They have a feudal attitude: as soon as they have the means, they become lazy. They want to get things without effort. They want instant initiations, opening the celestial eye, etc., without any training. To achieve anything in cultivation, you must undergo great hardship. One Daoist monk came up once, saying he wanted to stay in one of the caves, but he then realized how hard it would be. He didn't realize that my talkativeness and humor is the fruit of my loneliness. It's not like with you foreigners. Foreigners go around the world cultivating, they are not concerned with mundane things. With you foreigners, we can speak about Dao! It's not like that with Chinese, not even with other Daoist monks. Even they are only interested in a more comfortable life. When I go down and into the cities, I never visit Daoist temples. Quanzhen Daoism is in a state of acute decline, because they are always closed to the world. We are now like a small family who know each other so well that we are sick of each other. We have to go out and meet people of different countries and religions.[45]

For Master Hao, the Chinese have reached an extreme state of materialism. They are obsessed with physical sports, and starting to realize that something is missing at the level of spiritual cultivation. "Now, you Americans have already realized that, and come all the way to China to seek it. That's something the Chinese have not yet perceived. They do not yet know the Goddess of Liberty."

Master Hao's discourse now strangely echoed that of some Dream Trippers, who considered that the Dao had been lost in China, and could only be found in the free environment of the United States. But by appropriating the Statue ("Goddess") of Liberty as a manifestation of the Daoist goddess of the Dipper, he subsumed the entire American culture of freedom under the spirit of Chinese Daoism.

Indeed, when we came in August 2007, we found him carefully cleaning pine nuts on a stone outside his hut, and thought they were intended for some medicinal or alchemical diet, but he told us he was planning to string them together into necklaces, to offer as gifts to his foreign visitors. When we came in July 2008, we arrived at the Platform late at night. The next morning, we woke up to voices of men shouting. It was very noisy, unlike the quiet, deserted spot we knew from previous visits. There were a dozen workers, busy digging earth, cutting wood, and clipping at stone blocks. A little further behind, stone blocks had been chipped out like at a quarry. The sound of picking and chiseling went on all day. Master Hao joined in digging the earth, joking with the workers in their coarse Shaanxi dialect. The whole place had become a busy and noisy construction site. Master Hao was busy supervising and giving orders; he had little time for the long chats on Dao which we had had in our previous visits. The workers were less interested in speaking about Daoism with us than about the rapid spread of Christianity in the countryside surrounding Huashan. In the Cave of Purple Tenuity were altar tables which had just been repainted; the cave smelled of oil paint, and otherwise, besides the god statues, it was empty and tidy; it had visibly not been lived in for some time. All of the other caves were being used as dorms for the workers; high wooden platforms had been built in them and quilts laid on them for them to sleep in; signs of fires and their excrements were visible around the caves. All of this construction work aimed to build a house to accommodate larger numbers of visitors. The cost of 60,000 yuan had been donated by Hao's Taiwanese disciples.[46]

Master Hao had planned to complete the new structures by the end of summer. But when we returned again after four years, in June 2012, the site looked no different than before. Hao explained his disappointment at being unable to finish the project: since the government had begun a large-scale tourism redevelopment project at the foot of Huashan, the cost of building materials had more than tripled, as well as the cost of labor. The retreat center he had dreamed of building was now beyond his means.

The Jade Maiden and the Dream of the Bamboo Flute

One day in the 2012 Dream Trip, right after the wedding of Kent and Daisy on a large stone platform on the Central Peak of Huashan (see the epilogue), one of the Asheville participants, Peace, sat outside the Jade Maiden Temple next to the stone platform, and played a flute made from a knobby bamboo root. The soft, dreamy tune attracted the temple monk, Master Pu. He invited her to perform inside the temple, and videotaped her with his mobile phone. He was ecstatic at the sound of her flute, and, while listening, placed his hands in a meditative position, around his navel.

During the Dream Trip, she had always been hoping to play the flute in a temple. Now her dream had come true, and the fact that it had happened in the Jade Maiden Temple made it a very special and significant moment. Inside the temple, wall murals depicted the story of the Jade Maiden, in which bamboo flute playing figured prominently. As we relate below, this story, and the temple, would have unexpected significance for other Dream Trippers as well. The story goes as follows:

> In the Spring and Autumn period, the daughter of Duke Mu of Qin, when she was born, loved beautiful jades, so he called her Nong Yu—Playing with Jade. From a very young age, Nong Yu had an extraordinary ear for music, and loved to play the reed pipe. She grew up as a most seductive beauty. The duke wanted to marry her off, and she was courted by the counts from all over the land, but she declined all of their marriage proposals. One night, she dreamed of an elegant lad who lived on a stone crag, and was adept at playing the bamboo flute. They played the flute and the reed pipe in harmony and joy, and fell in love with each other, and were willing to commit to each other for hundreds of years. Nong Yu, on waking up, told her father of her dream. The duke sent his emissaries to all the mountains of the realm to find the lad, asking people everywhere if they knew of a mysterious, handsome young man who was a master of the bamboo flute. Finally, at Huashan, people pointed to a cave, in which they found a young flute-playing lad named Xiao Shi. The Duke invited him to the palace to meet Nong Yu. They fell in love. The Duke arranged for a magnificent wedding. But the two lovebirds didn't want to live in the court, with its elaborate ceremonies and restrictions. The night before the wedding, Xiao Shi and Nong Yu were playing the flute and the pipe in the garden behind the palace. A great phoenix flew over, and carried them both to the peak of Huashan. That night, they settled in a cave under the West Peak, consummated their marriage, and began their happy life together, living on *qi* alone.[47]

Master Pu told Peace, "The Jade Maiden is your ancestor." Peace now felt a deep connection with this temple on Huashan. This interaction occurred just after the Dream Trippers had staged a wedding just outside the temple. The newlyweds, Kent and Daisy, then stepped into the temple, and Master Pu improvised a short wedding ceremony in front of the shrine, asking them to bow to each other and to the statue of the Jade Maiden. Kent and Daisy had first met during the 2006 Dream Trip, and had now joined the 2012 trip for their wedding, as we describe in the epilogue. When Daisy heard us translating the monk's account of the Jade Maiden's story, she instantly connected the Jade Maiden's dream to her own: it was in a dream that her mother had told her to join the 2006 Dream Trip, telling her that she would meet Superman (Clark *Kent*)—on the trip. As it happened, she had met *Kent* on that trip. And this time, she had married her "Superman"—at the very temple commemorating a love story beginning with the Jade Maiden's dream of her own, Daoist superman.

Caroline, whom we have already encountered at the Cloud Platform, stepped into the temple at this moment, knowing nothing about the story on the temple murals. The murals of the Jade Maiden instantly caught her eye, and she exclaimed, "It's her! She is my teacher!" Caroline was a practitioner of dream meditation, and she had already had several dreams prior to the Dream Trip in which she had seen herself as assisting with a wedding on a mountain in China, and had also seen herself meeting with Immortals showing her scrolls in Chinese. She frequently had dreams of a figure she called "a Jade Maiden of some sort," who, in her dreams, taught her breathing and meditation techniques. This "Jade Maiden" was her "teacher in dream practice." During the Dream Trip, she had been seeking to locate and identify the Jade Maiden:

> I knew that was her name. The whole trip we were on, I was looking for her, the whole trip. I'm like, where was she? Where is this Jade Maiden? Every time I would see a maiden, and one of the names in the places that we would go, I would look for her. And then when the wedding happened, I knew it had to do with a wedding. . . . And then I walk into the temple, and see those beautiful images. And I see her dreaming of her beloved . . . I'm like, this is my dream. This has already happened to me. This is what I have been researching. This is what I have felt. This is what I have been looking for for the last five years.[48]

For Peace, the coincidence of all of these connections was "so phenomenal, so humbling . . . to bring three Western women in, each has one of the pieces that completes the myth": Daisy's mother had dreamed of the wedding, the Jade Maiden had been Caroline's teacher, and Peace played the bamboo flute. None of them had previously known of the story of the Jade Maiden. Master Pu had called them into the temple, right after Daisy's wedding, and drawn their attention to the mural that depicted the story that all three could deeply relate to.[49]

✶

In Turner's conception, the unstructured and unmediated interactions that produce "communitas" contain the potential of generating a new social structure. To what extent do the encounters we have described here generate new structures? In all of the stories related above, the Dream Trippers made special connections with monks and temples at Huashan, causing them to break out of the Dream Trips' bubble, in which the tours were structured to offer only a superficial exposure to the living Daoist culture at Huashan. We should note that the majority of the moments of "communitas" described above involved Master Hao, the most marginal of the monks on Huashan, in his interactions with those Dream Trippers who chose to make the extra three-hour hike to the Cloud Platform—those who were more committed to different forms of spiritual practice. These experiences saw the Dream Trippers communicate in personally significant ways with living Chinese Daoists, and sometimes connected them with the Daoist history, stories, and named deities associated with specific places on the mountain. Often, Dream Trippers made plans to return to Huashan alone, to spend time with Master Hao—but, in the rare cases when they actually did so, the return trips did not lead to a deepening or sustaining of the relationship, if anything, owing to their inability to speak Chinese. In other cases, very personal and spiritual links were made, through dreams and unexpected circumstances. A deity appeared to Caroline in a dream, expressing its desire that she revive its cult in the cave in which she stayed. Caroline also recognized the Jade Maiden as the teacher who had been guiding her in her dreamwork in America. Peace performed her bamboo flute meditation in the temple of the flute-playing Jade Maiden, and Master Pu affiliated her to the Maiden by stating that she was her ancestor. Kent and Daisy had married at the same temple, after a dream that paralleled the dream of the Jade Maiden. Those individuals gave a special spiritual significance to these unexpected encounters, which became important and even "life-changing" parts of their own spiritual biographies after their return home.

Several of the 2012 Dream Trippers—including Caroline, Blackfeather, and Winn's bride Jem, were students of the Daoist Traditions College of Chinese Medical Arts, located in Asheville and founded by Jeffrey Yuen, one of the leading teachers of Daoist medicine and acupuncture in the United States. Yuen is a Daoist-trained Chinese doctor who had immigrated to the United States from Hong Kong. His master had fled to Hong Kong at the time of the Communist takeover in 1949, and there adopted Yuen as a young, four-year-old boy. Yuen had later moved to the United States with his father, and became very active in the American TCM and tai chi circles, eventually becoming the chair of the US Tai Chi Quan Association. Yuen's master and adopted grandfather had been based at Huashan prior to 1949, living at the Purple Cloud Monastery at the end of Huashan valley, where he had

learned his Daoist arts, and been initiated into both the Longmen lineage of
the Quanzhen order and, he claims, into the eighty-eighth generation of the
Jade Purity (Yuqing) lineage of the Supreme Clarity (Shangqing) sect of Daoism. Thus, several of the Dream Trippers, had they perceived themselves as
having a lineage identity, would have had, through their significant personal
experiences at Huashan, another basis for reestablishing the connection of
their own lineage with Huashan. But they did not see themselves as having
such a lineage affiliation with Huashan.

While their experiences remained dear to their hearts, none of them returned to Huashan; at the time of this writing, none of them engaged with
Chinese Daoism or Daoists in a more sustained way after returning to the
Americas. It may be too early to tell, as all of them expressed a willingness to
do so, if the opportunity were to arise—in a "Daoist" spirit, Caroline said, "I
am not seeking, I'm allowing. And I feel I am in the place of responding. If an
offer came my way to go back there, and spend time there, and to be there, I'd
be there in a heartbeat."[50] But for the time being, the "transnational communitas" remained ephemeral; it led to a more significant, but still largely virtual,
connection between those Dream Trippers and Chinese Daoism at Huashan.

Perhaps more than the other Dream Trippers, Peace considered that the
experience and encounters at Huashan had transformed her life. Peace was
not only a practitioner of Daoist meditation, but also of Kundalini yoga and
channeling, often receiving messages from the "archangel Ariel." At various
locations on the trip to China, she had "channeled" Chinese "fairies," who
had given her the mission of connecting East and West. After returning to the
United States, inspired by her spiritual experiences in China, she started a new
career, performing music through the vibrations of multicolored crystal bowls,
going on tours across America, and launched the international "Beloved Wa-
ters Project" described on her website as: "A Global Network of Sound Healers, Grid Workers and Realm Walkers Using Crystal Sound Instruments together with the Vocal Sound Frequencies of Our Water Blessing Mantra to
Enhance and Unify the Sacred Water Grid As It Flows through Our Mother
Earth's Beautiful Body Planet and Our Own Beautiful Living Body Temples."[51]
When we interviewed Peace in 2013, almost two years after her Dream Trip,
she pulled out her diary and read aloud her experience of leaving Huashan:

> When I came out . . . I stayed an extra day in the temple. I did not want to go
> to the city. . . . I knew I was reborn. I knew that things were going to change in
> my life. I just did not know what. . . . Because when I came down, I was stop-
> ping, and doing water blessings all the way through—we have a mantra that
> we use. . . . Coming out of the womb, knowing that life would not be the same

again, knowing that things were going to leave my life that I was not ready to let go, and knowing that it was part of the journey. . . . Oh, my God, I am down at the bottom. I am at the ticket gate. [Reading from her diary:] "So amazing, Mount Huashan. I left the monastery alone at 5:30. I seem to need to walk out alone. Still I am not ready to leave her. I stopped along the way for an exquisite practice, an expression of gratitude, a call for blessing for all who come to this sacred beautiful place. My practice touched me so deeply. I am not knowing all that has occurred in these last five days, yet I know that I walked out as a caterpillar emerges from her cocoon, as a majestic butterfly. I know I emerged from this mountain reborn in radiance—a transformation is taking place. Of that, I am quite certain. In what ways, I did not know. The biggest transformation in my life so far has been through my gemstone balls. . . . And now, I should play my last flute offering on this mountain—may it reflect my deepest gratitude. I have made my offering—my gifted flute. . . . This has been a deliciously humbling journey. Am I ready to reemerge from my inner place? Am I ready to integrate myself back to the peoplehood? When I walk through that gate, I will be out. . . . Deep breath." I asked for a message—I needed one. [Reading "channeled" messages:] "*You are one. You are whole. You are divine presence. Feel it. Know it. Own it. You have now experienced another aspect of that divine essence. You are holy—a holy vessel to be tasted. Savored, you are she. Open it. Allow your sweet nectar to flow from every pore. Bless all you touch. Bless with your eyes. Bless with your sound. Bless with your words. You are a vessel of blessings. Bestow them generously.*" I just wept, because for me, that was the scariest thing. That was the scariest, scariest thing—humbling and scary, because that is a huge contract. That's a biggie. [Laughing] And when I came out—you know, where the village is down below, there was a monk, playing an instrument. And I stopped. And it was a tall string instrument. . . . The monk invited me to sit there, and brought out sheet music. And the two of us sat and sang together for like an hour. . . . It was just, you know, life changing. . . . So we played. I played flute. We sang together.[52]

6

The Scholar-Practitioners

"This is the end of Daoism," lamented Louis Komjathy, a professor of Daoist studies who is also a Daoist practitioner and founder of the Daoist Foundation, an American nonprofit organization dedicated to fostering authentic Daoist study and practice, and to preserving and transmitting traditional Daoist culture. While he was referring specifically to the participation of "New Age" practitioners at an academic conference in 2010, his words could just as well have applied to the Huashan encounters that we have just discussed. As we described in the opening section of the first chapter of this book, Komjathy had met Masters Chen and Hu at Huashan in June 2004 just days after avoiding the Dream Trippers, in a life-changing encounter that would lead him to becoming Chen's disciple and to seek formal ordination into the Huashan lineage of the Complete Perfection order. At that time, after over ten years of studying Daoism in the United States, in both practitioner and academic settings, Komjathy had become "disillusioned and disgusted" with the Daoist scene in the United States, and did not know where to go next. Such was his state of mind when, along with the Dream Trippers, we had bumped into him at Louguantai, and suggested that he find Chen and Hu at Huashan. He went, and was impressed. Komjathy inquired about the importance of lineage and ordination for Daoist identity and affiliation. Master Chen emphasized that while these were important as "outward forms," true Daoist identity rested on personal practice and attainment, including the correct "orientation" (*fangxiang*). As he relates his experience: "I asked them, 'How can I know that I have a real connection to Daoism?' They answered, 'Because you are sitting here with us.' And that answer cleared away all my doubts and uncertainties."[1]

For Komjathy, Huashan is an important Daoist sacred site and a pivotal way station on his personal initiatory journey. It is one of the key links in his Daoist lineage and transmission, the precious and precarious connection between an authentic Chinese tradition and his own project of establishing Daoism in faraway America. Strongly critical of the "designer hybrid spirituality" of New Age spiritual entrepreneurs and energy tourists, he has sought to establish an authentic, "tradition-based" Daoist practice and community in the United States. For him, there is also a visceral connection and physical similarity between Huashan and places in the American West where he traces his earliest spiritual experiences, such as California's Yosemite National Park.

In this chapter, through the case of the scholar-practitioner Louis Komjathy, we present an alternative construction of American Daoism to that of Winn and Healing Tao USA. This "tradition-based" American Daoism challenges the Dream Trippers' claims to Daoist authenticity by embodying the dual authority of formal lineage transmission and rigorous academic scholarship, combined with the discipline of personal practice.

The last chapter of Komjathy's 2013 textbook on Daoism, "Daoism in the Modern World," begins with two epigraphs: one each from Guy Debord's *Society of the Spectacle* and Jean Baudrillard's *Simulacra and Simulation*, about "substituting the signs of the real for the real."[2] Komjathy does not treat "popular American Taoism" as a continuation of the historical tradition he describes in the previous three hundred pages of his book, but as an illusion or fraud that has replaced the genuine thing. Indeed, he says as much on the next page: "Most of what goes by the name of 'Daoism' in the West, especially throughout the Internet and popular publications, are forms of appropriation and fabrication. They are rooted in colonialist, missionary, and Orientalist legacies."[3] For Komjathy, there is a question of "connection," "continuity," and "translation" of tradition. In contrast to what he considers to be more "tradition-based" Western Daoist associations, mostly in Europe,[4] he describes Winn's Healing Tao as follows:

> Healing Tao (Healing Dao), also known as Tao Yoga and Universal Tao, was first established in the United States in 1979 by Mantak Chia (b. 1943), a Thai citizen of Chinese ancestry who lived in America during the formative moments of the movement. [. . .] It included a hierarchically ordered credential system and offers various "dream trips" to China, which represents a form of spiritual tourism. It has been instrumental in contributing to the Western construction of Daoism as reducible to techniques, specifically sexual methods with no connection to Daoism as a living Chinese and now global religion.[5]

Komjathy appears to be eminently qualified to pass judgment on Healing Tao, the Dream Trips, and on the encounters at Huashan: not only is he a

Daoist practitioner who has a spiritual connection with Huashan and its Daoist monks, he is also a professor of Religious Studies, trained in the sinological
study of Daoist texts. Komjathy has been one of the key voices in emphasizing
the importance of studying global Daoism, "American Daoism" in particular,
including "anything identified as Daoist"; and he was among the first scholars
to conduct such research. Komjathy has called himself, in a public biographical statement, "a scholar-practitioner of Daoism with particular interests in
contemplative practice and mystical experience." As a scholar, he received his
doctorate from Boston University under the direction of Livia Kohn, and focused on the history of early Quanzhen Daoism and on the translation of its
texts. He is the author of an authoritative study of the Quanzhen order,[6] and
the first translator of many of its key scriptures and literature.[7] He also has
training in methodological issues in comparative religion, and has written
some of the first scholarly articles on Daoism in America. As a practitioner
with over twenty years of experience, he is committed to "dietetics, health
and longevity methods, quiet sitting (apophatic meditation), philosophical
reflection, and scripture study."[8] Much of Komjathy's scholarship can be read
as a map for Daoist practice, which he describes as "holistic" and "integrated."
For example, his *Daoism: A Guide for the Perplexed* is organized into nine
thematic chapters: tradition, community, identity, view, personhood, practice, experience, place, and modernity. He thus exemplifies the figure of the
"scholar-practitioner," which he defines as scholars "with deep subjective
connection to what they study," and he increasingly self-identifies as one:

> Without formal academic training, I would not be able to historically con-
> textualize and accurately translate classical Daoist literature. Without formal
> Daoist training, I would not be able to interpret such texts in a technically
> accurate way, specifically with respect to actual practice. On a deeper, and per-
> haps more esoteric, gnostic* and mystical* level, I would not have understood
> other layers of Daoist adherence, affiliation, community, ordination, tradition,
> and so forth. I may not have been open to experiences that revealed the Daoist
> tradition as a community of practitioners connected to each other as a histori-
> cal and energetic continuum.[9]

Michael Winn would probably agree with Komjathy on the value of scholarship in compensating for the insecurity of the Western practitioners' doubts
about the authenticity of the methods taught by immigrant Chinese masters.
As he told us,

> The Healing Tao felt ungrounded until more and more [academic studies]
> got published, and backed up what we'd received from our oral tradition. This
> is probably from the Song dynasty—Lü Dongbin's formulas are these Seven

Formulas here. Now we have a context where our tradition comes from. When
we first got it, we didn't have any context. That makes me feel a little uneasy.[10]

Winn's words point to a key aspect of the predicament of modern spirituality: the uncertain authenticity of many of its practices. For Winn, academic
research plays a validating role, merely confirming and contextualizing the
accuracy of the Seven Formulas of One Cloud.

But academic research can also have the opposite effect of relativizing or
even undermining such authenticity claims. Komjathy, for example, who has
conducted significant academic research on inner alchemy, claims that Healing Tao has very little, if any, connection to late medieval internal alchemy.
He has identified Indian Tantric and New Age esoteric influences and has
been explicitly critical of other "American Daoist" attempts to establish legitimacy through what he calls "inaccurate and selective" readings of scholarship. In an article on "Qigong in America," Komjathy identifies four "ideal
types" of American *qigong* practitioners. These include "traditionalists,"
"medicalists," "spiritualists," and "positivists," with Winn being placed in the
third category.[11] However, Winn subsequently cited Komjathy on the Healing Tao website and identified himself as the embodiment of *all four types*.
For Komjathy, "This pattern of self-promotion, hybridity, and syncretism is
an ever-shifting construction, as his search for the supposed 'history' of One
Cloud's methods and his later 'rhetoric of lineage' indicate."[12]

On the other hand, Winn points out the irony that he was the one who
first met with Master Chen, and that it was through the 2004 Dream Trip
that we came to know him and then connected Komjathy to Chen and Hu,
leading to his becoming Chen's disciple and finding his spiritual path in the
Huashan lineage. "That effectively puts me and the Dream Trippers into his
personal energetic lineage of evolution for which he should be grateful and
include me/us in his daily invocations and prayers."[13]

In this chapter, we explore the role of scholarship in the formation of
American Daoist authenticity and authority, and the history of border cross-
ings between Daoist "secular" scholarship and religious practice. After trac-
ing the genealogy of early scholarly contributions to what has become the
Daoism of the Dream Trippers, and reviewing Komjathy's precursors as
scholar-practitioners in the world of Daoist Studies in the West, we recount
the story of Komjathy's "anti–Dream Trip"—a scholar-practitioner's own
trips to Huashan, his encounters with Chen and Hu, and his search for a
Daoist authenticity grounded in practice, lineage, and scholarship. This is
an approach that defines itself in conscious opposition to that of the Healing
Tao and its Dream Trips, and yet parallels it in certain ways. Indeed, both

Komjathy and Winn are educated, articulate, and passionate about Daoism. Both have been to China many times. And both were introduced to Daoism while in college—in fact, they both studied at Dartmouth College—through a combination of reading the *Daodejing* and learning meditation. Both teach a message of spiritual independence: "You shouldn't be dependent on the teacher—he is just a transmitter of the Dao." Master Chen has been a key figure in both of their connections to Chinese Daoism. And both played an indirect role in each other's trajectories—Komjathy by introducing Winn to the world of Daoist scholarship, and Winn by opening the door for Komjathy to enter the world of Quanzhen tradition at Huashan. The tensions between their approaches to Daoist cultivation and authenticity highlight the highly contested and fragile foundations of authority claims in the emerging field of global Daoism.

Scholarship and "Eating Daoism"

When Komjathy looks for positive ideals of Westerners traveling to Daoist sites in China, he wants to avoid the path taken by the Dream Trippers and other Western spiritual tourists whom he sees as "looking for confirmation of their own mistaken views and deficient practice. They are not interested in authentic, tradition-based Daoist practice-realization."[14] He has given thought to leading his own group tour, but this presumptive trip would be referred to as a pilgrimage, would focus exclusively on important Daoist and Quanzhen sacred sites (e.g., Louguantai, Chongyanggong, Kunyushan, Long-mendong), with particular emphasis on key Quanzhen ones, and would embody "tradition" as opposed to "hybrid spirituality," to use Komjathy's own terms. When Komjathy discusses this, he emphasizes "reverence," "propriety," and traditional Chinese "host/guest protocol," specifically with respect to the place and its resident Daoist community. One might imagine that if Komjathy were to lead such a trip he would heed the advice of Brock Silvers, the American businessman (mentioned in chapter 2), who gave general advice on embarking on a "Taoist pilgrimage" that is completely ignored by Dream Trippers, such as "Do not ask to stay!" "Do not photograph Altars," and "females should refrain from entering the altar area of any Taoist temple while experiencing their menses."[15] In fact, Komjathy understands his own visits to Daoist sacred sites as pilgrimages, during which he recalls important historical personages and events, offers incense, bows before the altars, and occasionally makes donations.

In 2007, Komjathy wrote an unpublished essay about his life among the Quanzhen monks of Huashan that, by stressing the purity of the motives of

Chen and Hu, indirectly downplays the possibility of real connection between them and Dream Trippers:

> Both Chen and [Hu] enjoyed the company of their fellow adepts, with the qualification that they were committed to a Daoist religious life and to self-cultivation (*xiulian*). Many contemporary Daoists use a "rhetoric of practice"; that is, they talk about the importance of certain practices, but there is little evidence of such a commitment or fruition in their presence [. . .] One very interesting aspect of Daoist practice here focused on "virtue" (*dexing*) and "atonement" (*chanhui*). From the perspective of these Quanzhen monastics, practicing Daoist techniques without cultivating virtue (internal goodness and external benefit) and rectifying past misdeeds is a fruitless undertaking. Here they pointed toward negligent monks and Western "spiritual tourists" (Qigong practitioners) as anti-exemplars.[16]

When we told Komjathy that Chen, Hu, and other monks were willing to engage with the "spiritual tourists," he responded that "Chinese Daoists often understand themselves as 'transmitting the Dao' (*chuandao*), regardless of who is present. It is their religious commitment that is primary." And when it became apparent that Chen, Hao, and other monks enjoyed the company of what Komjathy calls "New Age Qigong practitioners," and to some extent were drawing closer to them, as we described in the previous chapter, Komjathy explained this as "a case of (romantic?) misunderstanding of the Dream Trippers" as possessing "similar expressions of 'naturalness' (*ziran*) and 'being carefree' (*xiaoyao*)." Komjathy argues that the monks depicted in this book are disillusioned with institutional monastic corruption, which leads them to mistakenly embrace Western tourists as seemingly more pure, at least in terms of intention, sincerity, and opportunity.[17]

When asked what he thought the Dream Trippers were gaining from the moments of "transnational communitas," he does not dismiss them out of hand. As he notes, "The Dao works in mysterious ways, and Daoism is far larger than any individual. Ultimately, one can never know the end result, and trusting in the Dao with open receptivity is most important."[18] But he wrote that, from his perspective, "One of the major problems with these types of 'encounters' (are they really encounters?) is that they involve spiritual colonialism and Orientalist appropriation." Komjathy goes on to argue that "Western spiritual tourists" use such transmissions as vehicles for their own legitimation. For Komjathy, this is an example of "The Oriental Monk" phenomenon as analyzed by cultural theorist Jane Iwamura, whereby "recognition of any Eastern spiritual guide (real or fictional) is predicated on their conformity to general features paradigmatically encapsulated in the icon of the Oriental

Monk: His spiritual commitment, his calm demeanor, his Asian face, and oftentimes his manner of dress."[19] For Komjathy, Healing Tao's "Yi Eng [One Cloud] legacy" and narratives of "spiritual exchanges" with Complete Perfection monks as sources of imagined legitimation are "quintessential examples" of this Orientalizing process.[20]

According to Komjathy, opinion was divided among monks at Jade Spring Monastery about Chen's departure from Huashan: "Those who were committed to Quanzhen religious practice lamented it as a loss, while those whose primary motivations simply involved living as ordinary people in Daoist robes in a Daoist monastery, those who were 'eating Daoism' (*chi daojiao*), were delighted."[21] In a footnote, Komjathy explains the meaning of that unusual phrase:

> This phrase was first introduced to me by Professor Jiang Sheng of Shandong University.[22] In my conversations with Chen and [Hu], it quickly became utilized as a way of referring to Daoists not oriented toward the Dao and not committed to Daoist religious practice. It was applied to "Daoists" whose motivations were non-Daoist, whether Quanzhen monastics without a true vocation or New Age American spiritualists who are "selling Daoism" (*mai daojiao*) on their "spiritual tourism" trips to China. Strangely, some of the latter actually include meetings with Chen and [Hu], formerly unbeknownst to them, as one of their products.[23]

"Eating Daoism" can thus be applied to monks who wear their robes and perform their offices without any inner cultivation practice, and, paradoxically, to Westerners who think only of their personal spiritual practice and know nothing about Daoist forms, ritual, or dress. Komjathy thus questions the authenticity of most "Daoists" in America, including the Dream Trippers, and that of most Chinese Daoist communities as well. By such standards, the number of authentic Daoists in the world seems vanishingly small. Master Chen might have concurred: at one point he told us, "Actually, the entire Chinese people (*zhonghua minzu*) are 'eating Daoism.'"[24]

For most scholars of Daoism—whose work focuses on the history of texts and practices, or on the ethnography of complex ritual traditions—the phenomenon of American Daoism can hardly be taken seriously: in the words of one eminent scholar, "these are crackpots." If our study has been welcomed by our academic colleagues in Daoist studies, it has been seen, at best, as comic relief after the dry, but serious business of textual analysis and ritual studies; at worst, as a necessary record of the tragic corruption of China's ancient Daoist traditions under the onslaught of modernity and globalization.

After all, what could a small band of Westerners who have tried a few "tai chi" and "chi kung" moves, watched a couple of DVDs, and perhaps read a book or two on energy healing and the Tao of Multiple Orgasms possibly pretend to understand about this rich and complex tradition, over two thousand years old, having over 1,400 scriptures in its Canon, some of the most elaborate liturgies in the world's religions, meditation systems said to take a lifetime to master, and deep connections with all aspects of Chinese history, culture, and civilization? For the scholar-practitioner Louis Komjathy,

> I find most of these people to be generally well-intentioned and sincere, but unconvincing from a historical or normative perspective on Daoist lifeways. On the most basic level, one may say that it is possible to practice "Daoist techniques" in a non-Daoist way. It is also possible to speak from a place of turbidity and agitation (a yin condition), and thereby confuse oneself and others.[25]

Other academics have gone farther by claiming that there can be no such thing as American Daoism. To make the distinction clear, the sinologist Terry Kleeman, at a panel at the American Academy of Religion in 2001, once proposed that the "true"—i.e., Chinese—practitioners be called "Daoists" (with a D), while the Americans should be labeled as "Taoists" (with a T), reflecting their preoccupation with Orientalist tropes having little connection with the reality of Daoism in China.[26] Louis Komjathy was on this panel and, perhaps in his first public "coming out" as a scholar-practitioner, challenged the notion that it would be impossible for an American to be a Daoist.[27] But he agreed with Kleeman that most so-called American Taoists have little connection with the true Daoist tradition.

Unlike Komjathy, most of the other academic critics of American Daoism are not participant-observers and certainly not "scholar-practitioners." Thus, Komjathy considers himself marginal in the Daoist academic circle, and remains critical of "the academic tendency toward hyper-intellectualism and authoritarian discourse"—a kind of disembodied scholarship that focuses on dry historicism, textual reconstruction or ethnographic description without taking into account actual experience.[28] As he wrote in his book *Daoism: A Guide for the Perplexed*, he asserts a principled stance that is critical of both "neutral" academics and those who claim Daoist identity:

> As I believe that there are ethical and political dimensions involved in the Western construction and appropriation of Daoism, including among those who choose to be "neutral" or "objective," here I apparently depart from academic conventions and take an ethico-political stance: anyone who claims to be Daoist while simultaneously denying the defining characteristics of Daoism and disempowering actual Daoists and Daoist communities has negated his or her claim of religious identity and affiliation. I choose not to provide

tacit legitimation by accepting self-promoting identity narratives. Developing this social critique further, if one were more daring and willing to take Daoist views seriously, one might recognize that something important is actually at stake, and such a recognition may require that one take a stand. It is not mere "fundamentalism," "factionalism," "sectarianism," and "exclusivism."[29]

For Komjathy, the "something important at stake" is "the Daoist tradition as a soteriological path, rooted in psychosomatic transformation, and the transmission of the numinous presence of the Dao."

Scholarship and the Construction of Authenticity in American Daoism

Although Komjathy does not consider academic training or Chinese language proficiency to be a condition for authentic Daoist practice, it is the path he has personally followed. Faced with the predicament of an ever-elusive, ever-counterfeited Dao, one solution is the mutual reinforcement of paths to legitimate authority and authenticity: lineage affiliation and tradition, academic training, and personal practice.

Komjathy is not the first to incorporate scholarship into a search for Daoist authenticity—indeed, the relationship between Daoist scholarship and religious practice has a complex history. This issue is an acute one in the search for and construction of an authentic Daoism—not only because Chinese Daoists express themselves through a very different culture and language than their Western counterparts, but because their own training and religious work is focused on embodied practices rather than intellectual discourse—a condition that has been amplified by the political turmoil and the marginalization of religious institutions in the twentieth century. While Daoism does have a scholastic dimension,[30] this is very different from other religious traditions, in which clergy are trained in textual study and scholarship according to the internal norms of the religious tradition, so that the position of the "scholar-practitioner" is much more common, even the norm. Rabbis who teach Jewish Studies and Jesuit priests who teach the history of Christianity are so common as to be unremarkable. Indeed, in the seminary model of teaching Religious Studies in the United States, a professor of Christianity was required to profess Christianity.

A closer parallel to Daoist Studies might be Buddhist Studies in the West: "The silent sangha" is what Charles Prebish calls academics who are also practicing Buddhists, and there are many of them.[31] The closest comparison with Daoism may be the case of Tibetan Buddhism. Like Daoism, it is a rich

textual tradition, widely misunderstood, popularized in the West, and influenced by "Orientalist" concerns, in the sense of trying to preserve the original
meaning of the text and saving the tradition from itself.

But the differences are instructive. The academic study of Tibetan Buddhism grew through refugee lamas coming to the United States via India who
taught Tibetan language at universities and, frequently, religious practices off
campus. It also grew through Americans who not only received doctorates
in Buddhist Studies but also trained in Tibetan monasteries in India; these
Americans include, most famously, Robert Thurman (b. 1941), who holds the
Je Tsongkhapa Chair of Indo-Tibetan Buddhist Studies at Columbia University. There are also substantive differences with respect to the status of such
scholar-practitioners in both the associated religious traditions and fields of
study.

In the modern context, Daoism has little tradition of the intellectual/
monk; most Daoist monks today are not well educated and it would be hard
to imagine them teaching at a Chinese university, let alone a Western one. As
well, unlike the all-but-mandatory training period for Western scholars of
Buddhism in Tibetan learning centers in exile in India, there have been virtually no opportunities for scholars of Daoism to train in Daoist monasteries
(until the last few years perhaps), which are not really teaching institutions
anyway. In fact, in China, Daoist temples and associations often outsource
their intellectual work to secular scholars: Chinese university researchers are
called in to teach Daoist textual traditions to young monks. Komjathy himself witnessed this while he was a visiting professor at Shandong University,
where he noted that secular academics taught "Daoist history" to monks in
inaccurate and unsophisticated ways.

In the absence of a strong Daoist institutional and discursive voice of authenticity and authority, secular academic institutions and training have thus
occupied a crucial place in the Daoist religious field. The formal academic
study of Daoism is in its infancy compared with, say, the academic study of
Hinduism or Buddhism, and the practice of Daoism in America is much less
hierarchical, institutionalized, and directly connected to a living tradition than
American Buddhism or Hinduism. And yet, paradoxically, American Daoist
practitioners have arguably been more influenced by secular scholars than the
practitioners of other non-Western spiritual traditions. Scholars, of course, are
never neutral observers or arbiters but always active participants in the debate
to shape the definition of their object of study. This is even truer when the object of study is something as poorly understood and as undefined as Daoism.

The attitudes the Dream Trippers hold and expressed to us on Huashan
and afterward are in many ways inherited from late nineteenth-century sinol-

ogy: Daoism as a cure for the illnesses of the modern West, and Daoism as a degenerate perennial philosophy that could be conserved in the West and restored to its original purity. As Norman Girardot put it, "The question to be asked about the perennial query of 'what is Taoism?' really comes down to asking how sinologists [. . .] could have gotten the answer so horribly distorted and lopsided, so grotesquely a corrupt gloss on this exceedingly rich and complex tradition."[32]

The emblematic figure of this influence is the sinologist James Legge (1815–1897), a Scottish Congregationalist missionary who became the leading scholar of Chinese religion from the late 1870s until the end of the nineteenth century. Unlike previous missionary-scholars, Legge admired the "Daoism of Laozi and Zhuangzi" as serious and worthy. Returning from his many years in China to occupy the first professorship in Chinese at Oxford University, Legge introduced a substantial knowledge of Chinese religions to the West. He was the first scholar to translate into English the great Chinese classics, the ones that are still found in every bookstore and taught in any survey course on Asian religions, including the *Yijing*, the *Zhuangzi*, and the *Daodejing*. These works were published as part of F. Max Müller's (1823–1900) monumental series *The Sacred Books of the East* (1879–1894; 49 vols.), thereby placing Daoism and Confucianism into the emerging category of "Religions of the World."

Legge allowed himself to understand, even to be moved, by the texts of classical Daoism (the so-called "philosophical Daoism"), while at the same time denigrating the present-day Daoist religion, thus instituting a conceptual dualism in thinking about Daoism that persists to this day. From the 1890s until quite recently, Americans who wrote on religions of the world relied mainly on Legge for their information on Chinese religion, and on Daoism in particular. Komjathy has characterized this received "philosophical Daoism"/"religious Daoism" distinction as the "Leggean" or "bifurcated view" of Daoism.[33]

Another subject of scholarly interest was investigation into body cultivation and alchemy. Although less research was done on these topics than on "Daoist philosophy" (i.e., the *Daodejing* and the *Zhuangzi*), this theme, by providing fodder for further Orientalist fantasies, had a huge impact on the formation of American Daoism. In this case, China was fantasized, not as it had been in the Enlightenment as a rational, ethical kingdom, but as a romantic land of alchemists, hermits, and Immortals.

The Swiss psychologist Carl Gustav Jung (1875–1961) was the person most responsible for popularizing Chinese alchemy in the West. Jung was never terribly interested in Confucianism; however, he had demonstrated excitement toward, and sympathy with, Daoism, which he tended, erroneously, to look upon as typical of Chinese thinking as a whole. Jung was first attracted to Daoism through the *Jinhua zongzhi* (Secret of the Golden Flower), a Qing-dynasty internal alchemical text, possibly produced through spirit-writing, for which he wrote an introduction in 1922.[34]

Later, in the mid-twentieth century, the ideas advanced by scholars such as Henri Maspero, Joseph Needham, and Robert van Gulik about Daoist conceptions of health, longevity, immortality, transcendence, and sex appealed to the West's growing interest in body-centered spirituality. Joseph Needham's (1901–1995) romanticized view of early China influenced the subsequent study of Daoism. Needham was editor and chief author of the monumental multivolume work *Science and Civilisation in China*, which includes book-length studies on many areas of science and technology in China including textiles, agriculture, and mining. Writing at the end of the Second World War, he saw Chinese alchemy as an antidote to the disease of the West, and Daoist sexual cultivation as "a therapeutic and healing force for Western culture."[35] Some of Needham's most thorough and important work was on Chinese alchemy. Needham also helped to edit and wrote the preface to the earliest popular book in English on "Daoist sex," *The Tao of Love and Sex: The Ancient Chinese Way to Ecstasy*, written by his friend and longtime correspondent Jolan Chang (1917–2002).[36] Needham saw in Daoism the potential for an archaic revival in the modern world.[37] Daoism might restore what modernity had broken: the connection between morality and science, between man and nature, and between branches of knowledge.

All of these scholars' writings inform the dispositions of popular American Daoists, although they generally do not know it. Popular practitioners' notions about Daoism have been shaped by some scholarship, often of the outdated Victorian variety. Yet, this shaping is rarely acknowledged and may even be disavowed, given that many American practitioners consider "book learning" to be "un-Daoist." Indeed, for Komjathy, "There is actually systematic ignorance and even attempts to shield people from informed sources."[38] But, of course, practitioners need ongoing scholarship: when they reach the limits of their own master's techniques, they often look for "new" (yet preferably labeled as very old) Daoist practices—and they need to rely on scholarly translations to find them, since almost none of them read Chinese.[39]

More sophisticated practitioners, like Michael Winn, acknowledge the debt practitioners have to scholarship. He told us he values Daoist scholars because he sees himself as one:

> I am not just a practitioner, I'm also a scholar. I'm interested in knowing the history, in knowing the context. Because of the depth of my practice, I'm able to pull out very small items that might give me different perspectives on this

practice or the context in which it was taught. . . . I like to look at the context.
I like to see how a practice evolves. Scholars keep practitioners honest. Practitioners tend to lie to boost their lineage status or whatever else or exaggerate
claims about how long has this been going on. . . .

   I have so many [scholarly] books and I keep reading them, because they
keep refining me and taking me deeper and deeper inside the Chinese culture and the Chinese mind, which is a very deep topic, that's changed over
time also. I enjoy reading a wide range of scholars and I keep finding out new
things, details I can incorporate into my teachings and give that [as] a perspective to Western Daoists.[40]

In fact, Winn considers himself to have "solid credentials as an independent
Daoist scholar," as evidenced by his membership on the editorial board of the
Journal of Daoist Studies, his articles published in that journal and in books
edited by Livia Kohn,[41] and his "private Taoist University" that offers courses
that integrate Daoist theory and practice.[42] And if he remains an "independent"
scholar without formal academic credentials, it is because, he claims, he would
prefer to sacrifice academic authority to maintain his personal authenticity:

   When I presented my paper on Quest for Spiritual Orgasm at a conference of
   Daoist and Tantric scholars, the inclusion of my personal sexual experiences
   raised many eyebrows. "I would get fired if I published that paper," several
   told me. Of course, that is one reason why I've stayed an independent scholar
   as well as independent teacher—to free myself from institutional pressures to
   conform or bend the truth to suit convention.[43]

However, from Komjathy's perspective, Winn is "the archetypal New Age
appropriator, seeking legitimation through his own misrepresentations and
selective reading of 'scholarship' in a relentless exercise in self-promotion . . .
actual scholarship requires systematic study and reflection, including formal
academic training in the case of Daoist Studies." Komjathy had Winn and
similar individuals in mind when he spoke of a "conspiracy of ignorance" in
The Daoist Tradition.[44]

Schipper and Saso: Ordination in the Field

The first century of Western textual scholarship played a key role in shaping
the popular Western understanding of Daoism. But Komjathy clearly situates
himself within a more recent generation of scholarship that rejects the "Orientalism" of the earlier sinological tradition. Part of this critique is based on a
new wave of ethnographic studies conducted since the 1960s, which have confronted the bookish fantasies of earlier scholars with contextualized data from

the field. By claiming to have been "ordained" as a "Daoist priest," Komjathy uses the terms that have been employed by the pioneers of ethnographic research on Daoism as a living tradition in Taiwan in the 1960s, Kristofer Schipper and Michael Saso. Saso's public presence as a Daoist initiate, self-cultivator, and scholar makes him a model for Komjathy. In fact, Komjathy met Saso at the 2010 conference discussed below, and they have since become close friends and collaborators. Komjathy writes, in his 2013 textbook on Daoism, that "Saso (b. 1930) and Schipper (b. 1934) were among the first known Westerners ordained as Daoist priests. They are both ordained members of Zhengyi, and they have also helped to establish a model of Daoist scholar-practitioners inside of Daoist Studies."[45] Indeed, it is this model that Komjathy seems to be claiming for himself. Just as Saso and Schipper were the first "Zhengyi scholar-practitioners," Komjathy presents himself as the first to be ordained as a Quanzhen priest, the first "Quanzhen scholar-practitioner." At a time when scholarship was exclusively textual and the received wisdom was that Daoism had already disappeared as a lived religion, Schipper and Saso made waves by "discovering" a living ritual tradition in Taiwan, and by becoming "ordained" as priests of the Zhengyi tradition. As Komjathy puts it, "both Saso and Schipper decided to become 'insiders' (adherents) in order to more fully understand Daoist ritual as 'outsiders' (scholars). Such early 'ethnographic' examples thus reveal an emerging trajectory of participant-observation,"[46] one that began to be seen as conferring academic authority based on initiation into the tradition. Komjathy sees his own ethnographic studies, discussed below, as a Quanzhen parallel to the work of Schipper and Saso.

Schipper's story is related by Norman Girardot in the foreword to the English translation to Schipper's book *The Taoist Body.*[47] In 1962, the twenty-eight-year-old French-trained Dutch sinologist first ventured to Taiwan as a researcher for the École Française d'Extrême-Orient. After two years at the Academia Sinica, he decided to "leave his official life as a research scholar in Taipei to live, as the Taoist saying goes, 'hidden among the people.'"[48] He went to the southern part of the island where he witnessed a *jiao* ritual; having impressed the local masters with his knowledge of obscure texts of the Daoist Canon that he had studied in Paris, he was admitted into formal apprenticeship as a priest. In 1968 he was ordained by Chen Rongsheng (b. 1927). Gradually, Schipper's initiation became known, and it contributed immensely to his charisma as an authority on Daoism, at a time when no other scholars of Daoism had ever ventured into the field. But unlike Saso, Schipper did not make his initiation experience a cornerstone of any published work; he built his academic authority through historical and textual studies on Daoist ritual, by training other renowned ethnographic field workers such as John

Lagerwey and Kenneth Dean, who were not practitioners, and by leading a
monumental study of the Daoist Canon.[49] The story of his ordination became
part of the legend surrounding the scholar, but it never became part of his
own subsequent scholarship. It also created a pattern, visible in the larger
field of Religious Studies as well, of scholars and scholar-practitioners as "sur-
rogates of tradition."

Where Schipper let the story of his initiation be recounted by another
scholar, based on his unpublished memoir, Michael Saso describes his own initiation as the centerpiece of one of his influential monographs.[50] Saso describes
his first meeting with his soon-to-be lineage master, Chuang-Ch'en Teng-yün
(Zhuang-Chen Dengyun, 1911–1976), as a "traumatic scolding. 'What purpose
could a foreign scholar possibly have,' Chuang demanded, 'other than to destroy
the traditions of his ancestors?'"[51] Chuang was mollified when Saso brought a
photocopy of a ritual text from the British Museum. Saso stresses that Chuang
gave lessons on Daoist philosophy and inner alchemy, not only ritual.

In Saso's narrative, similar to Komjathy's of thirty years later, the Westerner is the most diligent student, while many of the Chinese Daoists (in
Saso's case, Taiwanese priests-in-training) are lazy: "The motley crew whil-
ing away the hours between liturgical performances in the neighboring pool-
room, the lectures on breath control, exercise, macrobiotic diet, and the like
were wasted."[52] Here one might hear a precursor to Komjathy's "eating Daoism" comment, referring to monastic corruption and "temple rascals" in the
Quanzhen order. Komjathy also mentions the frequent playing of Mahjong
and incessant use of cellphones by monastics.

Like Schipper, Saso studied with his ritual master for several years until
he understood the "perfection and beauty of his liturgical performance"[53]
and could describe life among the community of Taiwanese Zhengyi Daoist
priests. Saso, in a subsequent book, revealed some texts supposedly only available to initiates. He also published a collection of Daoist liturgical texts. In a
scholarly work originally published in 1972, he, in fact, specifically argues that
only as a practitioner could he discover and elucidate the Daoist tradition:

> This tradition usually is taught only to disciples who have been accepted by a
> master and have learned how to do Taoist Meditation ("Ting hsin" [*dingxin*]
> as Master Shih of Mao put it). Consequently, a scholar conducting scientific
> investigations in this area may find it necessary to be accepted as a student of
> a Taoist master and actually practice ritual meditation in order to experience
> the "emic" approach to esoteric ritual.[54]

But, at least as a scholar, Saso paid for such outspokenness. Identifying as a
scholar-practitioner means performing a complicated dance. Whereas scholarly

credentials might help one's status as a practitioner, the reverse is not often true. Scholars tend to be careful to present their identity as practitioners some- what discreetly, or else they could find both of their identities called into ques- tion. Indeed, in an infamous takedown in the form of a forty-nine-page review essay, the sinologist Michel Strickmann (1942–1994) suggested "that there are serious problems concerning the manner in which Saso obtained information from his teacher-informant. There is already a basic question of objectivity in the case of an anthropologist who is at the same time a participant (and perhaps also a believer) in the rituals he describes. But there are also a number of clear indications that Saso influenced Chuang, and supplied the 'informa- tion' he was given."[55]

Komjathy explicitly identifies with both Saso and Schipper. In addition to providing models for the Daoist scholar-practitioner, they represent poten- tial "alternative fates." Like Schipper, this hyphenated identity could lead to authority and prominence; like Saso, it could lead to disempowerment and marginalization. Given his respect for Saso's work, Komjathy has also dis- cussed the possibility of writing an article titled "Revisiting the Strickmann- Saso Debate," in which he would question the views of the former and re- visit the contributions of the latter.[56] Along these lines, it is significant that Komjathy has an enduring interest in the larger phenomenon of the "scholar- practitioner" in Religious Studies and has written explicitly on the "insider/ outsider question."[57]

Livia Kohn: From Classical Scholar to Spiritual Entrepreneur

While Komjathy had early on looked to Schipper and Saso as models of the scholar-practitioner, he had not expected his own academic and doctoral advi- sor, Livia Kohn, to follow that path, albeit in a very different style and direction: while Schipper and Saso were initiated into community ritual traditions that almost nobody practices in the West, Kohn, after a distinguished academic career, became, after her retirement, an important actor in the "New Age" milieu of American Daoism with its focus on individual meditation and the body. We can say that she moved from being a colleague of Schipper the sinologist to a colleague of Winn the spiritual entrepreneur, and has played a significant role in trying to break down the barriers between Western scholars and practition- ers of Daoism.

Besides her voluminous scholarly publications, Kohn has produced numer- ous translations of important, useful texts to practitioners. Until the 2000s, Livia Kohn was considered to be very much a classical sinologist, German- trained, textual, and narrowly focused. But she then became more interested in

Western Daoism,[58] and then in effect became a popular Western Daoist herself. After she retired from full-time teaching at Boston University in 2004, a year before Komjathy completed his doctoral work, she opened a center in New Mexico where she lived from early 2006 to late 2008 to devote more time to teaching Daoist practice—her "Daoist immersion program" was mentioned by the scholar of religion and tourism Michael Stausberg as an example of "crossing the boundaries."[59]

In fact, Kohn had been a practitioner of one sort or another since the mid-1970s, when she began to practice tai chi as an exchange student at UC-Berkeley. After receiving her PhD from Bonn University in 1980, she moved to Kyoto, where her "meditation horizon widened considerably and [she] came in contact with Buddhist practice: insight meditation, tantra, and Zen. [She] participated in a 10-day Vipassana course by S. N. Goenka, sat with the local Dharmadhatu group, read every book of Chogyam Trungpa."[60] As a full-time professor at Boston University in 1988, she "published several books in Daoist meditation and Chinese mysticism while continuing insight practice."[61] During her formal academic career, she was primarily a dedicated Vipassana practitioner, consistently engaging in daily meditation and attending various retreats of both the ten-day and thirty-day varieties. This was the case when Komjathy was her graduate student from 1998 through 2005.[62]

But she was a scholar first and foremost, and her Buddhist meditation practice was kept discreet. After retirement, however, she self-published books (via her own Three Pines Press, devoted to works on Daoism), marketed herself as a practice teacher (in her biography on the website of a now defunct nonprofit she set up, she writes: "Livia Kohn has practiced taiji quan, qigong, meditation, and other cultivation practices for over twenty years"),[63] and led workshops—much like any New Age teacher, albeit with indescribably more historical, textual, and academic knowledge. Recently, she became a facilitator for a new eclectic form of energy healing called Core Health (cf. CorePower Yoga).[64]

As Livia Kohn's trajectory began to parallel Michael Winn's, it is not surprising that they have become friends and colleagues, and that she and Komjathy have become distant. Winn invited Kohn to his China Dream Trip and, though she had to cancel, she later led her own version of a Dream Trip in June of 2011, "The Footsteps of Laozi," with stays at Huashan and other Daoist sacred sites. Winn has contributed to two of Kohn's Three Pines Press anthologies, on body cultivation and inner alchemy.[65] Indeed, he has reviewed these books on his website and sells them there as well. Kohn, though certainly not a student of Winn's, has praised him as a good writer—"articulate" and well read, who learns from Kohn's books.

Livia Kohn has organized a series of conferences where scholars and practitioners of Daoism can interact with each other. The first was the Daoism
and Ecology conference at Harvard University in 1998[66] that was a part of a
series of ecology conferences, one devoted to each major world religion. It
was at this conference that Komjathy first met Livia Kohn, Kristofer Schipper,
and Liu Ming. In fact, Komjathy had specifically come to the conference to
explore the possibility of graduate studies with Kohn. Discussions at that conference eventually gave rise to a by-invitation-only meeting on Daoist Cultivation on Vashon Island near Seattle in May 2001. This was the first time that
Daoist scholars and practitioners were deliberately brought together. Livia
Kohn was the official convener, with the support of Mary Evelyn Tucker, a
professor of religion and ecology who organized the Harvard conference,
and Harrison Moretz, the founding director of the Taoist Studies Institute.
However, the key organizer was Kohn's graduate student, Louis Komjathy.
Partially rooted in a dissatisfaction with the "practitioner representatives" at
the Daoism and Ecology conference,[67] Komjathy specifically wanted to gather
"tradition-based Daoist adherents" and leading scholars. However, the endeavor proved to be challenging and, in the end, Komjathy had to settle with
some "New Age Daoists."[68] The event is where Kohn and Komjathy first met
Michael Winn.[69]

The invitation to Winn (originally intended for Mantak Chia) gave him a
context for defining himself as a scholar-practitioner as well, able to engage in
serious conversations with academic researchers. As Winn recounts,

> [Kohn and I] met at Vashon Island for the first time. She sent an invitation for
> Mantak Chia to come and I wrote back and I said, he's not available and he
> wouldn't be the right person anyway. He wouldn't relate to scholars. And I said
> I think the right person is me. And she said, OK, you come. Then she read my
> first paper, and she said, OK, this guy is kind of a private scholar. And he's a
> serious practitioner. . . . So she kept inviting me back, and I kept offering more
> perspective on that, and we became good friends. And it's been a good rela-
> tionship. I appreciate her role in bringing this into the academic community.[70]

The invitation was actually sent by Komjathy, who later saw the presentations of Winn and other "New Age" *qigong* practitioners as one of the major
deficiencies of the conference.[71] Indeed, inspired by the Vashon Island retreat, Kohn began holding international Daoist conferences roughly every
two years, and thus became the one person most responsible for bringing
together scholars and practitioners, and possibly for helping to legitimize
popular Western Daoism, often in scenic spots such as Daoist mountains in
China or lakes in Germany. She rates the conferences as "vastly successful" in

their attempts to reconcile scholars and practitioners, including "psychologists and business people."[72] Ideally, they engender exchanges of ideas and
practices, a widening of horizons. Sometimes, however, one gets the impression of two communities that speak past each other or through each other,
rather than with each other. For Komjathy, "They are undermining the Daoist tradition as such." Winn, however, is enthusiastic about the opportunity to
challenge scholars with knowledge derived from the experience of practice:

> [Kohn has] been a real mover and a shaker and I really appreciate her role in
> this of honoring practitioners. That's essentially what she's doing. I was at the
> Boston conference [Kohn's first international conference on Daoist Studies in
> 2003], and I presented a paper on the greatest Kan and Li formula, which
> deals with the planets and tones and things like this.[73] And Steve Eskildsen [a
> textual scholar of Daoism] is one of the readers and he says, "I've never heard
> of this; I can't believe this. I just have trouble, sorry." And I'm just saying this is
> an oral tradition here, which I'm putting into writing. I understand it was kept
> very secret and it wasn't put in writing before. So you don't know that. Now
> you do. That was a shock for him to see that elucidated. Or even to understand
> that the *Yijing* might be a musical notation system. I come at these things from
> a different perspective. We share the same interests. I'm just coming from a
> different perspective. They're trying to find the text, and the cultural context
> of the text, and I'm trying to locate the practitioner's point of view and how
> it's applied. So we're both interested in the same fact, we just have a different
> conclusion about its relevance.[74]

Ironically, by organizing the Vashon Island conference, Komjathy introduced
Kohn to Winn, and also set the template for the Daoist Conferences that he
now decries. Now he sometimes regrets his share of responsibility for what
he considers to be highly problematic subsequent developments. From his
"tradition-based" perspective, Kohn and Winn are collaborators in the self-
perpetuating, insular cycle of the spiritual capitalist and popular construction
of Daoism—"the end of Daoism."

The Loyola Marymount Conference

The sixth in the series of Livia Kohn's Daoist Studies conferences took place in
June 2010 at the prestigious Jesuit institution Loyola Marymount University
(LMU) in Los Angeles, on a gently sloping hill, covered in manicured grass,
overlooking the marina and the inevitable tangle of freeways. The gathering of Daoist scholars, practitioners, and scholar-practitioners did not dispel
the golden state's reputation as a center of spiritual individualism: here were
a mix of independent scholars, each hawking their own translation of the

Daodejing; martial arts and *qigong* masters with various groupies; and other seekers and sages dressed in various types of Chinese-style costumes. And there were several top scholars, American and Chinese, in the fields of Religious Studies and sinology, experts in Daoist Studies. While Komjathy had stayed away from Winn during his trip to China in 2004, he couldn't avoid him at the LMU conference. Komjathy presented a paper titled "Towards a History of Early Daoist Visualization Practice"; Michael Winn, who had just flown back from China after leading his 2010 Dream Trip, led a workshop titled "Qigong for Scholars: Grounding the Mental Body." The two of us were also there: we presented the first iterations of this chapter and chapter 7 of this book; Kohn had appointed Winn as the official panel chair, and Komjathy was in the audience.

The first morning at LMU, Livia Kohn's keynote address attempted to link Daoism to a list of trendy book titles in business and popular psychology. Addressing her audience "we, as Daoists," she exhorted us to become "change agents." The other keynote speaker was a self-styled Daoist master who had emigrated from China to southern California. He performed something called "dragon sword calligraphy," writing a talisman on a piece of paper "in honor of peace." For Komjathy, who walked out of this quasi-mediumistic "energy reading," it was yet another moment of "Daoist charlatanism" and "spiritual exhibitionism."

After the keynote, participants broke into groups for three days of panels and practice sessions. Panels focused on topics such as "Daoist Leadership Education" and "Daoism and Quantum Physics"; practice sessions included "Willow Waist: Women's Alchemical Practice" and "Chinese Astrology: Learning about Your Destiny." A panel on dietetics brought together academics (Livia Kohn and her former student Shawn Arthur) and practitioners (a doctor of traditional Chinese medicine) giving papers.

One might have expected that Komjathy, as a scholar-practitioner, would have found this conference, bringing together both scholars and practitioners, to represent a significant advance for the development of American Daoism. In fact, Komjathy was highly critical of the whole enterprise, and remarked that this conference represented "the end of Daoism." He was also disappointed that none of the attendees sought his own perspective as a scholar-practitioner. As he confided in us toward the end of the conference, as a Daoist, he had developed spiritual discernment—and he could tell as he sat at dinner with the conference participants, that "there is no cultivation in all these people. I wouldn't call them Daoists, or call this Daoism." To him Daoism "is about emptying the self. Here at the conference, people are filling the self." Instead of seeing the LMU conference as an encounter of scholars and practitioners, he saw it as an "extension of the activities of the National Qigong Association (NQA)"—in other words, a collection of *qigong* technicians (among whom he would include Michael Winn), each with a *qigong* form to market.

Komjathy's Story

Although Komjathy has been critical of certain expressions of so-called "American Daoism," his own path to Daoism conforms to many of the recurring patterns. After his parents divorced when he was twelve and his mother decided to move out of Michigan, he grew up in a middle-class home in California's Central Valley. From his early teens, he practiced aikido, enjoyed backpacking, and had an enduring interest in poetry. On one solo backpacking trip, when he was seventeen, he slept outside in the wilderness for seven days, and fasted for five of them. He also read "spiritual classics," including the *Dhammapada*, *Upanishads*, and *The Prophet*. There were various moments of deep stillness and expansions of consciousness. Ex post facto, Komjathy calls this an experience of nature mysticism, without any particular framework or vocabulary to express it. It changed his notion of space; when he came back to civilization, he felt boxed in by the corners in the rooms of buildings.[75] He also recalls having a unitive mystical experience while rock climbing the granite peaks at Yosemite National Park.

As a student at the University of California at San Diego, Komjathy majored in literature and philosophy. In his sophomore year, he spent a semester at Dartmouth College where he met an African American tai chi and Buddho-Daoist teacher, Deneal Amos (1928–2003), who led a residential quasi-monastic community. He began practicing Yang-style *taiji quan*. He felt a visceral connection between his *taiji quan* and his rock climbing, "Because if your body is not fully connected when you're flat against the rock face, you may not survive." Amos also gave Komjathy his first copy of the *Daodejing*, the R. B. Blakney translation (1958) titled *The Way of Life*, as well as a reading list of "spiritual classics," including J. Krishnamurti's *Freedom from the Known*. He studied the *Daodejing* while backpacking on the Appalachian Trail, and found that its message apparently confirmed his previous mystical experiences. He now had a theological language. In addition to feeling a deep affinity with the views expressed in the text and developing an emerging "wilderness ethic," Komjathy's time with Amos was noteworthy in two other respects. First, he often says that he "converted to Daoism through movement." His "conversion" to Daoism, which he formally identifies as having taken place in 1994, was as much about Amos's presence and Komjathy's experiences of "energetic harmonization" during tai chi classes as about the textual study of the *Daodejing*. Komjathy contemplated returning to Hanover, New Hampshire, after graduation to engage in full-time training.[76]

In college, he stopped drinking and eating meat because of his own philosophical reflection and spiritual inquiry; as he describes it, these restrictions lost him many of his friends. He was beginning to follow a quasi-ascetic way of life. After graduating in 1993, Komjathy moved to Seattle to start graduate school at the University of Washington, where he planned to study ecological themes in English romantic and American transcendentalist literature. He didn't get funding so he took a series of menial jobs, including driving recycling and juice delivery trucks, to make a living. He also began studying Daoism, Chinese internal martial arts, including *taiji quan*, and Chinese language at the Taoist Studies Institute (TSI) under the direction of Harrison Moretz, a longtime Euro-American practitioner of Daoism and internal martial arts. According to Komjathy, since leaving Dartmouth, he had been searching for a teacher with a "similar form" as Amos's Yang-style *taiji quan*; Moretz was the first such teacher. Komjathy practiced Daoist meditation and cultivation, including *qigong* and *taiji quan*, about twenty hours a week. Here, he also began reading various publications on Daoism. He recalls Kohn's *Taoist Meditation and Longevity Techniques* and Schipper's *The Taoist Body* being especially influential. He also read Thomas Cleary's *Vitality, Energy, Spirit* (1991), the first popular anthology on Quanzhen Daoism. Komjathy sees his own later work, *The Way of Complete Perfection* (2013) as an academic development of or counterpoint to Cleary's publication. At TSI, he also met Kate Townsend, who had been practicing Daoist cultivation and Traditional Chinese Medicine since the early 1980s.

Komjathy and Townsend began a relationship, eventually getting married. In 1997, they went to China together. On the way to an internship at the Chengdu University of Traditional Chinese Medicine, Komjathy and Townsend traveled to Shaanxi Province with the purpose of visiting Huashan. They decided to hike up the traditional pilgrimage route, beginning at the Jade Spring Monastery and ending at the summit. As they passed through the base-monastery in the predawn hours, Townsend noticed a monk practicing standing meditation, almost invisible near a tree. (After they later met Master Chen in 2004, Townsend wondered if it was him.) It was late autumn and chilly, not tourist season: they saw only a handful of people on the mountain. At the top, they reached the ruins of the temple of the Southern Gate of Heaven which was full of shards of Daoist material culture and garbage. "For some reason, we started to clean it up." On the Eastern Peak, Komjathy and Townsend encountered a ten-year-old boy monk, sitting on a bench, his legs spread and his hands on his knees, in the proper meditative posture. The boy took them to his master, an old, weatherworn monk, and they had tea in the temple. Then the old monk led Komjathy down the cliff on a stone ladder to a cave. The old monk went down the stone rungs facing forward; the attendants discouraged Komjathy from going, but he went anyway. This was the spot where a major figure of Huashan Daoism had meditated; Komjathy felt it had great significance for him. And it also reminded him of the places where he had rock climbed as a youth. It was also while staying overnight on the summit of Huashan that Townsend and Komjathy had another significant encounter. At dusk in the guesthouse, a single Daoist nun appeared, opened the largely defunct Daoist temple, and lit candles and incense before the Daoist altar. There was no actual Daoist icon or material culture, only a broken-down doll on a table. The nun chanted the entire Quanzhen liturgy by herself in the dimly lit cave-temple. Komjathy and Townsend discussed how this provided a clear insight into Daoism at the time: While it appeared diminished and in jeopardy of extinction, there remained dedicated Daoists engaging in self-cultivation and chanting before unknown altars. For Townsend, the nun was keeping a Daoist energetic presence and light alive. Still, at that time, Komjathy didn't feel a strong spiritual connection with the mountain, and didn't anticipate ever going back to Huashan.[77]

Later that year, after attending the Daoism and Ecology conference at Harvard University and meeting with Livia Kohn, Townsend and Komjathy moved to Boston, so that he could begin a PhD in Religious Studies with Kohn. By that time, Komjathy had read most of the literature published in English on Daoism. He had reflected on potential academic mentors, wishing to study with someone with a "practice-oriented" and more experiential perspective. He had identified Isabelle Robinet (1932–2000), Kristofer Schipper, and Kohn. In addition to the fact that Robinet and Schipper were in France, Komjathy's decision centered on Kohn's interest in Daoist meditation and her mastery of translation. Komjathy wanted to devote himself to the study of Daoism and especially to the translation of Daoist literature, and graduate school in a secular institution offered the only avenue for systematic study. (He subsequently described this as a quasi-seminary education.) He was not necessarily interested in an academic career; he was more concerned about how he could do academic studies while maintaining his practice.[78] Using original texts, he prepared his thesis on Wang Chongyang, the founder of the Quanzhen movement, and the practices of his early community of followers. After finishing his courses and qualifying exams at Boston University in 2001, but before finishing his dissertation, he returned to Seattle where he offered to teach courses on Daoist history and texts at the Taoist Studies Institute, partially as a gesture of gratitude toward

Moretz and partially to help community members develop a deeper understanding of Daoism. The organization provided a forum for him to teach,
but showed no real interest in or commitment to what he was teaching. Only
a few persons attended his classes. However, he channeled his energy into a
translation project. This resulted in his self-publication of the *Handbooks for
Daoist Practice*,[79] which were originally released in 2003 under the imprint
of Wandering Cloud Press and later formally published in 2008 by the Yuen
Yuen Institute in Hong Kong. This was the first translation series specifically
intended for individuals interested in Daoist practice. The project also revealed his increasing interest in what he would identify as a central part of
committed Daoist practice, namely, "scripture study" (*jingxue*). It was also
in 2003 that Komjathy and Townsend began the nascent Center for Daoist
Studies. At this time, Komjathy gave himself the Daoist name Xiujing ("Cultivating Stillness"), in order to express his affinity with clarity-and-stillness
(*qingjing*) practices.

Now Komjathy felt at a crossroads. He had completed his academic
training, and there was nowhere for him to go in the United States to learn
more about the Daoist tradition. He would have to look both further within
and farther afield—and that meant going to China. It was 2004. He had not
planned to go to Huashan, having already been there (Wudangshan was his
intended primary destination)—but, as we have already described, after we
unexpectedly bumped into him and Townsend at Louguantai, they changed
their itinerary, went to Huashan, and met Masters Chen and Hu.

This time, Huashan became a key location in his spiritual trajectory. For
Komjathy, Huashan not only resembles Yosemite physically and energetically,
but both are places where he "grew up spiritually." However, he generally de-
clines to speak of his personal spiritual experiences there, saying only that he
is critical of Winn for using his Dream Trip promotional materials to focus
on visionary and transcendent experiences in the hidden caves of Huashan.
"The energetics of Huashan is not in the caves," Komjathy told us. "Why is
it beneficial to meditate in a cave?" he asked rhetorically. "Are the desires to
meet Immortals and to achieve immortality for oneself better than drinking
tea with Master Hu?" As a follower of a "non-theistic form of Daoism," Komjathy is "not interested in making contact with gods."

The path Komjathy has chosen for himself at Huashan is a rigorous one,
one without the dazzling promise of the Dream Trippers' encounters. Perhaps
it is something akin to the pilgrimage route that he and Townsend first took
in 1997 and his third ascent with Master Hu in 2006.[80] It is a path of lineage
affiliation and serious study. It is a path of quiet sitting, a path Komjathy also
sees in his monastic mentors: "For Chen and Hu, solitary meditation was

the root of self-cultivation. They were committed to and emphasized daily personal meditation practice in a quiet and secluded place. Both were proficient in lineage-based *neidan* systems of self-transformation, but both also preferred 'quiet sitting' (*jingzuo*)."[81]

When Komjathy and Townsend first met with Masters Chen and Hu, they discussed Daoist adherence, identity, and practice. There was an immediate connection, partially because of Komjathy's deep knowledge about Daoism and his ability to converse in Chinese with questions related to Daoist practice. For Komjathy this meeting seemed to confirm his aspiration to be a scholar-practitioner. Komjathy mentioned that his Euro-American birth name was "Louis Komjathy" (the latter transliterated as Kang Siqi), but that many of his friends called him "Lou." He then told the monks that his self-given Daoist name was Xiujing. Chen and Hu laughed, saying "Lu (Lou) Xiujing," alluding to one of the most important Daoist systematizers in Chinese history, who lived in the fifth century (406–477). At the end of their initial meeting, Komjathy mentioned that he wanted to return alone the following year to live at the Jade Spring Monastery and to study with Master Chen. Master Chen provisionally agreed.

A year later, Komjathy returned to China as a visiting professor at Shandong University for the 2005–2006 academic year. He had planned to work as a professor and to conduct fieldwork on the material culture of Shandong Quanzhen for the first half of the year, and to work as an ethnographer and participant-observer of contemporary Daoist monasticism for the second half. Specifically, he had planned to live at the Jade Spring Monastery of Huashan with Masters Chen and Hu for four to six months. Within a week of arriving at the university, located in the city of Jinan, Komjathy called Master Chen to inform him that he was in China. However, Master Chen communicated an unexpected development: "I'm not at Huashan. I'm in Jinan, living with my parents." In yet another interesting twist of fate, Komjathy and Chen were living almost around the corner from each other. This encounter served to reinforce the sense of predestined affinities (*yuanfen*) necessary for a master and disciple to meet each other. They later met for tea, and Master Chen informed Komjathy that he had left Huashan for an indeterminate amount of time. Perplexed, Komjathy inquired if he would eventually go back. Master Chen said that he was unsure, but probably would not return. He was probably leaving the Quanzhen order as well. This uncertainty apparently pervaded the monastic community at Huashan after Master Chen's initial departure; for example, when Komjathy later met Master Hu, he constantly expressed hope for Chen's return. Chen's monastic friends imagined that he was only going into temporary seclusion.

Chen's decision to leave the monastery surprised Komjathy, and derailed his plans to live as a "visiting monastic" and to conduct ethnographic fieldwork as a participant-observer of contemporary Daoist monasticism. But Chen's explanation to Komjathy allowed Komjathy access to a different tradition. As Komjathy later reported it, in Daoism giving up monastic vows is usually referred to as "returning to the mundane" (*huansu*), but Chen told him that he preferred to refer to his own decision as "hiding his radiance" (*yinguang*) or "going into seclusion" (*yintui*). In other words, Chen's reasons for leaving "were not connected to desire for earthly pleasures unavailable (in theory) to monks: Meat, alcohol, sex, but rather as a way to intensify his own practice without the politics involved in running a monastery."[82]

In the late summer of 2005, Chen moved to Chengdu, as we narrated in chapter 4. Komjathy followed him there in the early spring of 2006, and they met often in teahouses to "discuss various dimensions of contemporary Quanzhen monastic life as well as the parameters of a Daoist religious way of life." According to Komjathy, "These meetings provided the necessary background for critically reflecting on appropriate questions" about Daoism and his relationship to it. They also traveled together to the nearby Daoist Mount Qingchengshan, where Chen "discussed Quanzhen monastic life from his own perspective and experiences as the vice-abbot of [the Jade Spring Monastery]."[83] During one particularly poignant exchange when they were discussing the current condition of Daoism, Komjathy commented, "Perhaps Daoism will die." Master Chen laughed, almost embarrassed by the matter-of-factness, and paused. He then responded, "Daoism may die, but the Dao will last forever."[84]

The "Ordination"

That summer, Komjathy was initiated into the Huashan lineage of Quanzhen Daoism. The initiation took place at the Heming ("crane call") teahouse in the People's Park in Chengdu. Komjathy remarked on the coincidence of that name, which is the name of the mountain in Sichuan where the divinized Laozi revealed himself to Zhang Daoling in the second century CE, a revelation that is considered by many scholars as marking the birth of Daoism as an organized religion.

During these meetings, Komjathy again inquired about Daoist adherence and identity, including lineage and ordination. He expressed interest in the possibility of being ordained as a "Daoist priest" (*daoshi*). Master Chen explained that lineage should reflect one's own affinities and commitments, especially with a particular teacher. They moved into a deeper discussion about the defining characteristics of the Longmen and Huashan lineages. Chen explained that, in addition to their associations with Qiu Chuji and Hao Datong, respectively, Longmen is more about precepts but Huashan is more free and spontaneous. Komjathy said that he was specifically interested in the Huashan lineage, partially because of the mountain locale and association with the solitary practice of hermits. He also expressed his deep respect for and recognition of Chen. This included a request to become Chen's disciple (*dizi*; *tudi*). Chen agreed. So began their formal master-disciple relationship, although Komjathy also frames this in terms of "companions of the Dao" (*daoyou*). Komjathy also had mentioned to Chen that he hoped to establish a Daoist community and center in the United States. It would include a new Daoist contemplative order called Qingjingdao (Way of Clarity and Stillness), due to Komjathy's affinity with the *Qingjing jing* (Scripture on Clarity and Stillness), belief that "clarity-and-stillness" (*qingjing*) is a major connective through the Daoist tradition, and emphasis on related "quietistic practices." However, Komjathy expressed reservations about using the name because of the existence of the Qingjingpai (Clarity and Stillness lineage), a Quanzhen lineage associated with Sun Bu'er and primarily consisting of Quanzhen nuns (*kundao*). Chen dismissed the problem, and said that Komjathy could use the Qingjing lineage poem for his own order. Surprisingly, Chen then informed Komjathy that he had been a disciple of a female master of this lineage in Shandong, Cui Jingyi (1912–2008) of Laoshan, so he could transmit an ordination name of this lineage as well.

Master Chen said he would have to go home and choose Daoist names for him. They met again at the same teahouse a few days later, and Chen told him the two names he had chosen for him: a Huashan lineage name (Wanrui, "Myriad Blessings"), and a Qingjing lineage name (Changde, "Constant Virtue"). The name Wanrui locates Komjathy as a twenty-sixth-generation lineage affiliate, with Chen Yuming as his "master-father" (*shifu*), and Xue Tailai, Master Chen's master, as his "master-grandfather" (*shiye*). As discussed in chapter 4, Xue Tailai was featured in Bill Porter's *Road to Heaven*. For Komjathy, such lineage names, if bestowed with intent and discernment, are highly significant: they both identify one's innate capacities and suggest areas for spiritual development. Komjathy often jokes that *wanrui* is a fascinating and difficult practice: accept everything as a blessing. This connects with Komjathy's view that "everything is cultivation." Now, in an information sheet, Komjathy describes himself and his wife Townsend as "founders and lineage-transmitters of the Clarity and Stillness Order, a new American Daoist religious order."

There was no other ceremony. But at that moment, Komjathy felt a new space opening between Chen and him. He felt a transmission taking place, he felt his own and Chen's "original nature" (*benxing*) open up and "an exchange beyond words" took place;[85] he could sense his heart and Master Chen's heart opening up and *daoqi*, the numinous presence of the Dao, flowing between them. He had had such an experience on a number of other occasions, with various other Daoists, and it is one of the key influences on his views concerning Daoist being and identity.

Komjathy then asked for a certificate (*zhengmingshu*, lit., "certificate of authenticity"). Chen said that wasn't necessary, and that besides, ordination certificates are no longer conferred now in the PRC. If he really wanted one, Master Chen would need to ask the gods if they accepted. But he could obtain a certificate at Huashan. In a later interview, Komjathy recollected the dialogue that ensued when he asked Chen for a certificate because "everybody has a document." Chen replied, "Do you think that's necessary?" Komjathy then asked, "Isn't it part of the tradition?" to which Chen replied, "The tradition is me informing heaven." Komjathy recalled he said something to the effect that the "world of charlatans" wouldn't believe him, to which Chen said, "That's fine." Komjathy took the latter insight as an important teaching.

As Chen recalled to us, "Komjathy wanted 'proof,' a written certificate of his initiation. But I refused to do so. *I* am the proof. I think all of this ordination business is useless. I told him: if God (*shangdi*) or Lü Dongbin appeared to save you, would you ask him to show his certificate (*daoshi zheng*)? . . . In China, now, anyone can get certificates and go through such ceremonies. There is nothing special about it at all. There are so many fake ordinations. Nowadays, it doesn't mean anything at all. You have to rely on yourself."[86]

Komjathy often refers to this transmission as his "ordination" as a Daoist "priest." Using traditional Daoist categories, he characterizes this experience as "entering the Dao" (*rudao*), "transmitting the Dao" (*chuandao*), or becoming a "Daoist priest" (*daoshi*; lit., "adept of the Way"). Alluding to his own process, he discusses ordination in terms of lineage and transmission, with particular attention to Chinese Daoist terms, in his recent textbook. Here, he explains, "Less well known are ordinations that do not involve formal public ceremonies, but rather direct transmissions between a master and disciple."[87]

However, the terms "ordination" and "priest," often used in Daoist Studies but borrowed from Catholic usage, do not easily translate back into Chinese. In the academic study of Daoism, the term "ordination" typically refers to the complex rites of the Zhengyi traditions, in which the authority is conferred on disciples to become "priests" (*daoshi*, masters of the Dao) conducting communal, healing, and exorcistic rituals, using specific talismans and registers, an authority that is obtained from the gods and signified by the conferring of "ordination certificates" (*dudie*, *dulu*). When we asked Master Chen the name of the "ceremony" that occurred in the People's Park teahouse, he explained that it was *baishi*—which literally means, "to show reverence for a master." It is the formal recognition of a master-disciple relationship by both parties, in which the conferring of a Daoist name, following the order of characters of the generational poem of a lineage, marks one's affiliation and membership in the lineage. According to Chen, this did not make Komjathy into a "Daoist master" (*daoshi*)—the term often translated into English as "priest," but which Chen understood to mean a celibate monk certified by the Chinese government—but rather gave him the status of a "formal disciple of a Daoist lineage" (*zhengshi de daomen dizi*). "It would be impossible for a foreigner to become a *daoshi*—it would need to be approved by the Daoist Association and so on."[88] For Chen, not only are ordination certificates meaningless, but so is the title of "Daoist master" or *daoshi* which now has no existence other than as a title and function conferred by the socialist state.

Komjathy stresses that he was never concerned about having a "ceremony" for his ordination; but that the transmission that occurred did, at an ontological level, make him into an ordained Daoist priest, albeit not according to Chen's governmental and institutional definition. As he wrote us,

> Ordination, or the formal process of becoming a Daoist priest or monastic (*daoshi* 道士), is a vocation, a calling. Ideally, this involves deep inquiry, formal training, and eventual confirmation. In the modern world, this is generally not the case. Individuals can buy (and have bought) ordination in modern mainland China. One finds a similar problematic and disturbing pattern among self-identified Daoist priests who use ordination and lineage as sources of legitimacy and authority, something akin to a TCM [Traditional Chinese Medicine] degree or Qigong certification.
>
> From my perspective, ordination is both an event and a continuing commitment. It involves specific roles and responsibilities. Daoist clerical identity is both ontological (about being) and functional (about enactment). The former relates to one's existence and transmission, while the latter relates to one's role and performance. These dimensions merge together in teaching, spiritual direction, and ritual activity. Daoist priests embody and transmit the Dao and the Daoist tradition in the world; they support individuals' inquiry into the Dao and Daoist ways of being; and they offer services and perform ritual when requested or required.[89]

Even though Komjathy had asked Chen for a "certificate" (*zhengmingshu*), he explained to us, a few years later, that although he did seek it out of a desire for legitimation, his main purpose in stating his position in the Huashan lineage in his public presentation was "to give a clear indication of my location within the tradition. Sometimes I speak as a Daoist, sometimes as a Quanzhen

Daoist, sometimes as a member of the specific lineage [Huashan]. It tells people exactly where I stand." However, Komjathy increasingly emphasizes that this has become problematic. Komjathy also does not believe that one *must* be ordained or have lineage to be a Daoist adherent or affiliate;[90] a root in tradition-based practice and deep study have been and remain his primary concern. He removed the references to his lineage affiliations from his website after other American Daoist commercial operators saw the marketing potential of such ordinations and asked him how to obtain one. As he wrote us,

> The challenge here is the high degree of corruption and distortion at work throughout much of modern Daoism, whether in China, Europe, the United States, or somewhere else. For example, in the case of the United States, one finds many self-identified Daoists using lineage and ordination as sources of legitimation and promotion. This includes individuals who received no formal training, who apparently purchased ordination, and who have no actual commitment to the charism (spiritual characteristics) of the corresponding Daoist movement or lineage. For example, one finds self-identified "Longmen" (Dragon Gate) Daoists who adhere to neither basic Quanzhen (Complete Perfection) monastic commitments[91] nor specifically Longmen lifeways.[92] This is not to mention actual self-cultivation and spiritual realization. The easiest way to avoid charlatans and deluded individuals is to educate oneself about the Daoist tradition.[93]

So now, he downplayed the importance of ordination titles and certificates, claiming that Western scholarship on Daoism has missed the real meaning of ordination and priesthood, based on studies of the Zhengyi order in which ordination certificates and rituals are the defining characteristics of the status of a priest. For Komjathy, the shift away from an emphasis on ordination is simply an expression of the fact that, for him, "Daoist inner cultivation, spiritual realization, and mystical attunement with the Dao have always been and remain my primary concern and orientation. It is also clearly influenced by Chen's teachings."[94]

> Ordination into priesthood is not only based on ordination certificates. This is a misunderstanding of the facts. The scholars take priesthood in a functional sense, but I understand it in an ontological sense. When Master Chen gave me the transmission, I felt an ontological transformation in myself. After that I felt ideas coming to me that were from the Quanzhen Order, that were not from my own path. The Huashan lineage started to work on me, to work through me. To be a priest means to have a commitment to the lineage, to its transmission, to knowing that it is not oneself. To be a priest is a burden: it is better not to be one, to be simply a practitioner, because then you are free, you do not have this responsibility.[95]

In that same interview, Komjathy spoke about the changes that took place after this "ordination" in the Heming teahouse: he began to "see the world from a Quanzhen perspective," and become infused with a kind of "Quanzhen DNA," thereby "getting rid of family karma."[96]

A few years later, we asked Komjathy how a claim to an "ontological transformation" can make one a priest. Can't Michael Winn also say that he has been ontologically transformed? "I can tell, and so can you," replied Komjathy, "that he has *qi*, not *daoqi*. He also does not have lineage. You need to be a manifestation of Dao." For Komjathy, it is not that "ontological transformation" makes one into a priest; it is, rather, that being a priest involves an ontological transformation. The ordinand ideally becomes a *new being*. Some of Komjathy's critique of "spiritual entrepreneurs" like Winn, and their supposed lack of *daoqi*, centers on "virtue" (*de*). From Komjathy's perspective, virtue is both a prerequisite for and a manifestation of Daoist cultivation. "One would not engage in certain types of behaviors or have certain character qualities if one had fruition of practice." Komjathy points toward the high degree of commercialism, materialism, and narcissism at work in much of "so-called Daoism"—including in spiritual tourism to Daoist sacred sites—as indicative of deficiency.[97]

Experiences of Monastic Life

After his initiation by Master Chen, during the spring of 2006, Komjathy stayed for a week at Taiqinggong (Palace of Great Clarity), the base-monastery at Laoshan in Shandong, through the assistance of Shandong University. They did not know that he had been a committed Daoist practitioner for over ten years and that he had recently become a formal disciple of Master Chen. In fact, he was advised by his sponsor not to mention any of this, especially to the official representative of the local Bureau of Religious Affairs. For almost everyone involved, Komjathy was "just a scholar" who wanted to understand Quanzhen monastic life from an academic perspective. Some feared that he was a "government mole." Nonetheless, they welcomed him in with some reservations and gave him a set of formal Quanzhen dress, including long robes, hat, shoes, and stockings. "They took me in to humor my foreigner's fancies, because I was connected to [a professor at Shandong University], and the Bureau of Religious Affairs told them in advance that they needed to act properly and to avoid eating meat or drinking alcohol in my presence."[98] During his week at Laoshan, Komjathy participated in the daily morning and evening liturgical recitation, ate in the refectory, and developed relationships with the administrator monks. The latter taught him the correct order of dress, different styles of topknots, as well as the various symbolic associations. Komjathy also climbed the mountain, during which he had tea conversations about Daoist cultivation with a number of senior monastics.

Komjathy was on the "inside" of monastic life as a visiting scholar-monk, but he was on the "outside" as a foreigner. Given the endless throngs of tourists, Komjathy often found himself as an object of curiosity, with frequent requests to take pictures with the "foreign Daoist" (*yang daoshi*). Komjathy began to develop a deeper understanding of the experience of Chinese Daoists, and their reticence to be seen or known. After a few days, one of the assistant directors asked about Komjathy's interest in Daoism. Komjathy self-identified as a Daoist and mentioned his Daoist name of Xiujing. He then said that he was a disciple of Master Chen, and that his Huashan lineage name was Wanrui. This rumor spread through the monastery, and many of the residents began to warm to Komjathy. One group of younger monks asked who his Chinese teacher was. When Komjathy identified Master Chen, but said that he had left Huashan, the monk replied, "This is terrible. Quanzhen needs Chen Yuming." For Komjathy, the fact that distant Laoshan monks knew of the Huashan monk Chen confirmed Komjathy's sense of Chen's rarity and importance.

He then went to Huashan where he stayed at the Jade Spring Monastery. According to his own report, he "participated in daily ritual activities, specifically the Complete Perfection liturgical services; discussed Daoist cosmology, literature, philosophy, and practice with senior Complete Perfection monks; visited and documented the layout and iconography of these sacred sites; and learned about the daily life of Complete Perfection monastics."[99]

Chen's decision to leave the monastic order meant that Komjathy's main "companion in the Dao" (*daoyou*) and supporter at Huashan could no longer give him permission to live at the monastery. He arrived at Huashan, wearing his Daoist robes, and found Master Hu. After having tea together, Hu offered him a room in the junior monk quarters. Later, Komjathy asked Master Hu about obtaining the "certificate," but Hu took him to meet the new vice-abbot, Master Hei. Hei, Hu, and five or six other leading monks all came, and they told him that it would not be possible to provide him with one. It would not only require permission from the Bureau of Religious Affairs, but one also needed to be a resident Chinese monastic. In the modern PRC, what Komjathy was requesting was the equivalent of a government identification card. However, in a gesture of compassion and generosity, Master Hu then took him aside and told him he would do it himself. Hu finally gave the certificate to him. The document is a "Huashan jushi zheng" (i.e., a "Huashan lay Daoist") membership card.[100] Hu explained that he could not provide an actual *daoshi* certificate, which could only be legally issued by the government. Nonetheless, for Komjathy, Hu's bestowal confirmed his connection to Master Chen, the Huashan lineage, and Huashan itself, and he remains deeply grateful.

In his report, Komjathy describes his two-week stay at the Jade Spring Monastery at Huashan:

> I was welcomed there by [Master Hu], who was also a close friend of Master Chen. Here my relationship with Chen was both beneficial and detrimental. With respect to the former, Hu knew me from previous visits and knew that I had been ordained. From his perspective, I was a Huashan Daoist, and so I should be received in a gracious way. This meant that I could live within the monastic compound as a visiting Daoist. At the same time, I had to be circumspect about my connections with Chen. I received different explanations about Chen's decision to leave Huashan, including the laxity among Huashan monastics, the political nature of monastic administration and Daoism in China, and the volume of tourist activity and visitor reception.[101]

For Komjathy, living at Huashan was a profound experience. He had daily tea conversations with Master Hu, during which they discussed Daoist cultivation. One of Komjathy's favorite moments was when they meditated next to the monastic compound's Koi pond and they talked about the "joy of fish," an allusion to the *Zhuangzi*. During this time, Hu often discussed his deep friendship with and fondness for Master Chen, including their earlier "poetry exchanges." Hu gave a set of these poems to Komjathy. Komjathy also explored the deeper history of Quanzhen at Huashan, including the associated lineage. Specifically, he found the tomb of Xue Tailai with an epitaph written by Master Chen and a side temple dedicated to He Zhizhen (1212–1299), a disciple of Hao Datong and possibly the formal founder of the Huashan lineage. Now Komjathy made offerings at sacred sites associated with his own lineage: from Hao to He to Xue to Chen to Komjathy. Finally, he and Master Hu made the pilgrimage up to the summit, during which Hu showed him various secret locales and explained the mountain's "inner history." They stayed inside of mountain monasteries and often meditated together. When he returned to Huashan about a week later, Komjathy gave a photobook and seal carving to Master Hu as a sign of his appreciation.

A few months later, when the 2006 Dream Trippers came to Huashan, Master Hu told us of Komjathy's visit: "He now has his hair in a topknot, like a Quanzhen monk. But this is of his own volition, not on Master Chen's instructions. But he is too passionately opposed to what is happening in American Daoism: he should calm down and become more detached."

Later that summer, Master Chen's comments to us were much in the same vein:

> He was very disappointed when I left monastic life. He is very much a scholar, a bookworm. This is not a bad thing. He has very fixed ideas, he is too sectarian, and too strongly attached to Quanzhen. He has many dogmatic ideas about the way Daoism should be, much of which is his own ideas. This is bookish, scholastic knowledge. Real cultivation must be based on true experience, not theory. He always talks about how there are so many fake Daoists in America, using Daoism for their own purposes, teaching tai chi in the name of Daoism. But I said, what's wrong with that? Practicing the zither can be an excellent form of cultivation, why shouldn't people practice tai chi as well as a form of self-perfection? But I really like him, because he reminds me of the way I was when I had just become a monk, so full of passion for Daoism, so full of hope and optimism for what can be done in society. He is just the way I was when I was beginning: totally bookish, sectarian, so earnest. His plan to establish Quanzhen Daoism in the US will be very difficult and may or may not succeed, but it doesn't matter. In this process, he will have many tests and experiences that will make him know more about the true nature of Daoism. This will be very good for his cultivation and this is more important than whether or not he succeeds.[102]

Komjathy returned to the United States and full-time teaching at Pacific Lutheran University. He next saw Chen in the summer of 2009, when his wife Kate Townsend was also initiated by Chen at the teahouse in People's Park. She received the Huashan lineage name of Wanqing ("Myriad Clarities") and the Qingjing lineage name of Changrong ("Constant Acceptance"). Afterward, Komjathy and Townsend independently went to Qingyanggong (Azure Ram Temple) and made offerings to the Three Purities and the external Three Treasures (Dao, Scriptures, Masters), and Komjathy gave her the Daoist name of Baojing ("Embracing Stillness"). For most of July of that year, Komjathy and Townsend met with Chen almost daily, either in the teahouse or in their room at a hostel near the park. Their meetings usually lasted for several hours at a time, with Komjathy translating. They discussed many topics: self-cultivation, of course, but also atonement (*chanhui*). Townsend stressed that Chen does more than articulate Daoist teachings; he embodies them, especially with regard to his patience in the face of slow back-and-forth translation. The overall slowness of the conversation—Komjathy being more at ease in the written classical language than oral Chinese conversation, combined with the time taken for Komjathy to translate for Townsend—would make the conversations with Chen take on an effortful quality, requiring a patience and commitment akin to meditation. Chen mentioned that he too learns from these sessions: Komjathy and Townsend's questions enable him to go deeper in his knowledge.[103] Komjathy and Townsend always make a donation to Master Chen when they meet. Although Chen often refuses, the pair urges him to use it to help others. For Komjathy, "This 'giving' approach stands in contrast to the 'taking' approach of the spiritual tourists. It is the difference between reverence and colonialism."[104]

Later that summer, Chen told us that Komjathy "has made lots of progress. . . . He used to be a total bookworm. He kept on getting angry, especially at those people he considered to be 'false' Daoists, but now he's mellowed out a lot. He understands more."[105] Chen later also said that he was moved by Komjathy's "sense of mission toward the religion. His steadfastness, his willingness to sacrifice, his devotion to his cause are all most praiseworthy qualities."[106]

But Komjathy felt that the communication with Chen in 2009 had not been as fruitful as previously. "Master Chen is now moving away from Quanzhen Daoism; he's more interested in talking about 'Dao' than about Daoism. The time before [in 2006], it was better because we were at closer points in our cultivation, with me moving closer to the Quanzhen tradition and him having just left it."[107]

The Daoist Foundation

Meanwhile, in September 2007, Komjathy and Townsend had established the Daoist Foundation, which they describe as a "nonprofit religious and educational organization dedicated to fostering authentic Daoist study and practice and to preserving and transmitting traditional Daoist culture." They hope to form a viable Daoist community "that is not dependent on a charismatic leader and that will survive any particular individual."[108] In many ways, the Foundation allows them to fulfill their roles as Daoist priests as opposed to mere practitioners, which includes, as Komjathy told us, switching one's allegiance from birth family to a spiritual family (including getting a new name); acting as spiritual director (your practice of self-cultivation is not just for you, but also for your teachers, your students, the community); and therefore practicing one-on-one spiritual direction, "that is, helping each individual understand his or her own connection with the Dao and life-destiny (*ming*), the way in which the Dao unfolds in/as/through oneself."[109] Komjathy explained the "dream" and "vision" of the Daoist Foundation as follows:

> Through the Daoist Foundation, we are working to establish and maintain
> an authentic and viable tradition-based Daoist community in America, one

that is connected to, but independent of, Chinese Daoism. This involves establishing a Daoist mountain retreat center, which will offer authentic Daoist training in various forms and at various levels, including seminary training with ordination and nonordination tracks. It involves offering opportunities to deepen spiritual training and forms of communal participation. Our hope is eventually to have a Daoist place with Daoist aesthetics. We are also working to establish a new contemplative order, the Clarity-and-Stillness Order (Qingjing dao 清靜道; CSO), which will involve formal training and eventual ordination. The Clarity-and-Stillness Order is rooted in both the Quanzhen movement and its Huashan (Mount Hua) lineage. It emphasizes the *Qingjing jing* (Scripture on Clarity and Stillness) as its primary text and the cultivation of interiority, energetic attunement, meditative absorption, and spiritual insight. Another dimension of CSO charism is mountain contemplation (*shanguan* 山觀). Potential CSO ordinands will have religious affiliation with Quanzhen, the Huashan lineage, and the Clarity-and-Stillness Order.[110]

The Daoist Foundation is a registered nonprofit organization and public charity, with the aspiration to eventually secure "church" status. Challenging the logic of the marketplace, Komjathy refuses to adapt his teachings to supply-and-demand forces and emphasizes the importance of giving. He compares both to offering incense before a Daoist altar. In fact, Komjathy and Townsend hope to fully establish a donation-based model and community.

The more communal part of the Daoist Foundation as it operated during the time of our research is the Gallagher Cove Daoist Association, named after the location of the home in Olympia, Washington, where the group meets. Generally, five or six people would meet monthly for an all-day session until Komjathy relocated to San Diego, when the association met around four times a year. In San Diego, Komjathy also teaches through a new association he formed, the Floating Bridge Daoist Association. Komjathy instructs his students on standing meditation, *qigong*, dietetics (seasonal eating), scripture study, as well as seated meditation and self-massage. Here, scripture study begins with the *Laozi* and *Zhuangzi* as foundational Daoist texts, but the community also uses Komjathy's *Handbooks for Daoist Practice*.

On one Saturday in March 2011, we attended one of the seasonal retreats of the Gallagher Cove Daoist Association. Besides Komjathy and Townsend and a senior community member whose house they were using and who also served as a chief patron, there were eight people in attendance. "I don't know what some of them are really looking for; for some of them it may simply be for health and contentment. I don't know if any of them would be interested in going any farther," he later told us.[111] After friendly chatting, Komjathy began with Yangsheng ("nourishing life"), which was essentially standing meditation and *qigong*. He instructed us on empty standing; "expelling the old and ingesting the new"; "Three Elixir Field standing"; and ingesting and circulating *qi*, which included harvesting celestial and terrestrial *qi* and storing *qi* in our three *dantians*. Overall, these were similar to Michael Winn's practices. However, the content of the next few hours was quite different from anything Winn would teach in Asheville or on a Dream Trip. After the first break, Komjathy put on robes and the Daoist headband (*yizi jin*) associated with "cloud wandering" and commenced what he calls "Lundao" or "discoursing on the Dao." Komjathy spoke about proper orientation (*fangxiang*), as well as several references to "my teacher in China" (that is, Master Chen) who, he said, emphasized that spiritual orientation should be primary. Komjathy also contrasted his primary approach to Daoist meditation, which is quietistic—the idea of returning to or going deeper into stillness—versus the alchemical approach. Finally, he spoke of "innate nature" (*xing*) and "life destiny" (*ming*), associated with "stillness practice" (*jinggong*) and "movement practice" (*donggong*), respectively. Overall, the Lundao was conducted like a good college seminar.

The next part of the retreat, Dietetics, was Townsend's main verbal contribution. She recited from a long list of correlates to "spring" (wood, east, liver, etc.), which led into lunch, a simple vegetarian meal of rice, pea greens, smoked tofu, and asparagus. After lunch, the participants went for a walk around the property.

When the group reconvened, Komjathy led them in Scripture Study (*jingxue*). Having completed the *Laozi*, they had now been going through the *Zhuangzi* chapter by chapter, a modified version of Burton Watson's translation with some adaptations and retranslations by Komjathy. Komjathy led us story-by-story and sometimes line-by-line through chapters 18, 19, and 20. Clearly, Komjathy has a real affinity toward textual exegesis, something quite rare in American Daoism.

The retreat ended with seated meditation, which Komjathy usually refers to as "quiet sitting" (*jingzuo*), and self-massage. Overall, this retreat was Komjathy's ideal of what a retreat, and a Daoist life by extension, should look like. He was not concerned with attracting a mass audience.[112]

The Normative Daoism of the Scholar-Practitioner

Meanwhile, as Komjathy's path of adherent cultivation and academic career both progressed and matured, aspects of his personal presentation and scholarly agenda underwent some changes. Most notably, Komjathy began publishing essays where he explicitly discussed his identity as scholar-practitioner.

For example, in an article on Daoist vegetarianism, Komjathy advances a "normative Daoist perspective": "I speak as a Daoist scholar-practitioner—as an adherent. . . . After some twelve years of commitment and practice, in 2006, I received ordination in the Huashan (Mount Hua) lineage of Complete Perfection Daoism. I am thus writing this from the perspective of someone with formal lineage affiliation in the Daoist religious tradition." From that perspective, he writes, "*anyone* who claims to have ecological commitments or environmental concerns, vegetarianism is a *minimal requirement*. . . . To bring about a larger ecological shift, people may have to remain strict vegetarians, even if this leads to premature death. I have taken such a vow."[113] Komjathy ends with a catechism: "I endeavor to follow a Daoist way of life, a life based in attentiveness, reverence, and connection. . . . As inhabitants of community, place and world, let us cultivate ways of nourishing life."[114]

In another essay, "Field Notes from a Daoist Professor,"[115] he again speaks as an advocate and "theologian" for Daoism. In the introduction, Judith Simmer-Brown and Fran Grace, the editors, write that Komjathy "speaks of the allure of his meditation 'hut' and the difficulty of coming out of it into the conventional academic world of discursive debate, multitasking, and institutional politics."[116] In this essay, Komjathy writes as someone with a "formal commitment to and affiliation with the Daoist religious tradition" who might find a model in the Immortal Lü Dongbin who "abandoned an official career in order to practice internal alchemy."[117] Komjathy consistently finds himself standing at the proverbial crossroads. But, at least until the time of our completing this book, he has chosen an academic career, and so wonders, "When I stand in front of [my students] as their teacher, does it make a difference that I am a Daoist and a contemplative?"[118] In fact, for Komjathy, being a Daoist professor means taking pedagogy seriously, listening to his students, and finding a humility that will "temper the academic tendency toward hyperintellectualism and authoritarian discourse."[119] Komjathy is here advocating a model of the scholar-practitioner, one whose Daoist practice informs his Daoist scholarship and vice versa, and both inform his teaching of Religious Studies to undergraduates.

A few years later he found a new academic position at the University of San Diego, an independent Catholic university, and was told that he was partially hired because he is an adherent and practitioner, and could engage in interreligious dialogue with them on matters of theological concern. His first post, at Pacific Lutheran University, was also in a church-affiliated university. Komjathy's professional work has thus largely involved teaching and writing in the company of Christian theologians. Thus, it is not surprising that his positive vision of Daoism owes something to comparative theology: "In the context of the United States, I locate Quanzhen in the context of the emerging 'new monasticism' movement. Here it involves sexual propriety, sobriety, and vegetarianism. Without these, Quanzhen loses both its charism and its spiritual power."[120] It is significant that Komjathy locates this normative American Quanzhen within the new monasticism movement, given that that movement is associated with emergent evangelical communities.[121] Komjathy's influence specifically comes from Beverly Lanzetta, the founder and senior teacher of the Community for a New Monastic Way, who relocated to San Diego and eventually began a spiritual friendship with Komjathy. Equally significant is Komjathy's use of the word "charism," a term used by Catholic monastic orders to denote the orientation or characteristics of their spiritual mission.

As Komjathy more and more clearly expresses his identity as a Daoist in his scholarly writing, it seems he sees an ethical obligation not to remain neutral about what might be called "fraudulent" Daoists, but instead to call them out. At our request, Komjathy commented on our narrative of the Dream Trippers in his role as scholar-practitioner:

> Through deep self-cultivation, one becomes an embodiment of the Dao and the Daoist tradition, and one becomes a conduit through which the Dao is transmitted in the world. This involves a movement from habituation and delusion to spiritual realization. For Daoists, the Dao manifests as numinous presence, as what is often referred to as *daoqi* 道炁. This is a specific form of qi associated with the Dao, the Daoist tradition, and Daoist communities and practitioners. It is not mere rhetoric—no amount of oration can conceal its absence or disclose its presence. Although pseudo-Daoists make various self-promoting claims, those claims themselves reveal the absence of *daoqi*. Realized Daoists recognize each other through the Dao's numinous presence, which pervades their being and is expressed in their lives, including through virtue.[122]

Komjathy's Dream

Livia Kohn's transformation disappointed Komjathy, since she seemed to be going in the direction of the "self-filled" marketers of the "American Daoist" scene. When asked separately about Komjathy's trajectory as a scholar and "tradition-based" practitioner, both Kohn and Winn made similar remarks: Kohn thought Komjathy's position was "not tenable" if you "look at the modern market." "Americans mix and match," she told us, "and for them Louis's way is too scholarly. One can't just be an apologist for your lineage."[123] And Winn asked, "My point is how many people is he reaching? What's the value he's adding that's not here already? That's the question. Maybe there is some value, doing it the way the Quanzhen sect does it. But my observation is that most Westerners are not interested in joining Quanzhen and never will be. Quanzhen has no future here. Not in its current form."[124]

By speaking the language of the market, both Kohn and Winn simply confirm Komjathy's belief that neither of them understands the roots of Daoist practice, which is based in dedicated and prolonged cultivation and resides beyond consumer considerations. "It is, first and foremost, about transpersonal communion with the Dao, which is energetic." What makes it even more difficult for Komjathy on a personal level is that all his mentors have left the authentic path of lineage and tradition that he has been seeking. His scholarly mentor Livia Kohn, having revealed herself as a spiritual eclectic and enjoying her retirement from teaching, seems to be accepting of the whole spectrum of popular American Daoism, unlike Komjathy. One of his dearest models and mentors, Master Hu is, as of 2016, fully enmeshed in Daoist bureaucracy. His closest mentor in Daoist practice and his lineage master, Master Chen, will teach a wide variety of Daoist seekers, including Dream Trippers, while living a reclusive life unconstrained by institutional demands. Both Kohn and Chen had continuing transactions with Michael Winn, whom Komjathy has little regard for. After Chen met Kohn during her Footsteps of Laozi tour of China in 2011, he was very impressed and told us, "I respect her very much . . . Komjathy should be like her. He is far too rigid."[125] Komjathy, for his part, increasingly understands his path as a largely solitary undertaking, "something akin to winter mountaineering and peak ascents." Amid the criticisms, he attempts to cultivate "nonattachment" and "spiritual discernment."

While all too aware of the criticisms from his mentors, Komjathy thus maintains his stance:

> You need to see Chen Yuming's and Livia Kohn's anti-institutionalism in the context of where they are located. They have been completely embedded in an institution, and so they have the possibility of moving out of it. It is not the same if you say you don't need structures, but have not been trained within one. For me, it's the opposite from Chen. In the US, there is no structure whatsoever. There is no structure to get out of; we need to establish structure. . . . Structures are necessary to tell people about the Dao; without such structures it would be difficult for the Dao to manifest itself.[126]

At the LMU conference, Komjathy told us, referring to his own situation, "Some people may have to be straw dogs for Daoism in America."[127] Later, he clarified his statement as follows:

> I mean that Daoism as a religious tradition is only beginning to take root in America. Those of us committed to the tradition and who hope to preserve

THE SCHOLAR-PRACTITIONERS

and transmit that tradition may have to sacrifice an easy life based on personal fulfillment in order to take a stand for Daoism as such. That is, as was the case of being a Daoist priest at the LMU conference, some tradition-based Daoists may have to accept being perceived as "sectarian" (a very funny category being among New Age Qigong teachers), "arrogant," or whatever other categories are used to preserve ignorance, delusion, and commercial success.

I hope this is clear.[128]

One might say that Kohn, Winn, and Chen have found workable personal solutions to the predicament of modern spirituality, whereas Komjathy exemplifies this predicament. In a telling moment, he once told us, "For me, giving up alcohol and meat is an essential condition for cultivation."—"Why do you say 'for me'?" we asked. "Why not because the Daoist scriptures or deities say so?"—"Because there is no commonly recognized authority in today's culture," he replied.[129]

Komjathy has been trying to inherit and transmit a structure that would locate authority in tradition, text, and lineage, rather than in the self, in that individualistic "for me." But at this moment at least, he continued to express himself in the idiom of personal subjectivity. And while the story of his journeys to China can be construed as an apprenticeship leading to initiation and transmission of an authentic lineage and tradition, the "authenticity" might also be located in pure subjectivity, or in a mystical realm: from Chen's statement, the day Komjathy first met him, that a mystical Daoist connection was evident "*because we are sitting here*" to his claim that "*I* am the proof" of the ordination, to Komjathy's experience of "an exchange beyond words," of their "hearts opening up" and the "*daoqi* flowing between them."

In a self-reflexive moment, Komjathy acknowledges that his vision of modern Daoism is also a dream: "Daoism thus gives me specific insights into the contributions and limitations of knowing and learning, including those of university education and academic intellectualism. It reminds me there are many dreams, from Zhuang Zhou's dream of a butterfly's life to Lü Dongbin's dream of millet. I am dreaming too."[130]

Back to America

In the summer of 2011, Kohn's "Footsteps of Laozi" tour arrived at Huashan; we were assisting on the tour, responsible for a group of American college students who had joined the tour for course credit. At the Jade Spring Monastery, they unexpectedly bumped into Komjathy, who was staying there as a visiting monastic and wearing his Daoist robes. He seemed embarrassed to be seen by the big group, but he readily agreed to come to dinner in the group's hotel to answer questions about his ordination. That evening, he changed out of his robes, and we walked over to the nearby hotel where Kohn, his former doctoral mentor, and her group were staying.

He chatted about his ordination with the group over dinner. Later, we strolled in the hotel's outdoor courtyard. We ran into American university students with their class materials out. They were part of Kohn's tour, but receiving course credit for it; their pack of readings about Daoism in modern China included a rough draft of sections of the manuscript for this book. The discussion with the students turned to Daoism in America, the Healing Tao, and the Dream Trips described in the reading. Komjathy remarked that he did not want to be identified with Dream Trippers while in China. A student exclaimed, pointing at the xeroxed typescript in front of him: "That's just what this person said!"—not realizing that the person quoted in the text, speaking in 2004, was now standing in front of him. Komjathy laughed, finding humor in a student talking to him about himself, and realizing that he had been saying some of the same things for seven years.

Later that evening, Komjathy told us that he had been in an "existential crisis," and had come to China for a summer of "cloud wandering," looking for Daoist hermits. He had recently stopped doing most forms of external practice. And the Daoist Foundation's practice group in Olympia was in jeopardy—it was hard to be the spiritual director that his calling as Quanzhen priest demanded of him when he lived more than 1,200 miles away from some of his community members.[131]

But traveling in China in the summer of 2011 turned out not to provide the imagined or complete answer; indeed, Komjathy said he was tired of the country, of being hot and sweaty. The likely locations for Daoist hermits where Komjathy had gone—Louguantai and the Zhongnan mountains, where Bill Porter had found hermits twenty years earlier and written about them in *Road to Heaven*, were "crawling with tourists."

Komjathy had come to Huashan to cement his relationship with Master Hu and to thank him; he had also hoped to deepen his connection with the monastic community and tradition at the Jade Spring monastic community. But in the seven years since Komjathy first met Hu, Master Hu had become less eager to interact with foreigners (see chapter 4) and, now promoted to a leadership position within the Huashan Daoist Association, had taken the airs of a Chinese official. Nonetheless, Komjathy did once again follow the traditional pilgrimage route, though this time on his own. Along the way, he veered off the path, passing by the multiple "do not enter" and "tourists prohibited" signs. Perhaps against the wishes of his teacher Chen and his monastic friend Hu, Komjathy was on his way to Master Hao's cave-hermitage at the

Cloud Platform. He and Hao had tea, conversing on the Dao and discussing Hao's plans and situation. Komjathy thanked Master Hao, offered a donation, and departed. Along the way of descent, this time toward rather than away from the lowlanders from whom he sought retreat, Komjathy contemplated the "lessons of Huashan." While lamenting the tensions between the three primary monastic protagonists of our story, who had so many shared commitments and values, he also recognized models of Daoist adherence and being: Master Chen embodied spiritual refinement; Master Hu monastic dwelling; and Master Hao mountain seclusion. Each maintained his Daoist cultivation while following his own way, and Komjathy also recognized something important, "a transmission if you will."

Later that summer, Master Chen took the train from Chengdu to visit Komjathy at his hostel in Xi'an. As is always the case, Komjathy and Chen discussed Daoist cultivation, and Komjathy offered his gratitude, including in the form of a donation. They also visited Chen's zither teacher, which provided yet another insight into his approach to practice-realization. However, later, when the conversation turned toward the *Dream Trippers* book project, Komjathy seemed disappointed to learn that Chen continued to have dealings with Michael Winn, and to get paid for imparting specific cultivation techniques. Indeed, while Chen was in Xi'an, he was also talking with representatives of a new religious movement based in Russia, called INBI, which, though drawing from a typically eclectic selection of spiritual traditions, seems mostly focused on inner alchemy.[132]

Komjathy maintained his dream of a Daoist place, perhaps a coinhabited place in the United States, where Chen might live as a Daoist recluse and teach Daoist cultivation to actual Daoists. He hopes to help develop a "tradition-based American Daoism" and a "viable Daoist community in the United States." Rooted in the aspiration "to foster authentic Daoist study and practice" and "to preserve and transmit traditional Daoist culture," this dream includes an ordained American Daoist clergy and a mountain retreat center offering holistic and integrated training.[133] Still, within this dream, it is difficult to know where Komjathy's "trip" will ultimately lead. By the end of the summer of 2011, Komjathy felt there was not much more he could learn in China: his Daoism was in America.

7

The Predicament

After dancing with the locals at Chen Tuan plaza, as described in chapter 3, the 2012 Dream Trippers proceeded to another dance session, this time in the ballroom of their hotel, a five-minute walk from the plaza. The lights were turned off, and Bethany instructed the Dream Trippers to sit in a circle. "This will be a free-flowing, freeform dance. Just let yourself go, follow your true self, follow your own Dao." And she dedicated this dance to the harmonious union of yin and yang of the two couples who would get married on Huashan the next day, as we describe below. The music, she explained, "will start soft, gentle, feminine, yin, and will become more rapid, more yang, masculine. It will rise to a climax, and then gradually calm down." And she turned on a mix of music on a boom box that included whooshy new age tunes that slowly shifted to more throbbing, rapid beats. It felt like a high school dance, except for the dance forms. People were moving in all ways. Some appeared to be dancing, but others did cartwheels, or push-ups; some moved in sync with the rhythm of the music, others were attuned to their own beat, or none at all; some fell onto their backs with their legs in the air, spinning their legs around, like an overturned beetle. Some even rolled onto the floor and over each other, graying boomers at play like wrestling toddlers. Some stayed in one place, while others glided and swished around the room, flowing beside each other, or bumping into each other, rolling onto each other's bodies. The scene could be described as a harmonious, roly-poly chaos, an expression of unbridled but gentle individualism.

The Dream Trippers had introduced to Huashan a sacred ritual that is practiced every week in Asheville, NC. Bethany, the deputy leader of the 2012 Dream Trip, is one of the founders and leaders of the "Asheville Movement Collective," which is also called the "Dance Church." "Dance waves," such as the one described above, are held every Sunday morning in the Asheville Masonic Hall, and are an important communal gathering for the town's extensive alternative healing and spiritual networks. Michael Winn, Peace, and several other of the 2012 Dream Trippers live in Asheville, and some of them first met each other at the Sunday Dance Wave—notably Winn and his fiancée Jem Minor, whom he would marry at the top of Huashan.

The Asheville Movement Collective (AMC) is inspired by the work of Gabrielle Roth, an American dancer known for the 5Rhythms® approach to ecstatic dance, which she developed in the 1960s after spending several years as a masseuse and dance instructor at the Esalen Institute in Big Sur, California, later joining the faculty at the Kripalu Center for Yoga & Health and at the Omega Institute for Holistic Studies. The AMC aims to create community through the free expression of the body. Its website describes its purpose as follows:

> We practice the dance wave as a transcendent experience, and acknowledge that this links us to our individual and collective healing and creates community. We gather and dance with authenticity, personal responsibility, and sensitivity to others. In doing so we are creating a beautiful, vibrant, and ever-evolving community. We believe each dancer is a cherished part of the whole and each experience matters.[1]

The weekly Waves, as we observed in Asheville in the fall of 2013, begin and end with ritual "opening and closing circles." At the beginning, all participants—some sixty people—must sit on the floor, in a large circle, as the facilitator makes some announcements and explains the guidelines of the activity. The music is turned on, and for ninety minutes, the participants dance and bob, swoosh and roll, lie and flow. Then, at the conclusion of the session, participants must again sit in a circle, and offer testimony. The facilitator enumerated rules to be followed in giving testimony:

> Your testimony must not be pre-scripted, it must be spontaneous and genuine.
> Your testimony must be in the present tense.
> Your testimony must be true.

And then, half a dozen or so participants shared their feelings. "Thank you so much for the love, the community, for sharing," said one, referring to the "sharing" of embodied experiences, since speaking is not allowed during the dance wave. And another: "Thank you for this chance to honor myself, and to be honored in honoring myself." Finally, various participants made announcements: of healing workshops they would give in the coming week, of objects for sale or bedrooms for rent—sharing practical information for the community.

The AMC explicitly describes its aim as fostering a community for the expression of a "transcendent experience" of the "authentic self," and has created rituals, rules, and guidelines to ensure that all participants will be spontaneous and authentic, creating a community while banning any trace of conformity and artificiality. The AMC website describes its vision as: "A world that moves in harmony where all are free to be their authentic selves within a loving community."[2] This community is based on the proper management of the boundaries between its members, as prescribed below:

Boundaries and Dancing with Others:

You have the right and responsibility to maintain your own boundaries. Ask non-verbally for permission to dance with, or touch, someone else. Please honor their boundaries and be willing to get a "no" or no response at all. If you choose to dance with someone, how long you remain in the dance is up to you. Please move on when you know you are ready. When you dance with AMC you dance in a community. Your personal dance exploration is the essence of this practice. We ask for your sensitivity to how your expressiveness impacts others. Please be aware of the dance we do between authenticity and community culture. The expressive nature of our practice naturally means that we encounter each other's energy along the way. We encourage feedback between dancers, whether incidents are supportive or confusing. Facilitators are available to help.[3]

The Movement Collective is a perfect example of the culture of "self-spirituality" out of which Healing Tao USA and the Dream Trippers have emerged. This is a "self" whose authenticity practitioners discover within the depths of their inner being—a bounded self, that interacts with others on the condition of its boundaries being maintained and respected—a self that, in spite of its assertion of autonomy, remains so fragile that facilitators are on hand to help in case of "confusing" encounters with the energy of another individual.

For Bethany, "Ecstatic dance is a beautiful, authentic, very Daoist form of movement, expression, self-enquiry and discovery, and turning to original self."[4] For Michael Winn, there is an overlap between the Movement Collective and Healing Tao, "but the differences may be like a child versus an adult version of the same spiritual self ... The western Taoist 'Self' is NOT fragile and in need of facilitators to protect its boundaries; the neidan-qigong adept is deeply grounded, [and] has merged into the larger [cosmic] field."[5] In one sense, indeed, Daoism may appear as a natural or "mature" expression of the values of the "movement collective" and American spiritual individualism—but from another perspective, nothing could be farther from the Dao than the "self-expression" of these American spiritual seekers and ecstatic dancers.

How could "Taoism" have become the fullest expression of American spiritual individualism? It comes from China, which has such a different history and culture from America's. This raises the question: Does Daoism represent an individualistic strand within Chinese culture? Are Chinese Daoists ontological individualists? What kinds of spiritual subjects are constituted through Daoist practice in the Chinese context? This chapter explores these questions, showing that while the Daoist tradition in China can be considered to have an individualistic dimension, it does not seek to assert the ontological autonomy of the self. The Daoist approach to social and political relations, and the structural location of Daoism in the Chinese religious field, have oriented the evolutionary trajectory of Chinese Daoism in the direction of embedding into locality, tradition, and Chinese indigeneity—all of which are in sharp contrast to the disembedding, detraditionalizing, and universalizing tendencies of popular American Daoism. The difficulties of sustaining either approach lead us into our concluding discussion of the "predicament" of modern spirituality, and of the alternative promises of a "third culture" that our protagonists evoke to imagine the solution to the predicament. But we question whether this "third culture" merely expresses and reinforces the hypermodern global order that it claims to transcend.

*

From our conversations with the Quanzhen monks, which we have discussed in the first part of chapter 5, their discourse on Daoist cultivation seems to be far from a perfect fit with American spiritual individualism! They talk of the authority of lineage, of the power of the masters, of the imperative of moral virtue, of the important role of ritual. Body cultivation techniques and the experience and work with "energies" are of value only when embedded in the cosmology and institutional structures of the Quanzhen order. What happened to Zhuangzi's happy-go-lucky mockery of all forms of authority, and to Laozi's preaching of a Dao that transcends virtue and tradition? Is not Daoist thought, at its origin, individualistic and subversive? And if so, would American Daoists such as Michael Winn not be correct in affirming that the true spirit of Daoism has been lost in the accretions of China's monastic and ritualistic institutions, and that it is from America that the true Dao can once again be released into the world? In this vein, Winn told us:

The role of the Daoist [in Chinese culture] was to hold the pole of individuation. That's what becoming an Immortal is. You become an Immortal and you've actually taken yourself out of the culture, raised yourself above it. That's why the guys, according to legend, like Zhang Sanfeng refused to go serve the emperor. If they were really part of Chinese culture, when the emperor called them, they would be like, "Sure, boss, what do you need? I'll give you all my secrets, you're the emperor." But they go: "Ah, I'm going to go off in the woods here and talk to my boss, which is the Dao, and you don't have any real power over me." So, they're basically spitting in the face of Chinese culture.[6]

Spiritual Individualism in China

If we avoid a monolithic view of Chinese culture, might it not be possible to identify a strand of spiritual individualism in the Chinese tradition, one that is precisely incarnated by certain strains of Daoism? The historian of Daoism Vincent Goossaert claims that the order of Complete Perfection, with its focus on inner alchemy, marks the beginning of "modern Daoism"—even though it appeared in the twelfth century![7] In one essay, he asked: "Integrated into popular literature, open to all, freely taught in temples, adaptable to all lifestyles, emphasizing individual choice instead of collective belonging, giving much more authority to experience than to faith, does not inner alchemy deserve to be considered a resolutely modern spirituality?"[8]

Daoist body cultivation is perhaps the most prevalent form of a more individualistic facet of Chinese culture, in which the individual turns inward, into observing, monitoring, and nurturing his body and its powers, in a discourse that is critical of conventional social obligations. From such a perspective, then, the "fit" between Daoism and American spiritual individualism would not simply be the result of decontextualization and reinvention. Rather, one might trace parallel strands of spiritual individualism in both the Chinese and Western traditions, and it is thus inevitable that the affinities between them would become evident with their connection and convergence in the era of globalization. Or, considering the technologies of the body themselves, one might consider their universal psychosomatic base, as argued by Jeffrey Kripal:

> The cross-cultural correspondences and actual borrowings that we can see between Asian Tantra [a broad category within which Kripal includes Daoist psycho-sexual technologies] and American counterculture can best be explained by one simple but astonishingly complex fact, that both the phenomenology of consciousness as witness of all human experience and the anatomical, hormonal, sexual, molecular, genetic, and subatomic processes of the human body display similar dynamics and structures across all known human cultures and recorded times. This is why human beings in different cultures and times can

experience similar, if probably never identical, forms of the enlightenment of the body. This is why Tantric traditions can and do migrate from culture to culture: everywhere they go, they find the same psychosomatic base.[9]

But, in contrast to Western conceptions of the self as an ontological reality, the Chinese Daoist understanding of the self has tended to be fluid, embodied, and dynamic; it is a composite of numerous entities, energies, and flows, in an unfolding relationship with other beings, objects, forces, and dimensions of the cosmos. It has no fixed "being." "Self-cultivation" in a Daoist context implies shedding the illusion of the self's ontological autonomy and boundedness, and returning to, or aligning with, an *original, prenatal self* that is at one with the Dao, through cultivating relationships between dynamic patterns and cycles in the body, the land, and the cosmos. Daoists never speak of "cultivating the self" but rather of "cultivating Dao" (*xiudao*) or "cultivating perfection" (*xiuzhen*), which implies a process of spiritual self-transcendence, of spiritual individuation that grows out of but ultimately transcends the physical body. This cultivational process involves a dissolving of the experience of the bounded self and body, until the body is experienced as a field of locations and forces, that are correlated with cosmic patterns, recombined with each other, and refined to produce a purely spiritual being. Enchantment consists in the ability to communicate with spirits and Immortals, and, at a higher level, to become one; to decode the significance of cosmic patterns, and to manipulate cosmic forces. Spiritual subjects are formed through their affiliation to masters and lineages, through their relationships with deities and places, and through their conscious work with cosmic forces in and through their body.

Here, we are far from modern individualism which, from a Daoist perspective, can be seen as an extreme form of dissipation and differentiation: Daoist cultivation in the framework of cosmological attunement is not simply a question of "follow your instincts," "be yourself," "be different," and "relax"—all of which may well be expressions of "going with the flow" of one's ego and desires, rather than any true self-transformation or alignment with Dao. As explained by Master Chen, "This does not mean that you can just be who you want—there is a work of self-transformation, to reach your true self which is at one with Heaven and Earth and all beings. You can't just take spontaneity (*wuwei*) and say it means you make no effort, do whatever you want. *Wuwei* refers to noninterference, not imposing your self on others; but you still need to make an effort on your self." He criticized another American *qigong* operator—whom he was, otherwise, very fond of as a person—for writing, in a book, that one can be wild and carefree in Daoism. "But what he doesn't understand is that being carefree (*xiaosa*) is not an attitude a Daoist takes toward *oneself*, but only a way *to deal with the world*. In their dealings with other people, Daoists may appear careless, easygoing, even unconventional, getting drunk and so on, but this can only be connected to a strong inner discipline, otherwise it is not Daoist at all."[10]

Master Chen, at times, spoke of reaching the "true self," for example, "the truest, the most free, the most original self, which is the most beautiful. It is in communion with all beings, with Heaven and Earth, it does not need to be controlled. . . . We want to attain the independent, free, true self." This search for the true self must pass through the stage of attaining tranquility (*jing*)— "Before that, there is no true self (*zhenshi de ziwo*). The attachment to that self is very dangerous. It's not a stable self, it's changing here and there. Today it might think this, and tomorrow it doesn't agree. It is pulled in different directions by different things." But when he describes the nature of this "true self" that is attained through tranquility, there is no stable ontological reality, only a fragile union between multiple *hun* and *po* souls that are associated with different organic systems and locations in the body, and express different ethical orientations, in line with the correlative cosmology.

Chinese Daoists are *not* ontological individualists in the American sense— but this does not mean that they are the *opposite* of individualists. Our comparison of the Western and Chinese trajectories does not aim to contrast a Chinese "collectivism" to American individualism. Rather, the "individualistic" dimension of Chinese Daoism has interacted with selfhood, authority, and tradition in ways that cannot be described through the lens of Western dichotomies of the individual versus the institution, resistance versus authority, or innovation versus tradition.[11] Where American self-spirituality posits the care of the *self* as a bounded and unique being endowed with interiority within the framework of the naturalist ontology, Chinese Daoism begins with the quest for attunement with a cosmic pattern that transcends the self, within the framework of a correlative cosmology. In Master Chen's words, the "lesser self" (*xiaowo*) is abandoned for a "greater self" (*dawo*), the "true self" that encompasses the entire cosmos.[12] Where the American "religion of no religion" is founded on the rejection of the authority of the church, Chinese Daoism has, in the course of history, repeatedly created alternative structures of authority, always in a dynamic interaction with the dominant authorities of the Chinese state and its official doctrines of Confucianism or, later, of Socialism. Where the American "New Age" strives for a universalistic detraditionalization and decontextualization of exotic spiritual techniques and symbols,

Chinese Daoism has typically been the vehicle for processes of *localization* and *contextual traditionalization*.

The Cosmic Self

What is now known as the Daoist tradition can be traced back to early Chinese texts of the Warring States period, especially the *Neiye*, the *Zhuangzi*, and the *Laozi*, around the third and fourth centuries BC. These texts appeared at a time when the dominant mode of human interaction with the divine was through sacrificial ritual. Spirits were seen as having power over natural phenomena; humans needed to establish relationships with them in order to avoid misfortunes and ensure prosperity and success. This relationship, however, was not "harmonious"; as Michael Puett has argued, "This results in seemingly endless attempts by humans to placate, coax, and influence the spirits through sacrifice and divination."[13] Ritual systems were elaborated to domesticate these forces, to anthropomorphize them as ancestors, to fix them into a hierarchy, and to regulate their interactions with humans. This ritual system was also the foundation and pattern of social and political order. Central to the functioning of this system were the priests—the ritual specialists whose technical knowledge was required to operate the communications with the spirits, and to orchestrate the ceremonial enactment of sovereignty.

The early Daoist texts challenged this sacrificial order, claiming that humans themselves could transform into divine beings. Without employing ritual arts, through practices of cultivating the body and consciousness, humans could access spiritual power, and acquire the knowledge of fortune and misfortune.[14] What emerged was a notion of "self-divinization," which could be accomplished through practices of the body and of consciousness. These practices were theoretically accessible to anyone. In the *Zhuangzi*, there is no concern for social rank; in its stories, we meet men and women, lettered gentlemen, farmers and artisans, freemen and servants, who all aspire to transcendence. The questions they discuss revolve around concerns of the individual—the meaning and purpose of life, the nature of death, and how to deal with the vicissitudes of the world.[15]

The Daoist texts do, then, point the way to a process of individuation, of awakening the consciousness of one's self, one's desires, one's illusions, and of the patterns and forces of the cosmos—and point to a path of transformation through individual meditation and cultivation, leading toward divinity. This is a path that openly mocks the priests and their sacrifices. There is a clear resonance here with modern individualism, both in terms of the inward turn to self-knowledge and development, and of the rejection of traditional and institutional authority.

But the divinization process advocated by the early Daoists involves attunement with a pattern of broader cosmic forces. A condition for attaining Dao is transcending the self; only when we become "empty" can we become "filled" with Dao. The natural process of life, leading toward death, is one of differentiation, moving ever farther from the undifferentiated state of Dao; the Daoist path of self-transformation involves turning around and returning to the undifferentiated state of the infant or the "uncarved block," "returning to the One." A precondition to the effortless, spontaneous "going with the flow" of Dao, one must "reverse the flow" (*ni*) of dissipation and differentiation.

But as Daoist traditions of self-cultivation evolved, they became integrated with the analogical cosmology of correspondences that was systematized during the Han dynasty. This process involves passing through a stage of redifferentiation, as the body/mind aligns itself with the categories of the correlative cosmology: first one learns to respond to the forces of the Eight Trigrams, the Five Phases, of the Heaven-Man-Earth triad, of the Yin-Yang duality, and to identify their correspondences with locations, forces, energies, and time cycles in one's body, one's environment, and in the universe. Then, it is through the combination of these forces in the body that their differentiation is transcended, and unity with Dao is attained.

The Shadow of Authority

The "Daoist" stance had clear political implications in ancient China. One implication was that accessing the powers of Dao was a more effective strategy of governance for rulers than relying on the sacrifices conducted by the ritualists. Daoist cultivation was something that could be learned as an art of government. Another implication, however, was that whoever attained oneness with Dao, aligned with the patterns and powers of the cosmos, was a true ruler; and such a state was theoretically accessible to anyone who mastered the techniques of Daoist transcendence. Both scenarios undermined the authority of the court ritualists. The early emperors of the Han dynasty had affinities with Daoist approaches to governance, but by the second century BC, especially under the influence of the minister Dong Zhongshu (195–105 BC), state orthodoxy turned to Confucian ritualism and textual study.

While the structural position of Confucianism has, since then, been one of a top-down concern with governance, orthodoxy, rationalization, and strengthening the state, Daoism acquired its institutional forms within a structural position among the people, in the villages and in the mountains, away from the centers of political power.[16] While emanating from the imperial center, a rationalizing Confucianism tended toward a relative, but far from complete, disenchantment; the body and local ritual became the locations of Daoist techniques of enchantment, with a whole pantheon of deities populating the body itself, to be invoked by the practitioner, and spirit soldiers to be commanded by the priest in exorcistic rites. Daoism was politically marginalized; out of favor in most imperial administrations, it spread among the common people. Daoism became the "religion of the subaltern" in China. China's first millenarian rebellions—the Yellow Turban (AD 184–205) and Heavenly Master movements (AD 142–215)—were led by divinized savior figures who had "attained the Dao."[17]

The Repository of Local Tradition

Pierre Bourdieu, drawing on Max Weber, hints at the differentiation of the Chinese religious field:

> At the heart of the same social formation, the opposition between religion and magic . . . conceals the opposition between differences of religious competence tied to the structure of the distribution of religious capital. This is best seen in the relationship between Confucianism and the religiosity of the Chinese working classes, which was rejected as magic out of the spite and suspicion of the well-educated who elaborated the refined ritual of state religion and who imposed the domination and legitimacy of their doctrines and social theories, despite some local and provisional victories of Taoist and Buddhist priests whose doctrines and practices were closer to the religious interests of the masses.[18]

Here, let us discuss those "local" victories of the Daoist priests—which were definitely not "provisional," having endured for centuries—showing how Daoism organized itself as the "higher religion" of *local* society. When Daoism penetrated the culture of the common people, it merged with local religious customs and lore; at the same time, it provided local traditions with an overarching cosmological and liturgical structure, integrating them, through ritual organization, into the common correlative cosmology.[19] Eminent Daoist cultivators and hermits acquired fame as healers while they were still alive or after their deaths, becoming deities and the focus of temple cults. The Heavenly Masters movement of the later Han dynasty created a liturgical system that, in many ways, mirrored Han court ritual, creating a structure of community self-governance and access to the celestial bureaucracy through

m of ritualized audiences and petitions to the gods, officiated by Dao-
sts. The Daoist priest acted as an official mandated to send forms and
ıs on behalf of the people to the relevant offices of the celestial government. Daoist ritual mediates a celestial world of official documents, record
keeping, and lawsuits, combined with a concern with healing and immortality. Through further changes and transformations, Daoist ritual evolved
in many directions, ranging from refined court ceremonies to integration
with the local deities and spirit-mediums of village religion. The Daoist priest
played a dual role, as minister (*chen*) in the sublimated court of Dao, and
as general (*jiang*) vis-à-vis the local spirits and demons—a complementary
distinction played out in the civil-martial (*wen/wu*) structure of much village
ritual today. Local spirits may be either absorbed into the Daoist hierarchy as
lower-ranked minions, or fought as unruly, bloodthirsty demons. The role of
the Daoist ritual institution in negotiating relationships, alliances or conflicts
between local and universal deities and forces is clear. It thus played an indispensable role both for local communities and for the imperial throne in their
formation of religio-political alliances, providing a common but multifocal
ritual and symbolic language for working through their relationships.[20]

The spiritual powers acquired by Daoist cultivators were thus deployed
in the service of the people, as they used their magic to empower, summon,
and marshal deities and spirits to fight demons, illnesses, and misfortunes.
The more attuned they were to Dao and cosmos, the better they mastered the
techniques of cultivation, and the more powerful they would be to heal and
protect the people and negotiate between local and universal forces. Daoism
became deeply woven into both local and imperial culture and ritual traditions. It may appear as if this type of Daoism evolved far from the early texts
that discounted the need for ritual—but we need to remember that Daoism
does not *oppose*, but *integrates* and *transcends*. Communal rituals might not
be required for the individual cultivation of Dao—but one who cultivated
Dao would be solicited to serve the people by performing their communal rituals for healing, protection, and prosperity. Daoist ritual became the
means for the collective salvation of communities, mediated by masters able
to manipulate and combine the powers of an analogical cosmos. Attuned to
energies and forces not only within their bodies but in their surrounding environment, serving the local people according to their needs and customs
for ritual and magical protection, positioning themselves in a field of local
deities, powers, and lore, Daoists became fully integrated into local tradition.

Daoism has thus become the most localized "religion" in China. Often,
as noted by Master Chen, the local embeddedness has become so deep that
the local people and masters have even forgotten that their ritual traditions

and techniques come from Daoism.[21] And yet, a common set of cosmological principles, practices, and texts has preserved a certain degree of unity that transcends local diversity. Daoism shared the basic correlative cosmology with the imperial state, but applied it differently, incorporating local deities and ritual traditions into its structures,[22] and affording direct access to its powers through the authority of its priests. Thus, to use the formulation of Anna Seidel, Daoism became China's "unofficial high religion."[23] Daoism became the religion of an "other" China, not the vertical China of the Imperial and civilizing Center, but a horizontal web of localities, each rooted in myriads of particular histories integrated through liturgical structures and practices of the body that shared a common cosmology. At times, Master Chen intimated that it is in this Daoism "among the people" (minjian) that the most authentic Daoism can be found, given that a long history of interference from the state has distorted the Daoist pantheon of deities and the canon of scriptures, and has arbitrarily elevated some branches, such as Zhengyi and Quanzhen, into prominent positions of state-structured orthodoxy while others were ignored and transmitted among the people. At the same time, Chen stressed that the local orientation of Daoists has also been the result of a voluntary choice to stay away from the centers of political power, staying in obscurity and blending into the people.[24]

This "Daoist China" was enriched at times of political upheaval and "barbarian" dynasties. At these times, many of the literati lost their positions in the capital and retreated into the popular realm. During the Six Dynasties (AD 222–589) following the downfall of the Han dynasty (206 BC–AD 220), when northern China was ruled by non-Han tribes, aristocratic families and court officials fled to the South. There, unable to serve as (Confucian) state administrators, they turned their attentions to cultivating the body, health, and immortality, and communicating with the spirit world. It was through Daoist texts, traditions, and practices that they could explore these realms. New Daoist movements appeared, such as the Supreme Clarity and the Maoshan traditions, which combined earlier Daoist traditions with local spirit cults and Buddhist teachings. Indeed, at a time when Buddhism was rapidly spreading in China, Daoism consciously defined itself in opposition to the foreign religion, simultaneously absorbing parts of it, but also, for the first time, developing its own identity as a distinctive "teaching" in contrast to Buddhism. Daoism became the self-conscious repository of China's indigenous religious traditions. It was during the conquest of north China by the "barbarian" Jin dynasty (1115–1234) of the Jurchen tribe that the Quanzhen movement emerged under Wang Chongyang, seen by some scholars as a movement of Song-dynasty (960–1279) Han loyalists; then, during the Mongol Yuan invasion, the

Quanzhen order used its influence to maintain social peace and to save the lives of Han Chinese.[25] Under the Yuan, the Quanzhen order secured the favor of the ruling court, becoming the leading institutional interface between the government and all religious orders. In relation to the political Center, Daoism thus structured *local* tradition; in relation to foreign culture, Daoism structured *indigenous* religious traditions and practices. (and nationalizing)

This tendency became acute during the non-Han, Manchu-led Qing dynasty, when Daoist practices became forms of resistance to the foreign regime. The martial arts and *taiji quan* developed and flourished at this time, through the integration of Daoist body cultivation practices with fist fighting techniques. As Wile and Shahar have shown, Daoist-inspired martial arts were primarily a form of cultural resistance to the Manchu through the embodiment of Chinese cosmology and power.[26] Daoist technologies of body cultivation aimed to form *Chinese* spiritual subjects.

Chinese Spiritual Modernity

In the early twentieth century, as China struggled with Western cultural hegemony, several individuals and groups recast the indigenous orientation of Daoism into a more modern, "nationalist" orientation. With the complete transformation of the outer world and the destruction of traditional social structures, the body becomes the last refuge for the preservation of the indigenous Chinese spirit. The leading modernizer of inner alchemy, Chen Yingning, for instance, strove to purify Daoist body technologies of all foreign, even Buddhist, influences—which he considered to be the source of China's weakness—while turning inner alchemy into a distinctively Chinese science.[27] Another approach was exemplified by the wave of redemptive societies of the first half of the twentieth century, new religious movements that tried to integrate all of China's spiritual heritage into a new, Chinese-centered universalism. Although these movements, such as the Fellowship United in Oneness (*Tongshanshe*), the Court of the Dao (*Daoyuan*), and the Way of Pervasive Unity (*Yiguandao*), all had strong Confucian and Buddhist elements, their cosmology and core esoteric texts were primarily Daoist; they were among the main propagators of Daoist inner alchemy in Republican China (1912–1949).[28] During the same period, the martial arts and Chinese medicine, both of which are based on the same correlative cosmology as Daoism, underwent nationalist revivals, renaming themselves "national martial arts" (*guoshu*) and "national medicine" (*guoyi*), respectively. Daoist body cultivation in modern China is thus profoundly linked to the embodiment of

Chinese-ness, in an environment in which the essence of Chinese-ness is seen as having been destroyed or lost under the onslaught of Western modernity.

In the post-Mao era of the 1980s and 1990s, China experienced a craze for *qigong*, as thousands of *qigong* masters appeared, each promoting his own *qigong* practice method, and tens of millions of Chinese congregated in parks and public spaces in the mornings for collective *qigong* practice. Until the mid-1990s, the movement was supported by the Chinese government, which saw mass *qigong* as a means to provide cheap health care to the people. While *qigong* is deeply enmeshed with Daoist history, culture, and cosmology, the state's project was to invent a modern, secularized, Chinese *qigong* in the service of the nation. Although the state aimed to cut *qigong* off from its Daoist context, the practices were promoted as fruits of a 5,000-year Chinese tradition and wisdom, and operated as a vehicle for a mass movement of rediscovery of *Chinese* spiritual culture after decades of revolutionary destructions.[29]

By the time the Dream Trippers started coming to China in the early 2000s, however, the *qigong* movement had largely collapsed in China, with almost all of the most famous *qigong* masters having emigrated to the West in the wake of the state's suppression of Falun Gong, one of the largest *qigong* movements, that was perceived by the Communist Party as posing a challenge to its authority in 1999.[30] *Qigong* was now a rather politically sensitive category, and many masters avoided the label; instead, they taught and promoted the techniques commercially, often under the label of Daoist health and life-nurturing *yangsheng* practices. The main *qigong* sanatoria and training centers were allowed to stay in business, but primarily to cater to a growing clientele of Western practitioners!

The Chinese Communist Party could not overtly and explicitly support Daoism, which is the incarnation of the traditional cosmology against which modernist Chinese thought and the Communist Party of China have struggled against for over a century. But by the early twenty-first century, the Chinese state began to adopt a more positive attitude toward traditional culture, and Daoism began to enjoy more legitimacy than in the past. This was part of an increasingly explicit nationalist strategy that aimed to arrest the rapid growth of Christianity in the rural areas, and to strengthen Chinese "soft power" in the international arena.

The Politics of Cosmological Attunement

The localizing, indigenizing, and nationalizing trajectory of Daoism in China can be contrasted with the cosmopolitanism of the Western esoteric tradition.

European esotericism, from the eighteenth century onward, largely followed a path parallel to secular modernism and universalism, away from rootedness in local and ethnic tradition. The notion of the "perennial philosophy" favored decontextualization rather than constructing ethnic identity, while alliances with science and modernism distanced the New Age from any connection with lived tradition.[31]

Daoism and the European esoteric traditions that are the precursors of contemporary Western spiritual individualism both share a long history of tension with political and religious orthodoxy. European esoteric traditions were branded as heretical by the Catholic Church; they sustained a current of spiritual resistance to ecclesiastical authority. But the medieval Roman Catholic Church was far less tolerant of "heresies" than the Confucian orthodoxy; in reaction, this led to a much stronger revulsion to religious authority in Western alternative spiritualities than has ever existed in China. Daoism, in China, found itself in a "yin" position of dynamic tension but nonopposition to the dominant orthodoxy. Within this positioning, the body becomes the locus of the empowerment of the subaltern who, lacking in political power or position, can aspire to divinity. The Daoist stance has not been one of seeking an independent position from which to *reject* orthodoxy, rather, an independent *attunement* with Dao that *transcends* convention, but does not oppose or reject it. The hermit ideal in Daoism is certainly one of cutting oneself off from social conventions and attachments—but the hermit, by moving away from the scene of society, precisely avoids challenging its orthodoxies and conventions. And when popular Daoist movements have precipitated into millenarian rebellions,[32] it has typically been to *defend* and *restore* conventional moral norms that the morally corrupt emperor or dynasty is perceived to have violated.

Wang Chongyang, the founder of the Quanzhen movement, stressed that "you must be loyal to the ruler and king, and be filial and reverent to parents and teachers. This is the method of cultivation. Then and only then can you practice the exercises of perfection." In addition to upholding these Confucian social principles, Wang Chongyang also stressed the necessity of practicing Buddhist ethics of selflessness and universal compassion as a prerequisite to cultivating Daoist inner alchemy.[33] In the Quanzhen writings, the practices of morality and conventional ritual obligations are means of learning selflessness and compassion, which are essential foundations to higher stages of spiritual cultivation. Master Hu emphasized the same point in his teaching to the Dream Trippers in 2006: to always consider others, to do meritorious deeds and virtuous acts, to practice moral behavior, justice, loving respect, filial piety, service, giving, and generosity.

The key difference between cosmological attunement and ontological individualism is that the latter finds its origin and affirmation through rejecting social convention and authority, and then seeks to find a new spiritual ground for the self that is independent of that convention and authority. Daoism takes the opposite tack: its point of departure is the search for connection and alignment with a higher cosmic pattern—the process of self-transcendence then leads one to let go of attachment to conventional norms and authority, while continuing to uphold them. While ontological individualism starts with *rejection*, Daoism begins with *attunement*.

Cosmological attunement in the Daoist tradition is not limited to a direct relationship between the individual body and the cosmos, but includes political relationships. Political, social, and cosmic structures—as well as the structure of the body itself—are conceived as analogous to each other; cosmological attunement precisely involves the mutual alignment of all of these relationships. As Chen described, the heart is the "sovereign" (*jun*) of the body, with other organ systems as its "ministers" (*chen*); the regulation of a political system and of the body should follow the same principles. By the same token, the Pole Star is the "sovereign" of the constellations, and other stars are seen in Daoist astronomy as its "ministers" that rotate around it. Just as the Pole Star is the unmoving pivot of the cosmos, the Sovereign rules through clarity, stillness, and noninterference (*qingjing wuwei*), unmoving while his ministers move in rotation around him, executing the functions of government. The same principles apply to the human body. Thus, the Sovereign governs by quieting and aligning his heart with Heaven, unifying the government of the cosmos, of the society, and of the body.

For Chen, cosmological attunement (*ganying*) in ancient Daoism, at the time of the Yellow Emperor, involved the observation of the stars and of nature, and the administration of the people. In a critique of inner alchemy, he detected a tendency toward greater individualism in the historical evolution of Daoism—in which the observation of the Heavens and the governance of society became unimportant; Daoist cultivation could now be conducted exclusively by looking into oneself, with the cosmos entirely encapsulated within the body. So, for Master Chen, the turning inward to an increasing emphasis on individual subjectivity is not an exclusively Western phenomenon; it has been a tendency in the history of Daoist cultivation practice in China. This, for Chen, is a sign of the decline of Daoism, as the state has, since the political centralization of the Qin dynasty (221–206 BC), for centuries restricted the space for cultivation to within the body and disempowered people from participating in the cosmological attunement of social and political relations. Thus, by this logic, the authentic Daoist tradition has been broken and corrupted, not only since the socialist regime, but for over two thousand years![34]

The Predicament

Some Westerners are critical of the excessively self-centered and superficial aspects of American Daoism, and seek lineage and tradition from the Chinese side. Some are unsatisfied with a primarily technical orientation to Daoist practice, and go to China seeking affiliation and initiation into a more deeply embedded tradition. Some have formally taken Daoist monks as their masters, and at least one other has even taken the step of becoming a Daoist nun herself, taking residence in a monastery. But the reality is that Daoist lineage and tradition in China are damaged, hurting, and inseparable from the whole of Chinese culture, history, and ethnocentrism. Can they find the authentic Daoist tradition they seek in such a context?

The encounters between the Dream Trippers and the Cloud Wanderers thus produce an interference and interpenetration between two trajectories of contemporary spirituality: an ultramodern radicalization of ontological individualism, or an encapsulated stepping outside of modernity with an orientation toward tradition, local embeddedness, and ethnic Chinese-ness. These encounters, and the mutual attractions, resistances, connections, and interpenetrations they generate, reveal the precariousness of *both* ultramodern and encapsulated constructions of spirituality today—what we call the "predicament" of modern spirituality.

Both orientations, however, are under strain: one the one hand, the fragility of a completely self-centered and ungrounded spiritual subjectivity; on the other hand, the breakdown of the traditional authority and structures of transmission, which exist precisely to provide a framework for the self-transcendence as a spiritual subject. Under classical modernity, ontological individualism had meaning within the grand narrative of the liberation of the rational self from traditional institutions, in which the modern utopia was characterized by free and autonomous individuals, firmly grounded in their reason and their personal alignment with the teleology of progress. But what happens when both traditional *and* modernist certitudes have collapsed? In the "liquid modernity" theorized by Zygmunt Bauman, social forms and institutions are no longer stable enough to provide a solid frame of reference for peoples' lives, which become ever more fragmented and uncertain. People need to constantly change commitments, jobs, relationships, and interests; so that their lives are no longer progressive "careers" but often haphazard successions of experiences and opportunities. They need to be constantly on the move, ever more uprooted and nomadic. They spend more and more of their time in generic "nonplaces" such as shopping malls, fast food restaurants, and airports.[35]

Under such conditions, the need to find a stable ground to the self becomes ever more acute, and groups such as the Healing Tao promise a path to this ground through Daoist inner alchemy. But can the ground of the self be found within oneself? We have discussed above how the Healing Tao continues a long American tradition of spiritual individualism that locates authenticity and authority within the self. Can some fleeting experiences in the body, no matter how frequent, or on a mountain, no matter how powerful, provide a stable grounding for the self? Are the Dream Trips a cure to the fragility of the "liquid self" of ultramodernity, or are they a symptom?[36]

The Dream Trips seem to exemplify the paradox of ultramodern spirituality: on the one hand, they appear as a mere commercial packaging of individual experience, offering a new backdrop for people interested primarily in their own embodied subjectivity, with virtually no concern for the historical, cultural, and religious context of the Daoist tradition that has generated the very practices and the sacred sites that make the "Dream" possible. On the other hand, the trips are premised on connecting to the source of Daoism, to an authenticity that can only be found in sites such as Huashan, and that there is a deep significance to the connections—personal, energetic, and spiritual—that can be made at the mountain. This authenticity also brings a much-needed legitimation to an organization such as Healing Tao USA that is still struggling to establish its Daoist credibility. As Winn puts it,

we had our ears open for everything coming out of China that was real, verifying our path too, because the big insecurity we had as Healing Taoists in the West was we were in a vacuum and we weren't connected to China except through Mantak Chia, and there wasn't any other background stuff published in English to verify what we were being taught. It's like, wow, we've got this incredible transmission but where's the support team? . . . I'm reminded in the early years, we were a little sensitive about this stuff, we were saying, "Where's our tradition? Where's our role in this thing?" Basically, you get heavyweight scholars—I think it was Schipper—saying these New Age Daoists aren't really Daoists. If they're not Quanzhen or Zhengyi then they aren't really Daoist. And us having to take that from people who are authorities in their field. Fortunately, I knew that they've got scholarly blinders on, and they're limited to the main traditions and the big things, and they can't see that this tradition of one wandering Daoist has become mainstream over here. It came in through the back door, from a wandering Daoist, One Cloud, to Mantak Chia.[37]

At the same time, Winn wants to return to China to find additional Daoist techniques: "Is there more to be exchanged here? Can we get more from the motherland than just what we got from Mantak Chia? And certainly, yes, I've gotten a lot more. Just learning other forms, like the *wujigong*, I got from Zhu Hui. Lots of teachers there that I've picked up pieces from that are essential to my filling out, rounding out, and strengthening of my teachings here."

Whether at the individual or the institutional level, then, the Dream Trips appear to be a search for an authenticity that is located outside the self and outside America. At Huashan, they meet the Cloud Wanderers, Daoist cultivators whose spiritual path is grounded in genealogy and tradition. But they, too, embody a paradox: the very lineages and transmission that constitute their identity and are the foundation of their authority, have been broken over the decades of revolutions, campaigns, and reforms—broken by the very state that has "frozen" the Quanzhen tradition, preserved its forms and created the encapsulated structure within which the monks can build their religious identity and evade or transcend the modern world.

We have argued that the tendency in Chinese Daoist spirituality, in contrast to that of American self-spirituality, has been toward embeddedness in local tradition and culture on the one hand, and toward the embodiment of the essence of Chinese-ness, on the other. But today, the local context and culture around Huashan is one of a countryside where the fastest-growing religion is Christianity, a town that is being developed into a commercial resort of "Daoist health and life-nurturing," and a mountain that is being exploited for mass tourism. Is there any room for the Quanzhen order to become embedded in these contexts? To the extent that there is local interest in the Huashan Daoists, it is as little more than as costumed actors in what may become a Daoist-ecological theme park. Would such "embedding" not lead to the end of the encapsulation of Quanzhen Daoism, to the further erosion of its authenticity? Very few people are genuinely interested in the Daoist spiritual significance of Huashan and in the practices of its monks—and among those few, a significant proportion are . . . Westerners!

For some Quanzhen monks, the national context of Daoism, with its damaged sacred places and politicized institutions, is not a suitable environment for true Daoist cultivation; and they see a new space for reaching students and potential disciples among the global spiritual seekers. Alienated by the corruption and breakdown of authority in the monastic institution, they are tempted by the unencumbered freedom of the Western practitioners, by a Daoism with no institution or authority. Hu, Hao, and Chen are very different individuals, whose paths came together for a few years at Huashan, where they interacted over a few years with Winn's Dream Trippers, but, since then, they have been moving in increasingly divergent directions. The three of them are passionate about cultivation—a passion they acutely sense is not shared by many of their fellow Daoist monks.

Master Hu has chosen to remain at the foot of Huashan at the Jade Spring Monastery, firmly in the path of politically orthodox monasticism, even if this means suffering the backbiting and intrigues of his fellow monks. As a Daoist official at the Huashan Daoist Association, he has become firmly embedded in a "religious work unit" of socialist China, contributing to the maintenance and construction of China's "traditional culture" and "indigenous religion" in the context of state nation-building. Master Hao has assumed the exile that was imposed on him, finding in the life of a mountain hermit the fulfillment of his early dreams of spiritual freedom; living in the cave complex, he has been trying, stone by stone, to build dormitories near his caves, in order to better accommodate larger groups of Western and Taiwanese practitioners. At the same time, he lives in fear of his cave complex becoming the target of tourist development. And Master Chen—who, more than the other three, was successful in the political and social scene at the Huashan Daoist Association and had largely benefited from it—simply quit the life of a Daoist monk, but not to return to the secular life of finding a job and building a family. Rather, as an urban hermit, he would devote himself even more ardently to his spiritual destiny. Catering to the needs and expectations of a handful of local Chinese disciples, he played the role of a magician and exorcist—while, at the same time, giving teachings and talks to American, Russian, and Belgian practitioners and organizations, and repudiating the Daoist community within which he had been trained.

Solving the Predicament: A Third Culture?

Our protagonists have each tried to find their own solutions to the predicament of modern spirituality. The predicament is most consciously and acutely felt by the scholar-practitioner Louis Komjathy, whose solution has been discussed in the previous chapter. Master Chen, given his rejection of Daoist institutions and his refusal to launch a new or reformist organization, gave the following answer when asked how a true seeker can connect to Dao in the absence of any legitimate institutions:

> Ever since the beginning of the universe, there has been differentiation. The myriad beings are not equal. Some will find the true Dao and others never will. No matter the institutional reality, the seeker after Dao needs to take refuge in the Three Treasures of Daoism: Dao, Scriptures, and Master (*dao, jing, shi*). Dao is everywhere and everything can be an opening to Dao. Therefore,

if our heart is open, it will connect with Dao. The difference here is only between the spiritual condition of each individual and his capacity to accept
Dao. As for Scriptures, so many people spend decades practicing all manner
of strange techniques, but never make any effort to read any scriptures. One
should immerse oneself in the authentic Scriptures, those that have endured
the test of time, and whose truth has been demonstrated. I tell my disciples,
they should obtain Scriptures, and read them, understand their teachings, and
place them on the altar near where they burn incense, and treat them reverently. And as for the Master, it is very hard to find a good master. But one
should think of what kind of disciple the most accomplished master would
choose, a master with infinite powers. A true master would accept disciples
who are pure hearted, people of virtue, willing to serve others, people of in-
tegrity and humility. So, even before finding a master, one should strive to be a
good disciple, and acquire those virtues, and do good deeds. Then, when one
has already acquired the qualities of a good disciple, undoubtedly a master
will come along and choose you.[38]

His answer tries to maintain the mystical and virtues-oriented framework of
traditional Daoism, while leaving it entirely to the imagination of the individual: one seeks refuge in the "Three Treasures" of Dao, Scriptures, and Master,
but not in a formal or ritualized fashion, only in one's heart. But on another
occasion, he did stress the fundamental importance of taking precepts in a
Daoist lineage, as discussed in chapter 5; and even after he had left the monastic order, he stressed the importance of his monastic training:

> Daoist religion is a kind of incubator. When I was a monk, I went through
> many tests in an artificial environment, which I couldn't have had elsewhere.
> For example, to break away from your family, to break all emotional ties, is a
> real experience of torture. At the same time, you become "brother" to all the
> other monks who have also cut their emotional ties, even to each other. This
> is a real training experience.[39]

Speaking of those people who make a distinction between "religion" and
"spirituality," Master Chen warned, "You have to be careful about *who* is advocating this distinction, and their motivations for doing so. Some religious
people say so, and when they say so it's from a position of understanding both
from the inside, having attained a certain level of cultivation. But for most of
those who make such a distinction, it's simply because they want to take and
to use things from religion for other purposes, such as their health, career,
fame, money, etc. They just want to pick and choose without any discipline,
so they advocate discarding religion and choosing 'spirituality' (*lingxing*)."

So, even though Chen's discourse, over the years, became increasingly "individualistic," he always spoke from the vantage point of someone who had

been trained in the monastic institution, and he still affirmed its importance. His discourse thus presented the paradox of affirming the spiritual corruption and degeneration of the monastic institution, while insisting on the value of monastic training for spiritual progress. Later, he clarified that "some type of form is important and essential; you can't just pick something out of nothing. But we need to accept that there are many forms, they come and go, and we should not be overly attached to them." So for Chen, some kind of "form" is essential to draw the person into a structure and authority transcending the ego—but no specific form is absolutely essential.[40] And, to find one's form, his answer is to advocate a purely individual approach, in which one engages in the spiritual path of moral self-transformation and waits for the Dao to operate without any active attempt to connect to a social community.

On the other hand, Winn argues for the necessity of a proactive approach. Critical of the passive and secretive attitude of Chinese Daoism, he argues that, just as it was the West that fully exploited the potential of Chinese inventions such as the printing press, gunpowder, and the compass, the same will happen with Daoist inner alchemy:

Why did the Westerners surpass the Chinese? It's because they shared the knowledge. It's because they would publish it. They said, "Hey, this is what I found out. Here's my scientific treatise." And everyone else would read it and go, "OK, you found that out, but I did this experiment based on your stuff and I found *this* out. And I'm publishing *my* results." So there was a sharing and a synergy, which catapulted the West ahead. And that's why the West is ahead in technology right now. Because of this creative edge and this sharing.

And this is what's happening now in spiritual technology. We're taking the Daoist technology, which is topflight, planetwide as far as I'm concerned. But it's embedded and hidden and, kind of, not lost but . . . mostly lost to the world, I'd say. And so we're taking that on, and we're sharing it, and we're testing it. And putting it into a new context and saying, "Here are the principles, let's try them this way, in our culture. Apply them to sexuality, apply them to depth psychology. Apply them to healing, apply them to all these things." Because of that project, of westernizing it, you could say, we're improving it; we're making it more accessible. We're actually rebirthing it. We're ensuring its ongoing viability and its presence on the planet.[41]

Part of this work of publicization, for Winn, involves putting yourself out in a very commercial manner, fully entering the spiritual marketplace that Chen and Komjathy so deplore. "Unless things get marketed in the West, they get lost." Putting as much information as possible on the Web, trying to make it accessible to the masses, even if, of those people, only 1 percent come to appreciate and practice the complexity of Daoist inner alchemy. Using sex as a gimmick is fine, if it can attract people to Daoism. "Of course it was the book on sex that really got a lot of people's attention and made [Mantak Chia] famous, the one I wrote on cultivating male sexual energy. That really got their attention, because, 'Hey, wow, this is the cultural role of sex. It's like important!' We became famous. Some people called him the sex guru, the Daoist sex guru. That doesn't really matter if that's the reason the people first came. Then when they got into it they found out, 'Oh, wow, I actually have to learn all this other stuff to manage my sexual energy and to get to a higher level.' It was just a hook. In China, all that's kind of suppressed." And this marketing, commercial dimension is also a structural requirement: Daoism in the United States, unlike in traditional or modern China, enjoys neither the state support of the large monasteries, nor the community support of small temples, nor the ritual needs of common people for funeral, healing, and exorcistic rituals. "We don't have that. We have to market, to create an infrastructure that will endure. We don't have state support."[42]

Winn claims that this process is leading to the emergence of a "third culture" between the American Protestant Christian culture and the Chinese Daoist culture, one that draws on American freedom and creativity to produce something more dynamic than Chinese Daoism. "The future of Daoism globally is here in the West, because we are fresh. We can look at it with new eyes, we can take out what is most alive in it and find what's relevant—the truly energetic science we want out of it." This "energetic science" is a bridge between scientific and religious cultures, as expressed by his vision of a replica of Beijing's Temple of Heaven that he hopes to build near his property in Asheville:

> My idea is to create an alchemical retreat center. Basically, there's a portal between spirit and matter—that's what alchemy's about. How do I open that doorway and move to both sides, back and forth? Move the contents, from the spirit side and the matter side, heaven and earth, without ever leaving, just staying right in the middle of the portal, not going all the way to one side or another. In the West, an environmentalist would be somebody who stays just in the earth side, and a religious faith type would say, "no, I want to cross over and go into the spirit side," and an alchemist is right there in the middle.[43]

This third culture takes Daoist techniques and applies them to new areas, notably to Western understandings of the psyche,

> because we want to know who we are. We want to develop that self, that individual self. That's part of our culture. We are using those techniques to do so . . . And I think the Healing Tao is kind of right in the center of it, in terms

of integrating Western psyche with this deep . . . I call it Daoist depth psychology, which integrates this Western impulse to individuate with the Daoist
technology and their principles—yin-yang, five elements. That's the cosmology. Completely accepting that cosmology but applying it to the Western
principle of "yeah, we're going to do this to individuate ourselves."[44]

What Winn seems to be proposing is a hybrid between the two integrative
schemas, of ontological individualism and cosmological attunement, that we
have compared in this book. It is an encapsulation of cosmological attunement
into the individual body and subjectivity. But cosmological attunement as it
evolved in the Chinese Daoist tradition posits and enacts correspondences
not only with the individual body and subjectivity, but also between social
and political structures, sacred geographies, and the cosmos. Cosmological
attunement is enacted not only through exercises of the body and spiritual
technologies, but also in social life, communal ritual, and political relationships. But little of this is present in the "third culture" of the Healing Tao, in
which cosmological attunement is embodied through individual exercises and
is subjectively experienced, but need not have any external expression or implications. One might say that the "third culture" uses the Daoist cosmology
to deepen and enchant the embodied subjectivity of the bounded individual.

Winn's Third Culture appears to conform to the paradox of Western religious exoticism analyzed by the sociologist Véronique Altglas: the contemporary wave of exotic and alternative spiritualities grew out of the counterculture
and the Human Potential movement, which rejected the mechanistic, dualistic, and materialistic features (all expressions of the naturalist ontology) of
Western culture, and sought an alternative in Asian and other exotic religious
traditions. And yet, they reject much of what makes those religious traditions
precisely different from Western culture; they find themselves oscillating between fascination and repulsion for their Otherness, and ultimately decontextualize them and standardize them into the framework of post-Freudian
bodywork and psychotherapy. The individual spiritual freedom and autonomy
they offer is an illusion that masks the marketing of disciplinary techniques to
cultivate versatile, adaptable, reflexive, and self-reliant neoliberal consumers
and producers.[45] Or, put in other terms, they reproduce the very ontological
individualism whose alienating effects they aim to repair, reinforcing it by offering a path to reenchantment and spiritual subjectivity that affirms the original
ontology of free, autonomous, and subjectively unique human agents.

For Winn, the challenge for Westerners is precisely to break beyond this
ontological individualism: "This requires that a westerner internalize Daoist

Qi-based cosmology, and abandon western ontological assumptions of separate beings. That is a huge shift. Much hard energetic work is required to become an 'authentic' western Daoist (my view) able to expand beyond the confines of their old ontologically bounded self-view."[46] The question is, does such a shift have implications beyond experience, perception, and embodiment at the strictly individual level?

The historian Jeffrey J. Kripal, in his study of the Esalen Institute, offers an optimistic prognosis by affirming the utopian political potential of this individualistic "religion of no religion" that has a "deconstructive power" to undermine ethnic nationalism and religious literalism. As he writes,

> the deepest psychological, social, and spiritual implications of democracy are *far* more radical than any society—including our own—has yet realized. . . . Thus, even as we speak of human rights, of individual freedoms and spiritual liberties, and of the inviolable integrity of the individual, many religious traditions continue to obey, worship, bow down to, and piously submit to a whole panoply of divine lords and kings, so many oppressive monarchies in the sky.
>
> Much of the planet, in other words, lives within one immense anachronism or superstition, literally a "left-over" in this sense: whereas our political ideals have evolved over the last three hundred years into different democratic and egalitarian forms, many of our most popular images of the divine remain stuck in the political past and so continue to encourage and justify grossly hierarchical, authoritarian, and violent practices.[47]

Perhaps Master Chen would have been interested in Kripal's argument: one day as we sat in a teahouse, he began a rant about the "slave mentality" of Chinese people that, in his view, the Chinese state has nurtured over 2,500 years, while distorting the teachings of the "independent-minded" Confucius; and he lashed out at Buddhism for its "eagerness to ally itself with slave owners" because "it believes that everything is emptiness, and has no reality, and so it is indifferent to injustice." When I mentioned to him that Daoism, too, has been criticized for doing nothing to restrain this authoritarian culture, Chen brought up the topic of human rights, emphatically stating that "Daoism absolutely upholds human rights because it is opposed to asking the individual to sacrifice himself for others, for the collectivity." He praised the philosopher Yang Zhu (440–360 BC) who famously said that he would not pluck a hair from his body to benefit others, and Zhuangzi's teaching that we should model ourselves on the useless old tree. For Master Chen, notions of service to others are used as pretexts to sacrifice individual rights and freedoms for the benefit of political power, in the name of the collective.

> You take a few people who have sacrificed themselves, you make them iᵗ heroes, you say it is very good to sacrifice yourself, and then you ask everyoᵤ. to sacrifice themselves for the political authority. Even if you offer yourself up in sacrifice, you are setting yourself up as an example, and saying that either you are morally superior to others, or that others should sacrifice themselves too. . . . You will expect others to follow you and obey you in return. That's what so many saints and sages have done. They act so selfless, but then they want you to worship them. And then those who don't sacrifice themselves are labeled as evil; they will be oppressed and killed.[48]

Master Chen's discourse was actually not about "rights," but a scathing critique of the notion of "duty." While his discourse is inflected by his lived experience in socialist China, in which notions of sacrifice and "serving the people" have been deployed in the service of political authoritarianism, it is consistent with both his explications of Daoist spiritual cultivation and with a streak of libertarianism that can be traced back to the *Zhuangzi*.[49]

For Kripal, the political significance of the Human Potential movement—to which American Daoism is closely tied—lies not in a specific political agenda or organization, but in the fact that the spiritual subjects cultivated through its practices are, in a deeply spiritual sense, *democratic political subjects*. Their nurturing of individuality through spiritual technologies gives a sacred foundation, experiential depth, and embodied substance to the abstract subjects of democratic rights and political processes. This provides the foundation for a universal ethic based on the body:

> It is the integrity of our human bodies that grants us our surest philosophical base from which *both* to appreciate and encourage the plurality of human practices *and* to resist any amoral relativism that does not distinguish between cultural practices that nurture and those that harm these same bodies. . . . It is also the welfare of this same body that allows us, that *calls* us to condemn cultural practices that endanger or harm this *corpus mysticum* in any way.[50]

But while Kripal lauds the utopian potential of this new universalism and democracy of the body, in the same breath, he also stresses how deeply *American* it is.[51] Winn is also unapologetically American in his style, approach, and appropriations of the Daoist tradition. We have seen how this appropriation may serve to repair and ultimately reinforce the ontological individualism underlying American culture by encapsulating the correlative cosmology of Daoism into the circumscribed limits of the body and personal subjectivity. The result would seem to be the formation of *American spiritual subjects*.

entitlement

rof Borchept

Thus, the question raised by Altglas remains highly pertinent: "Behind aesthetics and pleasure, religious exoticism implies implicit power relations and prompts questions about who can appropriate symbolic resources, who can be appropriated, and who defines the terms of the appropriation."[52]

But Kripal, as would Winn, turns the tables around, offering a new vision of "America" as a mystical ideal for all of humanity:

> Can we revision "America" not as a globally hated imperial superpower, not as a "Christian nation" obsessed with mad and arrogant apocalyptic fantasies abroad and discriminatory "family values" at home, not as a monster consumer of the world's ever-dwindling resources, but as a universal ideal yet to be actualized, as an empty and so creative space *far* more radical and free than the most patriotic or religiously right among us have dared imagine? . . . Can we also see that this same democratic vision of the religion of no religion will inevitably result in a free combination and recombination of ideas and beliefs that some might decry as a form of spiritual capitalism or as a debasement of religion but that others will recognize as the familiar and necessary evolutionary pattern of every new religious creation? "I am spiritual, but not religious." Are we really ready for such an affirming spiritual denial, for a radically American mysticism, for an "America" *as* mysticism?[53]

In counterpoint to this vision of an American-centered global spirituality, Komjathy advocates a different type of "third culture," one that is rooted in Chinese Daoism as "source-tradition" but that does not privilege either Chinese or American practitioners: It would "participate in a global Daoist tradition characterized by multiculturalism, multiethnicity, multilingualism, and multinationalism. Here there would be mutual respect and mutual support among tradition-based Daoists, especially committed practitioners, affiliated teachers, and actual elders. That is, although 'trans-Chinese' in an ethno-cultural sense, this 'third culture' would be a 'new Daoist culture,' one that would retain Daoist values, practices, aesthetics, orientations, and so forth."[54]

But are these two rival visions of a Daoist "third culture" both different expressions of *global* modernity? The sociologist of religion Peter Beyer, in his study of religion and globalization, has written that "modernity results simultaneously in the increased individuation of persons and the increased impersonal power of the overarching social systems."[55] These "overarching social systems" are those of functionally differentiated fields such as the economy, law, medicine, science, various professional specializations and norms, and so on. Under globalization, the norms, institutions, specialized knowledge, and networks of these systems become planetary in range and in authority. However, none of these specialized systems focuses on the "total lives of the people that carry them." But much of individual experience and social life takes place in those areas that are underdetermined by the overarching social systems. Philosophers and social scientists have called this domain the "private sphere" or the "life-world"; it is in this domain that people attempt to build themselves into spiritual subjects, able to connect the totality of their fragmented lives into a meaningful and purposeful whole. This process internalizes and relativizes the subjectivities of individuals; at the same time, it also generates, reinforces, and relativizes collective groups, based on ethnic, geographic or religious particularisms, that try to find a common identity and purpose, but always in conscious contrast to other collective groups in the world. There is thus a dual normative constitution of our modern, globalized world: it is constituted of billions of individuals, whose uniqueness is sacralized through the regime of human rights and freedoms; and it is also constituted of thousands of cultural, ethnic, or national communities, composed of people who are seen as sharing a common subjectivity that is often constructed as a "national spirit" or as finding its authenticity in the spirit of its traditional culture and religion. Each of these individual and collective subjectivities is constructed as unique and equally deserving of respect and protection. Both individuals and collectives are relativized, existing alongside and conscious of the differences of others, none having any ontological ground of authority or supremacy over others; the unique subjectivity of each is the source of its being deserving of respect. Outside of this diversity of individual and collective units, the common foundation for the operation of the global system is constituted by the outer, material world that follows identical laws, has no interiority, and can be instrumentally governed by the rational rules of the overarching social systems.

These are precisely the characteristics of the naturalist ontology formulated by Descola. To the two types of spiritual subjects—individual and collective—that are constructed within this ontology and modern global system, correspond the ultramodern spirituality of most Dream Trippers and popular American Daoists on the one hand, and the encapsulated monastic institutions of the Chinese Quanzhen order, on the other—each of which seeks to live out the Daoist correlative cosmology, but within the circumscribed limits of the individual body or a marginalized institution.

The spread and growing hegemony of the modern overarching social systems has been challenged by a succession of antisystemic movements since the rise of Romanticism in the eighteenth century.[56] These include the new alternative spiritualities from Thoreau to the Western counterculture and environmentalisms; as well as nationalisms, anticolonialist movements, and ethnic and indigenous revival movements. But ultimately, these movements tend to become encapsulated within the space afforded them by the naturalist ontology of the global system—as one religion among others, one nation among others, one culture among others; or as one spirituality among others, one spiritual experience or path among others. Is this the ultimate fate of the different Daoists in our story—whether it's monks holding the sacred space at temples and mountains, tradition-based scholar-practitioners, or hypermodern spiritual individualists? The overarching social systems that they ontologically challenge continue to expand. The cosmic energies the Dream Trippers generate, the deeper subjectivities they nurture, and the cosmic orgasms they enjoy (as described in the epilogue) only serve as a few drops of oil—or of *jing*, the vital fluid—to lubricate the operation of the global system. Are they, for better or for worse, "healing," reenchanting, and reinforcing the very global order they strive to transcend?

Epilogue:
The Cosmic Orgasms

"This is merely a cynical view of humanity as being on a downward spiral of devolution," wrote Winn in response to the above analysis. "It sees all individual progress as being co-opted by the Dark Side and converted into the agenda of some New World Order—rather than as the causal seeds of change which can take decades or centuries to fully mature." He continued:

> Witnessed externally, one cannot see the cause and effect that is occurring energetically, one only sees physical cause-and-effect of global physical institutions and organizations controlling the material aspect of life. But everything is born from within; the energetic shifting of the template of human consciousness is the first step to changing its material expression. That is the Great Work of alchemists, East and West: to drop a pearl of concentrated elixir/distilled soul consciousness into the larger field, and allowing it to ripple like a pebble tossed into a lake. This is why alchemists have traditionally remained hidden, so that they could NOT be compromised and encapsulated by the outer social-religious-political system.[1]

Contemporary academic social theory is itself based on a naturalist ontology, according to which the only common reality is exteriority, while interiority is purely subjective, unique to each individual or group, and in which there is no direct communication between interiorities that is not mediated through exteriority. Any analytical framework based on these foundational assumptions of social theory can only reach a similar conclusion to the one we have written at the end of the previous chapter. But we readily admit that this ontology is itself a social construction, and, as we have seen throughout this book, the quest to perceive, to preserve, to enact, and to redeploy alternatives to this ontology is very much alive. And, while social theory can provide critical insights, no theory or conceptual system can fully capture the complexity of reality and the infinite depth of life experience.

Our Dream Trippers, indeed, do not worry about academic critiques and debates. Consciously or not, they put the "third culture" into action, embodying the Daoist cosmology in new ways, turning life into a stream of spiritual lovemaking and ecstatic (or sometimes tongue-in-cheek) cosmic copulation. When they climbed Huashan on June 3, 2012, their purpose was not only to connect with the powerful energies of the Five Peaks: this was the spot and the time chosen by Michael Winn to hold his "alchemical wedding," which he highlighted in the promotional literature of the trip. On reaching the West Peak after six hours of climbing, the Dream Trippers dropped their bags on their assigned bunks in the rickety wooden dorm rooms of the Emerald Cloud monastery—but they were given only a few minutes to catch their breath. They still needed to climb for another thirty minutes, to reach the "secret spot" selected by Winn to conduct the alchemical ritual. The steps followed a ridge along the western cliffs of the summit, and reached a huge protruding boulder that marks the South Peak. Tourists in their scores crawled over the boulder, taking pictures, but the Trippers passed them by. They continued apace and disappeared into a nearly invisible bushy path.

The trail wound its way through a forest over the gnarly roots of pine trees until, after a few minutes, it opened onto a cascade of rocky platforms, forming a natural amphitheater protruding over the cliffs of Huashan and drawing the gaze across the abyss into an infinitely expansive view of the myriad peaks of the Zhongnanshan range, each a tower of surging white froth, the petrified form of seas of lava thrown out eons ago by the entrails of the Earth. Under the evening sun, shades of pink, yellow, blue, and gray spread their hues over the bulging cliffs of the mountains. The Dream Trippers, though tired from the long climb, were in a lighthearted mood. Several started practicing *qigong* forms, gliding past each other, until they frolicked in a spontaneous dance, and broke into song. A young woman in her twenties, slim of body, stood still at the cliff's edge, facing the void. Her arms embraced the immensity, moving with grace, caressing invisible flows. This was Jem—the alchemical bride.

Jem Minor, some thirty years Winn's junior, was about to become Winn's third wife. His first wife, from Ethiopia, was a "green card marriage" that "turned out to be true love."[2] He met his second wife, Joyce Gayheart, in 1983 at a Healing Tao workshop. They were married in 1987, at the edge of the Grand Canyon. Michael asked a well-known American Daoist Master, Ni Hua-Ching, to marry them but he was unavailable; so, as he told us, "We ended up writing our own Daoist wedding ceremony. My wife and I created a fire and water and five elements ceremony that we wrote ourselves."[3] They called in cosmic forces and Daoist Immortals, and served an Eight Trigrams pie with a big yin-yang figure in the middle. "What I discovered, and what wedding participants later told me, was that the ceremony was so powerful, they said, 'You will never be able to get divorced.' . . . We opened up some higher level of consciousness and energy that made us both feel reborn. . . . That night, on our wedding bed, we felt like virgins again. The feeling of having a pure energetic sexual connection was so intense that we didn't have physical sex."[4]

Encouraged by the powerful experiences generated by the ritual, Winn started holding alchemical Daoist ceremonies for others as well. After some time, in order to legalize the ceremonies, Winn obtained a religious minister's license from an online church.

The Invention of a Daoist Wedding Liturgy

The "Daoist" weddings at the Grand Canyon and Huashan are hybrid: they combine the very American idea of a "personalized" wedding and an experiential, destination wedding. More than that, this wedding crystallizes the complete merging of the commercial and the spiritual, the public and the private. Choosing your own dress—really a "costume" (Winn dressed as an Ethiopian prince for his first wedding), writing personal vows, and the use of eclectic readings, such as Khalil Gibran and the classic "Apache wedding" vow—these are sources which are commonly used by nonsectarian ministers everywhere in the United States. There is a profound irony that a wedding marketed as "Daoist" and also conceived by Winn as Daoist-alchemical-cosmic-energetic, and held at a secret, sacred spot on a Daoist mountain, was completely cut off from any Chinese Daoist institution or person.

But this observation raises the question: What would an "authentic" Daoist wedding ceremony look like anyway? In fact, there is no such thing, at least not traditionally. Theoretically, it might be possible: in China, Daoist priests and other ritual technicians are often called in for all kinds of auspicious rituals—opening a new business, for example—which are based on Chinese cosmology. But in China, marriage has traditionally been under the Confucian domain. Winn's Daoist weddings, however, are notable for their explicit gender equality—with a woman, Bethany, officiating, and no hints of gender hierarchy. While Daoist cosmology, perhaps more than any other major religion, accords ontological primacy to the feminine, in social practice, Chinese Daoism traditionally did not challenge the social relations of Confucian patriarchy. Daoism created a space for women in its nunneries, but again, this was in a celibate, monastic context. The Dream Trippers' weddings socially enacted a gender equality that was only suggested, but never realized, in traditional Chinese Daoism.

Perhaps the only remotely "Daoist" aspect to a traditional Chinese wedding is that before the wedding, matchmakers would have checked for cosmological compatibility and determined an auspicious date, using the almanac and the "eight characters" of the prospective bride and groom's time of birth—similar to customs found in many other cultures, which position the union within the correspondences and harmonies of an analogical cosmology. This "Daoist" element of a traditional Chinese wedding (including its concept of predestined affinities, *yuanfen*) is not romantic by any measure. But the Huashan weddings recast Dao and alchemy as supporting the modern Western idea of romance and personal fulfillment. Nor do Chinese weddings use the Daoist alchemical metaphor. But, at the same time, the use of alchemical imagery for these weddings is consistent with Daoist cosmology: the weddings are creative recastings of Daoist cosmology, in a new context and setting. As explained by Winn,

> If there is anything I want to add about the marriage, it is that in alchemy, I realized that there are basically two sets of polarities that you are working with. One is the horizontal, which is male and female. And the other is vertical, which is spirit and matter. So it's a vertical and horizontal axis. You will find that in the I-Ching and the eight trigrams. The early heaven arrangement of just fire and water, left and right, heaven and earth. . . . That's essentially what I feel alchemy is about. How do you resolve both of the polarities at the same time so they all meet at the center? That's the portal to immortality, essentially. That's where you're going to crystallize your inner sage, your essence. It can become indestructible and continue to create. Having a marriage that can stabilize the horizontal level, which is very changeable and volatile here. Male and female relationships are notoriously volatile. Having a sacred spiritual marriage, I feel, anchors that horizontal aspect of it. And, of course, the vertical aspect is to be cultivated internally, but you see, a lot of people meditate, and try to work with this on the vertical axis, and I feel their success is going to be limited somewhat, because they haven't really resolved their own sexual identity and those polarities. They will try to create an identity at the vertical spirit-matter meeting point, but it won't be stable without their horizontal inner male and female alchemically conjoined at the same point. That is where the Elixir forms, the soul is made tangible.[5]

Winn's commitment to monogamous married life represented an evolution from his earlier days, when he rode the wave of the sexual revolution that fueled his rise to prominence as the coauthor of Mantak Chia's *Taoist Secrets of Love: Cultivating Male Sexual Energy*. He explains that it was precisely sex that led him to Daoist cultivation: "I used to be obsessed by sex. The reason I got into this practice is because I was spending 70 percent of my time thinking about women. Every woman who walked past, I was like undressing them—where am I going to have sex with her? I was just obsessed. So I started to do the Daoist sexual practice. I was trying to alleviate this kind of chronic, perpetual horniness. This was too distracting." So Winn had gone celibate, trying Chia's methods on himself solo, and it did "get rid of my horniness and solve my problem. I discovered I could recycle my sexual energy into my organs or different meridians. It put me into different states, including a very embodied kind of bliss." Through his practice, he learned to go beyond his old fixation for "the kind of very salient, external, projected sexual *qi*—the never-ending chase for the sexually aroused 'I-am-turned-on' state." Instead, he grew to value a long-term, monogamous partnership "in which a man and woman cultivate and share together a sexually balanced Energy Body. The ironic thing that I have observed time and again is that guys come to the Tao because it deals with sex, which most paths do not. But once they engage their sexual energy, they realize it is not really about sex, it is just about cultivating energy. They realize they can creatively use internal sexual energy without chasing after women."[6] He repudiated the "vampirism" of the Chinese tradition of the "arts of the bedchamber," which teaches men how to use Daoist techniques to preserve their seminal essence in order to keep the stamina for sex with as many women as possible:

> I discovered that in China Daoist sexual practice has a very bad reputation. There's a history of vampirism, of "stealing virgins' *qi*," but I found even if you're not a vampire, if you just like having sex or have a healthy need to absorb Yin energy from a woman—that sexual promiscuity is very risky. Sexual pleasure may stimulate your *qi*, but during sex you also get your partner's psychic garbage as it is embedded in their sexual essence or *jing*. You may even think you're stealing their sexual energy, but in fact it comes at a high price. You have to creatively transform it. If you don't, all of your sex partner's buried issues and stress will be embedded in your psyche. That's why I tell my students don't mess around. You are better off finding one partner. If you both refine your *qi*, then you can actually exchange something to a higher level. Your lovemaking clears out all that subconscious junk as the male-female polarities neutralize it. If you are promiscuous, and go around dipping in here and there, you will be pulling in a lot of unrefined, raw, unconscious energy from these women. Or women may do the same with men. It's a kind of energetic self-punishment. You think you're getting fresh sexual energy from them, but you are actually their slave as you have to transform it. It doesn't support a high-level spiritual practice, as you are starting over with each partner. It's

much better to find a long-term partner who is committed to refining their *qi* with you into higher and higher realms. My last wife and I did dual cultivation practice together for 25 years. It takes time to clear out unconscious, biological urges and transmute them into a whole mind-body integration. . . . So the more refined you get, the more permanent a male-female relationship you want. You realize it is too slow to continually start over with someone's unrefined and unconscious sexual energy.[7]

Winn and his second wife, Joyce Gayheart, were both Healing Tao teachers and heavily involved in alternative spiritual and health practices. They spent thousands of hours meditating together, sublimating (or, in Winn's words, "cooking") the sexual impulses into spiritual refinement:

We had a very high-level practice together, where we didn't have to have sex often. We just lay down next to each other and exchanged *qi*. And, of course, this is polarized, male and female. We would be there for hours. . . . We could lie and feel our bodies and exchange our energy. So it's actually subtle body sex—with clothes on or with clothes off, it really didn't matter. And we discovered this actually on our wedding night. We were so tired, and we lay down. We thought wedding night, we're going to have sex. And the next morning, we didn't want sex. We just had this beautiful exchange. For six months, after our wedding, we never made physical love once. We just found this so pure, deep, and so rich. So we just kept doing that exchange of *qi* rather than physical friction sex. This part requires even the right partner, or at least some level of cultivation. But most people will not have that right away, because they are too object-oriented.[8]

Joyce wanted children, Michael did not. In February 2008, Joyce died of brain cancer. Three days later, in Winn's narrative, Joyce's heart spirit (*shen*) merged with Michael's. Winn wrote in detail about their life, her death, and this transference, in a memorial page within his commercial Healing Tao website.[9]

In Winn's view, "This merging of heart spirits felt like we were continuing our marriage, only now it was in heaven, as Joyce didn't have a body on earth." According to Winn's newsletter: "Spirit was pushing me to find another woman and birth some kind of 'divine love child,' who held the potential to also be my next spiritual teacher. I did not feel any need for children, who are messy and a lot of work (thanks Mom and Dad for doing it for me!). But I agreed to the fathering task, on the condition that the Spirit-Child find me the right Mother. I asked that the Mother would be attuned to an alchemical process of Conscious Conception."

Ultimately, according to his online newsletter, it was Winn's mother, two days after her death, who communicated to him that he would meet his mate in Asheville in six months. So he canceled his 2011 China trip in anticipation—which, in any case, had poor enrollment. And, at the predicted time, Winn met Jem in the spring of 2011 at the Asheville Movement Collective, which we described at the opening of chapter 7.

Jem, part Cheyenne Indian, was born in Alaska, started practicing *qigong* at the age of 11, was a member of a witches' coven as an undergraduate student at Mount Holyoke University, and was now enrolled in the acupuncture college at Asheville founded by Jeffrey Yuen, whose own lineage master had been based at Huashan prior to 1949.

Winn's newsletter posted Jem's narrative on their first meeting: "In that split second of seeing the man in question, an inner voice told me that I could have a child with him. This loud and clear internal declaration took me completely by surprise. I was neither seeking any romance nor felt likely to have children any time soon. I had two intensive years left in acupuncture school, and had recently committed to a year of celibacy. [. . .] Over the following months, I watched and felt how he held and moved *qi* at dance, on the few occasions he appeared."[10]

She finally agreed to visit him. A note greeted her on Winn's front door: "Welcome Home." We pick up the story with Michael's narrative:

After spending just ONE day with her, I invite her to move in, certain that we will marry. We are not even lovers yet. That sounds totally CRAZY, especially for someone as PICKY as me. One of my trusted female advisors to my Partner Search had already warned me: "You have so many conditions, I wonder if anyone exists that could meet them all." I told her: "There are 3 billion females on planet Earth. Tao only needs to deliver one unique female to me. Why accept less?" [. . .] And it turned out that Jem is equally picky as well, if not more so. But from the outside, it looks irrational. Some loving friends tried to warn Jem and I to double-check whether our decision to marry, after only another 3.5 months, was hasty. But the reality is, we already felt married.[11]

This entire story and the accompanying wedding announcement was part of the advertisement to Winn's China Trip 2012—sent via his e-newsletter "Chi Flows Naturally," read by 20,000 people. The wedding was marketed as a special added feature to the 2012 Dream Trip. Who else was invited? "I expect a host of Tao Immortals and Dragon Spirits to show up for the ceremony," Winn wrote in the wedding invitation/tour advertisement/love story. His assistant tour leaders were his fiancée (her first time in China), and Bethany, who was to perform the wedding ceremony. Also invited to the wedding, besides anyone who could pay between five and six thousand dollars for the two-and-a-half-week trip, was the spirit of Michael and Jem's child-to-be:

Jem and I are very clear that our spiritual mission involves a Water (birthing) phase. This could take many forms, and includes the potential for Conscious Conception of a divine love child with a destiny filled with harmony and spiritual grace. We'll invite this child-spirit to attend the wedding ceremony, and hope it comes riding in on a fire-breathing Water Dragon. The child has already revealed its spirit name to us as "Emerald" (speaking to us from a voice in deep Earth).[12]

But no Chinese Daoists were invited. Indeed, the whole wedding was hidden from the Daoists who actually live at Huashan. Winn did not want any bureaucratic involvement, which would have been inevitable had any Huashan Daoists been informed. He had not invited Master Hu, fearing a repeat of the interrogation Hu had been subjected to in 2006, as described in chapter 4.

The Weddings

It was time for the wedding to begin. The Dream Trippers had the entire platform to themselves—no tourists, and no Daoist monks. Three young Chinese lads, however, had followed the group to this spot. Dressed in military camouflage, these teenagers worked as helping hands at the Emerald Cloud monastery. Curious, bored, and amused by the strange aliens, they had followed the group from the monastery, all the way to this spot, pushing each other, joking, and laughing aloud. Winn allowed them to stay, and entrusted them with a sacred mission, albeit unknown to them: they would be the Chinese witnesses of the wedding. "Look at how thirsty they are for this. I realized that the transmission would go through them to the Chinese people."

A colorful cloth was placed on the rock surface, marking the ritual space for the ceremony; various implements were laid onto it. As the Dream Trippers sat or stood in the natural amphitheater formed by the terraced stones, an older American woman, her silver hair in a bun, wearing a black skirt, a traditional-style white Chinese shirt, and Chinese slippers, performed a standing *qigong* routine, "warming up the ritual space." Winn's assistant Bethany, wearing a bright yellow and purple Chinese robe, stepped in to officiate, rang a small bell, and called on the newlyweds to approach. *"Friends, we are all here today, in this most beautiful, spectacular moment, to witness and participate in the wedding of Jem and Michael Winn. Each of your presences is what makes this special moment, a perfect special moment in all eternity. Your presence is crucial. We are not witnesses, but participants to all create, and hold and strengthen the field of divine love."* Right after those few words of welcome, she guided the Dream Trippers into a visualizing *qi* meditation. *"And we will bring our hearts together, to bring this energy, beginning each in our own hearts. If you will, for a moment, close your eyes, and welcome a stream of golden light, into your head, into your forehead, beautiful golden light, flowing down across your face, passing and warming your eyes, your nose, your mouth, your whole face, down your throat, golden light pouring across the front of your body, flowing all the way down your chest, all the way down to your feet, until it absorbs and flows back up.*" She repeated the cycle three times, guiding the flow down the back and middle of the body, then invited the participants to bring the stream of light "*down to the dantian, we anchor and ground the divine love in our dantian, with ha, ho, hum three times.*" And all participants, in unison, melodiously chanted the "healing sounds" of "haaaaaaa," "hohhhhh," and "hummmm." And then, she invited them to raise their hands and point toward the couple: "*We will now extend this energy field to create a pearl, a pink pearl, surrounding us all. Each person holding onto the same pink pearl, the ground of divine love, the same way that we potentiate the pearl inside our dantian, we create and hold this collective field of divine love, anchored. One more ha—*" And all, in unison, chanted: haaaaaaaa. . . .

The next rite was the "purification by water and fire." Winn's sister, grayhaired, wearing a burgundy silk Chinese-style shirt, holding a white bowl, sprinkled water onto the newlyweds and onto Bethany, and then onto the Dream Trippers in the front rows. Bethany rang the bell, and her companion, holding a little plate of incense, waved it around the newlyweds, front and back, up and down, as their arms stretched downward, their hands facing outward, Jem smiling radiantly. She swooshed the incense in circles in the direction of the audience. Bethany rang the bell, and invited the newlyweds to invite those invisible entities they wished to be present. Jem began: "*I welcome Amache* [Jem's Cheyenne great-grandmother], *and all of my ancestors, male and female, I welcome my mother, and my sister, I welcome my priestess sisters, I welcome Guanyin, and Doumu, I welcome Gaia, all aspects of Goddess, my inner sage, the spirits of all directions, and all of my shen and my shadow.*" She brought her hands up to her navel, and Winn followed: "*I call on the spirits of my first guides on this planet, my parents Dean and Shirley Winn, they have been married for sixty years plus. I call in the spirits, the gods and the goddesses of all directions, and all dimensions, who have been guiding me on my path, and all my invisible ancestors, human and nonhuman, and I call in Taiyi the great central sun, radiating the purity of love, the divine, primordial love, and its emanations as Doumu, the primordial mother, the Eight Trigram forces of the Yijing, maintaining balance and harmony, wuxing, the five elements, responding to my life as the seasons, within and without, the Three Pure Ones, all the Zodiacal star beings, spirits, sun, moon, earth, planets, all of my vital organ spirits, requesting them to be fully present, fully conscious, and I invite in all of my shadow aspects, yet waiting to come into the light. I welcome you, come play,"* he said, as many Trippers chuckled.

Other friends approached and recited a love poem by Dorothy Walters, a reading from the I Ching, and a poem "on marriage" by Khalil Gibran. Then, a Belgian dance instructor and *qigong* practitioner, dressed in black, performed a "dragon dance" based on graceful tai chi forms, shifting suddenly between slow and fast movements, swiftly turning her body around the newlyweds and in front of the Dream Trippers. Joan, a friend of Winn, then recited a Cherokee prayer "in honor of the lands where the bride and groom reside, the sacred mountains at the other end of the spectrum of Huashan." She called on all present to "find themselves a sacred space," placing themselves in position for a collective practice of *wujigong*, *"and center ourselves on this mountain, this sacred mountain where we have come together for this ceremony of love. Let's set our intention for the union and bringing and gather the divine love here in this space and time. As we stand in wuji, let us all tone the sacred seven sounds, to come together."* All the Dream Trippers moved in unison, chanting the six healing sounds in melodious, soothing tones.

Now Michael Winn pronounced a blessing: *"Jem and I invite the primordial powers of fire and water to bless us with their copulation."* There was a moment of silence, then Winn and some of the Trippers laughed. *"This is what drives all creation. A lovemaking between yin and yang, male and female, we are dancing in that stream, each of us. We ask to celebrate that, and amplify it to the farthest reaches of the cosmos, the sun and moon making love, the inner sun, the inner earth, radiating their love, their juicy love to each soul that passes through on this macrocosmic journey. And all the star beings, the spirit beings, copulating with the material earth beings, in order to cocreate creation. We welcome this beautiful, intense cosmic sexual activity, and invite it to flow into our relationship, and into each and every relationship. It is the spark that drives all creation, all love, all transformation, all evolution. It is the alchemical process itself,"* Winn continued, as several Dream Trippers chuckled. *"Thank you, primal fire, thank you, primal mother, for blessing us, with your cosmic lovemaking, and may that love radiate to each and every heart here from atop Huashan, to everyone on this planet, to all the future souls who will be arriving on this planet as a result of that lovemaking, and especially that spirit we've named Emerald, feel that love radiating from the center of that lovemaking, perfect union of male and female, fire and water, heaven and earth, opening every heart."* Winn concluded, shaking in spasms of *qi*.

Bethany rang the bell and invited Winn and Jem to pronounce their wedding vows. Each professed their love for each other, in lyrical and alchemical terms. Winn placed a ring on Jem's finger, and she placed a necklace around his neck. They connected in deep kissing for several long seconds. And Bethany pronounced them married: "*With heaven and earth, the Dao immortals, the white ruler god of Huashan, goddess of the nine heavens, primordial mother Doumu, the Yellow Emperor, Taiyi, the central sun of love and oneness, assembled Daoist adepts, as witnesses, I pronounce you lifelong alchemical partners—* several Trippers laughed—*committed to fully realizing the Dao, and as husband and wife, within the human realm, may your divine union be blessed with harmony and virtues, children, and endless laughter.*"

The newlyweds ran up to a higher stone ledge behind the Dream Trippers. All the participants sang a song and clapped their hands: "*We shall go out with joy, and we set forth in peace, the mountains and the hills will break forth, there will be shouts of joy. And all the trees in the fields will clap, will clap their hands, and all the trees in the fields will clap their hands, the trees in the fields will clap their hands, and we'll go out with joy.*" Winn and Jem faced the sunset to the west, their black silhouettes waving in movements of *qigong*, and fell into embrace. The Trippers cheered. Jem threw a bouquet of flowers at them, and they scrambled to catch them. Winn came down and chatted with the Trippers, while Jem continued her slow motion dance above, on the ledge, her body a moving black shadow against the dusk.

All now returned to the monastery before dark. The three Chinese lads who had followed the group to the wedding were very excited, and intent on creating a joyful atmosphere, perhaps wanting a release after all the slow and gentle motions of the Dream Trippers. They put on some loud, Western rock music in the monastery courtyard. When one of the Americans, just for fun, shook a few beats to this music, the youth joined in, full of excitement, and pulled the Dream Trippers onto the "dance floor." Soon, all were dancing to the quick beat. Daoist "stillness and tranquility" vanished from the Emerald Cloud monastery, which became the setting of a booming dance party.

Winn later wrote an account of the wedding for his newsletter, and the honeymoon, with many photos. "June 3 ceremony atop Flower Mountain. It was the climax of a 3 week China Dream Trip into Taoist sacred mountains and caves with a wonderful group who bonded deeply, creating a secure cauldron for our wedding. In the ceremony we invited all souls to dive into the ocean of divine love, flowing from what Taoists call *Taiyi*, the Great Oneness. It was powerfully broadcast from Flower Mountain's highest peak, on what I feel is China's most powerful Taoist mountain." Referring to the night they spent in a cave to consummate the marriage, he wrote: "*My bride wakes up in our honeymoon suite: 3 nights in a hard, granite cave. We loved the emptiness! Just us and the spirit of the mountain. This is the same 'Snow Flower Cave' I spent a week in bigu (no food, no water) in 2002.*" Later, they took a more conventional honeymoon in Alaska, the Grand Canyon, the national parks of Utah, and Las Vegas.[13]

But while they were still at Huashan, the morning after Winn and Jem's wedding, the Dream Trippers hiked to the Central Peak of Huashan, for a second wedding. The Californian Kent, a friend of Winn's and former Dream Trip assistant leader, and the Mexican Daisy had both joined the 2006 Dream Trip, where they had met and begun their romance. Their wedding took place on a large natural stone platform, in front of the Jade Maiden Temple of the Central Peak, out of which the rhythmic sound of recorded sutra chanting could be heard. The temple keeper, Master Pu, came out to see the commotion as the Dream Trippers arrived and placed themselves in a large semicircle around the wedding ritual space. The monk joined the Westerners in observing the wedding, videotaping the ceremony with his mobile phone.

This ceremony followed a similar liturgy to the previous day's, this time with Winn acting as the officiant. Instead of the "purification by water and fire," this time it was the five elements which were highlighted, with five participants each acting as the "Dragon" of one of the elements, approaching the ritual space in turn with an object symbolizing the element. And instead of practicing *wujigong*, Kent himself, as a "gift to all present," directed the group in a practice of "Five Treasures *Qigong*," a form developed by the National Qigong Association of America. Following Kent's instructions and visualizations, the Trippers, in unison, engaged in "ocean wave breathing," "drawing up earth *qi*," "gathering starlight," "opening the fire," and "drawing down heavenly *qi*."

Winn then led the couple and the Dream Trippers into a visualization on love: "*The mountain itself is having an orgasm,*" Winn said, as some Trippers burst into laughter. "*And now, I invite you all to join in that sacred orgasm. Primal fire and primal water, which is the copulation of yin and yang, that drives the flow of all creation. Close your eyes, and seek within the mountain the fire rising up, deep within the earth, a ball of flaming passion, deep love radiating up from mother earth. And from the sky, the hidden heart, the water, blue pearls descending, embracing all of us. As the fire and the water copulate, massive clouds of bliss and radiant love. We are all floating in this cloud. Allow yourself to float for a minute, silently, feeling the fire below, the water above, and the true source, the connection, radiating to the center of the clouds of love.*" Here Winn shook in jerky movements, his hands gesturing around the "elixir field" at his abdomen. "*Now this blissful cloud of love and light penetrates into the hearts of Kent and Daisy, flows through all their blood vessels, to radiate deep into their bones, all of their bodily tissues, every cell, the nucleus of each cell is glowing with love and light, and the source of divine love. And may this inner love and*

light guide their relationship and their marriage, and their sacred path together,
as alchemical partners on the path of the Dao."

After the couple had said their vows and exchanged wedding rings, another participant performed a "sacred Eight Trigrams dance," a set of martial arts forms, jumping around the ritual space. Peace played a tune on her bamboo flute. And finally, Winn asked all the Trippers to form a circle around the couple, and to chant OM nine times—"the sacred Daoist number of completion and maximum yang." Kent and Daisy faced each other, holding hands. The others, in a wide circle around them, their palms turned outward, faced them, and chanted, in unison, "OOOOMMMMM," nine times. The bride and groom hugged, as the onlookers clapped. Winn invited them to join in the hug. The whole group came together for a group hug, thirty voices chanting in harmony: "OOOOOOMMMM. . . ."

Appendix:
Methodological Issues

This is not a study of a bounded religious community, but of encounters between individuals belonging to, or moving into or out of, at least three different cultural worlds—the Complete Perfection monastic order, global alternative health and spirituality networks, and western academic Daoist studies. The boundaries between the three worlds of monasticism, spiritual travel, and academia were challenged and undermined as our study progressed, and we inadvertently played a role in the way the encounters and trajectories unfolded.

Indeed, these encounters have been occurring through time, and inflecting changes in the protagonists' trajectories—so that this is not a holistic study of a cultural system in equilibrium, located in a timeless "ethnographic present," but rather of contacts, circulations, responses, and chain reactions between dissipating structures and emergent networks. These encounters are not repetitive cultural patterns but discrete events, moments in a history of transformation, points where much broader processes are constituted and manifested through the actions of unique individuals, moving within very specific social settings, and at concrete places. Our protagonists' situations have changed since we began this project, sometimes radically and unexpectedly.

Ethnography as Intervention

Pierre Bourdieu, discussing the challenges specific to the sociological study of religion, stressed that the researcher must make a choice between either understanding the struggles of the religious field, or taking part in those struggles.[1] In our experience researching and writing this book, however, we found that such a dichotomy does not hold. The researcher will be drawn into those

266   APPENDIX

struggles, even if he wishes to avoid it. Our study focuses on several players in the religious field of global Daoism, each of whom has his own stance and stake in the struggles over the definition and organization of Daoist authenticity, authority, and practice. We do not take sides—but we have inadvertently and inevitably been drawn into the struggles; indeed, this very book, even unintentionally, constitutes an intervention in this field, as a public work that will be read and invoked by the practitioners and scholars who constitute the field.

As the anthropologist Jean-Paul Dumont has noted, fieldwork is an illustration of the Heisenberg Uncertainty Principle: an investigator, through the very process of conducting an experiment, alters the conditions that he examines and is himself changed.[2] Over the past decades, anthropologists have engaged in a sustained critique of a traditional mode of ethnographic writing in which factual material was presented by an omniscient yet invisible author-narrator whose methods of fieldwork and data collecting were not always manifest, and who did not address the nature of his relationships, both personal and structural, with the subjects of the study.[3] Ethnographers have experimented with different approaches to writing, with a heightened sensitivity to the "politics of representation," the ethics of how, through writing, the author exercises control over how the voices of the research subjects are presented and interpreted.

Over the course of researching and writing this book, we have often reflected on these debates; in this appendix, we briefly consider some of the relevant aspects. Our research and writing approach is relevant to methodological discussions and experiments in "dialogical" or "collaborative" anthropology, which have attempted to move beyond the objectification of research subjects to engage them as equals.[4] Often, these discussions continue to posit a relatively undifferentiated community that can speak with a single voice (or with uncontested spokespersons) to represent its views and interests as a partner in dialogue or collaboration in producing a text with the ethnographer. Here, however, there is no collective interlocutor: each of our protagonists claims to represent the Daoist tradition, but could also be said to represent only himself. All of them, in their mutual positioning, whether through avoidance, dialogues, or debates—some of which were instigated through the process of our own research—help to constitute the global Daoist field.

Questioning the Insider-Outsider Dichotomy

Just as the encounters of this book represent the entanglement of the lifecourses of our protagonists, the conception and unfolding of this book's research and writing has been part of the trajectories of our own lives. Neither of us identifies as "Daoist"—Siegler is a secular Jew and Palmer is a practicing Bahá'í—but we have deep affinities (or perhaps, as Chinese Daoists might say, *yuanfen*) with the Daoist tradition. When we began this study, we were not "practitioners" in any regular or committed sense, but we had a sufficient experience of Daoist practice to say that we were not strangers to some of the types of experiences described by adepts, and could apprehend Daoist cosmology less as an intellectual system than as an embodied field of experience. Like so many others, our first encounter with Daoism was through the *Daodejing*, which we each discovered as teenagers. As high school classmates in Toronto, we shared an affinity with things Chinese; once, as teammates in an interschool impromptu debating tournament, we cast coins to use the *Yijing* as a source of arguments. A decade later, Siegler spent years researching the history and practice of American Daoism for his PhD in American religious history at the University of California at Santa Barbara, while Palmer was conducting his own field research in Chengdu on the *qigong* movement in post-Mao China under the direction of Kristofer Schipper and in the intellectual tradition of French anthropology and Daoist Studies at the École Pratique des Hautes Études in Paris. Notwithstanding our different academic trajectories and current disciplinary locations in the Academy (Palmer in a Sociology department, Siegler in Religious Studies), we have shared, for the purpose of this book, an approach that combines the anthropology, sociology, and history of religions. We conducted some of the field trips and interviews together and others alone; however, for the ease of reading, we have adopted the second person plural as the narrator's voice. In some cases "we" does refer to the two of us; and in others, only one of us was present observing or interviewing. Readers can refer to the endnotes to identify which of us is speaking in those cases.

Notwithstanding our intellectual, spiritual, and experiential comfort with Daoism in general, we began this study seeing ourselves clearly as outsiders to the specific groups and practices involved in the encounters. Our joint familiarity with both Chinese and Western Daoism and their broader historical and sociocultural contexts, as well as our critical historical, sociological, and anthropological gaze, led us to see the actors, their encounters, and their experiences from a different standpoint than the Dream Trippers or Chinese monks themselves.

However, the distinctiveness of our identity as outside observers has become less and less tenable with the passage of time. Dream Trippers are anything but a homogenous group; although they typically include some committed practitioners of the Daoist cultivation methods promoted by Michael

Winn or Mantak Chia, or of other forms of *qigong* or tai chi, many have, at best, a tenuous connection to Daoism, and others have more experience with other traditions of spiritual practice. Some of them know each other before joining Dream Trips, and may maintain friendships begun during the trip, but for the most part the groups are ephemeral communities that last only a few weeks before dissolving, upon leaving China, into the loose networks of Daoist and alternative spiritual practices. Thus, we hardly felt like aliens or outsiders when joining the Dream Trippers at Huashan or other points on their itinerary. Although some participants do join more than one Dream Trip, few, if any, have ever joined *four* trips, as we have (although we have only joined segments of trips, and never the complete journey). Siegler even helped Livia Kohn *organize* a trip, which had much in common with the Dream Trips.

Siegler knows basic Mandarin Chinese and Palmer is fluent in the language; he acted as interpreter in many of the conversations recorded in this book; it is difficult to know if they would have occurred differently, or even at all, under different circumstances. Michael Winn and the Dream Trippers do not speak Chinese; the Quanzhen monks and Master Chen speak no English. Winn always arranges for Chinese guides and interpreters for his Dream Trips, but they usually do not have the same cultural background and specialized knowledge on Daoism as Palmer, which could lead to differences in the way conversations are interpreted and oriented. Komjathy is more proficient in the classical written language of Daoist scriptures than in oral Chinese. Owing to these different sets of language skills, the content and flow of conversations between the Chinese interlocutors and Winn, Komjathy, and Palmer was surely different, and may inflect on their attitudes and biases.

When Palmer spent time with Masters Chen, Hu, and Hao, he engaged with them not only as a data collector, but also as a student of Daoism—and it was from this position that he prompted them to elaborate their discourses on Daoist cultivation and authenticity, and to comment on and evaluate those of Western practitioners. Palmer's relationship with them was one of a "friend in Dao" (*daoyou*), in which the Daoists took the role of teachers. Palmer approached them as embodiments of a living tradition, through whose lives the different pieces of the Daoist world all came together—its gods, its mountains, its body practices, its rituals, its mythology, and its philosophy. Although not a formal disciple, Palmer's learning was more than academic, and included teachings on practice. With time, this process so imbued his daily embodiment that it became an integral part of his experience and perception of the world.

Both of us learned some of Winn's and Chia's *qigong* forms, including basic moves of *wujigong*, which is important to the Dream Trip, and Siegler participated in a weekend retreat in Asheville organized by Winn in 2005. On three occasions in the caves of Huashan, Palmer also experienced powerful embodied visions that were as enchanting as those recounted by the protagonists in this book. We mention this here not to validate those accounts, which we refrain from passing judgment on, nor to claim any authority deriving from such experience, but to stress that we do not attempt to draw an artificial line between ourselves as scientific observers who would be "above" such experiences, and exotic "indigenous," "religious," or "spaced-out" ethnographic subjects who make unverifiable, inexplicable, or just plain silly claims.

Thus, by the time we completed this book, we were still far from being insiders to the Dream Trippers or to Complete Perfection Daoism—but we were not outsiders either. We could say that we were neither inside nor out, or both inside and out—but the same could be said of most of the Dream Trippers themselves, as well as of the scholar-practitioners. Rather than speaking of the "insider-outsider" distinction that has been a longstanding issue in religious studies, we can only speak of the different and changing positions of each of the actors—as well as the scholars who write about them—in the religious field and the networks that constitute it.

The same can be said of our main interlocutors among the Quanzhen Daoist monks. The culture of the Complete Perfection order reinforces a strong disposition to discretion and reserve toward strangers: it is not easy to enter into frank and in-depth conversations with Daoist monks. After repeated visits over a decade, however, we were able to build enough trust and familiarity with the main actors in the encounters described here to gain significant insights into the conditions and inner dynamics of the Daoist community at Huashan, the deeper motivations and concerns of individual Daoists, and their own spiritual and social trajectories during the period of interaction with the Westerners. Much of the information presented here, however, is largely based on the accounts of only a handful of individuals. How representative are they of Complete Perfection monks in general? It is difficult to say: by their own accounts, not very. During the more than ten years we have known them, Master Chen and Master Hao have become increasingly marginal to the Complete Perfection mainstream—a distance which is either voluntary or imposed by the Daoist community, and in which their ties with Westerners are a contributing factor. The marginality of these Daoists is thus significant, because it has been exacerbated by the global encounter which interests us here, and because it has given them a critical distance toward their own tradition and community. It is persons in such a position who are typically the ideal "informants" to the ethnographer. Master Chen became a pivotal figure in the social network within which this study was conducted—he had key relationships with each of the main protagonists of this story, but of a different nature: mentor to Master Hu; consultant and guest speaker to Winn's Dream Trippers; lineage master to Komjathy; and "friend in Dao" to Palmer.

From Informants to Protagonists

Thus, from our relationships with the main characters of our story, we see the limitations of the much-problematized concept of the ethnographic "informant"—or its substitute, the "consultant," with whom the participant-observer builds "rapport" to penetrate the community he is studying. Instead, we prefer to call them "protagonists" or "interlocutors," highlighting their individuality, their agency, and the roles they play in relation to each other in the sometimes dramatic unfolding of our narrative. And, rather than speaking of "rapport," the notion of "complicity," suggested by George Marcus, may be more apt.[5] At one level, we have found ourselves as accomplices of our protagonists in their subtle relations with each other, as they confided with us, and, at times, used us to send messages or debate with each other, either privately or through their proposed revisions to this book. At another level, we have become accomplices to all of our protagonists' projects. This book will be used by Winn for academic legitimation and promotion of his enterprise, while, for the urban hermit Master Chen, we have provided a platform to speak directly to a Western audience, pointing out what he sees as the errors and shortcomings of Western practitioners, and guiding them toward what he sees as a more full and authentic understanding of Daoism. We have been appointed to the advisory board of Komjathy and Townsend's Daoist Foundation, and this book provides Komjathy space to air a counter narrative to the Dream Trippers' construction of Daoism.

Research as a Chain of Encounters

This study is not only *about* encounters, it is constituted by a chain of encounters with our protagonists that took place, not in a single, geographically bounded "field site," but at an array of locales—monasteries, caves, peaks, parks, teahouses, hotels, spas, ranches, retreats, universities, and conference centers at Huashan, Xi'an, Louguantai, Chengdu, Qingchengshan, Chiang Mai, Asheville, Olympia, and Los Angeles.

Siegler was present at the first encounter between Michael Winn and Louis Komjathy in 2001 at the Vashon Island conference discussed in chapter 6. This invitation-only conference aimed to bring scholars and practitioners of

Daoism, all based in North America, together to discuss Daoist cultivation. At the conference, the practitioners divided into two camps, which by the afternoon of the first full day engaged in heated discussion. Michael Winn was at the core of the "nontraditional" camp, versus the group that valued lineage and initiation. Komjathy, along with the rest of the scholars, including Livia Kohn and Siegler himself, served as mediators and later chroniclers of this historic meeting. Siegler described this encounter in his PhD on Daoism in America, which he completed in 2003.[6] A year earlier, Palmer had finished his doctoral dissertation on the *qigong* movement in post-Mao China.[7] As an extension of his research, Siegler decided to study what happens when American Daoist *qigong* practitioners go to China, taking Winn's Dream Trips as a case. He teamed up with Palmer, whose role would be to focus on how Chinese Daoists perceived the American practitioners. Siegler contacted Winn and obtained permission to join the summer 2004 Dream Trip and interview participants; in exchange, we agreed, as scholars, to give a lecture on Chinese religion to the group. Palmer also acted as an interpreter in many of the conversations that are recorded in this book. We initially expected this to be a short field trip leading to an academic article. We ended up spending a decade following the twists and turns in the lives of our Chinese and American protagonists, joining several Dream Trips, until our research grew into a full-blown book.

We first joined the Dream Trippers in August 2004 at the Daoist mountain and temple complex of Qingchengshan, around 50 km northwest of Chengdu. At the very same time, at a resort at the bottom of the mountain, we also joined Livia Kohn's second academic conference on Daoism, which was sponsored by the Institute of Daoist Studies at Sichuan University. Louis Komjathy was there, as well as many of the leading scholars of Daoism in China and the West. Western scholars and practitioners were thus simultaneously to be found at the same Daoist sacred site, each engaging in their own transnational discourses on Daoism—the Dream Trippers with Daoist monks, in the temples at the top, and the Western scholars with their Chinese colleagues in the resort at the bottom. There was no communication between the two groups.

A few days later, we joined the Dream Trippers again, this time in Xi'an, traveled with them to Huashan, as described in the opening paragraphs of this book, and then followed them to Louguantai, where we bumped into Komjathy and Townsend. We had been impressed at Huashan by Master Chen and his fellow monk, Master Hu, and casually suggested to Komjathy that he and Townsend visit Huashan and meet them. Komjathy was initially planning to go to Wudangshan, another Daoist mountain, but he changed his itinerary on our suggestion. Little did we know that Komjathy's meeting with

Chen and Hu would change his life, and set him on a new course of initiation and transmission, as he became their formal disciple.

Palmer joined subsequent Dream Trips at Huashan in 2006 and 2012; Siegler also visited Huashan with Livia Kohn's "Footsteps of Laozi" tour—a "Dream Trip" with a more academic flavor—in 2011. The encounters at Huashan lasted around five days each time, at various locations at and around the mountain, including temples, caves, and peaks. Besides participating in the activities and interactions of the group—including hiking to various sites on the mountain, staying overnight in temples and caves, joining group *qigong* practice and individual meditation, and participating in conversations and lessons with Daoist monks—Palmer had private conversations with the Chinese monks in their living quarters, while Siegler, sometimes with Palmer, held semistructured interviews with the Dream Trip participants. A total of around thirty Dream Trippers from the USA, Canada, Mexico, France, Turkey, Romania, and Japan were interviewed in 2004 using a questionnaire, at rest stops during the ascent, in their hotel rooms, or in open spaces around the temples.

Either or both of us also accompanied the groups on other segments of their tours, notably to Louguantai, the city of Chengdu and its Qingyanggong Daoist temple, and the sacred Daoist mountain of Qingchengshan. Interviews were also conducted during these segments. Siegler conducted follow-up interviews with around twenty Dream Trip participants after their return home by e-mail and telephone and, in a few cases, in person. Further investigations and interviews were also conducted by Siegler and Palmer on the broader network and culture of Healing Tao, notably Mantak Chia's Tao Garden resort in Chiang Mai, Thailand, and the Healing Tao University outside Asheville, North Carolina. In July 2005 we both spent a week at the Tao Garden resort joining sessions and interviewing participants as well as Mantak Chia. We held several informal, in-depth conversations, as well as formal interviews, with Michael Winn over the years. Siegler also interviewed several other American Daoists who lead spiritual tours.

As our project advanced, some of our own academic colleagues in Daoist studies—Louis Komjathy and Livia Kohn—became increasingly active themselves as public teachers, and as organizers of Daoist retreats or spiritual tours. They were becoming a part of the phenomenon we were studying, but their status and training as sinologists gives them a different perspective from that of the Dream Trippers. With Komjathy's permission, we decided to include him in our narrative, especially in chapter 6, as a counterpoint to our main story focusing on the Dream Trippers.

The next time Palmer met with Komjathy was at Livia Kohn's fourth conference on Daoist Studies, held in Hong Kong in December 2007. Komjathy and Palmer were, unbeknownst to each other, placed on the same panel, each presenting papers on their respective ethnographic findings at Huashan, depicting the same monastic community and the same individuals. The "anthropologist" and his "subject" or "informant" appeared as academic colleagues presenting research on the same field site. We met the night before the panel to share notes and avoid any potentially embarrassing contradictions in our ethnographic accounts (fortunately, there were none, even though our presentations were from very different perspectives).

We had many conversations and interviews over the years with Kohn, Komjathy, and his wife Katherine Townsend, also a disciple of Master Chen, who serves as founding codirector of the Daoist Foundation and who operates a clinical practice in Traditional Chinese Medicine. At the sixth Daoist Studies conference at Loyola Marymount University in Los Angeles, in June 2010, mentioned in chapter 6, several of our protagonists were present, including Kohn, Winn, and Komjathy; in a two-day period, we interviewed them, wrote about them, and presented papers about them, in panels in which they were discussants and audience members. Their comments on our work were then incorporated into our future drafts. Beginning in 2011, Kohn organized a "Footsteps of Laozi" tour on an itinerary similar to that of Winn's Dream Trips. Siegler contributed to organizing the Laozi tour, which some of his students joined for college credit. He also joined a retreat of Komjathy's Gallagher Cove Daoist Association in March 2011.

Meanwhile, on the Chinese side, Palmer returned to Huashan alone five times. He stayed for a week at the monks' quarters at the Jade Spring Monastery at the base of the mountain in August 2004, where he had several long conversations with various monks including Master Chen and Master Hu. In the summers of 2006, 2007, 2008, and 2013, Palmer also stayed at the cave complex of the Cloud Platform with Master Hao. In addition, between 2005 and 2016, Palmer held intensive interviews every summer with Master Chen in Chengdu, where he had returned to secular life to live as an urban hermit. Palmer also conversed with and interviewed other Daoist monks at Beijing, Huashan, and Chengdu. In most cases we transcribed our conversations from memory as soon as possible after the fact (usually the same evening); in other instances we recorded the conversations and produced written transcripts.

Pseudonyms

A note about pseudonyms: Winn, Komjathy, Chia, Townsend, Kohn, and the other tour leaders we mention are public figures in the small circle of American Daoism; we identify them by name in our account. Our main Chinese protagonists, however, though they generously shared their time to collaborate with our research, do not seek publicity, in keeping with their Daoist vocation as well as their personal inclination. In consideration for their discretion, we use pseudonyms ("Master Hao," "Master Hu," "Master Hei," and "Master Pu") to identify them or, sometimes, do not specifically attribute their comments. We have also changed the name of the "Cloud Platform" at Huashan where Master Hao is the sole inhabitant. Master Chen had initially agreed to participate in this study on the condition of his anonymity being respected, and we called him "Master Wen" in the drafts of this manuscript. But, after Palmer narrated the content of the finished book to him, he changed his mind, and requested to be referred to by his real name, Chen Yuming 陈宇明. Other Daoists and Dream Trippers we interviewed are quoted anonymously or by pseudonym.

Reflecting on Bias

After finishing the draft of the book manuscript, we shared it with our main three protagonists—Chen, Winn, and Komjathy—for their feedback. Seeing oneself objectified is naturally a disquieting moment, and we are grateful for the magnanimity with which all three of them received a text that is not always flattering. Their responses confirmed the general structure of our narrative, and provided plenty of corrections and rich additional data. They also allowed us to reflect on the biases that inflect the way we have presented and structured our narrative, as well as our analytical conclusions. Each of them also refined their own discourse in relation to that of the other two, demonstrating an increased reflexivity about their identity and claims—an unplanned effect of this book on the discourses of authority and authenticity that it purports to describe.

Each of the three also responded with very different styles and emphases. Winn responded closely to every chapter, sending us a total of over sixty-five pages of comments in a series of e-mails. He engaged directly with our theoretical framework, which he broadly agreed with, but, where he disagreed, he supported his arguments with references from academic journals in Daoist Studies and anthropology. Notably, his comments helped us to critically refine our usage of Descola's comparative approach to ontologies. Winn also pointed out a few areas of bias in our account, criticizing the fact that, in our initial draft, we lumped all of the Dream Trippers into the same category of "New Age" practitioners and "spiritual tourists." He stressed that, among the Trippers, one could find both "tourists" with nothing more than a superficial desire to consume experiences, and dedicated practitioners of inner alchemy who are committed to transcend the subjectivist Western sense of self. This criticism led us to attempt to adopt a more nuanced formulation in our accounts of the Trippers.

Winn also detected a more fundamental bias in favor of the authenticity of Daoism as it is practiced in China:

> Your current thesis implies that it is impossible for a westerner to escape their cultural conditioning, and that their experience of Qi can ONLY reinforce the larger western cultural individualist identity. That any Qi a westerner feels is Consumable Qi, stimulated by the mountain, but still not authentic Daoist Qi. You are, in effect, reinforcing the common Chinese notion that I have encountered, the xenophobic bias many Chinese have, that it is impossible for a westerner to experience Qi, that Qi is something so deep and mysterious that it is only reserved for authentic Chinese people, not foreign barbarians.[8]

While we have tried to be as evenhanded as possible, we admit that our personal inclinations and academic training may make it difficult to escape some amount of bias. On a personal level, if we have studied Chinese, lived in China, and conducted field research on religion in China, it is precisely because, in our own lives and careers, we sought direct and rigorous access to Chinese culture and religion without Western intermediaries.[9] The academic fields of Religious Studies and Daoist Studies strongly privilege history, scriptures, and the ethnography of ritual traditions—all of which, in the case of Daoism, are still predominantly situated in China—over contemporary innovations in the West. Mainstream anthropology maintains a predilection for non-Western "indigenous" people. Sociology has shown a more sustained interest in modern religious innovation and globalization, but the highly critical theoretical approach of this discipline allows little space for a sympathetic treatment of the authenticity claims of Western practitioners. For this book, we have drawn on research and theories from these four disciplines, all of which seem to lead to some degree of structural bias against the Dream Trippers.

Komjathy's response to the manuscript focused primarily on correcting some factual errors and adding details and precision in his biography and in our discussion of his views. He directly typed numerous edits and additions into the manuscript document; we accepted most of them, as they consisted of very helpful additional data and clarifications. Komjathy wrote us, in reference to chapter 6, that "I found the chapter fair and accurate overall. I am grateful for that"; but he did have some issues with our narrative structure, writing that the "identity politics" we emphasize here is only one concern in Komjathy's larger life and project. In fact, he was critical of an earlier manuscript version of this book in which he identified a "triangulation tendency," a pattern of juxtaposing and intensifying the different viewpoints for narrative purposes. He suggested that certain dimensions of the writing overemphasized reactions that were not as central in the actual lives of the individuals in question. Komjathy's suggested changes aimed to remedy this situation; but we admit that the narrative structure we have employed does lead to highlighting those aspects of our protagonists' lives and views that are relevant to the story we tell. No narrative structure could do full justice to their lives, their practices, and their views, and we must remember that, as living humans, they are infinitely more than what any narrative or analysis could possibly convey. Komjathy also wrote us about chapter 6, that it "tends to privilege the authority of Hu, Kohn, Chen, and Winn." For him, our bias favors *both* the Chinese monks and the spiritual entrepreneurs. In the latter case, notwithstanding the general bias inherent in our academic disciplines, we have no qualms in affirming that we are sympathetic to religious innovation and global transmission, and that we find nothing fundamentally objectionable to Healing Tao USA and the Dream Trips, which are inherently *interesting* and *important* phenomena in the history of Daoism and religious globalization.

Since Chen Yuming does not read English, Palmer orally narrated the manuscript to him over several daylong sessions in Chengdu in October 2015 and May 2016, and recorded his comments. Chen's comments mostly consisted in further elaborations on conceptual aspects of Daoist cultivation and history; only on one minor chronological point did he suggest a correction concerning the story of his master, Xue Tailai. Regarding the details of his own life and opinions, he declined to propose any corrections or additions, stating that "this book has been an excellent mirror for me to look back and reflect on my own changes. Hearing you describe these things about me has been a little difficult to bear, oh! Over the years I have been through so many twists and turns, it has been a painful process." Asked to correct any factual errors about him in our account, he replied:

> This is of no concern, truly of no concern. The most important thing is to tell
> everyone the correct view. . . . Because there are so many bad things I have
> done, that I cannot tell anyone, nobody will know and I won't be criticized
> for them. If there are false things about me in this book, and I am criticized
> about it, well then it will compensate me [for the criticisms I deserve for other
> things]. So it's all for the best.[10]

Chen responded insightfully to the analytical framework of our book, and we have incorporated some of his statements on Daoist cultivation. However, unlike many Chinese intellectuals who constantly view Chinese civilization through the prism of a comparison between China and the West, the Other that Chen uses as a foil for his discourse on Daoism is not Western culture or religion, but Buddhism. It was through the lens of his critique of Buddhism that he (mis-?)interpreted the contrast we make between ontological individualism and cosmological attunement, associating ontological individualism with his understanding of Buddhism's exclusive focus on the self and extinguishing the self, in which cosmology is irrelevant. For Chen, this type of ontological individualism was introduced into China by Buddhism; it was a key cause of the decline of Daoism by turning it into an inward-focused practice with no concern for the world or cosmos, and this contributed to the subservience of the Chinese people to political authority. For Chen, the West is also in danger of falling under this corrosive influence. When we explained the Durkheimian, social constructivist theory of the sacred, he also assimilated it to Buddhism, in what could also count as a critique of postmodernism: "First they say that what you perceive has no intrinsic essence—it's just a product of your mind; then, once they have convinced you that your reality is nothing but a temporary mental construction, they make you believe in whatever mental world that they construct for you!"[11] Chen's deeper elaborations on Daoist cultivation and on Buddhism are fascinating, but they would use too much space and take us too far from the thread of our narrative, and so we unfortunately did not include most of them in our revisions. Our editorial decision shows the limits of how our dialogical approach could be integrated into our writing.

In response to our analytical conclusion to the book, Chen expressed that he was not interested in the question we posed about the possibility of a new Daoist "third culture" breaking through and transcending the structure of the current world system.

> Even if a breakthrough were accomplished that led to a change in society, it could not be sustained. This has nothing to do with China or America. All of these desires to change things emanate from the standpoint of the self—but what is the standpoint of Heaven and Earth? Why are the problems never solved? Because we are here. If we were not here, there would be no problem; actually, what we need to solve is ourselves. The Chinese people have an old saying: "There was originally no problem in the world; it is mediocre people who keep troubling it." Originally, the world is in a state of tranquility, without any problems; why are there so many controversies? Because foolish people keep stirring things up. . . . Embody Dao yourself, and don't worry about the prosperity or decline of the teachings. . . . The flower has dried up, but the root is alive.[12]

Notes

Acknowledgments

1. Siegler, "Back to the Pristine" and "Daoism Beyond Modernity"; Palmer, "Transnational Sacralizations" and "Globalising Daoism at Huashan"; Palmer & Siegler, "Healing Tao USA" and "Authenticating the Sacred Mountain."

Chapter One

1. Komjathy, *Cultivating Perfection.*
2. For ease of reading, we use the first person plural to designate either or both of the two coauthors of this book. See the appendix.
3. DP interview with Chen, Huashan, China, August 10, 2004.
4. ES interview with MW, Asheville, NC, December 22, 2010.
5. Frøystad, "The Return Path." While sociologists of new religious movements have begun a small but growing literature of studies on Western appropriations of Asian religious traditions as they are practiced in the West, this book is the first study to investigate the actual encounters between Asian and Western practitioners back on the Asian home soil.
6. See Palmer and Liu, eds. *Daoism in the Twentieth Century.*
7. Siegler, "Chinese Traditions in Euro-American Society," "Back to the Pristine," and "Daoism beyond Modernity."
8. Our use of the term "spiritual subject formation" is derived from the work of Louis Althusser, who examined how subjects are formed in relation to ideologies. "The term 'subject' contains a deep ambiguity, implying both (1) a free subjectivity, a centre of initiatives, author of and responsible for its actions; (2) a subjected being, who submits to a higher authority, and is therefore stripped of all freedom except that of freely accepting his submission." Adam Chau has applied this approach to Chinese religious practices, proposing the notion of "religious subjectification." The "spiritual subject formation" we speak of here is undoubtedly a form of religious subjectification, but not necessarily in relation to externally existing figures, teachings or texts— what we speak of here is often more subjectively experienced and felt to be directly emanating from an invisible, precognitive, energetic or spiritual realm; this "spiritual" realm may not be as clearly articulated and rigid as the "state ideological apparatus" or "Christian religious ideology" analyzed by Althusser. The key point we take from Althusser is the relational interplay between

subjectivity, interpellation, freedom, and alignment. See Althusser, "Ideology and Ideological State Apparatuses"; Chau, "Religious Subjectification."

9. Solignac, Aimé and Michel Dupuy, "Spiritualité."

10. Chau, "Modalities of Doing Religion," 72.

11. Foucault, *The Use of Pleasure*, 10–11.

12. Komjathy, *Cultivating Perfection*, 25.

13. Komjathy, *Cultivating Perfection*, 74–75.

14. Komjathy, *Cultivating Perfection*, 72.

15. Foucault, *The Use of Pleasure*, 44–45.

16. Csordas, *The Sacred Self*, 24.

17. In Ellsberg, *Modern Spiritual Masters*, 11; quoted in Gottlieb, *Spirituality*, 7.

18. Merleau-Ponty, *Phenomenology of Perception*; Csordas, *The Sacred Self*; Ingold, *The Perception of the Environment*.

19. See Yang, *Religion in Chinese Society*.

20. See van der Veer, *The Modern Spirit of Asia*.

21. See Duara, *The Crisis of Global Modernity*.

22. van der Veer, "Spirituality in Modern Society," 1097; *The Modern Spirit of Asia*.

23. Taylor, *A Secular Age*.

24. Csordas, "Introduction: Modalities of Transnational Transcendence," 4–5.

25. ES interview with MW, Asheville, NC, December 22, 2010.

26. Srinivas, *Winged Faith*, 335, 341.

27. Robbins, "Is the Trans- in *Transnational*."

28. Bourdieu, "Genesis and Structure." For the purpose of this study, we do not share Bourdieu's general conceptualization of social fields as clearly defined and institutionalized, in which the "rules of the game" of the field are embodied in the practice of all the actors within a field. Indeed, our account is one in which the rules of the game, and the boundaries of the field, have not been fixed, and are highly contested. See Goossaert and Palmer, *The Religious Question in Modern China*, 10.

29. For such treatments, see Madsen and Siegler, "The Globalization of Chinese Religions and Traditions"; Siegler, "Daoism beyond Modernity," and "Back to the Pristine"; Kenneth Dean, "Daoism, Local Religious Movements"; Murray and Miller, "The Daoist Society of Brazil."

30. Komjathy, "American Daoism," online at http://www.daoistcenter.org/america.html (accessed July 26, 2016).

31. Louis Komjathy, "Responses to *Dream Trippers* as an Adherent and Scholar-Practitioner," personal communication, 2015; see also *The Daoist Tradition*.

32. Louis Komjathy, "Popular Western Taoism," online at http://www.daoistcenter.org/pwt .html (accessed July 26, 2016).

33. MW e-mail to DP, February 19, 2016. We have slightly edited the passage for greater legibility.

34. MW e-mail to DP, February 22, 2016. We have slightly edited the passage for greater legibility.

35. See Carrette and King, *Selling Spirituality*; Lau, *New Age Capitalism*; Jain, *Selling Yoga*; Altglas, *From Yoga to Kabbalah*.

36. See the website "Native Religions and 'Plastic Medicine Men,'" online at http://web .williams.edu/AnthSoc/native/natreligion.htm (accessed July 26, 2016).

37. Morrison and Eberhard, *Hua Shan*; Deng, *Chronicles of Tao*.

38. Tsing, *Friction*, 5.

39. Srinivas, *Winged Faith*, 33–34.

40. See, for example, Huntington, *The Clash of Civilizations*; Nussbaum, *The Clash Within*; Sen, *Identity and Violence*.

41. See, for example, Pieterse, *Globalization and Culture*; Hannerz, *Transnational Connections*.

42. Giddens, *Modernity and Self-Identity*; Hervieu-Léger, *Religion as a Chain of Memory*.

Chapter Two

1. Weber, *The Sociology of Religion*, 270.

2. Taylor, *A Secular Age*, 30.

3. Taylor, *A Secular Age*, 33.

4. Taylor, *A Secular Age*, 29–41.

5. Descola, *Beyond Nature and Culture*, 104.

6. Descola, *Beyond Nature and Culture*, 107–11.

7. Granet, *La Pensée chinoise*, 297; quoted in Descola, *Beyond Nature and Culture*, 206.

8. Descola's use of Chinese cosmology as an example of analogical ontology has been criticized by scholars who stress that Chinese cosmology is not an ontology: see Feuchtwang, "Too Ontological"; a perspective that is shared by Michael Winn who referred the latter article to us. This critique is based on a restricted definition of ontology derived from Western philosophy. We do not wish to engage in these debates here, nor do we fully adopt Descola's structural framework or his complete typology. For the present purposes, we use the terms "ontology" and "cosmology" as more or less equivalent in meaning, referring in a broad sense to ideas about the basic constituents of the universe and their interrelations, rather than as specific branches of Western philosophy.

9. Stausberg, *Religion and Tourism*, 19–20.

10. Eliade, *The Sacred and the Profane*; Turner and Turner, *Image and Pilgrimage*.

11. Bremer, *Blessed with Tourists*, 32.

12. Graburn "Tourism: The Sacred Journey," 22, 26.

13. MacCannell, *The Tourist*.

14. Nyiri, *Scenic Spots*, 58.

15. Nyiri, *Scenic Spots*, 64–65.

16. Nyiri, *Scenic Spots*, 7–9.

17. See Nyiri, *Scenic Spots*, 18 for examples.

18. Lindholm, *Culture and Authenticity*, 48, summarizing MacCannell.

19. Lindholm, *Culture and Authenticity*, 50.

20. Stausberg, *Religion and Tourism*, 98.

21. Shackley, *Managing Sacred Sites*.

22. Todras-Whitehill, Ethan, "Touring the Spirit World," *New York Times*, April 29, 2007.

23. Timothy and Conover, "Nature Religion, Self-spirituality," 144.

24. DP field notes, Huashan, China, June 2–4, 2012.

25. ES field notes, Footsteps of Laozi tour, Huashan, China, 2010.

26. ES interview with MW, Asheville, NC, December 22, 2010.

27. Silvers, *The Taoist Manual*, 196.

28. Bernbaum, *Sacred Mountains of the World*, 29–30.

29. Blofeld, *My Journey in Mystic China*, 95.

30. Blofeld, *My Journey in Mystic China*, 98–99. This account is not well known, as it was taken from Blofeld's memoirs in Chinese, first published in 1990 by a Hong Kong Press as *Lao*

Pu You Ji. It was translated into English by Daniel Reid and published in English only in 2008 as *My Journey in Mystic China*.

31. Morrison and Eberhard, *Hua Shan*. The photos are online at the Harvard-Yenching Archive, http://library.harvard.edu (accessed August 27, 2015).

32. Morrison and Eberhard, *Hua Shan*, viii.

33. Deng, *Chronicles of Tao*. This book was originally published in three separate volumes: *The Wandering Taoist* (1983), *Seven Bamboo Tablets of the Cloudy Satchel* (1987); *Gateway to a Vast World* (1989).

34. Deng, *Chronicles of Tao*, 463.

35. The Daoist studies scholar Poul Andersen called *Chronicles of Tao* an "interesting forgery" (though it is not technically a forgery, but rather a fraud), and notes that its descriptions of Huashan were taken directly from the photographs taken by Hedda Morrison in 1935. More damning, American *qigong* teacher Ken Cohen has pointed out that the original edition of the first volume of *Chronicles of Tao* contains line drawings of the faces of Daoist monks. Some of these are clearly tracings of Morrison's photographic portraits.

36. Porter, *Road to Heaven*, 61.

37. ES interview with MW, Asheville, NC, December 22, 2010.

38. Winn, "Taoist Alchemy and Breatharians."

39. See Winn, "Taoist Alchemy & Breatharians" for testimony from two participants in the Healing Tao website.

40. Healing Tao USA Discussion Forum, online at http://forum.healingdao.com/general/message/860%5C (accessed August 19, 2015).

41. MW e-mail to DP, March 8, 2016.

42. MW e-mail to DP, April 8, 2016.

43. DP interview with MW, Huashan, China, June 3, 2012.

44. Stausberg, *Religion and Tourism*, 140.

45. ES interview with MW, Asheville, NC, December 22, 2010.

46. Winn, "Taoist Alchemy and Breatharians."

47. Michael Winn, "China's Crown Chakra: Mt. Changbai—Lineage & Origins of Healing Tao—PHOTOS," online at http://www.healingtaousa.com/cgi-bin/articles.pl?rm=mode2&articleid=168 (accessed September 23, 2013).

48. Herrou, *A World of Their Own*.

49. DP interview with Chen, Chengdu, China, June 18, 2013.

50. DP interview with Chen, Chengdu, China, June 18, 2013.

51. DP interview with Chen, Chengdu, China, June 19, 2013.

52. DP interview with Chen, Chengdu, China, June 19, 2013.

53. DP interview with Chen, Chengdu, China, June 18, 2013.

54. Naquin and Yu, eds., *Pilgrims and Sacred Sites*, 12.

55. Hahn, "The Standard Taoist Mountain."

56. von Glahn, *The Sinister Way*; Schipper, "Comment on crée un lieu saint local," in *La religion de la Chine*, 305–328.

57. See Yü, *The Spread of Tibetan Buddhism*.

58. As of this writing, there is no major modern scholarly account in English of Huashan, as there are of Emeishan (Hargett, *Stairway to Heaven*), Wudangshan (Lagerwey, "The Pilgrimage to Wu-tang Shan"), and Hengshan (Robson, *Power of Place*).

59. See Dott, *Identify Reflections*; Robson, *Power of Place*.

60. Robson, *Power of Place*, 185.

61. Robson, *Power of Place*, 17, 20.

62. Chen and Meng Hong, *Huashan: dongtian fudi.*

63. DP interview with Chen and Hu, Huashan, China, August 4, 2004.

64. DP interview with Chen and Hu, Huashan, China, August 4, 2004.

65. Chidester and Linenthal, "Introduction."

66. Ingold, *The Perception of the Environment*, 4–5.

67. MW e-mail to DP, March 8, 2016.

68. Naquin and Yü, *Pilgrims and Sacred Sites*, 22–23.

69. Wu, "An Ambivalent Pilgrim to T'ai Shan."

70. Ingold, *The Perception of the Environment*, 5–6.

71. MW e-mail to DP, March 8, 2016.

72. MW e-mail to DP, April 8, 2016.

73. MW e-mail to DP, April 8, 2016. Quote slightly edited for legibility.

Chapter Three

1. Farquhar, *Ten Thousand Things.*

2. Pseudonym. Her real name is similarly evocative.

3. DP & ES interview with Peace, Asheville, NC, November 14, 2013.

4. DP & ES interview with MW, Asheville, NC, November 16, 2013.

5. Winn, "Taoist Alchemy and Breatharians."

6. Winn, "Taoist Alchemy and Breatharians." The "urine incident" was also published in *QI Journal* 12, no. 1, spring (2012).

7. Jackson, *The Oriental Religions*, 96.

8. Tweed, "Asian Religions in the United States," 216.

9. Girardot, "Teaching Taoism."

10. Seager, ed., *The Dawn of Religious Pluralism*, 247.

11. J. J. Clarke is the best chronicler of these textual encounters. See Clarke, *The Tao of the West*; on the "Secret of the Golden Flower," 121–22; see also Merton, *The Way of Chuang Tzu*, 142–43.

12. van Gulik, *Sexual Life in Ancient China.*

13. See Kripal, *Esalen.*

14. See Kirkland, "Taoism of the Western Imagination"; Bradbury, "The American Conquest"; Girardot, *The Victorian Translation*; and Clarke, *The Tao of the West.*

15. Yang, *Chinese Christians in America*, 40.

16. See Watts, *Tao: The Watercourse Way.*

17. Winn, "Foreword," in Chia, *Awaken Healing Energy*, viii.

18. ES interview with MW, Vashon Island, WA, May 12, 2001.

19. ES and DP interview with Mantak Chia, Chiang Mai, Thailand, July 22, 2005.

20. Winn, "The Quest for Spiritual Orgasm."

21. ES and DP interview with Mantak Chia, Chiang Mai, Thailand, July 22, 2005.

22. Now called Healing Tao USA in the United States and The Universal Tao elsewhere, the name Healing Tao is used in this book for the sake of simplicity.

23. Belamide, "Taoism and Healing in North America," 263.

24. Belamide, "Taoism and Healing in North America," 270.

25. Winn, "The Quest for Spiritual Orgasm."

26. J. Gordon Melton, personal communication with ES, July 28, 2003. For more on the milieu of the 1970s (though with no mention made of Daoism), see Urban, *Magia Sexualis.*

27. In 1994, he founded the organizational consulting group Aspen Consulting Associates. Weil's biographical information comes from that website at http://www.aspen-consult.com/ACA Gunther.htm (accessed February 1, 2008).

28. ES interview with MW, Vashon Island, WA, May 12, 2001.

29. To Chia's credit, Tao Garden chooses to remain at a competitive disadvantage: food is served only in the dining hall and the entire Tao Garden is tobacco, alcohol, red meat, and white sugar free.

30. See the travel writer Caroline Robertson's description of the Gorgeous Tao Garden at http://www.getwellgetaways.com/taogarden-thailand.php (accessed August 25, 2015).

31. Wile, Art of the Bedchamber, 64.

32. Chia, Awaken Healing Energy, vii.

33. ES and DP interview with Mantak Chia, Chiang Mai, Thailand, July 22, 2005.

34. Winn, "The Quest for Spiritual Orgasm."

35. Winn, "Daoist Inner Alchemy in the West." Excerpt available online at http://www.healing taousa.com/blk7.html (accessed July 25, 2016).

36. Winn, "The Quest for Spiritual Orgasm."

37. ES interview with MW, Asheville, NC, December 22, 2010.

38. The website of Tao Garden: Health, Spa & Resort is at www.tao-garden.com (accessed August 25, 2015).

39. MW e-mails to DP, April 8, 2016, and July 24, 2016. According to Winn, in a members' vote, 96 percent of HTIA members had supported the "Tao of Democracy" campaign to preserve the independence of the HTIA.

40. Healing Tao University and Heavenly Mountain Retreats Catalogue, online at www .healingtaoretreats.com (accessed February 1, 2008).

41. MW e-mail to DP, March 6, 2016.

42. Online at http://www.healing-tao.com/tao-garden/universal/en/ (accessed May 6, 2008).

43. Online at http://www.healingtaousa.com/index.html (accessed May 6, 2008).

44. Healing Tao University and Heavenly Mountain Retreats Catalogue, online at www .healingtaoretreats.com (accessed February 1, 2008).

45. ES interview with MW, Asheville, NC, December 22, 2010.

46. ES interview with MW, Asheville, NC, December 22, 2010.

47. MW, mass e-mail, December 30, 2001.

48. ES interview with MW, Asheville, NC, December 22, 2010.

49. Michael Winn, mass e-mail, Dec. 30, 2001; "China Dream Trip—60 Amazing PHOTOS: May 16–June 3, 2010," online at http://www.healingdao.com/chinatrip2010.html (accessed November 9, 2010).

50. Abode of the Eternal Tao, "Empty Vessel China Tour," online at http://abodetao.com /china-tour/ (accessed March 2, 2017).

51. ES interview with MW, Asheville, NC, December 22, 2010.

52. ES interview with MW, Asheville, NC, December 22, 2010.

53. ES interview with MW, Asheville, NC, December 22, 2010.

54. Michael Winn, "China Dream Trip—60 Amazing PHOTOS: May 16–June 3, 2014," online at http://www.healingdao.com/chinatrip2010.html (accessed November 9, 2010).

55. MW, mass e-mail, December 30, 2001.

56. Said, Orientalism, 40.

57. Said, Orientalism, 99.

58. Said, "Orientalism Reconsidered," 104.

59. Said, *Orientalism*, 282.

60. Huang, "Once Again: A New Beginning."

61. ES interview with Maoshing Ni, Santa Monica, CA, May 4, 2001.

62. ES interview with Solala Towler, Vashon Island, WA, May 10, 2001.

63. ES interview with MW, Asheville, NC, December 22, 2010.

64. Towler, *Embarking on the Way*, xi–xii.

65. ES interview with Solala Towler, Vashon Island, WA, May 10, 2001.

66. Siegler conducted the surveys at three different American Daoist retreats. The first survey he conducted was at the USIW, Hua-Ching Ni's organization's 2000 Annual Retreat, led by Maoshing Ni, which was held at the Presbyterian Conference Center in Lake Arrowhead, California, from September 28 to October 1. A year later, he surveyed the Living Tao Retreat, led by Al Chung-liang Huang, held in Morro Bay, California, from November 9 to 18, 2001. Finally, he participated in the Orthodox Daoism of America (ODA) Winter Retreat, led by Liu Ming, held at Shennoa Springs, Mendocino County, California, from November 30 to December 3, 2001, and he also posted a similar list of questions to the USIW e-mail group during the summer of 2000. The surveys were anonymous, though they did request age and gender. There were eight questions: 1. How did you first hear about Daoism? 2. How did you first hear about the organization in question? 3. Do you identify yourself as Daoist? (If so, to whom: friends, family, application forms, etc.) 4. What Daoist practices do you engage in? 5. Do you engage in non-Daoist practices (i.e., going to Mass, sitting Zen meditation, etc.)? 6. How important to you is the Chinese origin of Daoism? 7. Can you recommend other North American Daoist individuals or groups I should contact? 8. Do you have general comments on the nature of this project? At the USIW retreat, fifteen responses were received out of approximately thirty-five participants. At the Living Tao retreat, twenty responses were received out of thirty-eight participants. At the ODA retreat, twenty-three responses were received out of approximately fifty-five participants.

67. See, for example, Kohn, *The Taoist Experience*, and Robinet, *Taoist Meditation*, for a detailed analysis of Shangqing scriptures. In his introduction to Robinet, Norman Girardot calls the scriptures "both an instruction on how to climb the mountain and a description of the view from the top." A more prolific and popular translator of Daoist scripture is Thomas Cleary.

68. Norman J. Girardot, in his unpublished article "My Way: Reflections on Thirty Years of Teaching Taoism," remarks that this has been the case for many of the students in his Daoism class over the years. For a close parallel with American Buddhism, see Nattier, "Who Is a Buddhist?" Nattier asks, "If a college sophomore buys a book on Zen by Alan Watts, reads it, likes it, and subsequently begins to think of himself as a Buddhist—but without ever having encountered any form of 'Buddhism' beyond the printed pages—should he be included within the scope of a study of Buddhism in America?"

69. The Wandering Taoist web ring was founded January 4, 1998. At one time it had 121 active sites, though currently the number is closer to 80. In the early days of the World Wide Web, before 1999 when Google made retrieving lists of related websites as simple as clicking a mouse, the "web ring" was a popular and useful way of linking similarly themed websites. The website is at http://M.webring.com/hub?ring=tao&id=1&hub (accessed March 3, 2009).

70. Online at http://reformtaoism.org (accessed December 15, 2009).

71. Online at http://www.reformtaoism.org/introduction.php (accessed December 15, 2009).

72. Online at http://members.tripod.com/~the_hermitage/index.htm (accessed March 3, 2009).

73. ES interview with Solala Towler, Vashon Island, WA, May 10, 2001.

286   NOTES TO PAGES 89–98

74. Roof, *Spiritual Marketplace*, 175.

75. Personal e-mail correspondence, September 7, 2005, translated by ES.

76. Winn, "Taoist Alchemy and Breatharians."

77. Althusser, "Ideology and Ideological State Apparatus."

78. Descola, *Beyond Nature and Culture*; Taylor, *A Secular Age*.

79. Kripal, *Esalen*, vi, 139, 141, 316.

80. Carroll, *Spiritualism*, 2; Albanese, *A Republic of Mind and Spirit*.

81. Bourdieu, "Genesis and Structure," 9.

82. Spiegelberg, *The Religion of No-Religion*.

83. Hervieu-Léger, *Religion as a Chain of Memory*.

84. Winn, "Foreword," in Chia, *Awaken Healing Energy*, viii.

85. ES interview with MW, Vashon Island, WA, May 12, 2001.

86. ES interview with MW, Asheville, NC, November 6, 2004. The Healing Tao's modernizing position that the ritual and "folk belief" aspects of the Daoist tradition are inessential, and that at the core of Daoism lies esoteric teaching and mystical philosophy, recalls the positions of the famous twentieth-century scholars of religion Gershom Sholem, Mircea Eliade, and Henry Corbin, who made similar arguments about Judaism, Christianity, and Islam, respectively. See Wasserstrom, *Religion After Religion*.

87. Chia, *Awaken Healing Energy*, 141.

88. Willaime, "Religion in Ultramodernity."

89. See Heelas, Martin, and Morris, *Religion, Modernity and Postmodernity*, 4–5.

90. Beyer, *Religions in Global Society*, 283.

91. Beyer, *Religions in Global Society*, 280. For a book-length exploration of how the New Age movement, of which the Healing Tao can be seen as a part, looks to the self as a source of authenticity and is thus quintessentially modern, see Heelas, *The New Age Movement*, 18–27.

92. Bauman, *Postmodernity and Its Discontents*, 70.

93. Carrette and King, *Selling Spirituality*, 23–24.

94. Heelas, *The New Age Movement*.

95. Kripal, *Esalen*.

96. Heelas, *The New Age Movement*, 28–29.

97. Roof, *Spiritual Marketplace*, 178.

98. Roof, *Spiritual Marketplace*, 203–212.

99. Bellah, *Habits of the Heart*, 20–21.

100. Bellah, *Habits of the Heart*, 55.

101. Bellah, *Habits of the Heart*, 71.

102. Bellah, *Habits of the Heart*, 233.

103. Bellah, *Habits of the Heart*, 221.

104. Altglas, *From Yoga to Kabbalah*, 238.

105. Altglas, *From Yoga to Kabbalah*, 226–35.

106. Altglas, *From Yoga to Kabbalah*, 327–28.

107. Altglas, *From Yoga to Kabbalah*, 241. This notion can be related to Foucault's conception of "governmentality," in which subjects become "self-governing" by internalizing specific modes of behavior, and the self-monitoring of such norms of behavior, through the practice of various disciplines, thereby contributing, in a noncoercive fashion, to the overall economy of power. See Chau, "Religious Subjectification," 76–77. See also Foucault, *Dits et écrits IV*, 237, discussed online at https://foucaultblog.wordpress.com/2007/05/15/key-term-conduct-of-conduct/ (accessed August 26, 2015).

108. ES interview with MW, Asheville, NC, December 22, 2010.

109. See Altglas, *From Yoga to Kabbalah*; Obadia, *Bouddhisme et Occident*; Srinivas, *Winged Faith*; Altglas, *Le nouvel hindouisme occidental*; Coleman, *The New Buddhism*; Lenoir, *Le bouddhisme en France*.

110. Brian Hodel, "Tibetan Buddhism in the West: Is It Working Here? An Interview with Alan Wallace," online at http://alanwallace.org/Tricycle%20Interview.pdf (accessed July 29, 2016).

111. Louis Komjathy, "Responses to *Dream Trippers* as an Adherent and Scholar-Practitioner," personal communication, 2015.

112. Tara Carreon, "Another View on Tibetan Buddhism," online at http://www.iivs.de/~iivs 01311/EN/deba05.html (accessed September 16, 2013).

113. Winn, "Taoist 'Dual Cultivation,'" vi.

114. Chia and Chia, *Awaken Healing Light of the Tao*, 1.

Chapter Four

1. See Palmer, "Dao and Nation."

2. This refers to the original film in Chinese, *Zhiqu Huashan* [The Conquest of Huashan], filmed in 1953, available online at https://youtu.be/kNLqG0pkIfQ (accessed August 26, 2015).

3. Andersen, "A Visit to Huashan."

4. On contemporary Quanzhen monasticism, see Herrou, *A World of Their Own.*

5. DP field notes, August 2004.

6. See Komjathy, "Living among Daoists," 9.

7. DP interview with Chen, Chengdu, China, June 20, 2005.

8. Herrou, *A World of Their Own.*

9. See Palmer, "China's Religious *Danwei.*"

10. DP interview with Chen and Hu, Huashan, China, August 11, 2004.

11. Komjathy, "Living among Daoists."

12. Palmer, "Dao and Nation."

13. DP interview with Chen, Chengdu, China, August 28, 2009.

14. DP interview with Chen and Hu, Huashan, China, August 12, 2004.

15. Yang, "Revolution of Temporality."

16. The United Front is an agency of the Communist Party Central Committee that is charged with co-opting non-communist elites, notably the leaders of overseas Chinese, ethnic minorities, religious communities, chambers of commerce, and non-communist political parties.

17. DP interview with Chen, Chengdu, China, July 15, 2011.

18. Yang, "Spatial Struggles."

19. Bremer, "Sacred Spaces and Tourist Places," 30.

20. Hu Jintao was president of the Peoples' Republic of China from 2003 to 2013.

21. Other than the interviews conducted by the authors, biographical data on Chen Yuming was also obtained from an account published online by the writer Liu Bai, "Huashan Daoshi," online at http://blog.sina.com.cn/s/blog_4b96867501000ajv.html (accessed July 29, 2016); http://blog.sina.com.cn/s/blog_4b96867501000ald.html (accessed July 29, 2016).

22. DP interview with Chen, Chengdu, China, October 23, 2015.

23. See Palmer, *Qigong Fever.*

24. According to comments left by a user on http://blog.sina.com.cn/s/blog_4b96867501 000ajv.html (accessed July 29, 2016).

25. Porter, *Road to Heaven*, 82.

26. DP interview with Chen, Chengdu, China, October 23, 2015.

27. DP interview with Chen, Chengdu, China, June 19, 2013.

28. DP interview with Chen, Chengdu, China, August 28, 2009.

29. DP interview with Chen, Chengdu, China, June 17, 2010.

30. DP interview with Chen, Chengdu, China, July 10, 2007.

31. DP interview with Chen, Chengdu, China, August 28, 2009.

32. DP interview with Chen, Chengdu, China, August 30, 2011.

33. DP interview with Chen, Chengdu, China, July 18, 2006.

34. DP interview with Chen, Chengdu, China, Oct. 23, 2015.

35. DP interview with Chen, Chengdu, China, August 28, 2009.

36. DP interview with Chen, Chengdu, China, August 28, 2009.

37. DP interview with Chen, Chengdu, China, June 17, 2010.

38. DP interview with Chen, Chengdu, China, July 10, 2007.

39. DP interview with Chen, Chengdu, China, July 10, 2007.

40. DP interview with Chen, Chengdu, China, August 28, 2009.

41. DP interview with Chen, Chengdu, China, June 17, 2010.

42. DP interview with Chen, Chengdu, China, June 20, 2013.

43. DP interview with Chen, Chengdu, China, Oct. 23, 2015.

44. DP interview with Chen, Chengdu, China, May 26, 2016.

45. On Quanzhen, see Liu and Goossaert, eds. *Quanzhen Daoists*; Goossaert, "La création du taoïsme moderne"; Marsone, *Wang Chongyang*; Komjathy, *Cultivating Perfection* and *The Way of Complete Perfection*; Eskildsen, *The Teachings and Practices*; Herrou, *A World of Their Own*.

46. Kohn, *Chinese Healing Exercises*; Shahar, *Shaolin Monastery*; Dean, *Lord of the Three-in-One*.

47. Pregadio, *The Way of the Golden Elixir*; Robinet, *The World Upside Down*.

48. Goossaert, "The Invention of an Order."

49. See Goossaert, *The Taoists of Peking*.

50. Kohn, "Quiet Sitting."

51. Liu, *Daoist Modern*.

52. Palmer, "Chinese Redemptive Societies."

53. Palmer, *Qigong Fever*.

54. Lee, "Transmission and Innovation"; Palmer, "Dao and Nation."

55. Goossaert, *The Taoists of Peking*.

56. Goossaert, *The Taoists of Peking* and "Daoists in the Modern Chinese Self-Cultivation Market."

57. Esposito, *Facets of Qing Daoism*; Goossaert and Liu, eds., *Quanzhen Daoists*.

58. DP interview with Chen and Hu, Huashan, China, August 4, 2004.

59. DP interview with Chen, Chengdu, China, June 17, 2013.

60. MW e-mail to DP, February 22, 2016.

Chapter Five

1. DP interview with Chen and Hu, Huashan, China, August 13, 2004.

2. Online at http://www.healingtaousa.com/tao_alchemy_formulas.html (accessed August 31, 2015). We are grateful to P. G. G. van Enckevort for bringing this passage to our attention.

3. Naquin and Yü, *Pilgrims and Sacred Sites*; Verellen, "Cultes des sites."

4. Stausberg, *Religion and Tourism*, 102.

5. DP field notes, Huashan, July 2004.

6. DP field notes, Huashan, June 2–4, 2012.

7. DP interview with Chen and Hu, Huashan, China, August 13, 2004.

8. DP field notes, Huashan, June 2–4, 2012.

9. DP interview with Chen, Chengdu, China, August 28, 2009.

10. DP interview with Chen, Chengdu, China, August 28, 2009.

11. DP field notes, Huashan, August 2004.

12. DP field notes, Huashan, August 2004.

13. DP and ES interview with MW, Asheville, NC, November 13, 2013.

14. DP interview with Chen, Chengdu, China, May 25, 2016.

15. DP field notes, Huashan, July 2004.

16. ES and DP interviews with Dream Trippers, Huashan, China, July 2004.

17. ES personal e-mail communication with a Dream Tripper, August 17, 2004.

18. DP interview with MW, Huashan, China, June 5, 2006.

19. MW e-mail to DP, February 22, 2016.

20. MW e-mail to DP, March 8, 2016.

21. MW e-mail to DP, March 8, 2016.

22. DP field notes, Huashan, June 2–4, 2012.

23. DP field notes, Huashan, June 2–4, 2012.

24. DP field notes, Huashan, June 2, 2006.

25. DP interview with Chen, Chengdu, China, August 28, 2009.

26. DP interview with Chen, Chengdu, China, May 25, 2016.

27. DP interview with MW, Huashan, China, June 5, 2006.

28. DP interview with Chen, Chengdu, China, July 17, 2006.

29. MW e-mail to DP, April 8, 2016.

30. Chia, *Taoist Secrets of Love*; Chia, Chia, Abrams, and Abrams, *The Multi-Orgasmic Couple*.

31. ES interview with MW, Asheville, NC, December 22, 2010.

32. DP interview with Chen, Chengdu, China, August 30, 2011.

33. Turner, *Dramas, Fields and Metaphors*.

34. Robbins, "Is the Trans- in *Transnational*."

35. DP interview with Chen, Huashan, China, August 13, 2004.

36. DP interview with Hu, Huashan, China, August 13, 2004.

37. DP field notes, Huashan, June 3, 2006.

38. DP field notes, Huashan, June 3, 2006.

39. DP field notes, Huashan, June 3, 2006.

40. DP field notes, Huashan, June 2–4, 2012.

41. DP and ES interview with Caroline, Asheville, NC, November 14, 2013.

42. DP field notes, Huashan, June 2–4, 2012.

43. DP field notes, Huashan, June 2–4, 2012.

44. DP field notes, Huashan, June 3, 2006.

45. DP field notes, Huashan, June 3, 2006.

46. DP field notes, Huashan, August 2008.

47. Chen and Meng, *Huashan: dongtian fudi*.

48. DP and ES interview with Caroline and husband, Asheville, NC, November 18, 2013.

49. DP and ES interview with Peace, Asheville, NC, November 17, 2013.

50. DP and ES interview with Caroline and her husband, Asheville, NC, November 18, 2013.

51. Online at http://www.belovedwaters.com (accessed August 27, 2015).

52. DP and ES interview with Peace, Asheville, NC, November 17, 2013.

Chapter Six

1. DP and ES interview with Komjathy, Los Angeles, CA, June 4, 2010.

2. Komjathy, *The Daoist Tradition*, 303.

3. Komjathy, *The Daoist Tradition*, 305.

4. Komjathy, *The Daoist Tradition*, 315.

5. Komjathy, *The Daoist Tradition*, 313. Compare with Livia Kohn's 2001 textbook, one of the first published indications of her sympathies, which concludes with a four-page summary of Daoism in the West that is uncritical, almost laudatory. See Kohn, *Daoism and Chinese Culture*, 222–26.

6. Komjathy, *Cultivating Perfection*.

7. Komjathy, *The Way of Complete Perfection*.

8. Komjathy, "Basic Information Sheet on Daoism," online at http://www.daoistcenter.org /Daoism_Information.pdf (accessed July 31, 2016).

9. Komjathy, "Möbius Religion: The Insider/Outsider Question."

10. ES interview with MW, Asheville, NC, December 22, 2010.

11. Komjathy, "Qigong in America," 226.

12. Louis Komjathy, "Responses to *Dream Trippers*."

13. MW e-mail to DP, February 22, 2016.

14. Komjathy personal e-mail to ES, March 8, 2015.

15. Silvers, *The Taoist Manual*, 192–93.

16. Komjathy, "Living among Daoists."

17. Komjathy personal e-mail to ES, March 8, 2015.

18. Komjathy personal e-mail to ES, March 8, 2015.

19. Iwamura, "The Oriental Monk in American," 27.

20. Komjathy, "Responses to *Dream Trippers*."

21. Komjathy, "Living among Daoists."

22. He later moved to Sichuan University.

23. Komjathy, "Living among Daoists."

24. DP interview with Chen, Chengdu, China, May 25, 2016.

25. Komjathy, "Some Reflections on My Location in the Daoist Tradition."

26. Terry Kleeman, comments at a panel reviewing Clarke, *The Tao of the West*, at the Annual Meeting of the American Academy of Religion, Denver, CO, November, 2001.

27. Komjathy, notes on *Dream Trippers* manuscript, December 1, 2015.

28. Komjathy, "Field Notes," 100.

29. Komjathy, *Daoism: A Guide for the Perplexed*, 209–10.

30. See Komjathy, *The Daoist Tradition*. Komjathy stresses that there are models of earlier scholar-practitioners *inside of* the tradition, and he personally identifies with such Daoist luminaries and models as Lu Xiujing (406–477), Tao Hongjing (456–536), and Li Daoqian (1219–1296). Komjathy, "Responses to *Dream Trippers*."

31. Prebish, *Luminous Passage*, 173–202.

32. Girardot, *The Victorian Translation*, 317.

33. See Komjathy, *The Daoist Tradition*.

34. Jung, *The Secret of the Golden Flower*. See Clarke, *Jung and Eastern Thought*; Esposito, "The Different Versions of the *Secret of the Golden Flower*." Komjathy discusses Jung and alchemy in "Daoist Internal Alchemy."

35. Handwritten notes by Needham stored in the Needham Archive, quoted by Rocha, "The Way of Sex," 614.

36. Chang, *The Tao of Love and Sex*. Needham's role is discussed in Rocha, "The Way of Sex."

37. See Needham's pseudonymous article: Holorenshaw, "The Making of an Honorary Taoist."

38. Komjathy, "Responses to *Dream Trippers*."

39. Noteworthy examples are translations published by Livia Kohn, whose role is discussed in *Taoist Meditation and Longevity Techniques*.

40. ES interview with MW, Asheville, NC, December 22, 2010.

41. Winn, "Daoist Methods," "Daoist Neidan," "Daoist Internal Alchemy," and "Transforming Sexual Energy."

42. MW e-mail to DP, March 6, 2016.

43. MW e-mail to DP, February 19, 2016. See Winn, "The Quest for Spiritual Orgasm."

44. Komjathy, *The Daoist Tradition*, 9.

45. Komjathy, *The Daoist Tradition*, 307.

46. Komjathy, "Möbius Religion: The Insider/Outsider Question."

47. This book was one of the most influential on Komjathy's early inquiries into the Daoist tradition. While studying at the Taoist Studies Institute in the early 1990s, when there was little reliable scholarship on Daoism, Komjathy found *The Taoist Body*. He was particularly interested in Schipper's discussion of Daoist views of "mountains": the mountain as mountain, altar, body, and stillness. Komjathy, "Responses to *Dream Trippers*." Komjathy often writes about this theme, and it informs his conception of "mountain contemplation" discussed below.

48. Schipper, *The Taoist Body*, preface, xii.

49. Schipper and Verellen, eds., *The Taoist Canon*.

50. Saso, *The Teachings of Taoist Master Chuang*.

51. Saso, *The Teachings of Taoist Master Chuang*, 89.

52. Saso, *The Teachings of Taoist Master Chuang*, 89.

53. Saso, *The Teachings of Taoist Master Chuang*, 101.

54. Saso, *Taoism and the Rite*, 114; see also Komjathy, *The Daoist Tradition*, 260.

55. Strickmann, "History, Anthropology and Chinese Religion," 237. For a comparable case, see Robert Buswell, *The Zen Monastic Experience*. It is interesting that Buswell explicitly mentions the mentorship of Strickmann.

56. Komjathy, "Responses to *Dream Trippers*."

57. Komjathy, "Möbius Religion."

58. See the last four pages of her textbook, Kohn, *Daoism and Chinese Culture*; and her sponsoring the Vashon Island Conference, "Conference on Daoist Cultivation."

59. Stausberg, *Religion and Tourism*, 142.

60. ES telephone interview with Livia Kohn, January 11, 2011.

61. Kohn, "Acknowledgments," in *Meditation Works*.

62. Komjathy, "Responses to *Dream Trippers*."

63. See the website of the Legacy of Dao, online at http://www.legacyofdao.org/organization .html (accessed March 6, 2015).

64. See the website of Core Health, online at http://corehealth.us/facilitator/facilitators/united -states/florida/saint-petersburg/ (accessed March 6, 2015).

65. Winn, "Daoist Internal Alchemy in the West"; "Transforming Sexual Energy." Komjathy also contributed to the first volume, but withdrew from the second due to the increasing "hybrid spirituality" tenor of many Three Pines Press publications.

66. The conference was co-organized with Norman Girardot and Mary Evelyn Tucker.

67. These presentations were sympathetically summarized by Kohn in Girardot, Miller, and Liu, eds. *Daoism and Ecology*.

68. For a summary, see Komjathy's unpublished paper "Conference on Daoist Cultivation: Summary Report." James Miller, another former student of Kohn, also video-recorded many of the participants and posted them on his "American Daoist Cultivation," online at www.dao iststudies.org/content/american-daoist-cultivation (accessed July 31, 2016). For Winn's paper at this conference, see Winn, "Daoist Alchemy as a Deep Language."

69. The conference became the basis for Kohn's edited volume titled *Daoist Body Cultivation*.

70. ES interview with MW, Asheville, NC, December 22, 2010.

71. Komjathy, "Responses to *Dream Trippers*."

72. ES telephone interview with Livia Kohn, January 9, 2011.

73. Winn, "Magic Numbers."

74. ES interview with MW, Asheville, NC, December 22, 2010.

75. DP and ES interview with Komjathy, Los Angeles, CA, June 4, 2010.

76. Komjathy, "Responses to *Dream Trippers*."

77. DP and ES interview with Komjathy, Los Angeles, CA, June 4, 2010.

78. DP and ES interview with Komjathy, Los Angeles, June 4, 2010.

79. Liu Ming, *The Blue Book*; Silvers, *The Taoist Manual*.

80. Komjathy has followed the pilgrimage route to the summit on each of his visits to Huashan: 1998 (with Townsend), 2004 (with Townsend), 2006 (with Hu), and 2011 (alone).

81. Komjathy, "Living among Daoists."

82. Komjathy, "Living among Daoists."

83. Details taken from conversations with Louis Komjathy; see also his unpublished paper, "Living among Daoists."

84. Komjathy, "Responses to *Dream Trippers*."

85. ES interview with Komjathy, Chengdu, China, July 11, 2009.

86. DP interview with Chen, Chengdu, China, June 17, 2010. Interestingly, Komjathy echoes these sentiments in his introductions to Daoism.

87. Komjathy, *The Daoist Tradition*, 251.

88. DP interview with Chen, Chengdu, China, June 17, 2010.

89. Komjathy, "Responses to *Dream Trippers*."

90. See, for example, his discussions in *The Daoist Tradition*.

91. That is, celibacy (no sex), sobriety (no intoxicants), and vegetarianism (no meat). Komjathy himself is not celibate, but he did make an intentional choice at a young age not to have children. As with his renunciation of alcohol and meat, this occurred prior to both Komjathy's formal "conversion" (1994) and formal "ordination" (2006). Still, as he says, "In a nod to the Confucian tradition," he has not severed ties to his family and maintains his "ancestral obligations" to his father and mother.

92. The official, "orthodox" Longmen lineage centers on three ordination ranks and corresponding monastic manuals and precept texts. See Komjathy, *The Way of Complete Perfection* and *The Daoist Tradition*.

93. Komjathy, "Responses to *Dream Trippers*."

94. Komjathy, "Responses to *Dream Trippers*."

95. DP and ES interview with Komjathy, Baltimore, MD, November 23, 2013.

96. DP and ES interview with Komjathy, Baltimore, MD, November 23, 2013. Komjathy also discusses this ongoing transformative unfolding in his "Möbius Religion": "Following my ordination, and without explicit discussion with my master-father (*shifu*) or extensive reflection, a whole series of insights emerged about the deeper layers of ancestral influences and family obligations. Specifically, I began to see through some of the disorientation and distortion that come through ordinary family entanglements, including biological and social demands for reproduction."

97. Komjathy, "Responses to *Dream Trippers*."

98. DP and ES interview with Komjathy, Los Angeles, CA, June 4, 2010.

99. Komjathy, "Living among Daoists."

100. DP and ES interview with Komjathy, Los Angeles, CA, June 4, 2010.

101. Komjathy, "Living among Daoists."

102. ES telephone interview with Livia Kohn, January 9, 2011.

103. ES field notes, Chengdu, China, July 24, 2009.

104. Komjathy, "Responses to *Dream Trippers*."

105. DP interview with Chen, Chengdu, China, August 28, 2009.

106. DP interview with Chen, Chengdu, China, June 17, 2013.

107. DP and ES interview with Komjathy, Los Angeles, CA, June 4, 2010.

108. Komjathy, "Some Reflections on My Location in the Daoist Tradition."

109. Komjathy, "Some Reflections on My Location in the Daoist Tradition."

110. Komjathy, "Responses to *Dream Trippers*."

111. DP and ES interview with Komjathy, Los Angeles, CA, June 4, 2010.

112. ES field notes, Olympia, WA, March 2011.

113. Komjathy, "Daoism: From Meat Avoidance." It should be noted that neither his fellow priest and wife, Kate Townsend, nor his chief student in Olympia, nor his master, Chen, are vegetarian. Nonetheless, Komjathy maintains that vegetarianism is a requirement for and a manifestation of spiritual realization. See Komjathy, "Responses to *Dream Trippers*."

114. Komjathy, "Daoism: From Meat Avoidance," 103.

115. Komjathy, "Field Notes."

116. Komjathy, "Field Notes," xxi.

117. Komjathy, "Field Notes," 97.

118. Komjathy, "Field Notes," 96.

119. Komjathy, "Field Notes," 96, 100.

120. Komjathy, "Responses to *Dream Trippers*."

121. See Samsom, "The New Monasticism."

122. Komjathy, "Responses to *Dream Trippers*."

123. DP interview with Chen, Chengdu, China, July 17, 2006.

124. ES interview with MW, Asheville, NC, December 22, 2010.

125. DP interview with Chen, Chengdu, China, July 15, 2011.

126. DP and ES interview with Komjathy, Baltimore, MD, November 23, 2013.

127. An allusion to chapter 5 of the *Daodejing*: "The heavens and earth are not humane;/They regard the myriad beings as straw dogs (*chugou*)."

128. Komjathy personal communication with DP, June 10, 2010.

129. DP and ES interview with Komjathy, Baltimore, MD, November 23, 2013.

130. Komjathy, "Field Notes," 102.

131. ES field notes, Huashan, China, June 15, 2011.

132. See the website of INBI World, online at http://www.inbiworld.com (accessed September 1, 2015).

133. Komjathy, "Responses to *Dream Trippers.*"

Chapter Seven

1. Online at www.ashevillemovementcollective.org (accessed November 18, 2013).

2. Online at http://ashevillemovementcollective.org/about-Asheville-Movement-Collective .html; http://ashevillemovementcollective.org/AMC-guidelines.html (accessed November 18, 2013).

3. Online at http://ashevillemovementcollective.org/about-Asheville-Movement-Collective. html; http://ashevillemovementcollective.org/AMC-guidelines.html (accessed November 18, 2013).

4. DP and ES interview with Alison, Asheville, NC, November 17, 2013.

5. MW e-mail to DP, April 8, 2016.

6. ES interview with MW, Asheville, NC, December 22, 2010.

7. Goossaert, "La création du taoïsme moderne."

8. Goossaert, "L'alchimie intérieure réhabilitée?," 507.

9. Kripal, *Esalen*, 22–23.

10. DP interview with Chen, Chengdu, China, June 17, 2010.

11. For a fuller discussion of this theme, see Brindley, *Individualism in Early China.*

12. DP interview with Chen, Chengdu, China, October 23, 2015.

13. Puett, *To Become a God*, 44.

14. See Roth, trans., *Original Tao.*

15. Schipper, *La religion des chinois*, 41.

16. This is not to say that Daoists were not present at the Court—on the contrary, they continued to be patronized by the emperor, which, in different periods, officially sanctioned specific Daoist sects such as Quanzhen and Zhengyi. Daoist lineage and ritual was consistently invoked by the emperor as a source of sacred authority and legitimacy (see Lagerwey, "Droit divin"). But the base of Daoist influence has always been away from the political capital.

17. Stein, "Remarques sur les mouvements du taoïsme"; Seidel, "The Image of the Perfect Ruler."

18. Bourdieu, "Genesis and Structure," 12.

19. Dean, *Taoist Ritual.*

20. Lagerwey, *China: A Religious State.*

21. DP interview with Chen, Chengdu, China, May 25, 2016.

22. Davis, *Society and the Supernatural.*

23. Seidel, "Taoism: The Unofficial High Religion."

24. DP interview with Chen, Chengdu, China, May 25, 2016.

25. Komjathy, *Cultivating Perfection*, 18; Goossaert, "La création du taoïsme moderne."

26. Wile, *Lost T'ai-chi Classics*; Shahar, *Shaolin Monastery.*

27. Liu, *Daoist Modern.*

28. Palmer, "Chinese Redemptive Societies"; Goossaert, *The Taoists of Peking*; Goossaert and Palmer, *The Religious Question.* For the contrasting case of Vietnam, see Jammes and Palmer, "Occulting the Dao."

29. Palmer, *Qigong Fever.*

30. Palmer, *Qigong Fever*; Ownby, *Falun Gong.*

31. There are, to be sure, other trajectories. The European esoteric tradition has fed into and provided symbolic and intellectual resources for ultranationalist European movements of the far right, while "traditionalism" as an intellectual school has drawn on esoteric sources to maintain a radical critique of modernity. Chinese Daoist "nationalism," however, has never taken a militant form.

32. Weller, *Resistance, Chaos, and Control in China.*

33. Wang Chongyang, *Jinguan yusuo jue* 金關玉鎖訣, quoted in Komjathy, *Cultivating Perfection*, 151.

34. DP interview with Chen, Chengdu, China, October 23, 2015.

35. Bauman, *Liquid Times*; Augé, *Non-Places.*

36. On this paradox, see Heelas, *New Age Movement*, 137.

37. ES interview with MW, Asheville, NC, December 22, 2010.

38. DP interview with Chen, Chengdu, China, June 17, 2010.

39. DP interview with Chen, Chengdu, China, July 17, 2006.

40. DP interview with Chen, Chengdu, China, June 20, 2013.

41. ES and DP interview with MW, Asheville, NC, November 16, 2013.

42. ES and DP interview with MW, Asheville, NC, November 16, 2013.

43. ES and DP interview with MW, Asheville, NC, November 16, 2013. As of March 2016, Winn still had not broken ground on his building project, but anticipated closing a deal with major investors for the project.

44. ES interview MW, Asheville, NC, December 22, 2010.

45. Altglas, *From Yoga to Kabbalah*, 271–81, 323–24.

46. MW e-mail to DP, April 8, 2016.

47. Kripal, *Esalen*, 10–11.

48. DP interview with Chen, Chengdu, China, June 20, 2013.

49. For a further discussion, see Palmer, "Daoism and Human Rights."

50. Kripal, *Esalen*, 223.

51. Kripal, *Esalen*, 9.

52. Altglas, *From Yoga to Kabbalah*, 327.

53. Kripal, *Esalen*, 464–65.

54. LK e-mail to DP, June 13, 2016.

55. Beyer, *Religion and Globalization*, 99.

56. Beyer, *Religion and Globalization*, 100–101.

Epilogue

1. MW e-mail to DP, April 8, 2016.

2. DP and ES interview with MW, Asheville, NC, November 16, 2013.

3. ES interview with MW, Asheville, NC, December 22, 2010.

4. DP and ES interview with MW, Asheville, NC, November 16, 2013; slightly edited in MW e-mail to DP, April 8, 2016.

5. DP and ES interview with MW, Asheville, NC, November 16, 2013, slightly edited in MW e-mail to DP, April 8, 2016.

6. DP and ES interview with MW, Asheville, NC, November 16, 2013, slightly edited in MW e-mail to DP, April 8, 2016.

7. DP and ES interview with MW, Asheville, NC, November 16, 2013, slightly edited in MW e-mail to DP, April 8, 2016. For an online video interview of Winn on Daoist sexual energetics, see https://vimeo.com/150606564.

8. DP and ES interview with MW, Asheville, NC, November 16, 2013.

9. Michael Winn, "Joyce Gayheart: Joyful Living Process," online at http://www.healing taousa.com/JoyceGayheart/ (accessed August 24, 2015).

10. Michael Winn, "Jem on the Tao of Love: Winter Solstice Dark Goddess," online at http://www.healingtaousa.com/cgi-bin/articles.pl?rm=mode2&articleid=147 (accessed August 24, 2015).

11. Michael Winn, "Come to My Wedding on Mt. Hua: China 'Water Dragon' Dream Trip," online at http://www.healingtaousa.com/cgi-bin/articles.pl?rm=mode2&articleid=142 (accessed August 24, 2015).

12. Michael Winn, "Come to My Wedding on Mt. Hua: China 'Water Dragon' Dream Trip," online at http://www.healingtaousa.com/cgi-bin/articles.pl?rm=mode2&articleid=142 (accessed August 24, 2015).

13. Michael Winn, "My Wedding Photos Atop China's Mt. Hua: 2012 China Dream Trip Photos," online at http://www.healingtaousa.com/cgi-bin/articles.pl?rm=mode2&articleid=152 (accessed August 24, 2015).

Appendix

1. Bourdieu, "Sociologists of Belief."

2. Dumont, The Headman and I, 60–61.

3. Robertson, "Reflexivity Redux," 785; see also Davies, Reflexive Ethnography, 40; Clifford and Marcus, eds. Writing Culture.

4. Lassiter, The Chicago Guide to Collaborative Ethnography.

5. Marcus, Ethnography through Thick and Thin, 105–32.

6. Siegler, "The Dao of America."

7. Palmer, Qigong Fever.

8. MW e-mail to DP, April 8, 2016.

9. This statement applies more for Palmer in terms of academic specialization, but Siegler has also studied Chinese as an undergraduate, lived and worked in China, and still visits China about once a year.

10. DP interview with Chen, Chengdu, China, October 23, 2015.

11. DP interview with Chen, Chengdu, China, October 23, 2015.

12. DP interview with Chen, Chengdu, China, May 26, 2016.

Glossary of Chinese Terms

baishi 拜師 : to kowtow to a master (become his disciple)
baiyuan tongbeiquan 白猿通背拳 : White Monkey Shadow Boxing
baiyuan zhenren 白猿真人 : White Monkey immortal
Baiyunguan 白雲觀 : White Cloud Monastery
Baojing 抱靜 : Embracing Stillness
Beidoujing 北斗經 : The Book of the Northern Dipper
Beidouping 北斗坪 : Northern Dipper Platform
benxing 本性 : original nature
bigu 辟穀 : fasting (abstention from grains)
bushi 布施 : donation
Changbaishan 長白山 : The Eternal White Mountain
Changde 常德 : Constant Virtue
Changrong 常容 : Constant Acceptance
chanhui 懺悔 : atonement
chen 臣 : minister
Chen Rongsheng 陳榮盛 : Taiwanese Daoist priest (b. 1927), master of K. Schipper
Chen Tuan 陳摶 : legendary Daoist sage (b. 929)
chi daojiao 吃道教 : to eat Daoism
Chia, Mantak 謝明德 : founder of Healing Tao (b. 1944)
Chiang Kai-shek 蔣介石 : president of the Republic of China (1887–1975)
chuandao 傳道 : transmitting the Dao
chujia 出家 : to leave the family and enter monastic life
conglin miao 叢林廟 : public monastery
Cui Jingyi 崔靜一 : Daoist nun of the Purity and Tranquility lineage
dantian 丹田 : elixir field
danwei 單位 : work unit
danyao 丹藥 : elixir pill
Dao 道
Daodejing 道德經 : The Book of the Way and Its Virtue
Daojia 道家 : Daoism; Daoists

Daojiao 道教 : Daoism; Daoist teachings
Daojiao xiulianjie 道教修煉界 : the circle of Daoist cultivators
Daojiao xueshujie 道教學術界 : the Daoist academic circle
Daojiao zongjiaojie 道教宗教界 : the Daoist religious circle
Dao, jing, shi 道經師 : Dao, Scriptures, Master; the "Three Treasures" of Daoism
daoqi 道炁 : primordial energy of Dao
daoshi 道士 : Daoist master, monk, or priest
daoshi zheng 道士證 : Daoist master certificate
Daoye 道爺 : master of Dao
daoyou 道友 : companion in Dao
Daoyuan 道院 : court of the Dao
dawo 大我 : greater self
de 德 : virtue
dexing 德性 : virtue
dingxin 定心 : to ground the heart
dixian 地仙 : earthly immortal
dizi 弟子 : disciple
dong 洞 : hole; cave
Dongdaoyuan 東道院 : Eastern Cloister of the Dao
donggong 動功 : movement practice
dongtian 洞天 : grotto-heavens
Doumu 斗姆 : Dipper Mother
dushi 度師 : accomplished master
enshi 恩師 : role-model master
Falun Gong 法輪功 : Qigong of the Dharma Wheel
fangshi 方士 : wizard
fangxiang 方向 : orientation
fengshui 風水 : Chinese geomancy
fudi 福地 : blissful realms
ganying 感應 : resonance; attunement
gongfu 功夫 : skill in practice
guadan 掛單 : registration of a traveling monk in a monastery
guanxi 關係 : social connections
Guanyin 觀音 : Bodhisattva Avalokitesvara
guoshu 國術 : national (martial) arts
guoyi 國醫 : national medicine
Jin Yong 金庸 : best-selling martial arts novelist, aka Louis Cha (b. 1924)
jingdian 景點 : scenic spot
jintian gong 金天宮 : Palace of Golden Heaven
Hao Datong 郝大通 : Daoist patriarch (1140–1213), founder of the Huashan lineage
Heming 鶴鳴 : crane call
Hengshan 衡山 : The Southern Marchmount, located in Hunan Province
Hengshan 恆山 : The Northern Marchmount, located in Shanxi Province
Heshanggong 河上公 : The Riverside Elder, a Daoist hermit of the first century AD, who wrote
     a commentary on the *Daodejing*
huanjie gongzuozu 換屆工作組 : election work group

Huashan 華山 : Mount Hua
Huashan Daoshi 華山道士 : Daoist master residing at Mount Hua
huansu 還俗 : to return to secular life
huidaomen 會道門 : sects and secret societies
hunyuan jin 混元巾 : cap of the original chaos
huoshen 火神 : fire spirit
jiang 將 : military general
jianghu 江湖 : errant knight of the rivers and lakes
Jiang Sheng 姜生 : professor of Daoist Studies at Shandong University and Sichuan University
jiao 醮 : communal offering ritual
jinggong 靜功 : stillness practice
jingxue 經學 : scripture study
jingzuo 靜坐 : quiet sitting
Jiutian xuannü 九天玄女 : The Mysterious Maiden of the Nine Heavens
jumin weiyuanhui 居民委員會 : residents' committee
jun 君 : sovereign
jushi zheng 居士證 : lay believer membership card
kaishan zushi 開山祖師 : founding patriarch of a sacred mountain
kan li 坎離 : kan and li trigrams
kundao 坤道 : Daoist nun
Kunyushan 崑嵛山 : Mount Kunyu
Kuomintang; KMT 國民黨 : Nationalist Party
Laoshan 嶗山 : Mountain and Daoist monastic complex in Shandong Province
Li Yujie 李玉階 : religious leader, entrepreneur, and politician (1901–1994), founder of the Heavenly Lord religion in Taiwan
ling 靈 : soul; numinous power
Longmendong 龍門洞 : Dragon Gate Cavern/Grotto
Longmen pai 龍門派 : Dragon Gate lineage
Louguantai 樓觀臺 : Lookout Tower Monastery
Lu Xiujing 陸修靜 : Daoist patriarch (406–477), compiler of the first Daoist Canon
Lü Dongbin 呂洞賓 : Tang dynasty Chinese scholar and poet (b. 796), worshipped as a Daoist Immortal and master of inner alchemy
lundao 論道 : discoursing on Dao
lunhui 輪迴 : reincarnation
Lüshan 閭山 : Daoist ritual tradition found in Southeast China
Ma Danyang 馬丹陽 : Daoist patriarch (1123–1184), one of the Seven Perfected Ones of Quanzhen Daoism
mai daojiao 賣道教 : selling Daoism
Meishan 梅山 : Daoist ritual tradition found in central and southeast China
miaohunzi 廟混子 : temple rascal
ming 命 : bodily life
mingmen 命門 : gate of destiny (acupoint)
mingshengqu 名勝區 : famous tourist attraction
minjian 民間 : among the people
muyu 木魚 : wooden fish
neidan 內丹 : inner alchemy

neigong 內功 : inner skill
nengliang 能量 : energy
panxi 磻溪 : stream in southern Shaanxi province
qi 氣 : cosmic energy, vital energy
qian 籤 : divination slips
qichang 氣場 : energy field
qigong 氣功 : vital energy practice
Qingchengshan 青城山 : famous Daoist mountain near Chengdu
qingjing 清靜 : clarity and stillness
Qingjingdao 清靜道 : Way of Clarity and Stillness
Qingjingjing 清靜經 : The Book of Clarity and Stillness
Qingjingpai 清靜派 : Clarity and Stillness lineage
Qingkeping 青柯坪 : meadow at the end of Huashan valley
Qingyanggong 青羊宮 : Azure Ram Temple
Qiu Chuji 丘處機 : Quanzhen patriarch (1148–1227), founder of the Dragon Gate lineage
qizhen 七真 : Seven Perfected Ones
Quanzhen 全真 : Complete Perfection monastic order
Ren Farong 任法融 : chairman of the China Daoist Association (b. 1936)
rudao 入道 : entering the Dao
samanjiao 薩滿教 : shamanism
Sanqing 三清 : Three Purities (supreme Daoist deities)
Shangdi 上帝 : God; the Lord on High
Shangshu—yugongbian 尚書愚公篇 : *Yugong* chapter of the Book of Documents
shanguan 山觀 : mountain contemplation
Shanhaijing 山海經 : The Book of Mountains and Seas
shanlin daoshi 山林道士 : Daoist master of the mountains and forests
shenqi 神氣 : spiritual *qi*
shenshou 身受 : receiving with your body
shifu 師父 : master
shixiong 師兄 : fellow disciple
shiye 師爺 : senior master (master's master)
shoujie 受戒 : precept transmission and ordination
shuangxiu 雙修 : dual cultivation
sixiang 思想 : thought
songbaipi 松白皮 : white pine bark
Songshan 嵩山 : The Central Marchmount, located in Henan Province
Sun Bu'er 孫不二 : Female Patriarch of Quanzhen Daoism (1119–1182), one of the Seven Perfected Ones
Suo Wu Sou 索無叟 : founder of the northern branch of the Huashan lineage of the Complete Perfection order
taiji quan 太極拳 : "Tai Chi" exercises
Taiqinggong 太清宮 : Palace of Great Clarity
Taishan 泰山 : The Eastern Marchmount
Taishang ganying pian 太上感應篇 : The Supreme Lord Lao's Treatise on Divine Retribution
Taishang Laojun 太上老君 : Supreme Sovereign Lord Lao (Laozi)
Taiyi 太乙 : The Supreme Oneness
Tao. *See* Dao

Tiande shengjiao 天德聖教 : The Holy Teachings of Heavenly Virtue
Tiandijiao 天帝教 : Heavenly Lord Teachings
tianxia 天下 : all under Heaven
tong 通 : communication; unobstructed flow
Tongshanshe 同善社 : Fellowship United in Goodness
tudi 徒弟 : disciple
Wanqing 萬清 : Myriad Clarities
Wanrui 萬瑞 : Myriad Blessings
Wang Changyue 王常月 : famous Daoist of the Dragon Gate lineage (?–1680)
Wang Chongyang 王重陽 : founding patriarch of Quanzhen Daoism (1113–1170)
Wang Liping 王立平 : famous Daoist *qigong* master in contemporary China
weiqi 圍棋 : go (a type of chess game)
wen/wu 文武 : civil/martial
Wudangshan 武當山 : Daoist mountain famous for its martial arts
wudao 悟道 : to understand intuitively
wujigong 無極功 : Primordial Qigong
wuwei 無為 : spontaneity; noninterference
wuxing 五行 : five elements; five phases
wuyue 五嶽 : The Five Marchmounts / Sacred Peaks
Xi'an 西安 : capital of Shaanxi province
xianjing 仙境 : realm of immortals
xiansheng 先生 : supplementary master
xiantian qi 先天氣 : prenatal *qi*
xiaosa 瀟灑 : carefree
xiaoshu 小術 : minor tricks
xiaowo 小我 : lesser self
xiaoyao 逍遙 : being carefree
xing 性 : spiritual nature
xingshi zourou 行屍走肉 : walking cadaver
xintu 信徒 : religious follower
xinxi 信息 : information
xinxing 心性 : heart-nature
xinyang 信仰 : faith
xiujing 修靜 : to cultivate stillness
xiulian 修煉 : cultivation and refinement
xuwu 虛無 : the void
xiyang danyao 西洋丹藥 : elixir pill of the Western Seas
xiyue dadi 西嶽大帝 : The Lord of the Western Marchmount
xiyuemiao 西嶽廟 : Temple of the Western Marchmount
Xue Tailai 薛泰來 : Master Chen's master at Huashan
Yan Xin 嚴新 : famous *qigong* master in contemporary China (b. 1950)
yang Daoshi 洋道士 : foreign Daoist master
yangsheng 養生 : nourishing life
ye 爺 : master
Yi Eng 一雲 : One Cloud
Yiguandao 一貫道 : Way of Pervasive Unity
Yijing 易經 : I Ching; The Book of Changes

yinde 陰德 : hidden virtue
yinguang 隱光 : to hide one's radiance
yinshi 引師 : inducting master
yintui 隱退 : to go into seclusion
yinxing 隱行 : hidden cultivation
yinyang 陰陽 : yin and yang
yiqie shenfo 一切神佛 : all deities and Buddhas
yiqie shenming 一切神明 : all deities and spirits
yizijin 一字巾 : Daoist headband
yuanfen 緣分 : predestined or karmic affinity
Yuanhuang 元皇 : Daoist ritual tradition found in Hunan
yunyou 雲遊 : cloud wandering
Yuquanyuan 玉泉院 : Jade Spring Monastery
zaiyi zehuo, zaiqi zezhi 在意則活，在氣則滯 : vitality begins in the intention, and ends in the *qi*
zaoke 早科 : morning recitations
Zhang Daoling 張道陵 : Daoist patriarch, founder of the Heavenly Masters movement in the
    second century AD
Zhang Sanfeng 張三丰 : legendary Daoist martial arts master of the Song dynasty
Zhang Xueliang 張學良 : Chinese general and Republican-era warlord (1901–2001)
zhengming shu 證明書 : certificate
zhengshi de Daomen dizi 正式的道門弟子 : formal disciple of a Daoist lineage
Zhengyi 正一 : Orthodox Oneness
zhenshi de ziwo 真實的自我 : true self
zhenwo 真我 : true self
Zhenyuegong 鎮岳宮 : Palace for Pacifying the Summit
Zhongnanshan 終南山 : mountain chain famous for its hermits
Zhuang-Chen Dengyun 莊陳登雲 : Daoist priest (1911–1976), master of M. Saso
Zhuangzi 莊子 : The Book of Master Zhuang
ziran 自然 : naturalness
zisun miao 子孫廟 : hereditary temple
Ziyou nüshen 自由女神 : Goddess/Statue of Liberty
zuodao 左道 : deviant ways
zuting 祖庭 : ancestral temple

Bibliography

Albanese, Catherine L. *A Republic of Mind and Spirit: A Cultural History of American Metaphysical Religion.* New Haven, CT: Yale University Press, 2007.

Altglas, Véronique. *From Yoga to Kabbalah: Religious Exoticism and the Logics of Bricolage.* Oxford: Oxford University Press, 2014.

———. *Le nouvel hindouisme occidental.* Paris: CNRS, 2005.

Althusser, Louis. "Ideology and Ideological State Apparatus (Notes towards an Investigation)." In *Lenin and Philosophy and Other Essays.* New York: Monthly Review Press, 1971. https://www.marxists.org/reference/archive/althusser/1970/ideology.htm (accessed July 13, 2015).

Andersen, Poul. "A Visit to Huashan." *Cahiers d'Extrême-Asie* 5 (1990): 349–54.

Augé, Marc. *Non-Places: Introduction to an Anthropology of Supermodernity.* London: Verso, 1995.

Bauman, Zygmunt. *Liquid Times: Living in an Age of Uncertainty.* Cambridge: Polity Press, 2007.

———. *Postmodernity and Its Discontents.* Cambridge: Polity Press, 2013.

Belamide, Paulino. "Taoism and Healing in North America: The Healing Tao of Mantak Chia." *International Review of Chinese Religion and Philosophy* 5 (2000): 245–89.

Bellah, Robert Neelly, Richard Madsen, William M. Sullivan, Ann Swidler, and Steven M. Tipton. *Habits of the Heart: Individualism and Commitment in American Life.* Berkeley: University of California Press, 1985.

Bernbaum, Edwin. *Sacred Mountains of the World,* 2nd ed. Berkeley: University of California Press, 1997.

Beyer, Peter. *Religion and Globalization.* London: Sage, 1994.

———. *Religions in Global Society.* London: Routledge, 2006.

Blofeld, John. 蒲樂道. *Lao Pu You Ji: Yi ge wai guo ren dui zhong guo de hui yi* 老蒲遊記：一個外國人對中國的回憶 [Old Pu's Travel Diary: The Memoir of a Foreigner in China]. Hong Kong: Ming Pao Publications, 1990.

———. *My Journey in Mystic China: Old Pu's Travel Diary.* Translated by Daniel Reid. Rochester, VT: Inner Traditions, 2008.

Bourdieu, Pierre. "Genesis and Structure of the Religious Field." *Comparative Social Research* 13 (1991): 1–44.

———. "Sociologists of Belief and Beliefs of Sociologists." Translated by Véronique Altglas and Matthew Wood. *Nordic Journal of Religion and Society* 23, no. 1 (2010): 1–7.

Bradbury, Steve. "The American Conquest of Philosophical Taoism." In *Translation East and West: A Cross Cultural Approach*, edited by Comelia N. Moore and Lucy Lower, 29–41. Honolulu: University of Hawaii Press, 1992.

Bremer, Thomas S. *Blessed with Tourists: The Borderlands of Religion and Tourism in San Antonio.* Chapel Hill: University of North Carolina Press, 2004.

———. "Sacred Spaces and Tourist Places." In *Tourism, Religion and Spiritual Journeys*, edited by Dallen J. Timothy and Daniel H. Olsen, 25–35. London: Routledge, 2006.

Brindley, Erica Fox. *Individualism in Early China: Human Agency and the Self in Thought and Politics.* Honolulu: University of Hawaii Press, 2010.

Buswell, Robert E. *The Zen Monastic Experience: Buddhist Practice in Contemporary Korea.* Princeton, NJ: Princeton University Press, 1992.

Carrette, Jeremy R., and Richard King. *Selling Spirituality: The Silent Takeover of Religion.* London: Routledge, 2005.

Carroll, Bret E. *Spiritualism in Antebellum America.* Bloomington: Indiana University Press, 1997.

Chang, Jolan. *The Tao of Love and Sex: The Ancient Chinese Way to Ecstasy.* New York: Dutton, 1977.

Chau, Adam Yuet. "Modalities of Doing Religion." In *Chinese Religious Life*, edited by David A. Palmer, Glenn Shive, and Philip L. Wickeri, 67–84. New York: Oxford University Press, 2010.

———. "Religious Subjectification: The Practice of Cherishing Written Characters and Being a Ciji (Tzu Chi) Person." In *Chinese Popular Religion: Linking Fieldwork and Theory, Papers from the Fourth International Conference on Sinology*, edited by Chang Hsun, 75–113. Taipei: Academia Sinica, 2013.

Chen Yuming 陳宇明 and Meng Hong 孟宏. *Huashan: dongtian fudi* 華山—洞天福地. Xi'an: Shanxi lüyou chubanshe, 2003.

Chia, Mantak. *Awaken Healing Energy through the Tao: The Taoist Secret of Circulating Internal Power.* New York: Aurora Press, 1983.

———. (Written with Michael Winn). *Taoist Secrets of Love: Cultivating Male Sexual Energy.* Santa Fe, NM: Aurora Press, 1984.

Chia, Mantak, and Maneewan Chia. *Awaken Healing Light of the Tao.* Chiang Mai, Thailand: Universal Tao Publications, 1993.

Chia, Mantak, Maneewan Chia, Douglas Abrams, and Rachel Carlton Abrams. *The Multi-Orgasmic Couple: Sexual Secrets Every Couple Should Know.* New York: HarperOne, 2002.

Chidester, David, and Edward T. Linenthal. "Introduction" to *American Sacred Space*, edited by David Chidester and Edward T. Linenthal, 6–19. Bloomington: Indiana University Press, 1995.

Clarke, J. J. *Jung and Eastern Thought: A Dialogue with the Orient.* London: Routledge, 1994.

———. *The Tao of the West: Western Transformations of Taoist Thought.* London: Routledge, 2000.

Clifford, James, and George E. Marcus, eds. *Writing Culture: The Poetics and Politics of Ethnography.* Berkeley: University of California Press, 1986.

Coleman, John. *The New Buddhism: The Western Transformation of an Ancient Tradition.* New York: Oxford University Press, 2001.

Csordas, Thomas J. "Introduction: Modalities of Transnational Transcendence." In *Transnational Transcendence: Essays on Religion and Globalization*, edited by Thomas J. Csordas, 1–30. Berkeley: University of California Press, 2009.

———. *The Sacred Self: A Cultural Phenomenology of Charismatic Healing.* Berkeley: University of California Press, 1997.

Davies, Charlotte Aull. *Reflexive Ethnography: A Guide to Researching Selves and Others*, 2nd ed. London: Routledge, 2008.

Davis, Edward L. *Society and the Supernatural in Song China*. Honolulu: University of Hawaii Press, 2001.

Dean, Kenneth. "Daoism, Local Religious Movements, and Transnational Chinese Society: The Circulation of Daoist Priests, Three-in-One Self-Cultivators, and Spirit Mediums between Fujian and Southeast Asia." In *Daoism in the Twentieth Century: Between Eternity and Modernity*, edited by David A. Palmer and Xun Liu, 251–73. Berkeley: University of California Press, 2011.

———. *Lord of the Three in One: The Spread of a Cult in Southeast China*. Princeton, NJ: Princeton University Press, 1998.

———. *Taoist Ritual and Popular Cults of Southeast China*. Princeton, NJ: Princeton University Press, 1993.

Deng Ming-Dao. *Chronicles of Tao: The Secret Life of a Taoist Master*. San Francisco: HarperOne, 1993.

———. *Gateway to a Vast World*. New York: Harper & Row, 1989.

———. *Seven Bamboo Tablets of the Cloudy Satchel*. New York: Harper & Row, 1987.

———. *The Wandering Taoist*. New York: Harper & Row, 1983.

Descola, Philippe. *Beyond Nature and Culture*. Translated by Janet Lloyd. Chicago: University of Chicago Press, 2013.

Dott, Brian R. *Identity Reflections: Pilgrimages to Mount Tai in Late Imperial China*. Cambridge, MA: Harvard University Press, 2005.

Duara, Prasenjit. *The Crisis of Global Modernity: Asian Traditions and a Sustainable Future*. Cambridge: Cambridge University Press, 2015.

Dumont, Jean-Paul. *The Headman and I: Ambiguity and Ambivalence in the Fieldworking Experience*. Austin: University of Texas Press, 1978.

Eliade, Mircea. *The Sacred and the Profane: The Nature of Religion*. Translated by Willard W. Trask. New York: Harcourt, Brace and World, 1958.

Ellsberg, Robert, ed. *Modern Spiritual Masters: Writings on Contemplation and Compassion*. Maryknoll, NY: Orbis, 2008.

Eskildsen, Stephen. *The Teachings and Practices of the Early Quanzhen Taoist Masters*. Albany: State University of New York Press, 2004.

Esposito, Monica. "The Different Versions of the *Secret of the Golden Flower* and their Relationship with the Longmen School." *Transactions of the International Conference of Eastern Studies* 43 (1998): 90–109.

———. *Facets of Qing Daoism*. Wil, Switzerland: UniversityMedia, 2014.

Farquhar, Judith. *Ten Thousand Things: Nurturing Life in Contemporary Beijing*. New York: Zone Books, 2012.

Feuchtwang, Stephan. "Too Ontological, Too Rigid, Too Ahistorical but Magnificent." *Hau: Journal of Ethnographic Theory* 4, no. 3 (2014): 383–387.

Foucault, Michel. *Dits et écrits 1954–1988: IV 1980–1988*. Paris: Gallimard, 1994.

———. *The Use of Pleasure: Volume 2 of the History of Sexuality*. Translated by Robert Hurley. New York: Vintage Books, 1990.

Frøystad, Kathinka. "The Return Path: Anthropology of a Western Yogi." In *Transnational Transcendence: Essays on Religion and Globalization*, edited by Thomas J. Csordas, 279–304. Berkeley: University of California Press, 2009.

Giddens, Anthony. *Modernity and Self-Identity: Self and Society in the Late Modern Age*. Stanford, CA: Stanford University Press, 1991.

Girardot, Norman J. "My Way: Reflections on Thirty Years of Teaching Taoism." Unpublished article.

———. "Teaching Taoism." Introductory comments in a panel of the *American Academy of Religion Annual Meeting*, Nashville, TN, November 18, 2000.

———. *The Victorian Translation of China: James Legge's Oriental Pilgrimage*. Berkeley: University of California Press, 2002.

Girardot, Norman J., James Miller, and Liu Xiaogan, eds. *Daoism and Ecology: Ways within a Cosmic Landscape*. Cambridge, MA: Harvard University Center for the Study of World Religions, 2001.

Goossaert, Vincent. "Daoists in the Modern Chinese Self-Cultivation Market: The Case of Beijing, 1850–1949." In *Daoism in the Twentieth Century: Between Eternity and Modernity*, edited by David A. Palmer and Xun Liu, 123–53. Berkeley: University of California Press, 2011.

———. "The Invention of an Order: Collective Identity in Thirteenth-Century Quanzhen Taoism." *Journal of Chinese Religions* 29 (2011): 111–38.

———. "La création du taoïsme moderne: l'ordre Quanzhen." PhD diss., École Pratique des Hautes Études, Section des Sciences Religieuses, 1997.

———. "L'alchimie intérieure réhabilitée? (Notes critiques)." *Revue d'histoire des religions* 215, no. 4 (1998): 493–507.

———. *The Taoists of Peking, 1800–1949: A Social History of Urban Clerics*. Cambridge, MA: Harvard University Asia Center, 2007.

Goossaert, Vincent, and David A. Palmer. *The Religious Question in Modern China*. Chicago: University of Chicago Press, 2011.

Goossaert, Vincent, and Xun Liu, eds. *Quanzhen Daoists in Chinese Society and Culture, 1500–2010*. Berkeley, CA: Institute of East Asian Studies, 2013.

Gottlieb, Roger S. *Spirituality: What It Is and Why It Matters*. New York: Oxford University Press, 2013.

Graburn, Nelson H. H. "Tourism: The Sacred Journey." In *Hosts and Guests: The Anthropology of Tourism*, edited by Valene Smith, 21–36. Philadelphia: University of Pennsylvania Press, 1989.

Granet, Marcel. *La Pensée chinoise*. Paris: Albin Michel, 1968 [1934].

Hahn, Thomas H. "The Standard Taoist Mountain and Related Features of Religious Geography." *Cahiers d'Extrême-Asie* 4 (1988): 145–56.

Hannerz, Ulf. *Transnational Connections: Culture, People, Places*. London: Routledge, 1996.

Hargett, James. *Stairway to Heaven: A Journey to the Summit of Mount Emei*. Albany: State University of New York Press, 2006.

Heelas, Paul. *The New Age Movement: The Celebration of the Self and the Sacralization of Modernity*. Oxford: Blackwell, 1996.

Heelas, Paul, David Martin, and Paul Morris. *Religion, Modernity and Postmodernity*. Oxford: Blackwell, 1998.

Herrou, Adeline. *A World of Their Own: Daoist Monks and Their Community in Contemporary China*. Translated by Livia Kohn. Dunedin, FL: Three Pines Press, 2013.

Hervieu-Léger, Danièle. *Religion as a Chain of Memory*. New Brunswick, NJ: Rutgers University Press, 2000.

Hodel, Bryan. "Tibetan Buddhism in the West: Is it Working Here? An Interview with Alan Wallace." Published in *Tricycle: The Buddhist Review* (Summer 2001), http://alanwallace.org/Tri cycle%20Interview.pdf (accessed September 16, 2013).

Holorenshaw, Henry. "The Making of an Honorary Taoist." In *Changing Perspectives in the History of Science: Essays in Honour of Joseph Needham*, edited by Mikuláš Teich, 1–20. London: Heinemann, 1973.

Huang, Al Chung-liang. "Once Again: A New Beginning." In *Tao: The Watercourse Way*, Alan Watts (with Huang), 123–27. New York: Pantheon Books, 1975.

Huntington, Samuel P. *The Clash of Civilizations and the Remaking of World Order*. New York: Simon & Schuster, 1996.

Ingold, Tim. *The Perception of the Environment: Essays on Livelihood, Dwelling and Skill*. London: Routledge, 2000.

Iwamura, Jane. "The Oriental Monk in American Popular Culture." In *Religion and Popular Culture in America*, rev. ed., edited by Bruce David Forbes and Jeffrey H. Mahan, 25–43. Berkeley: University of California Press, 2005.

Jackson, Carl T. *The Oriental Religions and American Thought: Nineteenth-Century Explorations*. Westport, CT: Greenwood Press, 1981.

Jain, Andrea R. *Selling Yoga: From Counterculture to Pop Culture*. Oxford: Oxford University Press, 2015.

Jammes, Jérémy, and David A. Palmer. "Occulting the Dao: Daoist Inner Alchemy, French Spiritism and Vietnamese Colonial Modernity in Caodai Translingual Practice." *Journal of Asian Studies*, forthcoming.

Jung, C. G. *The Secret of the Golden Flower: A Chinese Book of Life (with a European Commentary)*, 7th ed. Translated to German by Richard Wilhelm; translated to English by Cary F. Baynes; with a commentary by C. G. Jung. London: Kegan Paul, Trench, Trubner & Co., 1947 [1931].

Kirkland, Russell. "The Taoism of the Western Imagination and the Taoism of China: De-Colonializing the Exotic Teachings of the East." Unpublished paper, http://www.arches.uga .edu/~kirkland/rk/pdf/pubs.html (accessed February 1, 2009).

Kohn, Livia. *Chinese Healing Exercises: The Tradition of Daoyin*. Honolulu: University of Hawaii Press, 2008.

———. *Daoism and Chinese Culture*. Cambridge, MA: Three Pines Press, 2001.

———, ed. *Daoist Body Cultivation: Traditional Models and Contemporary Practices*. Magdalena, NM: Three Pines Press, 2006.

———. *Meditation Works: In the Daoist, Buddhist, and Hindu Traditions*. Magdalena, NM: Three Pines Press, 2008.

———. "Quiet Sitting with Master Yinshi: Religion and Medicine in China Today." *Zen Buddhism Today* 10 (1993): 79–95.

———, ed. *The Taoist Experience: An Anthology*. Albany: State University of New York Press, 1993.

———, ed. *Taoist Meditation and Longevity Techniques*. Ann Arbor: University of Michigan, 1989.

Komjathy, Louis. "Conference on Daoist Cultivation: Summary Report." Unpublished paper presented at the Conference on Daoist Cultivation, Vashon Island, Washington, May 9–13, 2001, http://www.daoistcenter.org/Cultivation.pdf (accessed July 31, 2016).

———. *Cultivating Perfection: Mysticism and Self-Transformation in Early Quanzhen Daoism*. Leiden, Netherlands: Brill, 2007.

———. "Daoism: From Meat Avoidance to Compassion-Based Vegetarianism." In *Call to Compassion: Reflections on Animal Advocacy in World Religions*, edited by Lisa Kemmerer and Anthony J. Nocella II, 83–103. New York: Lantern Books, 2011.

———. *Daoism: A Guide for the Perplexed*. London: Bloomsbury, 2014.

———. *The Daoist Tradition: An Introduction*. London: Bloomsbury, 2013.

———. "Field Notes from a Daoist Professor." In *Meditation and the Classroom: Contemplative Pedagogy for Religious Studies*, edited by Judith Simmer-Brown and Fran Grace, 95–103. Albany: State University of New York Press, 2011.

———. "Living among Daoists: Daily Quanzhen Monastic Life." Unpublished paper presented at the Fourth International Conference on Daoist Studies, Hong Kong Institute of Education, 2007.

———. "Möbius Religion: The Insider/Outsider Question." In *Religion: A Next-Generation Handbook for Its Robust Study*, edited by Jeffrey Kripal. New York: Palgrave Macmillan, forthcoming.

———. "Qigong in America." In *Daoist Body Cultivation: Traditional Models and Contemporary Practices*, edited by Livia Kohn, 203–36. Magdalena, NM: Three Pines Press, 2006.

———. "Responses to *Dream Trippers* as an Adherent and Scholar-Practitioner." Personal communication, 2015.

———. "Some Reflections on my Location in the Daoist Tradition." Personal communication, June 12, 2013.

———. *The Way of Complete Perfection: A Quanzhen Daoist Anthology, Selected, Translated, and with an Introduction by Louis Komjathy*. Albany: State University of New York Press, 2013.

Kripal, Jeffrey John. *Esalen: America and the Religion of No Religion*. Chicago: University of Chicago Press, 2007.

Lagerwey, John. *China: A Religious State*. Hong Kong: University of Hong Kong Press, 2010.

———. "Droit divin et crise dynastique en Chine: les fondements religieux de la légitimité politique." In *Religion et politique en Asie: histoire et actualité*, edited by John Lagerwey, 49–56. Paris: Les Indes savantes, 2006.

———. "The Pilgrimage to Wu-tang Shan." In *Pilgrims and Sacred Sites in China*, edited by Susan Naquin and Yü Chün-fang, 293–332. Berkeley: University of California Press, 1992.

Lassiter, Luke Eric. *The Chicago Guide to Collaborative Ethnography*. Chicago: University of Chicago Press, 2005.

Lau, Kimberly J. *New Age Capitalism: Making Money East of Eden*. Philadelphia: University of Pennsylvania Press, 2000.

Lee, Fongmao. "Transmission and Innovation: The Modernization of Daoist Inner Alchemy in Postwar Taiwan." In *Daoism in the Twentieth Century: Between Eternity and Modernity*, edited by David A. Palmer and Xun Liu, 196–227. Berkeley: University of California Press, 2011.

Lenoir, Frédéric. *Le bouddhisme en France*. Paris: Fayard, 1999.

Lindholm, Charles. *Culture and Authenticity*. Malden, MA: Blackwell, 2008.

Liu, Xun. *Daoist Modern: Innovation, Lay Practice, and the Community of Inner Alchemy in Republican Shanghai*. Cambridge, MA: Harvard University Press, 2009.

Liu, Xun, and Vincent Goossaert, eds. *Quanzhen Daoists in Chinese Society and Culture, 1500–2010*. Berkeley, CA: Institute of East Asian Studies, 2013.

MacCannell, Dean. *The Tourist: A New Theory of the Leisure Class*. Berkeley: University of California Press, 1999.

Madsen, Richard, and Elijah Siegler. "The Globalization of Chinese Religions and Traditions." In *Chinese Religious Life*, edited by David A. Palmer, Glenn Shive, and Philip L. Wickeri, 227–40. New York: Oxford University Press, 2010.

Marcus, George E. *Ethnography through Thick and Thin*. Princeton, NJ: Princeton University Press, 1998.

Marsone, Pierre. *Wang Chongyang et la fondation du Quanzhen: ascètes taoïstes et alchimie intérieure*. Paris: Institut des Hautes Études chinoises, Collège de France, 2010.

Merleau-Ponty, Maurice. *Phenomenology of Perception*. Translated by James Edie. Evanston, IL: Northwestern University Press, 1962.

Merton, Thomas. *The Way of Chuang Tzu*. New York: New Directions, 1965.

Ming, Liu. *The Blue Book: A Text Concerning Orthodox Daoist Conduct*, 3rd ed. Santa Cruz, CA: Orthodox Daoism in America, 1998.

Morrison, Hedda, and Wolfram Eberhard. *Hua Shan: The Taoist Sacred Mountain in West China, Its Scenery, Monasteries, and Monks*. Hong Kong: Vetch and Lee, 1973.

Murray, Daniel M., and James Miller. "The Daoist Society of Brazil and the Globalization of Orthodox Unity." *Journal of Daoist Studies* 6 (2013): 93–114.

Naquin, Susan, and Yü Chün-fang, eds. *Pilgrims and Sacred Sites in China*. Berkeley: University of California Press, 1992.

Nattier, Jan. "Who is a Buddhist? Charting the Landscape of Buddhist America." In *The Faces of Buddhism in America*, edited by Charles S. Prebish and Kenneth Tanaka, 183–95. Berkeley: University of California Press, 1998.

Nussbaum, Martha Craven. *The Clash Within: Democracy, Religious Violence, and India's Future*. Cambridge, MA: Belknap Press, 2007.

Nyiri, Pal. *Scenic Spots: Chinese Tourism, the State, and Cultural Authority*. Seattle: University of Washington Press, 2006.

Obadia, Lionel. *Bouddhisme et Occident: la diffusion du bouddhisme tibétain en France*. Paris: L'Harmattan, 1999.

Ownby, David. *Falun Gong and the Future of China*. Oxford: Oxford University Press, 2008.

Palmer, David A. "China's Religious *Danwei*: Institutionalizing Religion in the Peoples' Republic." *China Perspectives* 4 (2009): 17–31.

———. "Chinese Redemptive Societies and Salvationist Religion: Historical Phenomenon or Sociological Category?" *Journal of Chinese Ritual, Theatre and Folklore* 172 (2011): 21–72.

———. "Daoism and Human Rights: Integrating the Incommensurable." In *Religious Perspectives on Human Rights and Bioethics*, edited by Joseph Tham. Dordrecht, Netherlands: Springer, forthcoming.

———. "Dao and Nation: Li Yujie: May Fourth Activist, Daoist Cultivator and Redemptive Society Patriarch in Mainland China and Taiwan." In *Daoism in the Twentieth Century: Between Eternity and Modernity*, edited by David A. Palmer and Xun Liu, 173–95. Berkeley: University of California Press, 2011.

———. "Globalizing Daoism at Huashan: Quanzhen Monks, Danwei Politics, and International Dream Trippers." In *Quanzhen Daoists in Chinese Society and Culture, 1500–2010*, edited by Xun Liu and Vincent Goossaert, 113–40. Berkeley, CA: Institute of East Asian Studies, 2013.

———. *Qigong Fever: Body, Science and Utopia in China*. New York: Columbia University Press, 2007.

———. "Transnational Sacralizations: When Daoist Monks Meet Spiritual Tourists." *Ethnos: Journal of Anthropology* 79, no. 2 (2014): 169–92.

Palmer, David A., and Elijah Siegler. "'Healing Tao USA' and the History of American Spiritual Individualism." *Cahiers d'Extrême-Asie* 26 (2017).

———. "Authenticating the Sacred Mountain: Chinese Monks and Western Practitioners 'Connect to the Dao' at Huashan." In *Religion and Tourism in China and India*, edited by Knut Aukland, forthcoming.

Palmer, David A., Glenn Shive, and Philip L. Wickeri, eds. *Chinese Religious Life*. New York: Oxford University Press, 2010.

Palmer, David A., and Xun Liu, eds. *Daoism in the Twentieth Century: Between Eternity and Modernity*. Berkeley: University of California Press, 2011.

———. "Introduction: The Daoist Encounter with Modernity." In Palmer and Liu, *Daoism in the Twentieth Century*, 1–19.

Pieterse, Jan Nederveen. *Globalization and Culture: Global Mélange*. Lanham, MD: Rowman & Littlefield, 2009.

Porter, Bill. *Road to Heaven: Encounters with Chinese Hermits*. San Francisco: Mercury House, 1993.

Prebish, Charles S. *Luminous Passage: The Practice and Study of Buddhism in America*. Berkeley: University of California Press, 1999.

Pregadio, Fabrizio. *The Way of the Golden Elixir: An Introduction to Taoist Alchemy*. Mountain View, CA: Golden Elixir Press, 2014 [2012].

Puett, Michael J. *To Become a God: Cosmology, Sacrifice, and Self-Divinization in Early China*. Cambridge, MA: Harvard University Press, 2002.

Robbins, Joel. "Is the Trans- in *Transnational* the Trans- in *Transcendent*? On Alterity and the Sacred in the Age of Globalization." In *Transnational Transcendence: Essays on Religion and Globalization*, edited by Thomas J. Csordas, 55–72. Berkeley: University of California Press, 2009.

Robertson, Jennifer. "Reflexivity Redux: A Pithy Polemic on 'Positionality.'" *Anthropology Quarterly* 75, no. 4 (2002): 785–92.

Robinet, Isabelle. *Taoist Meditation: The Mao-Shan Tradition of Great Purity*. Albany: State University of New York Press, 1993.

———. *The World Upside Down: Essays on Taoist Internal Alchemy*. Translated and edited by Fabrizio Pregadio. Mountain View, CA: Golden Elixir Press, 2011.

Robson, James. *Power of Place: The Religious Landscape of the Southern Sacred Peak (Nanyue) in Medieval China*. Cambridge, MA: Harvard University Press, 2009.

Rocha, Leon Antonio. "The Way of Sex: Joseph Needham and Jolan Chang." *Studies in History and Philosophy of Biology and Biomedical Sciences* 43, no. 3 (2012): 611–26.

Roof, Wade Clark. *Spiritual Marketplace: Baby Boomers and the Remaking of American Religion*. Princeton, NJ: Princeton University Press, 1999.

Roth, Harold David. *Original Tao: Inward Training (Nei-Yeh) and the Foundations of Taoist Mysticism*. Translations from the Asian Classics. New York: Columbia University Press, 1999.

Said, Edward W. *Orientalism*. New York: Vintage Books, 2003 [1978].

———. "Orientalism Reconsidered." *Cultural Critique* 1 (Fall 1985): 89–107.

Samsom, Will. "The New Monasticism." In *The New Evangelical Social Engagement*, edited by Brian Steensland and Philip Goff, 94–108. Oxford: Oxford University Press, 2014.

Saso, Michael R. *Taoism and the Rite of Cosmic Renewal*, 2nd ed. Pullman: Washington State University Press, 1990.

———. *The Teachings of Taoist Master Chuang*. New Haven, CT: Yale University Press, 1978.

Schipper, Kristofer. *La religion de la Chine: la tradition vivante*. Paris: Fayard, 2008.

———. "Taoism: The Story of the Way." In *Taoism and the Arts of China*, edited by Stephen Little and Shawn Eichman, 33–56. Berkeley: University of California Press, 2000.

———. *The Taoist Body*. Berkeley: University of California Press, 1993.

Schipper, Kristofer, and Franciscus Verellen, eds. *The Taoist Canon: A Historical Companion to the Daozang*. Chicago: University of Chicago Press, 2004.

Seager, Richard Hughes, ed. *The Dawn of Religious Pluralism: Voices from the World's Parliament of Religion, 1893*. Lasalle, IL: Open Court Press, 1993.

Seidel, Anna. "The Image of the Perfect Ruler in Early Taoist Messianism: Lao-Tzu and Li Hung." *History of Religions* 9, no. 2/3 (1969–1970): 216–47.

———. "Taoism: The Unofficial High Religion of China." *Taoist Resources* 7, no. 2 (1997): 39–72.

Sen, Amartya. *Identity and Violence: The Illusion of Destiny*. New York: W. W. Norton & Company, 2006.

Shackley, Myra L. *Managing Sacred Sites: Service Provision and Visitor Experience*. London: Thomson Learning, 2001.

Shahar, Meir. *The Shaolin Monastery: History, Religion, and the Chinese Martial Arts*. Honolulu: University of Hawaii Press, 2008.

Siegler, Elijah. " 'Back to the Pristine': Identity Formation and Legitimation in Contemporary American Daoism." *Nova Religio* 14, no. 1 (2010): 45–66.

———. "Chinese Traditions in Euro-American Society." In *Chinese Religions in Contemporary Societies*, edited by James Miller, 257–80. Santa Barbara, CA: ABC-CLIO, 2006.

———. "The Dao of America: The History and Practice of American Daoism." PhD diss., University of California at Santa Barbara, 2003.

———. "Daoism beyond Modernity: The 'Healing Tao' as Postmodern Movement." In *Daoism in the Twentieth Century: Between Eternity and Modernity*, edited by David A. Palmer and Xun Liu, 274–92. Berkeley: University of California Press, 2011.

Silvers, Brock. *The Taoist Manual: An Illustrated Guide Applying Taoism to Daily Life*. Honolulu: Sacred Mountain Press, 2005.

Solignac, Aimé, and Michel Dupuy. "Spiritualité." In *Dictionnaire de spiritualité ascétique et mystique: Doctrine et Histoire*, edited by M. Viller et al., vol. 14, colonne 1142. Paris: Beauchesne, 1932–1995.

Spiegelberg, Frederic. *The Religion of No-Religion*. Stanford, CA: James Ladd Delkin, 1953.

Srinivas, Tulasi. *Winged Faith: Rethinking Globalization and Religious Pluralism through the Sathya Sai Movement*. New York: Columbia University Press, 2010.

Stausberg, Michael. *Religion and Tourism: Crossroads, Destinations and Encounters*. London: Routledge, 2011.

Stein, Rolf. "Remarques sur les Mouvements du Taoïsme politico-religieux au IIe siècle après J-C." *T'oung Pao* 50 (1963): 42–59.

Strickmann, Michel. "History, Anthropology, and Chinese Religion: A Review Essay of the Teachings of Taoist Master Chuang by Michael Saso." *Harvard Journal of Asiatic Studies* 40, no. 1, June (1980): 201–48.

Taylor, Charles. *A Secular Age*. Cambridge, MA: Belknap Press, 2007.

Timothy, Dallen J., and Paul J. Conover. "Nature Religion, Self-Spirituality and New Age Tourism." In *Tourism, Religion and Spiritual Journeys*, edited by Dallen J. Timothy and Daniel H. Olsen, 139–55. London: Routledge, 2006.

Towler, Solala. *Embarking on the Way: A Guide to Western Taoism*. Dallas: Abode of the Eternal Tao, 1998.

Tsing, Anna Lauwenhaupt. *Friction: An Ethnography of Global Connection*. Princeton, NJ: Princeton University Press, 2005.

Turner, Victor. *Drama, Fields and Metaphors: Symbolic Action in Human Society*. Ithaca, NY: Cornell University Press, 1974.

Turner, Victor, and Edith L. B. Turner. *Image and Pilgrimage in Christian Culture*. New York: Columbia University Press, 1995 [1978].

Tweed, Thomas A. "Asian Religions in the United States: Reflections on an Emerging Subfield." In *Religious Diversity and American Religious History*, edited by Walter H. Conser Jr. and Sumner B. Twiss, 189–217. Athens: University of Georgia Press, 1997.

Urban, Hugh B. *Magia Sexualis: Sex, Magic, and Liberation in Modern Western Esotericism*. Berkeley: University of California Press, 2006.

van der Veer, Peter. *The Modern Spirit of Asia: The Spiritual and the Secular in China and India*. Princeton, NJ: Princeton University Press, 2014.

———. "Spirituality in Modern Society." *Social Research* 76, no. 4 (Winter 2009): 1097–1120.

van Gulik, R. H. *Sexual Life in Ancient China: A Preliminary Survey of Chinese Sex and Society from ca. 1500 B.C. till 1644 A.D.* Leiden, Netherlands: BRILL, 1961.

Verellen, Franciscus, ed. "Cultes des sites et culte des saints en Chine." *Cahiers d'Extrême-Asie* 10, special issue, 1998.

von Glahn, Richard. *The Sinister Way: The Divine and the Demonic in Chinese Religious Culture*. Berkeley: University of California Press, 2004.

Wasserstrom, Steven M. *Religion After Religion: Gershom Scholem, Mircea Eliade, and Henry Corbin at Eranos*. Princeton, NJ: Princeton University Press, 1999.

Watts, Alan (with the collaboration of Al Chung-liang Huang). *Tao: The Watercourse Way*. New York: Pantheon Books, 1975.

Weber, Max. *The Sociology of Religion*. Translated by Ephraim Fischoff. Boston: Beacon Press, 1971 [1920].

Weller, Robert P. *Resistance, Chaos, and Control in China: Taiping Rebels, Taiwanese Ghosts, and Tiananmen*. Seattle: University of Washington Press, 1994.

Wile, Douglas. *Art of the Bedchamber: The Chinese Sexual Yoga Classics including Women's Solo Meditation Texts*. Albany: State University of New York Press, 1992.

———. *Lost T'ai-chi Classics from the Late Ch'ing Dynasty*. Albany: State University of New York Press, 1996.

Willaime, Jean-Paul. "Religion in Ultramodernity." In *Theorizing Religion: Classical and Contemporary Debates*, edited by James A. Beckford and John Wallis, 77–89. Aldershot, UK: Ashgate, 2006.

Winn, Michael. "Daoist Alchemy as a Deep Language for Communicating with Nature." Paper presented at Vashon Island Conference of Daoist Scholars and Adepts, May 2001, http://www.healingtaousa.com/articles/taoalchemy_idx.html (accessed July 25, 2016).

———. "Daoist Internal Alchemy in the West." In *Internal Alchemy: Self, Society, and the Quest for Immortality*, edited by Livia Kohn and Robin Wang. Magdalena, NM: Three Pines Press, 2009. Excerpt online at http://www.healingtaousa.com/cgi-bin/articles.pl?rm=mode2&articleid=209 (accessed July 25, 2016).

———. "Daoist Methods of Dissolving the Heart-Mind." *Journal of Daoist Studies* 2 (2009), http://www.healingtaousa.com/cgi-bin/articles.pl?rm=mode2&articleid=97 (accessed July 25, 2016).

———. "Daoist Neidan: Lineage and Secrecy Issues Challenge for Western Adepts." *Journal of Daoist Studies* 1 (Spring 2008), http://www.healingtaousa.com/cgi-bin/articles.pl?rm=mode2&articleid=210 (accessed July 25, 2016).

———. "Foreword" to *Awaken Healing Energy through the Tao: The Taoist Secret of Circulating Internal Power*, by Mantak Chia. New York: Aurora Press, 1983.

———. "Magic Numbers, Planetary Tones and the Body: The Evolution of Daoist Inner Alchemy into Modern Sacred Science." Paper presented at International Daoism Conference, Boston University, 2003, http://www.healingtaousa.com/pdf/39.pdf (accessed July 25, 2016).

———. "The Quest for Spiritual Orgasm: Daoist and Tantric Sexual Cultivation in the West." Unpublished paper, 2002, http://www.healingtaobritain.com/p67magazinequestforspiritual orgasm.htm (accessed February 3, 2008).

———. "Taoist Alchemy and Breatharians: Five Days in a Huashan Cave." *QI Journal* 12, no. 1 (Spring 2002). Also available at http://www.healingtaousa.com/cgi-bin/articles.pl?rm=mode2&articleid=32 (accessed November 4, 2010).

———. "Taoist 'Dual Cultivation' and the Quest for Sexual Love." In Mantak Chia and Michael Winn, *Taoist Secrets of Love: Cultivating Male Sexual Energy*. Santa Fe, NM: Aurora Press, 1984.

———. "Transforming Sexual Energy with Water-and-Fire Alchemy." In *Daoist Body Cultivation: Traditional Models and Contemporary Practices*, edited by Livia Kohn, 151–78. Magdalena, NM: Three Pines Press, 2006. Excerpt online at http://www.healingtaousa.com/cgi-bin/articles.pl?rm=mode2&articleid=103 (accessed July 25, 2016).

Wu, Pei-yi. "An Ambivalent Pilgrim to T'ai Shan in the Seventeenth Century." In *Pilgrims and Sacred Sites in China*, edited by Susan Naquin and Yü Chün-fang, 65–88. Berkeley: University of California Press, 1992.

Yang, C. K. *Religion in Chinese Society: A Study of Contemporary Social Functions of Religion and Some of Their Historical Factors*. Berkeley: University of California Press, 1961.

Yang, Der-ruey. "Revolution of Temporality: The Modern Schooling of Daoist Priests in Shanghai at the Turn of the Twenty-First Century." In *Daoism in the Twentieth Century: Between Eternity and Modernity*, edited by David A. Palmer and Xun Liu, 47–80. Berkeley: University of California Press, 2011.

Yang, Fenggang. *Chinese Christians in America: Conversion, Assimilation, and Adhesive Identities*. University Park: Pennsylvania State University Press, 1999.

Yang, Mayfair. "Spatial Struggles: Postcolonial Complex, State Disenchantment, and Popular Reappropriation of Space in Rural Southeast China." *Journal of Asian Studies* 63, no. 3 (2004): 719–55.

Yü, Dan Smyer. *The Spread of Tibetan Buddhism in China: Charisma, Money, Enlightenment*. London: Routledge, 2012.

Index